London
for Children
timeout.com

Published by
Time Out Guides Limited
Universal House
251 Tottenham Court Road
London W1T 7AB
Tel +44 (0)20 7813 3000
Fax +44 (0)20 7813 6001
email guides@timeout.com
www.timeout.com

Editorial
Editor Emma Perry
Copy Editors Ros Sales, Elizabeth Winding
Listings Editors William Crow, Emma Pritchard
Indexer Holly Pick

Managing Director Peter Fiennes
Editorial Director Sarah Guy
Series Editor Cath Phillips
Business Manager Daniel Allen
Editorial Manager Holly Pick
Assistant Management Accountant Ija Krasnikova

Design
Art Director Scott Moore
Art Editor Pinelope Kourmouzoglou
Senior Designer Kei Ishimaru
Guides Commercial Designer Jodi Sher

Picture Desk
Picture Editor Jael Marschner
Acting Deputy Picture Editor Liz Leahy
Picture Desk Assistant/Researcher Ben Rowe

Advertising
New Business & Commercial Director Mark Phillips
Magazine & UK Guides Commercial Director St John Betteridge

Account Managers Jessica Baldwin, Michelle Daburn, Ben Holt
Production Controller Christ Pastfield
Copy Controller Alison Bourke

Marketing
Sales & Marketing Director, North America & Latin America Lisa Levinson
Group Commercial Art Director Anthony Huggins
Circulation & Distribution Manager Dan Collins
Marketing Co-ordinator Alana Benton

Production
Group Production Director Mark Lamond
Production Manager Brendan McKeown
Production Controller Damian Bennett
Production Assistant Katie Mulhern

Time Out Group
Director & Founder Tony Elliott
Chief Executive Officer David King
Group Financial Director Paul Rakkar
Group General Manager/Director Nichola Coulthard
Time Out Communications Ltd MD David Pepper
Time Out International Ltd MD Cathy Runciman
Time Out Magazine Ltd Publisher/MD Mark Elliott
Group Commercial Director Graeme Tottle
Group IT Director Simon Chappell

Sections in this guide were written by
Nature Watch Rachel Halliburton. **London Stories Retold** Emma Perry. **Sleepovers With a Difference** Rosie Scammell. **Trips & Tours** Elizabeth Winding. **Festivals & Events** William Crow. **Attractions** Ronnie Haydon, Tom Howard, Emma Perry (*Great Days Out: Westminster* Elizabeth Winding; *Great Days Out: South Bank, Covent Garden* Emma Perry; *Butterfly World* Emma Perry). **Museums & Galleries** Nick Coleman, Meryl O'Rourke, Emma Perry, Peter Watts, Elizabeth Winding (*Great Days Out: Bloomsbury, South Kensington* Elizabeth Winding; *Great Days Out: Docklands* Emma Perry; *Florence Nightingale Museum, The all-new Jewish Museum* Emma Perry). **Parks & Gardens** Emma Perry (*Great Days Out: Camden, Chelsea* Emma Perry; *Great Days Out: Greenwich* Elizabeth Winding; *Pipe dreams, Dizzy heights, Go down to the woods, Bubble fun* Emma Perry). **Parties** Meryl O'Rourke (*Great places to party* Emma Perry). **Arts & Entertainment** Meryl O'Rourke, Elizabeth Winding (*Hare today, gone tomorrow; World of stagecraft, Full steam ahead, Wordplay* Emma Perry). **Sports & Leisure** Peter Watts (*Olympic legacy, Pooling resources* Emma Perry). **Eating** Fiona Barrows, Bruce Dessau, Sarah Labovitch, Anna Leach, Meryl O'Rourke and contributors to *Time Out Eating & Drinking Guide* (*Perfect pizza* Jenni Muir; *Get the scoop* William Crow; *Mad about mushrooms* Emma Perry). **Shopping** Fiona Barrows, Alex Brown, Emma Perry, Heather Welsh, Elizabeth Winding (*Toy libraries* Emma Perry).

Maps john@jsgraphics.co.uk
Backcover photography Alys Tomlinson, Christina Theisen.
Photography pages 2, 130 (left), 209 (bottom), 266 Scott Wishart; pages 5, 19 (right), 29 Nick Ballon; pages 6, 57, 62, 90, 91, 95, 132 (left), 137, 164 (right), 245 (bottom right) Tove K Breitstein; page 7 Ed Marshall; page 15 David Axelbank; pages 19 (left), 44 (bottom) Belinda Lawley; page 20 Michael Walter/Troika/Thames Festival; pages 25, 61, 110, 134 (right), 164 (left), 171, 179, 180, 181, 213, 223, 239, 246 Heloise Bergman; pages 27, 35 (top), 101 (bottom), 114 www.simonleigh.com; pages 30, 34, 40, 46, 72, 80 (top), 88, 102, 107, 131 (right), 229, 241, 242, 245, 268, 283, 287 Michelle Grant; pages 32, 148, 165, 182, 194, 196, 197, 209 (top) Andrew Brackenbury; pages 35 (bottom), 153, 157, 250 Rob Greig; pages 36, 69 (top left), 70 (bottom), 78, 108, 122, 132 (right), 138 (bottom right), 145, 176 (top), 201, 206, 285 Jonathan Perugia; pages 58, 60, 119, 112, 168, 200, 288 Elisabeth Blanchet; page 66 (left) Richard Eaton; page 69 (top right) www.alanwilliamsphotography.com; page 69 (bottom), 219, 235, 274 Alys Tomlinson; pages 78 (bottom left), 138, 236 Tricia de Courcy Ling; page 80 (bottom) Heike Bohnstengel; pages 84, 134 (left) Ben Rowe; pages 70 (top), 98, 101, 190 Susannah Stone; pages 133, 141, 144, 150, 151, 154, 161, 186, 205, 226, 273, 290, 291, 293 Christina Theisen; pages 185, 262 Britta Jaschinski; page 188 Karl Andre; page 202 London 2012; pages 229 (left), 234, 255, 279 Ming Tang-Evans; pages 229 (right), 265 Gemma Day; page 271 Jael Marschner; pages 44 (top), 249 Olivia Rutherford.

The following images were provided by the featured establishments/artists: pages 8, 9, 10, 11, 12, 14, 18, 21, 43, 49, 54, 66 (right), 75, 130, 136, 147, 152, 158, 173, 176 (bottom), 187, 193, 222, 224, 275, 280.

Printer St Ives Web Ltd, Roche, St Austell PL26 8LX.
Time Out Group uses paper products that are environmentally friendly, from well managed forests and mills that use certified (PEFC) Chain of Custody pulp in their production.

ISBN 978-1-905042-50-0

Distribution by Comag Specialist (01895 433 800).
For further distribution details, see www.timeout.com.

Contents

Introduction

TIME OUT LONDON FOR CHILDREN GUIDE

This is the tenth edition of the Time Out *London for Children Guide*, produced by the people behind the successful listings magazines and travel guide series. It is written by resident experts to provide you with all the information you'll need to explore the city, whether you're a local or a first-time visitor.

THE LOWDOWN ON THE LISTINGS

Addresses, phone numbers, websites, transport information, opening times, admission prices and credit card details are included in the listings. Details of facilities, services and events were all checked and correct as we went to press.

Before you go out of your way, however, we'd advise you to phone and check opening times, ticket prices and other particulars. While every effort has been made to ensure the accuracy of the information contained in this guide, the publishers cannot accept any responsibility for any errors that it may contain.

FAMILY-FRIENDLY INFORMATION

Having visited all the places with our children, we've added essential information for families. Where we think it's important, we've stated whether a building can accommodate buggies, or if there's a place to change a nappy. We've also listed the nearest picnic place.

Attractions are required to provide reasonable facilities for disabled visitors, although it's best to check accessibility before setting out.

PRICES AND PAYMENT

We have noted where venues accept the following credit cards: American Express (AmEx), MasterCard (MC) and Visa (V).

THE LIE OF THE LAND

Map references are included for each venue that falls within the area covered by our London street maps, starting on page 310. We would recommend that you also use a standard A-Z map of the city.

PHONE NUMBERS

The area code for London is 020. All phone numbers given in this guide take this code unless otherwise stated, so add 020 if you're calling from outside London; otherwise, simply dial the number as written. The international dialling code for the UK is 44.

LET US KNOW WHAT YOU THINK

We hope that you enjoy this book and we'd like to know what you think of it. Email us at guides@timeout.com.

ADVERTISERS

We would like to stress that no establishment has been included in this guide because it has advertised in any of our publications and no payment of any kind has influenced any review. The opinions given in this book are those of Time Out writers and editors and are entirely independent.

Out & About

Nature Watch

The evolution of Exhibition Road continues apace.

Streets ahead

By 2012, Exhibition Road will look completely different. The street's grand cultural institutions, the Mayor of London and the Royal Borough of Kensington and Chelsea have come up with a plan that will make it a much more pleasant place for visitors to inhabit. The new street design follows the 'Shared Space' concept gaining favour with town planners across Europe. The idea is that pedestrians are given greater priority by taking away traditional street furniture like kerbs and railings.

By 2012, Exhibition Road will be one large, level space; an expansive surface with enlarged pedestrian areas marked out simply by different coloured stone. The idea behind this design is that drivers and cyclists have to move through the zone more slowly and with more awareness, causing fewer accidents and making the area much more friendly for those on two feet.

Exhibition Road has been London's major museum hotspot since 1851's Great Exhibition raised the money to build its three great institutions: the Victoria & Albert Museum, the Science Museum and the Natural History Museum.

All three are undergoing major changes; the first of the V&A's planned new galleries are open (*see p68*), while the Science Museum's Wellcome Wing (*see p92*) reopened after an extensive refurb in June 2010, and will have a new rooftop extension and façade by 2015. Perhaps the most exciting news on Exhibition Road, though, is the brand new Darwin Centre at the Natural History Museum (*see p87*).

To go from Waterhouse's Romanesque 19th-century building into the 21st-century Darwin Centre feels like a journey into the future, in more ways than one. First, there's the vertiginous glass lift ride that zips you to the seventh floor where the tour of the collection begins. Then there's the vast translucent table that awaits you as you step out of the lift, with its mixture of insect displays and touch screens – the beginning of an interactive tour using technology that wouldn't seem out of place in a Spielberg movie. Before long, virtual figures are springing up on walls and screens in order to share their expertise on the vast array of creepy crawlies stored in this new extension. Insects – already a source both of horror and fascination to the small mind – have rarely seemed so glamorous.

The Darwin Centre opened with a great fanfare in September 2009. A £78 million centre for scientific research and collections, it is dominated by a 65-metre-high eight-storey cocoon, which is – for those who get excited about such things – the largest sprayed-concrete curved structure in Europe. Over 17 million insect and three million plant specimens are contained within the building – just one indication of the dizzying range of the ongoing projects here.

One of the most exciting aspects of the Darwin Centre is the way that it lets children and adults alike appreciate that the Natural History Museum is a dynamic centre for working scientists as much as a display facility for everything from dinosaurs to dung beetles. Malaria and climate change are just two areas of research dealt with here; not only can children investigate both of these through interactive displays, but they can also spy on the museum's scientists as they go about their work in laboratories clearly visible from the gallery.

The whole experience is completely free, and takes around 45 minutes. There's even a take-home aspect, through a Nature Plus Card – a credit-card sized device that allows you to scan information from any of the computerised displays, then take it home and relay the details to your computer.

In addition to the cocoon there is the Attenborough Studio, a communication centre where visitors can attend – for free – both screened and live events. Real-life animals and scientists are to be found prowling around there at certain points of the day in order to introduce visitors to research (on animal vision, for example). Visitors who want to indulge in science themselves rather than just be voyeurs can also go to the Angela Marmont Centre for UK Biodiversity. Here, amateur naturalists can not only look at some of the museum's collection, but can even (within reason) bring in specimens of their own, which will then be analysed by the Centre's enquiries staff. What better way to spend a day out?

Out & About

London Stories Retold

The new Museum of London galleries are bold, original, informative and fun.

For three years, the lower floor of the Museum of London has been shrouded in dust sheets and mystery. Visitors to the upstairs gallery have been able to snatch mere tantalising glimpses of men in hard hats discussing the vast project going on down below. In May 2010, the new Galleries of Modern London – telling the story of the great city from 1666 to the present day – were unveiled. It was worth the wait.

Visitors enter the new galleries through the Sackler Hall, where a specially commissioned LED art installation by the Light Surgeons, *LDN24*, an ever-changing picture of London over 24 hours that stretches right around the walls, has pride of place.

Once inside the galleries, the first thing you notice is the sleek design of the new interiors. Although only one per cent of the museum's collection is on display, each object plucked from the vaults to be seen by the public has been given due consideration and placed in a context designed to give maximum impact. There are some lovely touches. Glass panels in the floors reveal collections underfoot. Cubby holes in the walls are stuffed with interesting objects. Exhibits are mounted at odd angles and surprising heights, all the better to get your mind to think differently. Interactivity features strongly, and touchscreens allow visitors to ask questions about life expectancy during Hogarth's time, say, or to explore Charles Booth's poverty maps

Charles Booth poverty map

or find out what's in the water of a London well. A walk-through Georgian pleasure garden introduces a touch of theatre. Here, visitors can sit on elegant reproduction park benches and listen to the stories related by various characters as they walk past (on video projections around the walls). The popular Victorian section has been spruced up and there are small displays on the Suffragettes, World War II and the suburbs, before the exhibition reaches the present day. Memorable exhibits include the original (and magnificent) Selfridges lifts, the wall panels from an 18th-century debtor's prison featuring some interesting graffiti, and intimate artwork *The Ghetto* by Tom Hunter, a fascinating facsimile model of the squat-filled (and now demolished) Hackney street Hunter lived in during the mid '90s.

The exterior of the museum has changed too, with glass panels in London Wall allowing views into the museum from the outside. The most striking object passers by can see is the fabulously decorative Lord Mayor's State Coach. That said, it's still as difficult to locate the museum's entrance as it ever was. The most child-friendly route from the Barbican tube station involves ignoring traffic-heavy Aldersgate Street and instead going up to the Barbican Highwalks (the entrance is up the staircase on the left just before leaving the tube station) and following the discreet signs. Those with buggies should go to St Paul's tube and walk up St Martin's Le Grand to the lift and escalator near the roundabout.

There are plans for the museum shop, which will soon sell items designed uniquely for the Museum of London and based on the collections. The Benugo café is another plus, although there's a designated picnic area too.

By comparison, the upstairs galleries now look a bit old-fashioned, but once there, children will still enjoy the attempts made to get them involved in the history of London, from dressing up clothes, to a stylish video presentation about the Black Death to a walk-in reconstruction of a Saxon hut. It's London, but not as you know it.

For listings details, *see p84*.

Expanding City: 1666-1850s Gallery

Sleepovers with a Difference

Nights in a museum.

Want to sleep with dinosaurs? Bed down under an Elizabethan cannon? Or wake up beside the mummies? Here we round up the top attractions that will let your kids bed down for the night. Call venues to find out dates of upcoming sleepovers.

Science Museum

The veteran in city sleepovers, Science Night at the Science Museum (*see p92*) has been running for so long that some of the current staff first attended as children in the '90s. Activities are based around a different theme each month but a make-and-take workshop, a science show, and an IMAX film are guaranteed.

After breakfast, once the doors are opened to the public, those exhausted by all the excitement head home to show off their creations but kids with energy to spare are free to explore the museum, including the 50 interactive exhibits in the Launchpad area and the dazzling Exploring Space Gallery.

British Museum

These popular quarterly sleepovers at the British Museum (*see p73*) are open to Young Friends of the British Museum and their chums. Past highlights include a Terracotta Warrior night, which saw kids leave with their own warrior, some Kung Fu kicks and a phrase or two of Chinese.

Every sleepover brings temporary and permanent exhibitions to life with story-telling surrounded by centuries of world history, before kids bed down in the Egyptian and Mesopotamian Galleries. September's event is focused on the Enlightenment, and in November there's

Science Museum

Out & About

Our optometrists and dispensing opticians have been looking after children's vision for years and years. We have specially designed eye tests for little ladies and little gents. And we can fit contact lenses for over 10 year olds.

With frames and sunspecs from Lindberg and other specialist brands, your child will not only see properly, they'll look great too.

AUERBACH & STEELE

FOR THE APPLE OF YOUR EYE

129 KING'S ROAD, CHELSEA SW3 4PW   020 7349 0001

LINDBERG

an eerie walk through the afterlife to coincide with the BM's exhibition about the Book of the Dead.

In addition to sleepover invitations, Young Friends of the British Museum receive a magazine, a gift membership pack full of museum goodies and the chance to attend other fun events.

Natural History Museum

For anyone who fancies themselves as the next David Attenborough, Dino Snores at the Natural History Museum (*see p87*) is the hot ticket. Visitors are taken by torch-light into the darkest depths of the museum, discovering clues along the way to solve a nature puzzle. The pleasures of this new addition to the sleepover scene include the opportunity to be dwarfed by the enormous blue whale and to get the microscope out for the insect hordes in the Revenge of the Mini-Beasts.

Explorers can recover from their adventure by watching a film or a show by leading naturalists before falling asleep under the watchful eye of the 150-million-year-old Diplodocus, in the iconic Central Hall.

The Golden Hinde

An opportunity to sail the seven seas in the company of famous and infamous explorer Sir Francis Drake, sleepovers aboard the *Golden Hinde* (*see p32*), a replica of Drake's ship permanently moored on the southern bank of the Thames, offer a 'voyage' in search of hidden treasures, and perhaps a bit of plundering too.

On arrival at 5pm a quick change into Tudor sailor costumes gets everyone set for firing the cannons, before a traditional Tudor dinner and storytelling. After an exhausting evening on the high seas, the young crew bed down on the gun deck among the cannons. During the chilly winter months there are electric radiators and additional blankets available for families who don't fancy replicating the harsh conditions Drake and his crew would have endured. There's an SIA-registered security guard on board all night as well as the actors who lead the fun. Popular for birthday parties, the ship is also available for private hire.

Hamleys

Not a budget option, but if cost is not an issue what party girl or boy wouldn't relish the chance to join the teddy bears at Hamleys (*see p281*) for their picnic, save the world with the action heroes, or relax at a doll's pampering session? The world-famous toy shop is available for private hire on Saturday nights, when trained staff run treasure hunts and games galore and a chef serves a midnight feast before the partygoers head to the land of nod.

Natural History Museum

Trips & Tours

London on the move.

Getting around

If speed is of the essence, it's generally best to hop on the tube (*see p286*), but taking the bus is far more scenic. Good routes for city sightseeing are the 7, 8, 11 and 12 (all double-deckers) and, along the South Bank, the single-decker RV1. A couple of old-style Routemaster buses – numbers 9 and 15 – now run as Heritage Routes; the 9 runs from the Aldwych via the Strand, Trafalgar Square and Piccadilly Circus to the Royal Albert Hall, and the 15 from Trafalgar Square to Tower Hill, allowing passengers to get a glimpse of the Strand, Fleet Street and St Paul's Cathedral. Normal fares apply.

Tourist information

To get the most from the capital, a tourist information office is an essential port of call. **Visit London** (7234 5800, www.visitlondon.com) is the city's official tourist information service, with its main office in Lower Regent Street. There are also outposts in Greenwich, Leicester Square and just by St Paul's Cathedral.

If your programme takes in some of the city's pricier sights, a **London Pass** (01664 485020, www.londonpass.com) gives you pre-paid access to more than 50 attractions. Check the website for details and prices.

In our listings, the initials 'EH' mean that English Heritage members, and their kids, get in free. 'NT' means National Trust members get free admission.

Britain & London Visitor Centre *1 Lower Regent Street, SW1Y 4XT (7808 3800, www.visitbritain.com). Piccadilly Circus tube.* **Open** *Apr, May* 9.30am-6.30pm Mon; 9am-6.30pm Tue-Fri; 10am-4pm Sat, Sun. *June-Sept* 9.30am-6.30pm Mon; 9am-6.30pm Tue-Fri; 10am-4pm Sat, Sun. *Oct-Mar* 9.30am-6pm Mon; 9am-6pm Tue-Fri; 10am-4pm Sat, Sun.

London Information Centre *Leicester Square, WC2H 7BP (7292 2333, www.londontown.com). Leicester Square tube.* **Open** *Phone enquiries* 8am-10pm Mon-Fri; 10am-8pm Sat, Sun. *In person* 10am-6pm Mon-Fri, noon-6pm Sat, Sun.

Moving experiences

On the river

City Cruises *7740 0400, www.citycruises.com.* **Departures** check website for details. **Tickets** vary. **Credit** MC, V.
City Cruises' handy Rail River Rover ticket (£14.50; £7.25 5-16s, reductions; free under-5s) combines hop-on, hop-off travel on any of its regular cruises (pick-up points: Westminster, Waterloo, Tower and Greenwich piers) with unlimited travel on the DLR.

London Duck Tours *7928 3132, www.london ducktours.co.uk.* **Tours** daily; phone for details *Pick-up* Chicheley Street, behind the London Eye. **Fares** £20; £16 reductions; £14 1-12s; £58 family (2+2). **Credit** AmEx, MC, V.
For a unique perspective on the City of Westminster, climb aboard one of these bright yellow amphibious vehicles. The thrilling road and river trip, lasting 75 minutes, starts at the London Eye and plunges into the Thames at Vauxhall.

London RIB Voyages *7928 8933, www. londonribvoyages.com.* **Departures** check website for details. **Tickets** £32.50-£45; £19.50-£28 under-17s. **Credit** AmEx, MC, V.
Sightseeing is fast and furious with RIB's speedboat trips, which power passengers from the London Eye to Canary Wharf (50mins) or the Thames Barrier (80mins). Book in advance.

London Waterbus Company *7482 2660, www.londonwaterbus.com.* **Departures** check website for details. **Fares** *Single* £6.50; £5.20 3-15s, reductions. *Return* £9.30; £7.40 3-15s, reductions. Free under-3s. **Credit** MC, V.
Navigate Regent's Canal in a narrowboat. Trips run between Camden Lock and Little Venice, stopping off at London Zoo.

Thames Clippers *0870 781 5049, www.thamesclippers.com.* **Departures** 6am-midnight Mon-Fri; 8.30am-midnight Sat, Sun. **Tickets** vary. **Credit** MC, V.
Equipped with a River Roamer ticket (£12; £6 5-15s; free under-5s) you can hop on and hop off along the banks of the Thames between Millbank Pier and Royal Arsenal Woolwich pier, with stops at Waterloo, Embankment, London Bridge, Tower, Canary Wharf, Greenwich and the O2. The Family Roamer costs £25 (2+3).

On the buses

Big Bus Company *0800 169 1365, 7233 9533, www.bigbustours.com.* **Departures** every 10-30mins. *Summer* 8.30am-6pm daily. *Winter* 8.30am-5pm daily. *Pick-up* Green Park (near the Ritz); Marble Arch (Speakers' Corner); Victoria (outside Thistle Victoria Hotel, 48 Buckingham Palace Road, SW1W 0RN).

Fares £25; £10 5-15s; free under-5s. Tickets valid for 24hrs, interchangeable between routes. **Credit** AmEx, MC, V.
These open-top buses, with commentary, stop at the major tourist sights, where customers can hop on and off at will. Big Bus also runs cruises and walking tours.

Original London Sightseeing Tour *8877 1722, www.theoriginaltour.com.* **Departures** *Summer* every 5-10mins, 9am-8pm daily. *Winter* every 10-25mins, 9am-5pm daily. *Pick-up* Grosvenor Gardens; Marble Arch (Speakers' Corner); Haymarket (Piccadilly Circus); Embankment tube; Trafalgar Square. **Fares** £24; £12 5-15s; free under-5s. **Credit** AmEx, MC, V.
Another open-top bus operation, taking a circuit of the sights. The Kids' Club tours include a special activity pack.

Pedal power

London Bicycle Tour Company *1A Gabriel's Wharf, 56 Upper Ground, SE1 9PP (7928 6838, www.londonbicycle.com).* Waterloo tube/rail. **Open** 10am-6pm daily. **Hire** £3/hr; £19/1st day, £9/day thereafter. **Credit** AmEx, MC, V.
Bike and tandem hire; children's bike seats are free with an adult bike. There are guided tours covering major sights in central London beginning at 10.30am.

London Pedicabs *01737 812268, www.londonpedicabs.com.* **Fares** from £3 per person per mile. **No credit cards**. Hard-working cycle rickshaws, based in Covent Garden and Soho.

Take a hike

Guided walking tours are also offered by **And Did Those Feet** (8806 4325, www.chr.org.uk), **Performing London** (01234 404774, www.performinglondon. co.uk) and **Silver Cane Tours** (07720 715295, www.silvercanetours.com).
Original London Walks *7624 3978, www. walks.com.* **Tours** £7; £5 reductions; 1 free under-15 per adult. **No credit cards**.
These themed walks criss-cross the capital, revealing all sorts of fascinating facts along the way. Plenty appeal to kids, not least the Harry Potter walk (3pm Sun) and Ghosts of the Old City walk (7.30pm Tue, Sat).

'Taxi!'

Black Taxi Tours of London *7935 9363, www.blacktaxitours.co.uk.* **Cost** £100-£115. **No credit cards**.
This company runs two-hour tour by taxi for up to five people.

Out & About

Festivals & Events

Celebrate London all year round.

There's no doubt about it, Londoners love a good knees-up. Whether it's cheering the **London Marathon** runners on (see p26), getting down to the steel bands and sound systems of the **Notting Hill Carnival** (see p21) or staring skywards as fireworks usher in **Chinese New Year** (see p25), there's something to suit all ages and tastes: what's more, most of it won't cost you a penny.

While we've included the regular events and festivals that keep the city in a giddy social whirl, there's always more going on: check *Time Out* magazine for the latest one-off celebrations and cultural happenings. We've given exact dates for events where possible; phone or check websites nearer the time for unconfirmed timings.

SUMMER

Coin Street Festival

Bernie Spain Gardens, next to Oxo Tower Wharf, SE1 9PH (7021 1686, www.coinstreet festival.org). Southwark tube/Waterloo tube/ rail. **Date** June-Sept 2010. **Map** p318 N7.
This welcoming, family-friendly summer shindig brings a series of culturally themed weekday and weekend events that celebrate different communities in the capital. Festivities take place in the open spaces around Bernie Spain Gardens, Gabriel's Wharf and the South Bank and include music, dance and performances, as well as craft and refreshment stalls and workshops. Check the website for more information nearer the time.

Beating Retreat

Horse Guards Parade, Whitehall, SW1A 2AX (booking 0844 847 2435). Westminster tube/Charing Cross tube/rail. **Date** June. **Map** p317 K8.
Held on two June evenings, this spirited, stirring ceremony kicks off at 9pm, with the 'Retreat' beaten on drums by the Mounted Bands of the Household Cavalry and the Massed Bands of the Guards Division.

Trooping the Colour

Horse Guards Parade, Whitehall, SW1A 2AX (7414 2271). Westminster tube/Charing Cross tube/rail. **Date** 2nd Sat June. **Map** p317 K8.
The Queen was actually born on 21 April, but this is her official birthday celebration, for practical reasons. At 10.45am, Her Majesty makes the journey from Buckingham Palace to Horse Guards Parade, then scoots home to watch a Royal Air Force flypast and receive a formal gun salute from Green Park.

Open Garden Squares Weekend

Various venues (www.opensquares.org). **Date** 2nd weekend in June.
For one weekend a year, the London Parks & Gardens Trust opens locked and gated green spaces to one and all. Tickets (£9, £7.50 in advance, free under-12s) allow entry to all participating gardens, which range from secret 'children-only' play areas to allotments and exclusive garden squares. Many are wheelchair-accessible and host activities and plant sales; if you're lucky, there might be home-made cakes to munch on as you admire the greenery. Check online for the full list of gardens taking part.

City of London Festival

Venues across the City, EC2-EC4 (7583 3585, www.colf.org). St Paul's tube/Bank tube/DLR/ Cannon Street, Farringdon or Moorgate tube/ rail/Blackfriars rail. **Date** 21 June-9 July 2010.
Founded in 1962, with the aim of revitalising the City's cultural life, this summer festival stages indoor ticketed concerts and free outdoor events in and around some of the Square Mile's finest historic buildings. Outdoor events, including walks, street theatre, jazz concerts and dance performances, run until 7 August.

Wimbledon Lawn Tennis Championships

All England Lawn Tennis Club, PO Box 98, Church Road, SW19 5AE (8944 1066, 8946 2244 info, www.wimbledon.org). Southfields tube, Wimbledon tube/rail. **Date** 21 June-4 July 2010.
To nab tickets for this prestigious tennis tournament, you'll need to plan ahead. For Centre Court and Court Number One seats, request an application form from the All

All eyes on the ball at the **London Youth Games**.

England Lawn Tennis Club between August and mid December the year before; you'll then be entered into the public ticket ballot. Queuing on the day should gain you entry to the outside courts. In the afternoon, returned show-court tickets are available from the booth opposite Court One, so it may be worth hanging about to see the stars slicing, serving and mopping their perspiring brows on one of the world's most famous courts.

Greenwich & Docklands International Festival

Various venues (8305 1818, www.festival.org). **Date** 24 June-4 July 2010.

With its vibrant mixture of theatre, music and spectacle, this free festival has been bringing spectacle and colour to the varied backdrops of Maritime Greenwich, the Isle of Dogs, Canary Wharf and Woolwich since 2007. Last year's Water theme was the first in an elemental series – the 2010 focus is Earth (drawing on Greenwich's Prime Meridian fame) and the following two editions in 2011 and 2012 will be Fire and Air respectively.

Young Pavement Artists Competition

www.muscular-dystrophy.org/pavementart. **Date** Closing date 25 June 2010

Over 5,000 schools and community and youth groups take part in this national competition, which aims to raise awareness of muscular dystrophy and generate funds for the Muscular Dystrophy Campaign. Children aged four to 19 can compete at events across the country, with pitches costing a pound per entrant. Photos of the day's winners are then entered into the national competition, judged by members of Tate Britain and the Royal Academy of Arts, which is followed by a prestigious awards ceremony.

Henley Royal Regatta

Henley Reach, Henley-on-Thames, Oxon RG9 2LY (01491 572153, www.hrr.co.uk). Henley-on-Thames rail. **Date** 30 June-4 July 2010; 29 June-3 July 2011.

First held in 1839, and under royal patronage since 1851, Henley is still going strong; it's now a five-day affair. Boat races range from open events for men and women through club and student crews to the Princess Elizabeth race for juniors (boys under the age of 19). Straw boaters and blazers are *de rigeur*, as is bringing a picnic.

Watch This Space

Theatre Square, outside the National Theatre, South Bank, SE1 9PX (7452 3400, www. nationaltheatre.org.uk/wts). Waterloo tube/ rail. **Date** July-Sept 2010. **Map** p318 M7.

This superb free festival brings all manner of entertainment to an artificial lawn laid out on the South Bank. Lounge in the sunshine and catch the best street theatre, circus, cinema, music, art and dance from all over the world.

Big Dance

Various venues (www.london.gov.uk/bigdance). **Date** 3-11 July 2010.

This week-long, biennial celebration of all styles of dance sees hundreds of jumping, jiving free events and performances taking place in parks, museums, theatres and streets across London. Various dance-related records were broken at the 2008 event, including the biggest number of streetdance moves performed in one minute, and the biggest Bollywood dance class.

London Youth Games

Various venues (7717 1570, www.londonyouth games.org). **Date** (finals) 3-4 July 2010.

In 2008 this mini-Olympics attracted 27,000 sporting hopefuls, all of them under 17, representing their London borough in 30 different sports – including archery, fencing, canoeing, cycling, rugby and athletics. The finals weekend takes place at Crystal Palace Sports Ground, while other competitions are held at venues around the capital throughout the summer. Extra entertainments include dance performances, DJs, street sport demonstrations and graffiti art.

Streatham Festival

Various venues (www.streathamfestival.com). **Date** 3-11 July 2010.

From humble beginnings in 2002, this local festival has blossomed into a week-long community arts jamboree. More than 50 events are held in all sorts of locations, from churches and youth centres to parks and bars. There are family heritage walks and talks, garden parties and parades, along with poetry workshops, theatre, dance, comedy and film. Check the online programme for details.

Chap & Hendrick's Olympiad

Bedford Square Gardens, WC1 (www.hendricks gin.com). Tottenham Court Road tube. **Date** 12 July 2010. **Map** p315 K5.

Expect a surreally splendid afternoon out at this terribly silly, terribly English event, where children can watch adults engage in all manner of tomfoolery. Events kick off with the lighting of the Olympic Pipe, with 'sports' including umbrella hockey (with a bowler hat for a ball) and the three-trousered limbo.

BBC Sir Henry Wood Promenade Concerts

Royal Albert Hall, Kensington Gore, SW7 2AP (7589 8212. box office, www.bbc.co.uk/proms). Knightsbridge or South Kensington tube/ 9, 10, 52 bus. **Date** 16 July-11 Sept 2010. **Map** p313 D9.

While plenty of the concerts are broadcast on the radio or TV, there's nothing like seeing them in person. Choose carefully and you should find something in the main programme that will appeal to children; there are also special family events, and a young composers' competition. Under-16s get half-price tickets to every prom, bar the legendary Last Night.

Lambeth Country Show

Brockwell Park, SE24 0NG (7926 7085, www. lambeth.gov.uk). Brixton tube/rail, then 2, 3, 68, 196 bus/Herne Hill rail. **Date** 17-18 July 2010.

Notting Hill Carnival. *See p21.*

Out & About

Celebrating London's river at the **Mayor's Thames Festival**.

Hankering for the countryside, and an escape from the urban grind and grime? No need to leave town; instead, head down to Brockwell Park's free country show. Aside from meeting and greeting assorted farmyard beasts, children can cheer on horse and dog shows, watch sheep-shearing and birds of prey demonstrations and have fun on numerous bouncy castles and fairground rides. An international array of food stalls keep the masses well-fed (don't miss the jerk chicken), while the strains of brass bands fill the air.

Sundae on the Common

Clapham Common, SW4 (www.benjerry. co.uk/sundae). Clapham Common tube. **Date** 24-25 July 2010.
A family-friendly mix of fairground activities and live music, last year's Sundae featured banana jousting (fair-trade of course) and toe wrestling – not to mention free ice-cream all day. You can pet farm animals, make cookies, scoot down the helter-skelter, pelt the coconut shy and have your fortune told by Mystic Moo. See the website for the latest musical line-up; in previous years, headline acts have included the Charlatans, Badly Drawn Boy and Ash. Tickets (£15) go on sale in June.

Apple Cart Festival

Shoreditch Park (07812 147 547, www. theapplecartfestival.com). Old Street tube/ rail. **Date** 25 July 2010.
This newcomer to the London festival scene comes from the same stable as the popular Underage Festival held annually in Victoria Park (see below). St Etienne top Apple Cart's music bill,

but families will want to check out the House of Fairy Tales, a parallel world in which to play, conceived by artists Gavin Turk and Deborah Curtis. There's also a bill of family-friendly magic on stage, as well as chocolate-making and puppet workshops and wordy games courtesy of the London Word Festival. Tickets are £33 per adult; £15 for 13-17-year-olds and free for 12s and under (although they still need a ticket).

Carnaval del Pueblo

Burgess Park, SE5 (7686 1633, www.carnaval delpueblo.co.uk). Elephant & Castle tube/12, 25, 36, 68, 68A, 100, 172 bus. **Date** 1 Aug 2010.
The UK's largest Latin American celebration kicks off at noon with a colourful parade from Elephant and Castle, which makes its way to Burgess Park. Here, the entertainment runs until around 9.30pm, and includes over 100 food and crafts stalls, a children's zone and four stages; the live Brazilian samba, Latin hip hop, Mexican mariachi and Colombian salsa soon gets everyone dancing.

Underage

Victoria Park, Old Ford Road, E3 (0844 477 2000 tickets, www.underagefestivals.com). Mile End tube/Cambridge Heath or Hackney Wick rail/8, 26, 30, 55, 253, 277, S2 bus. **Date** 1 Aug 2010. **Tickets** £26.50.
Strictly for 14- to 18-year-olds, Underage attracts an enviable line-up of alternative, rock and electro bands. This year's hipper-than-thou acts include the Horrors, Santigold, Little Boots and Ladyhawke. The ban on alcohol (and adults) is firmly enforced.

Notting Hill Carnival

Notting Hill, W10 & W11 (7727 0072, www.thenottinghillcarnival.com). Ladbroke Grove, Notting Hill Gate & Westbourne Park tube. **Date** 29-30 Aug 2010.

Held over the August bank holiday weekend, the annual Notting Hill Carnival is as loud, colourful and chaotic as they come – and the Sunday is traditionally decreed to be children's day. Masquerades, steel bands, decorative floats and ground-shaking sound systems take over the streets of Notting Hill, and there's curried goat, roti and fried plantain to sample. Its reputation for bringing short, sharp spikes to the annual crime rate continues to court controversy, but increasing commercialism and a strong police presence have made the carnival safer than ever.

AUTUMN

Great River Race

River Thames, from Island Gardens, Greenwich, E14 to Ham House, Richmond, Surrey (8398 9057, www.greatriverrace.co.uk). **Date** 25 Sept 2010.

Vessels of every shape and size compete over a 22-mile (35km) course in this traditional boat championship, from Viking longboats to Hawaiian war canoes. The race begins at 11am and reaches the finish at around 4.30pm. The best viewing points are at Richmond Bridge, along the South Bank or on the Millennium and Hungerford Bridges; due to tides, the race will go from east to west in 2009.

Regent Street Festival

Regent Street, W1 (7287 9601, www.regent streetonline.com). Oxford Circus or Piccadilly Circus tube. **Date** 26 Sept 2010. **Map** p316 J7.

All traffic is banned from Regent's Street in honour of this annual event; in its place, fairground rides, storytellers, street entertainers and musicians take over the tarmac for a day of fun. There's usually plenty of input from Regent Street's resident toy emporium extraordinaire, Hamleys.

Mayor's Thames Festival

Between Westminster & Tower Bridges (7983 4100, www.thamesfestival.org). London Bridge or Waterloo tube/rail/Blackfriars rail. **Date** 11-12 Sept 2010.

This jolly celebration of the Thames brings a weekend of riverside stalls, performers, sand sculptures, environmental activities and creative workshops – plus the chance to milk a cow in the middle of Southwark Bridge. An atmospheric lantern procession and dramatic fireworks display bring proceedings to a close on Sunday evening.

Spitalfields Show & Green Fair

Allen Gardens & Spitalfields City Farm, Buxton Street, E1 (7375 0441, www.alternativearts. co.uk). Whitechapel tube. **Date** 12 Sept 2010. **Map** p319 S5.

Oodles of own-made produce, handicrafts, Fairtrade goods and healing therapies are on offer at this east London horticultural show, along with plenty of advice on growing-your-own, composting, and other ways to go green.

Out & About

Big Draw. *See p22.*

City Harvest Festival

Capel Manor Gardens, Bullsmoor Lane, Enfield, Middx EN1 4RQ (0845 612 2122, www.capel.ac.uk). Turkey Street rail (closed Sun)/217, 310 bus. **Date** 18 Sept 2010.

Every year, London's city farms and community gardens gather in the grounds of Capel Manor College to hold a harvest festival. Events and activities include an animal show (with entrants from various city farms), milking and shearing demonstrations, vegetable and plant sales, crafts displays and food stalls.

Horseman's Sunday

Church of St John's Hyde Park, Hyde Park Crescent, W2 2QD (7262 1732, www.stjohns-hydepark.com/horsemans). Edgware Road or Lancaster Gate tube/Paddington tube/rail. **Date** 19 Sept 2010. **Map** p313 E6.

The first Horseman's Sunday was held in 1967, when local stables, threatened with closure, held an outdoor service to protest. Since then, it's become an equine institution: at noon, after morning service, the vicar of St John's rides out to bless and present rosettes to a procession of horses and riders, then delivers a short service. There are children's activities, games and face-painting in the church grounds.

Story of London

Various venues (www.london.gov.uk/storyoflondon). **Date** 1-10 Oct 2010.

Now in it's second year, Story of London is a month-long festival of events and activities, celebrating the city's past, present and future. Involving a collaboration of institutions from all over the capital, led by the Mayor's office, the ambitious programme incorporates music, history, film, walks and architecture. Check online for the full list of events.

Big Draw

Venues across London & nationwide (www.thebigdraw.org.uk). **Date** 1-31 Oct 2010.

Pencils at the ready – this brilliant annual event aims to bring out the inner artist in everyone, with imaginative free events running in libraries, community centres, shopping centres, gardens and cultural institutions across the country. London's big museums and galleries always come up with some excellent offerings.

Punch & Judy Festival

Covent Garden Piazza, WC2 (0870 780 5001, www.coventgardenmarket.co.uk). Covent Garden tube. **Date** early Oct 2010. **Map** p315 L6.

That's the way to do it! Slapstick humour and violent altercations between Punch and his missus hold kids enthralled, with performances taking place around the market building. Call nearer the time to confirm this year's date.

Children's Book Week

8516 2977, www.booktrust.org.uk. **Date** 4-10 Oct 2010.

This festival aims to encourage children of primary school age to get reading – and enjoy it. Hands-on activities and author visits take place across the country, and there's always plenty going on in London's schools and libraries. National Poetry Day (www.national poetryday.co.uk) is on 7 October 2010.

Pearly Kings & Queens Harvest Festival

St Paul's Church, Bedford Street, WC2E 9ED (8778 8670, www.pearlysociety.co.uk). Covent Garden tube. **Date** 4 Oct 2010 **Map** p317 L7.

Pearly kings and queens – so named because of the shiny white pearl buttons sewn in elaborate designs on their dark suits – have their origins in the 'aristocracy' of London's early Victorian costermongers, who elected their own royalty to look after their interests. Now charity representatives, today's pearly monarchs gather in their resplendent garb an hour before the 11am thanksgiving service.

The Baby Show

Earl's Court Exhibition Centre, SW5 9TA (0870 122 1313 booking, www.thebaby show.co.uk). Earl's Court tube. **Date** 22-24 Oct 2010.

Earl's Court overflows with all manner of baby-related paraphernalia, with a mind-boggling array of pregnancy gear, nursery equipment and stimulating toys. Consult the website to search for your area of interest.

Trafalgar Day Parade

Trafalgar Square, WC2 (7928 8978, www.ms-sc.org). Charing Cross tube/rail. **Date** 24 Oct 2010. **Map** p401 K7.

Over 500 sea cadets parade with marching bands and musical performances, in celebration of the British victory at Trafalgar. Events culminate in a wreath-laying at the foot of Nelson's Column, in honour of the mortally wounded admiral.

London to Brighton Veteran Car Run

Start at Serpentine Road, Hyde Park, W2 (01327 856024, www.lbvcr.com). Hyde Park Corner tube. **Date** 8 Nov 2010. **Map** p311 F8.

There's no time for lie-ins if you want to see this parade of gleaming vintage motors leaving London, or join the crowds lining the route. The

Out & About

buffed-up fleet sets off from Hyde Park at 7am, with the first cars reaching Brighton around 10am. The rest arrive by 4pm; bear in mind that the average speed is a stately 32kmph (20mph). The vehicles are on display in Regent Street the day before (11am-3pm, Saturday 31 October).

Bonfire Night

Date 5 Nov.

The weekend nearest to 5 November see numerous public pyrotechnic displays commemorating Guy Fawkes and his ill-fated Gunpowder Plot. Those at Battersea Park, Alexandra Palace and Crystal Palace are among London's best; for an overview, book a late ride on the London Eye (*see p28*).

Lord Mayor's Show

The City EC2-EC4 (7332 3456, www.lord mayorsshow.org). Mansion House, St Paul's or Temple tube/Bank tube/DLR/Blackfriars rail. **Date** 13 Nov 2010.

This is the day when, under the conditions of the Magna Carta, the newly elected Lord Mayor is presented for approval to the monarch, or his or her justices. Amid a procession of around 140 floats, the Lord Mayor leaves the Mansion House at 11am and travels through the City to the Royal Courts of Justice on the Strand, then receives a blessing at St Paul's Cathedral before returning to Mansion House. The procession takes around 75 minutes to pass by. At around 5pm, fireworks are set off from a barge moored on the Thames between Waterloo and Blackfriars Bridges; anywhere along the Embankment affords a good vantage point.

Discover Dogs

Earl's Court 2 Exhibition Centre, entrance on Lillie Road, SW5 9TA (7518 1012, www. discoverdogs.org.uk). West Brompton tube/ rail. **Date** 13-14 Nov 2010. **Map** p312 A11.

They say every dog has its day – and this is a chance for mutts that don't quite fit Crufts' criteria to take centre stage. Visitors can meet around 190 pedigree pooches and their breeders, watch Heelwork to Music displays and see husky team and police-dog agility demonstrations. Competition categories range from 'dog that looks most like a celebrity' to Scruffts (family crossbreed dog of the year).

Children's Film Festival

Main venue: Barbican Centre, Silk Street, EC2Y 8DS (7638 8891 Barbican box office, www.londonchildrenfilm.org.uk). Barbican tube. **Date** Nov 2010. **Map** p318 P5.

This annual festival proves that kids are interested in more sophisticated film fare than big blockbusters. The line-up features foreign language films, documentaries and animations; seven- to 12-year-olds are invited to join a jury and become film critics. Check online for workshops and events, many of which are free.

State Opening of Parliament

House of Lords, Palace of Westminster, SW1A 0PW (7219 4272/www.parliament.uk). *Westminster tube.* **Date** Nov/Dec 2010 (exact date tbc). **Map** p317 L9.

In a ceremony that has changed little since the 16th century, the Queen reopens Parliament after its summer recess. Watch Her Majesty arrive and depart in her Irish or Australian State Coach, attended by the Household Cavalry.

Christmas Lights & Tree

Covent Garden (0870 780 5001, www.covent gardenmarket.co.uk); Oxford Street (7462 0680); Regent Street (7152 5853, www.regent-street.co.uk); Bond Street (www.bondstreet association.com); Trafalgar Square (7983 4234/www.london.gov.uk). **Date** Nov-Dec 2010.

The glittering lights on St Christopher's Place, Marylebone High Street, Bond Street and Kensington High Street add a magical touch to grey winter's days. The giant fir tree that stands in pride of place in Trafalgar Square is an annual gift from the Norwegian people, in gratitude for Britain's role in liberating their country from the Nazis during World War II.

WINTER

London International Horse Show

Olympia Exhibition Centre, Hammersmith Road, W14 8UX (01753 847900, www.olympia horseshow.com). Kensington (Olympia) tube/ rail. **Date** 14-20 Dec 2010.

Enthusiasts of all things equestrian can enjoy dressage, show-jumping, mounted military displays, dog agility contests and a Shetland Pony Grand National. The grand finale features Father Christmas (with a sledge pulled by horses) and there are over 200 trade stands, so you can also do some seasonal shopping.

Bankside Frost Fair

Bankside Riverside, next to Tate Modern, SE1 9TG (7928 3998, www.visitsouthwark.com). Southwark tube/rail/Blackfriars rail. **Date** Dec 2010. **Map** p318 O7.

In centuries gone by, the Thames regularly froze over – whereupon enterprising Londoners set up 'Frost Fairs' on the ice, with skating, puppet shows, mulled wine and roast meat stalls. This wonderfully festive revival of the

Chinese New Year Festival

tradition takes place by the river, rather than on it; in previous years it has involved food and craft stalls, ice sculptures, children's shows and a lantern parade, although changes are afoot for 2010 so check the website nearer the time for further details.

Peter Pan Swimming Race

The Serpentine, Hyde Park, W2 (7298 2000, www.royalparks.gov.uk). Hyde Park Corner tube. **Date** 25 Dec.
Established in 1864 by *Peter Pan* author JM Barrie, this chilly 100-yard race draws intrepid swimmers (Serpentine Swimming Club members only) and spectators every Christmas morning, competing for the Peter Pan cup. However mild the weather is, the Serpentine always looks less than inviting.

New Year's Eve Celebrations

Date 31 Dec.
London's New Year revelry has traditionally been concentrated around Trafalgar Square; the spectacular fireworks on the South Bank are a more recent draw. Both attract huge crowds, and can be nightmarish with younger children in tow.

London International Mime Festival

Various venues (7637 5661, www.mimefest. co.uk). **Date** 15-30 Jan 2011.

An international array of companies and artists perform visual theatre of every genre: circus skills, mask, mime, clown and visual theatre shows appeal to audiences of all ages.

Chinese New Year Festival

Around Gerrard Street, Chinatown, W1, Leicester Square, WC2 & Trafalgar Square, WC2 (7851 6686, www.chinatownchinese.co.uk). Leicester Square or Piccadilly Circus tube. **Date** 6 Feb 2011. **Map** p317 K7.
Riotous celebrations to mark Chinese New Year begin at 11am with a children's parade that weaves its way from Leicester Square Gardens to Trafalgar Square, where lion and dragon dance teams entertain the masses. Firework displays at lunchtime and 5pm fill the sky with colour (and loud bangs, which might alarm unwary tinies).

National Storytelling Week

Various theatres, museums, bookshops, arts centres, schools, libraries & pubs (8866 4232 Del Reid, www.sfs.org.uk). **Date** 29 Jan-5 Feb 2011.
This annual celebration of the art of storytelling, which has been around for over a decade now, sees theatres, bookshops, community centres and schools across the country hosting events for tellers and listeners. Catering to all ages, the stories are drawn from an array of global cultures.

Great Spitalfields Pancake Day Race

Dray Walk, Old Truman Brewery, 91 Brick Lane, E1 6QL (7375 0441, www.alternative arts.co.uk). Aldgate East tube/Liverpool Street tube/rail. **Date** 8th Mar 2011. **Map** p319 S5.
Relay teams of four toss pancakes as they race along Dray Walk, with heats starting at 12.30pm; all proceeds go to the London Air Ambulance charity. Register in advance if you fancy taking part and bring your own frying pan (pancakes are provided); everyone races together, so it isn't suitable for younger children. It's fun to go along as a spectator though, as fancy-dress clad teams get flipping and pancakes hit the pavement.

SPRING

National Science & Engineering Week

Various venues (www.britishscience association.org). **Date** 11-20 Mar 2011.
A week of scientific shenanigans, hosted by the British Association for the Advancement of Science. From hands-on shows, workshops and guided nature walks for youngsters to in-depth discussions for adults, each event celebrates different aspects of science, engineering and technology. Check the website for details.

St Patrick's Day Parade & Festival

Trafalgar Square, Leicester Square & Covent Garden (7983 4000, www.london.gov.uk). **Date** 17 Mar. **Map** p317 K7.
This good-natured, raucous parade departs from Hyde Park Corner at noon and continues to romp through the streets until 6pm. Expect lively performances of traditional Irish music in Trafalgar Square, a Covent Garden food market, ceilidh dancers in Leicester Square and lots of other activities for all ages.

Kempton Park Family Fun Day

Kempton Park, Sunbury-on-Thames, Middx TW16 5AQ (01932 782292, www.kempton. co.uk). Kempton Park rail. **Date** Apr and May 2011 (specific dates tbc).
Take the train from Waterloo for a day at the races. Free entertainment (simulator rides, crafts, a soft play area, face-painting, balloon-modelling) is laid on and previous years have seen lavish concerts to keep the youngsters happy while you blow their university fees on the gee-gees.

Shakespeare's Birthday

Various venues around South Bank & Bankside. **Date** 23 Apr 2011.

Celebrations of the Bard's birth date centre around Shakespeare's Globe and Southwark Cathedral, with performances, music, readings and walks marking his contribution to literature.

London Marathon

Greenwich Park to the Mall via the Isle of Dogs, Victoria Embankment & St James's Park (7902 0200, www.virginlondonmarathon.com). **Date** 17 Apr 2011.
Completing this 26.2 mile (42km) course is no mean feat, so the runners need all the support they can get. Energetic 11 to 17s can compete in the three-mile Mini London Marathon – check online for details of time trials.

Canalway Cavalcade

Little Venice, W9 (01494 783453, 07876 597941, www.waterways.org.uk). Warwick Avenue tube/Paddington tube/rail. **Date** 30 Apr-2 May 2011.
Decked out in bunting and flowers, more than 130 colourful narrowboats assemble in the pool of Little Venice to celebrate this three-day Bank Holiday boat bash. Stalls line the area, and events include a teddy bears' picnic, Punch and Judy shows, music and (of course) boat trips. The beautiful lantern-lit boat procession on Sunday evening is a must-see.

May Fayre & Puppet Festival

St Paul's Church Garden, Bedford Street, WC2E 9ED (7375 0441/www.alternative arts.co.uk). Covent Garden tube. **Date** 8 May 2011. **Map** p317 L7.
Marking the first recorded sighting of Mr Punch in England (by Pepys, in 1662), this free event offers puppetry galore from 10.30am to 5.30pm. A brass band procession around Covent Garden is followed by a service at 11.30am in St Paul's Church, with Mr Punch in the pulpit. Then there are puppet shows, booths and stalls, plus workshops for puppet-making and dressing-up. Folk music and maypole dancing, clowns and jugglers add to the mayhem.

Kew Summer Festival

Royal Botanic Gardens, Kew, Richmond, Surrey TW9 3AB (8332 5655, www.kew.org. uk). Kew Gardens tube/rail/Kew Bridge rail. **Date** May-Sept 2010.
Each season at Kew Gardens brings a new and varied programme of events and family activities. Among other things, this year sees the Plantasic Play area, where children can explore the inner workings of a plant by tunnelling through gigantic roots and up through the stem and flower parts of a plant – learning all about photosythesis and pollination along the way.

Sightseeing

Attractions

Big fun for small people.

There's no getting away from it: London is bursting with things to do. In this chapter, we've listed the city's most famous sights and its most iconic buildings – from the Tower of London (*see p41*) to the London Eye (*see below*) – and looked at how they can be best enjoyed from a child's perspective. At some of them, your children will learn something while they have fun; at others it's just about the fun (see our Thrills & Chills section).

London's top tourist attractions charge high fees, so pick and choose carefully so your child gets the most out of each experience. To help parents out, we've marked our recommended age range in green. Some attractions offer free entry to under-fives, but that doesn't necessarily mean they'll enjoy it.

ASTRONOMY

Royal Observatory & Planetarium
Greenwich Park, SE10 9NF (8312 6565, www.rognmm.ac.uk). Cutty Sark DLR/Greenwich DLR/rail. **Open** 10am-5pm daily (last entry 4.30pm). *Tours* phone for details. **Admission** free. *Space Safari* £6.50; £4.50 1-16s, reductions; free under-1s; £17.50 family (2+2). *Tours* free. **Credit** MC, V. 3+ (5+ for shows)
This imposing set of buildings is part of a World Heritage Site and grouped in with the National Maritime Museum (*see p100*). In the courtyard is the Greenwich Meridian Line, where visitors can stand with one foot in the Western Hemisphere and one in the Eastern; every place in the world is measured in terms of longitudinal distance from this point. The Observatory, originally built for Charles II by Wren in 1675, underwent a £15m refurbishment in 2007. The Peter Harrison Planetarium is the impressive result. Inside, shows about the stars are presented by a Royal Observatory astronomer who enjoys fielding knotty nipper questions. The shows are full of awesome facts: did you know there are more stars in the galaxy than the total number of heartbeats in the history of human existence?

Neighbouring galleries chart timekeeping since the 14th century, and the Observatory's dome houses the largest refracting telescope in the country. In the Observatory Courtyard is a small summerhouse, home to London's only public camera obscura. The moving, real-time view of Greenwich and the Thames is best seen on a bright day. *See also p114* **Great Days Out**. *Buggy access (courtyard only). Café. Nappy-changing facilities. Nearest picnic place: Greenwich Park. Shop.*

BIRD'S EYE VIEWS

London Eye
Riverside Building (next to County Hall), Westminster Bridge Road, SE1 7PB (0870 990 8883, www.londoneye.com). Westminster tube/Waterloo tube/rail. **Open** Oct-Apr 10am-8pm daily. *May, June, Sept 10am-9pm daily. July, Aug 10am-9.30pm daily.* **Admission** £17.88; £14.30 reductions (not offered at weekends, or July & Aug); £9.50 4-15s; free under-5s. Fast Track tickets £27.88. **Credit** AmEx, MC, V. **Map** p317 M8. All ages
2010 marks the tenth anniversary of the London Eye. The majestic circle rising above the Thames has become such a defining point on London's skyline, it's hard to believe it was originally only supposed to be here for half that time. No one wants to see it come down, and it's very near the top of every child's must-do list. Some kids, expecting a more white-knuckle affair, express disappointment that it turns so slowly, but there's no other view in London like it. Each ride (or flight, as the ticket office has it) is one complete revolution and takes half an hour – long enough to have a good look at the Queen's back garden and trace the silvery snaking of the Thames.

The queues for tickets can be long, especially on clear days, but you can book a Fast Track ticket online, which allows you to turn up just 15 minutes before the ride (there's a hefty tariff for the convenience though). Night flights provide a twinkly experience, and the Eye gets festive with fairy lights at Christmas; other holiday specials include Hallowe'en and Easter. Visit the website for special Eye and river cruise packages.

Sightseeing

Buggy access. Café. Disabled access: toilet. Nappy-changing facilities. Nearest picnic place: Jubilee Gardens. Shop.

Monument

Monument Street, EC3R 8AH (7626 2717, www.themonument.info). Monument tube. **Open** 9.30am-5pm daily. **Admission** £3; £1 5-15s; free under-5s. **No credit cards. Map** p319 Q7. 6+
The tallest freestanding stone column in the world was designed by Christopher Wren and is a monument to the Great Fire of London of 1666. It is 61m (202ft) high, and located 61m (202ft) west of the exact location of the bakery in Pudding Lane where the fire broke out. The Monument got an extensive makeover recently, and has already started winning awards. The stone has been cleaned, the golden orb re-gilded and there's an improved viewing gallery at the top (although we're not sure we like the talking telescopes). Children who make it to the top of the 311 steps can expect two treats: the spectacular view from the top and a commemorative certificate for the climb. At ground level, you can admire relayed views from the top.
Nearest picnic place: riverside by London Bridge.

Tower Bridge Exhibition

Tower Bridge, SE1 2UP (7403 3761, www.tower bridge.org.uk). Tower Hill tube/Tower Gateway DLR. **Open** *Apr-Sept* 10am-6.30pm daily (last entry 5.30pm). *Oct-Mar* 9.30am-6pm daily (last entry 5pm). **Admission** £7; £5 reductions; £3 5-15s; free under-5s; £16 family (2+2). **Credit** AmEx, MC, V. **Map** p319 R8. 6+

A popular urban myth doing the rounds in late 20th century had it that an American, Robert McCulloch, bought London Bridge thinking he was buying London's most iconic river crossing. Tourists often still refer to this bridge as London Bridge, but Londoners think the two enormous towers offer some clue as to its proper identity. It's a majestic, unforgettable structure, partly because of the bascules that raise when a ship needs to come through. It took eight long years to build, finally opening in 1894. At first, it was painted an unexciting shade of brown: only in 1977, in celebration of the Queen's Silver Jubilee, was it painted in jaunty red, white and blue. A lift transports you to the walkway foyer, 42m (138ft) above the Thames, where you watch a short film on the history of the bridge, then pass through both walkways to catch the stupendous views to the east and west. Large aerial photographs pinpoint famous landmarks (kids can take a playsheet and tick them off), and there are photo points where you can slide open the windows to get an unimpeded shot. Ring for details of occasional school-holiday storytelling events and for when the famous bascules will next be raised. From the walkways, it's a short stroll to the south tower and the Victorian engine rooms, for a more thorough explanation of the hydraulics involved. The summer exhibition of 2010 will display photographs of the Thames, taken along its entire 215 mile length.
Buggy access. Disabled access: lift, toilet. Nappy-changing facilities. Nearest picnic place: Potters Field, Tower of London Gardens. Shop.

Royal Observatory & Planetarium

Great Days Out
South Bank & Bankside

Tower of London

The majestic snaking Thames is the reason this great city exists. It was the trade hub on which all expansion and wealth were built. But when shipping went out of fashion for transporting cargo, the city turned its back on the river for several decades. Many of London's great cultural institutions, old and new, nestle along its banks and the opening of the Thames Path in the mid 1990s went a long way to making them more easily accessible.

The South Bank itself is a wonderful place for a family day out, even if you ignore the varied organised activities on offer at its various institutions. The wide, riverside promenade is perfect terrain for wheels of any sort (scooters, bikes or skates), while the sculptural landscaping is good for impromptu climbing adventures; children of all ages will want to watch open-mouthed in awe at the skateboarders' pit underneath the Hayward Gallery. Beyond that, Bankside's attractions – including Tate Modern, Borough Market and the Golden Hinde – stretch off towards the east.

The arts

The iconic **Royal Festival Hall** (*see p164*) often has free dance, music and poetry performances and events for families in the foyer or out on the terrace; check online for details.

Jeppe Hien's playful outdoor water sculpture *Appearing Rooms* has become an annual fixture and will be in residence until 19 September 2010 – walk inside the rooms as one wall of water disappears, then hide inside when it shoots up again. Endless fun. Since 2009, a large purple cow known as Udderbelly squats just the other side of Hungerford Bridge from the RFH in May and June, hosting a preview of Edinburgh Festival treats including comedy, music, circus, theatre and lots of children's shows and workshops.

The light, bright **Hayward Gallery** (*see p164*) is free for under-12s. Whatever the current exhibition, it's an intriguing place to explore. Further east is the **BFI Southbank** (*see p167*); on Saturday mornings, junior film screenings bring a mix of current and classic hits. You can also book a viewing station in the mediathèque and choose from over 1,000 films and TV programmes from the BFI archive.

The **IMAX** (*see p165*) is just around the corner. Kids enjoy wearing the 3D glasses for special features, but the storylines can be secondary to the fantastic effects that seem to leap from the screen.

Strolling past the National Theatre – home to the **Watch This Space Festival** (*see p18*) every summer – will take you to Gabriel's Wharf, where arts and crafts shops sit alongside cafés and restaurants. This area is always bustling, but never more so than during the **Coin Street Festival** (*see p17*), when it's overtaken by performers celebrating different communities in the capital. All events are free, taking place in and around the green spaces of Bernie Spain Gardens.

Head under Blackfriars Bridge, along Queen's Walk. Next stop for the arts is **Tate Modern** (*see p67*), once Bankside Power Station. Children absolutely love this vast gallery (which plans to expand dramatically by 2012). Even the sloping entrance to the Turbine Hall is exciting to young eyes and, once inside, the sheer scale of the hall gives them pause for thought.

Further along Bankside is the distinctive **Shakespeare's Globe** (*see p190*), which offers guided tours of the building and seasonal performances.

History writ large

At Southwark Bridge, one wall is covered with an etching depicting the frost fairs in the days when the Thames was 'frozen o'er'. Walk as far as you can by the river until you are diverted past the Vinopolis wine museum, down Clink Street and straight to the **Clink Prison Museum** (*see p95*), where unsettling exhibitions reveal what life was like for the prisoners incarcerated here from 1247 to 1780.

Straight ahead, in Pickfords Wharf, is a replica of the **Golden Hinde** (*see p32*), the tiny vessel in which Sir Francis Drake circumnavigated the globe in the 16th century. Just around the corner is **Southwark Cathedral** (*see p42*); its gardens are great for a picnic. Turn left

---

LUNCH BOX

Also in the area: Giraffe, Nando's, Pizza Express (four branches), Strada, Wagamama.

fish! *Cathedral Street, Borough Market, SE1 9AL (7407 3801, www.fishkitchen.com).* Posh fish and chips. *See p240.*

House of Crêpes *56 Upper Ground, SE1 9PP (7401 9816).* Flippin' lovely pancakes in sweet and savoury forms.

Riverside Terrace Café *Royal Festival Hall, Southbank Centre, SE1 8XX (0871 663 2501).* Arts centre café.

Table *83 Southwark Street, SE1 OHX (7401 2760, www.thetablecafe.com).* Superbly inventive salads, sarnies and hot meals, made from carefully-sourced ingredients.

Tate Modern Café 2 *2nd Floor, Tate Modern, SE1 9TG (7401 5014, www.tate.org.uk).* Highly recommended for children. *See p223.*

---

at the cathedral, taking the pavement studded with blue and green lights that goes under London Bridge (Montague Close). Keep walking until you emerge on Tooley Street, not far from the **London Dungeon** (*see p52*), where London's great disasters and grisly murders are brought garishly to life.

Those needing a pit stop and some 21st-century materialist diversions should follow the signs to **Hays Galleria**, a touristy enclave with shops and restaurants. It also houses a ship-like sculpture by David Kemp called *The Navigators*. A rather more substantial vessel looms up ahead, though. Rejoin the Thames footpath to see **HMS Belfast** (*see p99*), a floating wing of the Imperial War Museum. Carry on eastwards until you reach City Hall, the odd-shaped, glass-sided headquarters of Mayor Boris Johnson, the London Assembly and the Greater London Authority. This is part of a 13-acre riverside development known as More London, which has some sculptural fountains that children love to play in. Potters Fields Park is next door, and a great place for a picnic with views of **Tower Bridge** (*see p29*) and the **Tower of London** (*see p41*), just across the river.

London Eye. *See p28.*

LIVING HISTORY

Age Exchange Reminiscence Centre

11 Blackheath Village, SE3 9LA (8318 9105, www.age-exchange.org.uk). Blackheath rail.
Open 10am-5pm Mon-Fri; 10am-4pm Sat.
Admission free. Groups must book in advance; charges vary. **Credit** MC, V. 8+
Run by the charity Age Exchange, this living history centre comprises several different areas. A mock-up of a grocer's shop from about 60 years ago features drawers of comestibles; an old-fashioned sweetie shop stocks classics like rosy apples; and a 1940s sitting room features vintage toys, a stove and old-style furnishings. It's a low-key, cosy sort of place that aims to promote lively communication between the generations; there's also a small café and theatre space at the back. The Centre's programme of exhibitions is based on older people's memories and it also organises a variety of workshops; check the website for dates of future attractions.
Buggy access. Café. Disabled access: toilet. Nearest picnic place: centre gardens. Shop.

Dennis Severs' House

18 Folgate Street, E1 6BX (7247 4013, www.dennissevershouse.co.uk). Liverpool Street tube/rail. **Open** noon-2pm 1st & 3rd Mon of mth; Mon evenings (times vary; booking required); noon-4pm Sun. **Admission** £8 Sun; £5 noon-2pm Mon; £12 Mon evenings. No under-10s. **Credit** MC, V. **Map** p319 R5. 10+

As much art installation as museum, a visit here is an unusual experience to be savoured. Dennis Severs (1948-1999) was the artist son of a garage owner from California, who came to Spitalfields and fell in love with the area and this house. He restored the house to its original splendour (living day-to-day *sans* bathroom, electricity or modern cooking facilities), created a fictional Huguenot silk-weaving family to live in it and opened the doors to the public.

Each of the ten rooms is the scene of a drama, set between 1724 and 1914. Visitors make their way from the cellar to the kitchen, and on to the grander entertaining rooms above, hearing footsteps, whispers and doors closing, smelling the scent of pomanders and seeing strewn clothes and half-eaten meals. It's as if the inhabitants deserted the rooms seconds before; Severs himself called it a 'still life drama'. No museum can provide an experience quite like it. *Nearest picnic place: Broadgate Circus (Liverpool Street Station), Elder Street Gardens. Shop.*

Golden Hinde

Pickfords Wharf, Clink Street, SE1 9DG (7403 0123, www.goldenhinde.com). Monument tube/London Bridge tube/rail. **Open** daily; times vary. Phone for details. *Tours* phone for times. **Admission** £6; £4.50 reductions; £4.50 4-16s; free under-4s; £18 family (2+3). **Credit** MC, V. **Map** p319 P8. 4+
On a trip to trendy Borough, after you and the kids have secured some fresh produce from the market, walk around the corner to the river and take a look at this replica of of Sir Francis

Enjoy hundreds of great days out

in Lee Valley Regional Park

Family fun
Let the kids go wild at the farms, take a boat trip along the River Lee or enjoy a picnic, cycle ride or walk in picturesque countryside.

Get active
Try something new and burn off that excess energy with athletics, fishing, golf, horse riding, ice skating and watersports, there's plenty to keep you busy!

Events for all
Join us for a family event near you, from fun runs to outdoor theatres, cycle rides, scarecrow making and wildlife activities, there's plenty going on and many events are free.

Visit our website for further information on activities and events or call us on 08456 770 600

www.leevalleypark.org.uk

Lee Valley Park

Open spaces and sporting places

Christopher Wren's **Monument**. *See p29.*

Mon, Tue; 11.30am-7.30pm Wed; 10.30am-6.30pm Thur; 9.30am-3pm Fri. Closed bank hols. *House of Lords Visitors' Gallery* 2.30-10pm Mon, Tue; 3-10pm Wed; 11am-7.30pm Thur; 10am until close of business Fri. Check website for debate times. *Tours* summer recess only; phone for details for other times. **Admission** *Visitors' Gallery* free. *Tours* £11.70; £7.80 reductions; £4.80 5-15s; free under-5s; £29.20 family (2+2). **Credit** MC, V. **Map** p317 L9. 10+

The new coalition government in residence, might make a visit even more interesting for any youngster learning about politics. The building we see today, with its 1,100 rooms and three miles of corridors, was rebuilt by Charles Barry and Augustus Pugin. All that's left of the original Palace of Westminster that burned down in 1834 are the Westminster Hall (used for major ceremonial events) and the Jewel Tower. Tours run all year round for UK residents (overseas visitors must wait until summer opening), when Parliament is not sitting; visitors can also attend debates and watch committees in session. Children are usually satisfied by the mere proximity of the big old bell known as Big Ben, but only UK residents over 11 can climb the Clock Tower to take a closer look. All visits must be booked ahead through your MP.

Buggy access. Disabled access: lift, toilet. Nappy-changing facilities. Nearest picnic place: Victoria Tower Gardens. Shop.

Drake's 16th-century galleon. The first ship to circumnavigate the globe (in a voyage that began in 1577) it's surprisingly small, and looks almost like an expensive model toy. This thoroughly seaworthy replica *Golden Hinde* was built in 1973 to mark the admiral-pirate's 400th birthday – after which it sailed to San Francisco.

Pirate Fun Days offer storytelling, a treasure hunt and prizes for the best pirate costume. Families can also attend sleepovers, in which participants dress in period clothes, eat Tudor food, learn ancient seafaring skills and sleep next to the cannons. These take place on Saturdays and cost £39.95 per person (the minimum age for would-be recruits is six years old). Costumes and entertainment are provided; book ahead and bring a sleeping bag. During the school holidays there are storytelling sessions, craft activities and special workshops every weekend. You can also have a party here; ring or check online for details.

Nearest picnic place: Southwark Cathedral Gardens, riverside benches. Shop.

Houses of Parliament

Parliament Square, SW1A 0AA (Commons info 7219 3000/Lords info 7219 3107/tours 7219 4206/www.parliament.uk). Westminster tube. **Open** *(when in session) House of Commons Visitors' Gallery* 2.30-10.30pm

Linley Sambourne House

18 Stafford Terrace, W8 7BH (7602 3316 Mon-Fri, 7938 1295 Sat, Sun, www.rbkc. gov.uk/linleysambournehouse). High Street Kensington tube. **Open** *Tours* (groups only; maximum 12 people. Pre-booking essential) 11.15am, 2.15pm Weds; 11.15am, 1pm, 2.15pm, 3.30pm Sat, Sun; also by appointment. **Admission** £6; £4 reductions; £1 under-18s. **Credit** MC, V. **Map** p314 A9. 5+

There's plenty to enjoy here even if you're not particularly interested in Edward Linley Sambourne, the Victorian cartoonist and contributor to *Punch*. His classical Italianate house has almost all its original fittings and furniture and can be visited only by eccentric (and terrific) pre-booked tours. On Saturdays and Sundays these are guided by costumed actors, which goes down well with children. Gossipy housekeeper Mrs Reffle shines a cheeky light into Victorian family life and tells jokes along the way. There's also a visitors' centre, where children can take part in craftwork sessions relating to objects in the house.
Shop.

Shakespeare's Globe

*21 New Globe Walk, Bankside, SE1 9DT
(7401 9919, 7902 1500 tour information,
www.shakespeares-globe.org). Mansion House
tube/London Bridge tube/rail.* **Open** *Box office
theatre bookings* 10am-6pm daily. *Tours* 9am-
5pm daily. May-Sept afternoon tours only visit
the Rose Theatre, not the Globe. **Tickets** £5-
£33. *Tours* £10.50; £8.50 reductions; £6.50 5-
15s; free under-5s; £28 family (2+3). **Credit**
AmEx, MC, V. **Map** p318 P7. 8+

Shakespeare's Globe is a reconstruction of the
Bard's own theatre, less than 100m (328ft) from
where the original stood. It opened in 1997, the
brainchild of actor Sam Wanamaker. Tours take
place all year, and include the UnderGlobe
exhibition on the reconstruction, Elizabethan
theatres and Shakespeare's London; the theatre
season runs from late April to early October.
Historically authentic performances of
Shakespeare's plays make up the bulk of the
programme, but new theatre also gets a showing.

There's fun for all around the time of
Shakespeare's birthday (23 April) and at the
drama sessions for eight to 11s that accompany
the theatre season; see the website or ring 7902
1433 for details. The remains of the Rose
Theatre (www.rosetheatre.org.uk), where many
of Shakespeare's works were staged, are around
the corner in the basement of an office block.
*Café. Disabled access: lift, toilet. Nappy-
changing facilities. Nearest picnic place:
South Bank benches. Restaurant. Shop.*

PALACES & STRONGHOLDS

Buckingham Palace & Royal Mews

*SW1A 1AA (7766 7300, www.royalcollection.
org.uk). Green Park or St James's Park tube/
Victoria tube/rail.* **Open** *State Rooms* 27 July-29
Sept 9.45am-3.45pm daily. *Royal Mews* 20 Mar-
30 Oct 11am-4pm Mon-Thur, Sat, Sun (last
entry 3.15pm when palace is open); 26 July-29
Sept 10am-5pm daily (last entry 4.15pm).
Queen's Gallery 10am-4.30pm (closes 5.30pm)
daily. Closed during Ascot & state occasions.
Admission *State Rooms* £17; £9.75 5-16s;
£15.50 reductions; free under-5s; £45 family
(2+3). *Royal Mews* £7.75; £5 5-16s; £7
reductions; free under-5s; £20.50 family (2+3).
Queen's Gallery £8.75; £4.50 5-16s; £7.75
reductions; free under-5s; £22 family (2+3). *Joint
ticket* (Royal Mews and Queen's Gallery) £15;
£8.75 5-16s; £13.50 reductions; £38.50 family
(2+3). **Credit** AmEx, MC, V. **Map** p316 H9. All
ages (Royal Mews). 5+ (Queen's Gallery).

Shakespeare's Globe

Sightseeing

Great Days Out
Westminster

Westminster is London's centre of power. It is the London featured in storybooks, plastered over souvenirs and embedded in the perception of anyone who hasn't actually been here before. Westminster is the centre of politics, where the Queen lives and where most of the city's hotels are. It has remained largely unchanged for centuries. The iconic sights and sounds are endless, from the distinctive peal of Big Ben to the lions in Trafalgar Square, to the scarlet-clad Guards at Buckingham Palace.

Nelson's patch

Though the official centre of London is just south of here (marked by a small plaque behind the equestrian statue of Charles I), **Trafalgar Square** is the city's symbolic heart. Its delights are timeless: the great lions at the base of Nelson's column are often overrun with children, who shelter between their massive paws or try to clamber astride their surprisingly high sun-warmed backs. Above the throng, Admiral Nelson gazes across the city from atop his granite column.

There's plenty going on at his feet, with all manner of protests, performances and free festivals held here throughout the year. Dance a jig to lilting Irish fiddles in celebration of St Patrick's Day, see the famous fountains filled with floating lanterns for Diwali, or gawp at a fiery-mouthed dragon, weaving its way through the revellers welcoming in Chinese New Year.

While military dignitaries and royalty occupy three stone pedestals around the square, the fourth plinth showcases contemporary artworks. From May 2010, Yinka Shonibare's *Nelson's Ship in a Bottle* is in residence. It's impressive and commemorates the Battle of Trafalgar, although perhaps lacks the daring of some earlier commissions.

Art for all

At the northern edge of Trafalgar Square, follow the broad flight of stairs up to the splendid **National Gallery** (*see p61*). You can pick up various audio tours and trails around the glorious artworks, or design and print out your own bespoke route in the Sainsbury Wing's ArtStart room. Sundays and school holidays are our favourite times to visit, with free art workshops for five to 11s and story sessions for under-fives; enquiring minded toddlers can squeeze on to the magic carpet to learn about a selected painting.

Alternatively, scoot up past the National Gallery and on to the **National Portrait Gallery** (*see p61*), where all sorts of

Big Ben.

famous faces peer down from the walls: after checking your heroes have been honoured (we're glad to see Roald Dahl has no less than three likenesses), you can head to the rooftop Portrait Restaurant for a posh afternoon tea and truly magnificent views.

For more down-to-earth grub and prices, take the kids to the excellent Café in the Crypt at nearby St-Martin-in-the-Field – also home to the low-key but lovely **London Brass Rubbing Centre** (see p195).

All the queen's horses

Another option is to head down Whitehall, keeping your camera at the ready. Why? Well for a start, the dashing chaps of the Household Cavalry – and their trusty steeds – are headquartered here. At Horse Guard Parade, you can watch the mounted regiment change the Queen's Life Guard at 11am (10am on Sundays). With their shiny coats and well-polished hooves, the horses are every bit as dapper and professional as their riders; for a glimpse of them when they're off duty, visit the **Household Cavalry Museum** (see p99), which offers a sneaky peek into the stables.

Halfway down Whitehall, Downing Street is guarded by a rather less photogenic phalanx of policemen. Though the road is closed to the public, you can peep through the heavy iron gates to see No.10. The road leads on to Parliament Square, **Westminster Abbey** (see p45), and the **Houses of Parliament** (see p34) – home, of course, to **Big Ben**.

A palatial park

The Abbey and the home of British politics are interesting for older children, but on a sunny day we'd be tempted to forgo its suits and seriousness in favour of a stroll and a nice ice-cream in **St James' Park** (see p125), and a quick peek at **Buckingham Palace** (see p35). The Changing of the Guard, as witnessed by Alice and Christopher Robin in AA Milne's famous ditty, takes place in the palace forecourt. The ceremony begins at 11.30am, and is held every day from May to July, then on alternate days for the rest of the year.

LUNCH BOX

Also in the area: Pizza Express.
Café in the Crypt *St-Martin-in-the-Fields, Duncannon Street, WC2N 4JJ (7736 1158, www.smitf.org)*. Wholesome comfort food and nursery puds, with child-sized portions of main courses available on request.
Inn the Park *St James's Park, SW1A 2BJ (7451 9999, www.innthepark.com)*. Expensive but appealing back-to-British fare, in a sylvan setting; the self-service café area is cheaper than the proper restaurant. See p233.
Jom Makan *5-7 Pall Mall East, SW1Y 5BA (7925 2402, www.jom makan.co.uk)*. Noodles, curries and Malaysian street food for daring eaters, plus bite-sized side dishes and satay for cautious kids to try.
National Café *East Wing, The National Gallery, WC2N 4DN (7747 5942, www. thenationalcafe.com)*. Classic brasserie fare in smart but unstuffy surrounds, plus a simple kids' menu. See p222.
Thai Square *21-24 Cockspur Street, SW1Y 5BL (7839 4000, www.thai square.net)*. Hot and spicy fare, just off Trafalgar Square.

Crowds start to build behind the railings around half an hour before the start, and it can get very busy; if all you're really after is a spot of military marching and a gander at the famous bearskin hats, you might be better off mooching up to **St James' Palace** at elevenish. Here, you can get an unobstructed view of the Old Guard setting off along the Mall to Buckingham Palace.

A no less august ceremony in these parts is the daily feeding of the pelicans at St James' Park. At 2.30pm, the hungry birds gather by the lake to feast on fresh fish; in 2006 one swallowed a live pigeon, but hasn't been seen to repeat the alarming feat since. They're friendly creatures (so long as you're not a tasty-looking pigeon); if you sit on one of the benches by the lake, you might find one alighting next to you. Afterwards, take the bridge across the lake for a fairytale view of Buckingham Palace, beautifully framed by the trees.

Great Days Out

A world of experience on your doorstep

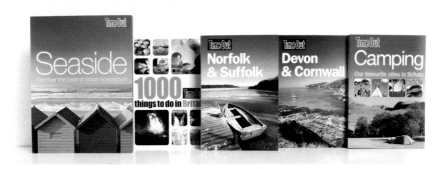

Queen Victoria was the first monarch to make Buckingham Palace her home and it remains the premier residence of the reigning Queen. While it's not the world's most beautiful palace, it is probably the most famous, drawing millions of visitors every year. The famous Changing of the Guard takes place daily in the palace forecourt at 11.30am from May to July, and on alternate days the rest of the year.

The State Rooms were first opened to the public in 1993 (the fire at Windsor Castle the previous year meant the Queen had to raise some cash for reconstructions) and can be seen during August and September, while the Queen is at Balmoral. There are 19 rooms to see in all, including the White Drawing Room. Designed by John Nash and furnished in opulent luxury with treasures from the Royal Collection, this will set the children's imaginations spinning. The Queen's Gallery, open all year round, has paintings by Dürer, Rembrandt, Canaletto, Rubens and Van Dyck, as well as some exquisite Fabergé eggs. Until October 31 2010 an exhibition examines Victoria and Albert's dedication to (and patronage of) the arts in The Queen's Gallery.

There's a nature trail for children in the gardens and a family activity room, also open throughout August and September. At the Royal Mews, children can watch the horses being groomed, fed and exercised, and examine the royal Rolls-Royces and the Gold State Coach, last used for the 2002 Golden Jubilee. *See also p36* **Great Days Out.**
Buggy access. Disabled access: lift, toilet (Buckingham Palace). Nappy-changing facilities (Buckingham Palace). Nearest picnic place: Green Park. Shop.

Eltham Palace

Court Yard, SE9 5QE (8294 2548, www. elthampalace.org.uk). Eltham rail. **Open** *Apr-Oct* 10am-5pm Mon-Wed, Sun. *Nov, Dec, Feb, Mar* 11am-4pm Mon-Wed, Sun. Closed week before Christmas-31 Jan. **Admission** *House & grounds* (incl audio tour) £8.70; £7.40 reductions; £4.40 5-15s; £21.80 family (2+3); free under-5s. *Gardens only* £5.60; £4.80 reductions; £2.70 5-15s; free under-5s. **Credit** MC, V. 5+
Eltham Palace was a full blown Tudor Palace until it fell out of favour in Henry VIII's reign; he was said to prefer nearby Greenwich. There's still a Tudor bridge over the moat, as well as evidence of earlier medieval ruins. The biggest draw now is the art deco beauty (one of London's architectural treasures), erected adjoining the Great Hall in 1936 by textiles heir Stephen Courtauld – like his more famous brother Samuel (who founded the Courtauld

Institute of Art in 1932), a collector of the arts. Stephen and his wife Virginia created a masterpiece, and the house was the scene of many a lavish party before World War II broke out and the building was commandeered by the War Office.

The furniture and fittings look like a film set – check out the pink leather chairs, ornate black and silver doors and moulded maple veneer in the dining room, or the onyx and gold-plated taps in Virginia's glamorous vaulted bathroom. The house was way ahead of its time when it came to mod cons, including underfloor heating, ensuite bathrooms and a quirky vacuum-cleaning system. Upstairs there's a chance to look at the Courtauld family's photos and artefacts and enjoy a home movie of Stephen and Virginia with their pet lemur, Mahjong (who had his own, specially designed quarters).

The grounds are beautifully restored and hold various events in summer, like an Art Deco fair and Tudor trails for kids. The quaint tearoom and shop have a distinctly 1930s flavour. *Café. Disabled access: lift. Shop.*

Fulham Palace & Museum

Bishop's Avenue, off Fulham Palace Road, SW6 6EA (7736 3233, www.elthampalace. org.uk). Hammersmith or Putney Bridge tube/ 220, 414, 430 bus. **Open** noon-4pm Mon, Tue; 11am-2pm Sat; 11.30am-3.30pm Sun. *Tours* phone for details. **Admission** *Museum* free; under-16s must be accompanied by an adult. *Tours* £5; free under-16s. **No credit cards.** 3+
A building as ancient as this – the official residence of the Bishops of London from 704 until 1975 – doesn't give up its secrets readily, so a tour is a good way to get the most out of a visit. The main house – more manor than palace – is Tudor (try out the echo in the courtyard), with significant Georgian and Victorian additions. Refurbishment has left the East Quadrangle looking beautiful, and the café is a particularly pleasant place to sit. The museum has plenty of new interactive features, lots more room to display treasures dug up in the grounds (including a mummified rat found in the roofspace of the Tudor Courtyard), and a programme of theatre, exhibitions and activities for families: music workshops for nippers between two and five, for example, or craft sessions where over-fives turn out hobby horses or soldier skittles. All must be pre-booked; most cost £5-£10 a head. Leave time to admire the gorgeous gardens and make sure the children look out for the Holm Oak, which would have been visible to Elizabeth I when she visited, and the Bishop's Tree, a sculpture on one of the

Sightseeing

An iconic feature of London's skyline: **St Paul's Cathedral**. *See p42.*

cedar of Lebanon trees on the North Lawn. From July 17-September 19, a temporary display explores the 1910 exhibition staged in White City to strengthen political bonds between Japan and Britain
Buggy access. Café. Disabled access: toilet (in palace). Nearest picnic place: grounds. Shop.

Hampton Court Palace

East Molesey, Surrey KT8 9AU (0844 482 7777, www.hrp.org.uk). Hampton Court rail/ riverboat from Westminster or Richmond to Hampton Court Pier (Apr-Oct). **Open** *Palace* Mar-Oct 10am-6pm daily. Nov-Feb 10am-4.30pm daily. Last entry 45mins before closing. *Park* dawn-dusk daily. **Admission** *Palace, courtyard, cloister & maze* £14; £11.50 reductions; £7 5-15s; free under-5s; £38 family (2+3). *Gardens only* £4.60; £4 reductions; free under-16s. *Maze only* £3.50; £2.50 5-15s; free under-5s; £10 family (2+3). **Credit** AmEx, MC, V. 6+

Henry VIII has a reputation as a tyrant, but as long as courtiers were on his good side, there was much revelry to be had. Hampton Court was a pleasure palace. Archeologists recently found the remains of a wine fountain in the largest of the courtyards, and a lovingly crafted four metre tall reconstruction started serving wine at weekends in spring 2010. You can get to the palace by boat from Westminster, or by train (which is considerably quicker). It's worth the trek. Henry VIII is always a favourite monarch with children, who are fascinated by his large girth, eccentric ways and habit of having his wives executed. He had many homes, but this one positively oozes with historical drama. Elizabeth I was imprisoned in the tower by her elder sister Mary; Shakespeare performed here; and Cromwell made it his home after the Civil War. The ghost of Henry's fifth wife, Catherine Howard, who was executed for adultery at the Tower of London, is said to shriek around in the Haunted Gallery.

The various Tudor and Baroque buildings sprawl over six acres, with costumed guides adding a lively dimension to the state apartments, courtyards and cloisters. The world famous gardens are truly wonderful, with the maze taking centre stage in any child's itinerary. It's the oldest in the country, having been planted between 1689 and 1694 – though it's virtually impossible to get lost in.

Themed activities are plentiful during the school holidays and on selected bank holidays and weekends, Tudor cookery demonstrations take place in the huge kitchens, where children love the bubbling cauldrons and game bird carcasses (see the website for dates). This year, Henry VIII's Council Chamber will be opened to the public for the first time, with a special exhibition on Henry's ill-fated wives.

Buggy access. Café. Disabled access: lift, toilet. Nappy-changing facilities. Nearest picnic place: palace gardens/picnic area. Restaurant. Shops.

Kensington Palace

Kensington Gardens, W8 4PX (0844 482 7777, www.hrp.org.uk). Bayswater or High Street Kensington tube/9, 10, 49, 52, 70 bus. **Open** *Mar-Oct* 10am-6pm daily. *Nov-Feb* 10am-5pm daily. Last entry 1hr before closing. **Admission** (incl audio guide) £12.50; £11 reductions; £6.25 5-15s; free under-5s; £34 family (2+3). **Credit** MC, V. **Map** p310 B8. 7+
Kensington Palace is another of London's landmarks striving to achieve major change before 2012. The multi-million pound refurbishment budget will see this Jacobean Mansion with a new suite of rooms at the entrance that visitors can explore for free. The Gardens are also being reinterpreted. For now though, the Palace has an exciting new exhibition to enjoy until January 2012. The Enchanted Palace is a dazzling multimedia interpretation of the history of the Palace and its inhabitants. The original mansion was turned into a palace by Christopher Wren, as commissioned by William III and his wife Mary when they came to live here in 1689. Mary II died of smallpox here in 1694, Queen Victoria was introduced to her beloved Albert here in 1836 and Princess Diana lived here before her death in 1997. At first the exhibition seems confusing – it's dark and hard to navigate – but you soon realise this is part of the thrill. Visitors are ushered up a back stairwell adorned with doodles and echoing with with whispering voices. Taking on the quest of finding the hidden names of the palace's princess inhabitants is a brilliant way to keep children occupied. Fashion plays a vital role in the exhibition and designers like Vivienne Westwood, Stephen Jones and William Tempest have been commissioned to create fabulous installations throughout the rooms. Theatre company Wildworks add to the fun by having actors dressed in grey monk-like uniforms walking around the rooms interacting with visitors.

The rest of the palace remains open for tours of the State Apartments (which you enter via Wren's lofty King's Staircase), the King's Gallery and the Queen's Apartments, where William and Mary lived quite simply. Family trails begin in the dressmakers' workshop, where children can begin an interactive quiz; there are special activities during the school holidays.
Buggy access. Disabled access: toilet. Nappy-changing facilities. Nearest picnic place: grounds. Restaurant. Shop.

Tower of London

Tower Hill, EC3N 4AB (0844 482 7777, www.hrp.org.uk). Tower Hill tube/Tower Gateway DLR/Fenchurch Street rail. **Open** *Mar-Oct* 10am-5.30pm Mon, Sun; 9am-5.30pm Tue-Sat (last entry 5pm). *Nov-Feb* 10am-4.30pm Mon, Sun; 9am-4.30pm Tue-Sat. *Tours* (outside only, weather permitting) every 30mins until 3.30pm (2.30pm Winter). **Admission** £17; £9.50 5-15s; £14.50 reductions; free under-5s; £47 family (2+3). Audio guide £4; £3 reductions. *Tours* free. **Credit** AmEx, MC, V. **Map** p319 R7. 5+
The Pool of London here on the Thames provides rich cultural pickings, including Tower Bridge and HMS *Belfast*, but few tourist attractions can top this centuries-old fortress, palace, prison and execution ground (two of Henry VIII's wives got the chop here) for sheer historical bounty. You can easily spend a whole day exploring. The Medieval Palace, where kings and queens stayed until the reign of Elizabeth I, has recently been restored, and uses smells and sound effects to whisk you back in time. Interactive displays reveal the ordeals of life as a prisoner, while outside on Tower Green is the place where unfortunates such as Anne Boleyn and Lady Jane Grey were beheaded; a glass pillow sculpted by artist Brian Catling marks the spot. Battle nuts love the gleaming armoury in the White Tower, and can learn about what it was like to be a soldier in medieval times; there are also replicas of two fearsome-looking siege engines (a special half-term event usually centres on the collection).

The crown jewels are the Tower's biggest draw, with 23,578 gems on display. Highlights include a model of the uncut, fist-sized Cullinan I – the largest diamond in the world – and an illustrated description of how it was cut into nine smaller diamonds. You can't miss the two-metre-wide Grand Punch Bowl – it's big enough to bathe in.

The beautiful vaulted chamber of the Bowyer Tower has been open to visitors since 2007. Legend has it the Duke of Clarence met a grisly fate here in 1478, drowning in a barrel of malmsey wine. The most entertaining way to hear such stories is to join one of the free tours, led by a Yeoman Warder (Beefeater). The Warders, photogenic in their black and red finery, are genial hosts and a mine of information.

Children's trails and quizzes tackle different themes, including Knights and Princesses and the Peasants' Revolt. Check the website for details of daily special events.
Buggy access (Jewel House). Café. Nappy-changing facilities. Nearest picnic place: riverside benches, Trinity Square Memorial Gardens. Shops.

PLACES OF WORSHIP

London Central Mosque

146 Park Road, NW8 7RG (7725 2213, www. iccuk.org). Baker Street tube/13, 82, 133 bus. **Open** 9.30am-last prayer daily (check website for details). **Admission** free. All ages
The golden dome visible across the treetops of Regent's Park belongs to the imposing London Central Mosque. Even while Churchill was busy with WWII, plans were going ahead to secure land and funding to build the city's first mosque. It was finally opened in 1944 by King George VI. Around a central courtyard, the Islamic Cultural Centre holds regular lessons, lectures and seminars (phone for details); there's also a library, bookshop and information booth. Visitors entering the prayer area must remove their shoes, while women are asked to wear a headscarf at all times. Tours can be arranged, but must be booked in advance.
Buggy access. Café. Disabled access: ramp, toilet. Nappy-changing facilities. Nearest picnic place: Regent's Park. Shop.

Shri Swaminarayan Mandir Temple

105-119 Brentfield Road, NW10 8LD (8965 2651, www.swaminarayan.org). Wembley Park tube, then BR2 bus/Neasden tube, then 15min walk. **Open** 9am-6pm daily. **Admission** free. Exhibition £2; £1.50 6-15s; free under-6s. **Credit** AmEx, MC, V. 5+
What is locally known as the Neasden Temple was voted Brent's most iconic building in 2010 in a competition organised by the London Olympic Committee across all of the capital's boroughs. Most of the stone used to build the incredibly decorative and intricate white structure was shipped from the quarries of Italy and Bulgaria to India, where it was carved by 1,500 master sculptors before being shipped to London. The temple has a permanent exhibition (with a video) called 'Understanding Hinduism', which is especially useful for children studying world religion. It also holds family seminars, and there's colourful kite flying for all the family every year on January 14, to mark the festival of Uttarayan.
Buggy access. Café. Disabled access: lift, toilet. Nappy-changing facilities. Shop.

Southwark Cathedral

London Bridge, SE1 9DA (7367 6700, 7367 6734 tours, www.dswark.org/cathedral). London Bridge tube/rail. **Open** 7.30am-6pm Mon-Fri; 8.30am-6pm Sat, Sun. *Restaurant* 8.30am-6pm Mon-Fri; 10am-6pm Sat, Sun. Closed 25 Dec, Good Friday, Easter Sunday.

Services 8am, 8.15am, 12.30pm, 12.45pm, 5.30pm Mon-Fri; 9am, 9.15am, 4pm Sat; 8.45am, 9am, 11am, 3pm, 6.30pm Sun. **Admission** *Guided Tour* £5; £2.50 1-11s; £4 reductions. **Credit** MC, V. Map p319 P8. 5+
This beautiful Anglican cathedral began life on this site more than eight centuries ago; the retro-choir and lady chapel and the north transept are the remaining medieval sections. The church fell into disrepair after the Reformation (one part was used as a bakery, another as a pigsty), but in 1905 it became a cathedral; it now has an Education Centre, a shop and a refectory. Memorials are devoted to the 51 people who drowned in the 1989 *Marchioness* accident; Shakespeare (and Sam Wanamaker who persevered for over 20 years to get the Globe Theatre built nearby); John Gower; and John Harvard. The windows show images of Chaucer, who set off on pilgrimage to Canterbury from a pub in Borough High Street, and John Bunyan, who preached locally. In the churchyard, hunt for the flattish, ribbed stone monument to Mahomet Weyomon, a Mohegan chief buried in the churchyard in 1735. He died of smallpox after travelling to London to state his case in the Mohegan Land Dispute.
The cathedral choir is one of the UK's best, and families cram inside to hear it at Christmas when the charismatic Dean indulges his love of theatre. You can also hear the choir sing evensong on Mondays and Thursdays (girls) and Tuesdays, Fridays and Sundays (boys). An all-male choir usually sings morning Eucharist, except on high days and holidays. Joining the choir gives kids a fantastic musical education; phone for audition dates.
Buggy access. Disabled access: lift, ramp, toilet. Nappy-changing facilities. Nearest picnic place: gardens. Restaurant. Shop.

St Paul's Cathedral

Ludgate Hill, EC4M 8AD (7236 4128, www.stpauls.co.uk). St Paul's tube. **Open** 8.30am-4pm Mon-Sat. *Galleries, crypt & ambulatory* 9.30am-4.15pm Mon-Sat. Closed for special services, sometimes at short notice. *Tours* 10.45am, 11.15am, 1.30pm, 2pm Mon-Sat. **Admission** *Cathedral, crypt & gallery* £12.50; £4.50 7-16s; £9.50-£11.50 reductions; free under-7s; £29.50 family (2+2). *Tours* £3; £1 7-16s; £2.50 reductions; free under-7s. Audio guide £4; £3.50 reductions. **Credit** MC, V. **Map** p318 O6. 5+
St Paul's is so large (that golden ball just beneath the cross is big enough to fit ten people inside), that despite the modern buildings crowding around it, St Paul's remains an iconic feature on the London skyline. It sits on top of Ludgate Hill, the highest point in the City. The world-

famous cathedral was thoroughly cleaned for its 300th birthday in 2008, as part of a £40 million restoration project that also included a complete rebuild of the organ and the creation of a new set of ecclesiastical robes by Royal College of Art designer Marie Brisou. The present building is the fourth to sit on the site, and was designed by Sir Christopher Wren after the previous incumbent was burned down in the Great Fire of London. Wren had to campaign vociferously to get it built to his specifications – it was nearly vetoed on several occasions as being too ambitious and expensive.

The audioguide recounts quirky facts about everything from the organ pipes (some big enough to crawl through) to Nelson's corpse (they had a hell of a time getting it back to England for the funeral) to enliven the tour. During Christmas and Easter holidays, there are trails that are rewarded at the end with a small prize; parents who need ideas for a self-guided tour can download the activity sheets for schools. Most fun of all is the Whispering Gallery, 259 steps from the ground, whose acoustics simply have to be heard to be believed. From there, it's a few more steps up to the Stone Gallery for an amazing

Butterfly World

In an unlikely setting, just minutes from the M25, lies the largest hommage to the butterfly in the UK. It makes London Zoo's Butterfly Paradise tunnel, and even the temporary Butterfly World at the Natural History Museum, look puny by comparison. The site is designed to look like an enormous butterfly head from the air and has been set up by property tycoon and butterfly obsessive Clive Farrell (he even has his own butterfly farm in Belize). Right now, the butterfly tunnel here is a sneak preview of what's to come in the huge Biome – a 100m diameter walk-through butterfly haven planned to open in 2011. But it's well worth a trip before then and ahead

of the crowds. Kids love the butterfly breeding house, where they can see first hand all the incredible stages of a butterfly's life cycle from egg to caterpillar to pupae to butterfly. Hunt around the potted plants and shrubs along either side for real life examples (the clever camouflage turns it into a treasure hunt). The Insect Study Centre is often used by school groups during the week, but casual visitors are just as welcome to observe the specimens inside the transparent containers. The butterfly tunnel itself is full of all kinds of varieties and has feeding tables full of semi rotten fruit to encourage the winged critters to sit still for observation.

The 20 acres of wildflower meadows (designed to attract and support native butterflies and insects) are a breathtaking blaze of colour during summer, and the specialist gardens that stretch down one side of the site are also lots of fun. Designed by award-winning gardener Ivan Hicks, who is celebrated for his eccentric ideas, they are a mix of the playful and the practical and should inspire visitors large and small. There's a playground under construction and the new café has a sheltered terrace that will prove popular with families on sunny days. What's more they don't make you walk through the well-stocked shop on your way out. It's an educational and fun day out.

Miriam Lane, Chiswell Green, Herts AL2 3NY 01727 869 203, www.butterflyworld project.com. **Admission** £6; £5 reductions; £4 3-16s, free under 3s; £19 family (2+2). (Prices will change on completion of the biome.)

Shri Swaminarayan Mandir Temple. *See p42.*

360° view of London. If you're likely to have the energy to ascend still further to the Golden Gallery, go early, or you may find yourself jostled by boisterous teens on the cramped balcony.

Down in the crypt are tombs of historical figures such as Nelson, Wellington and Wren; Lawrence of Arabia and Florence Nightingale are honoured with memorials. At the back is the shop and the Crypt Café. And if you want to experience the true spirit of St Paul's, come for evensong, held every day at 5pm.
Buggy access. Café. Disabled access: lift, ramp, toilet. Nappy-changing facilities. Nearest picnic space: garden. Restaurant. Shops.

Westminster Abbey

20 Dean's Yard, SW1P 3PA (7222 5152, 7654 4900 tours, www.westminster-abbey.org). St James's Park or Westminster tube/11, 12, 24, 88, 159, 211 bus. **Open** *Westminster Abbey* June-Sept 9.30am-3.30pm Mon, Tue, Thur, Fri; 9.30am-6pm Wed; 9.30am-3.30pm Sat. Oct-May 9.30am-3.30pm Mon, Tue, Thur, Fri; 9.30am-6pm Wed; 9.30am-1.30pm Sat. *Abbey Museum & Chapter House* 10.30am-4pm daily. *Cloisters* 8am-6pm daily. *College Garden* Apr-Sept 10am-6pm Tue-Thur. Oct-Mar 10am-4pm Tue-Thur (last entry 1hr before closing). *Tours* phone for details. **Admission** £15; £6 11-15s, reductions; free under-11s with adult; £30 family (2+1). *Chapter House* free. *Abbey Museum* free (audio guide free). *Tours* £3. **Credit** AmEx, MC, V. **Map** p317 K9. 5+
Westminster Abbey is a busy place – during a typical year it can hold up to 1,500 services and worship sessions. It has always had close links with royalty, not least because it has been the Coronation Church since 1066. The Queen was also married here. The body of Edward the Confessor, who built the first church on the site, is entombed in the abbey, though no one knows exactly where: it was removed from its elaborate shrine and reburied in an unmarked spot during the Reformation. Henry III was responsible for the Gothic splendour of the current building, which was heavily influenced by the French architectural style of the period. Poets' Corner is the final resting place of Geoffrey Chaucer, and you can also see the graves of Dickens, Dryden, Johnson, Browning and Tennyson. Statues of several 20th-century martyrs (including Martin Luther King) occupy 15th-century niches above the west door.

You can escape the crowds in the 900-year-old College Garden, one of the oldest cultivated gardens in Britain. The Abbey Museum (Broad Sanctuary; free if you have a ticket to the Abbey, £1 otherwise) is in the vaulted area under the

former monks' dormitory, in one of the oldest parts of the Abbey. Here you'll find a collection of effigies and waxworks of British monarchs such as Edward II and Henry VII, wearing the robes they donned in life; the Queen's Coronation robes are also on show. The Choir School is the only school in Britain exclusively for the education of boy choristers from eight to 13; voice trials are held twice a year. Its Christmas services are magnificent. Next door is St Margaret's Church, where the weddings of Samuel Pepys and Winston Churchill (in 1655 and 1908 respectively) took place; Sir Walter Raleigh is buried here.
Buggy access. Café. Disabled access: toilet. Nearest picnic place: college gardens (10am-6pm Tue-Thur), St James's Park. Shop.

SCIENCE

Centre of the Cell

4 Newark Street, E1 2AT (7882 2562, www.centreofthecell.org). Whitechapel tube. **Open** *Sessions* 10-11.30am, noon-1.30pm, 2-3.30pm, 4-5.30pm, 6.30-8pm daily. Session times may vary; phone to check. **Admission** free. 9+
Politicians and businessmen regularly complain that our school children aren't going into maths and sciences in sufficient numbers. Within the medical centre inside the RIBA award-winning Blizard Building there's an exciting educational resource for school-age children that might just inspire them. A glass-walled walkway takes visitors over the labs and their 400 white-coated occupants to a large multimedia 'pod' (designed to take 40 people), which is where the fun takes place. A film introduces children to the amazing work going on around them, then a huge silver tube opens up to reveal more audio-visual magic and interactive jollies illustrating different aspects of biomedical science for key stages 2, 3 and 4. One game compares the size of a cell to a five-pence piece (a quarter of the size of one of the little dots around the coin edge), another charts the growth of an embryo. Other features show how to repair a damaged spinal cord, or grow real skin for grafts; there are even (oo-er!) real body organs. The pod is intended to be regularly updated in line with the discoveries of the boffins in the labs below.

The whole experience lasts around 90 minutes; thanks to the unique setting and the theatricality of the presentation, young 'uns will be entertained throughout – and hardly aware that they're learning things.
Buggy access. Disabled access: lift; toilet. Café. Nearest picnic place: Whitechapel hospital grounds. Shop.

Great Days Out
Covent Garden

In the current age of conservation and appreciation of all things ancient, it's hard to believe this major tourist attraction was nearly bulldozed in the 1970s to make way for a masterplan of modern hotels and conference centres. Thanks to locals, who campaigned to save the market that had served the area with fresh produce and flowers for over three centuries, Covent Garden survived.

The name is most likely drawn from the 'convent garden' that once surrounded the historic abbey of St Peter. The land that belonged to the Convent of St Peter at West Minster was handed over by the Crown to John Russell, the first Earl of Bedford, following Henry VIII's dissolution of the monasteries.

In the 1630s, the Earl commissioned master architect Inigo Jones to design a series of Palladian arcades. These wonderfully elegant, stately terraces, opening on to a central courtyard, constituted the first public square in the country and proved popular with wealthy tenants, until the fruit and vegetable market expanded on to their exclusive patch.

These days the stalls are full of gifts and souvenirs (Londoners have to travel to Vauxhall to find the hearty barrow boy cries and the fruit, vegetables and bouquets of the original market) and the Piazza is an open stage for street performers. Covent Garden is usually thick with tourists, but it's still well worth a trip for its pedestrianised mooching opportunities, free entertainment (many of the clowns, acrobats and comedians get spectating children involved whenever they can) and the nearby cultural attractions of the Transport Museum, the Royal Opera House and various West End theatres.

Going underground

Weekdays in term time are best for exploring this area. Head straight down James Street from the tube exit, cut through the market, and start off at

London Transport Museum

one of London's most fun museums: the **London Transport Museum** (*see p83*). Inside, children tend to steam past the historic timeline that puts London's travel achievements in context with other major cities, straight on to the interactive rooms. For the under-sixes, the All Aboard! Gallery has climb-on model vehicles and soft play. For older children (seven to 11s), there are train carriages and buses to explore (from the horse-drawn Shillibeer's model to a sliced-through modern bus), tricky computerised driving games, costumes to try on, mystery objects to guess at and – the ultimate excitement – the possibility of driving a bus. There's also a fantastic shop with imaginative themed gifts.

If all that travelling has made you rather peckish, nip upstairs to the friendly **Upper Deck** café (*see p237*), overlooking Covent Garden Piazza. In addition to the Upper Deck, the Museum also has a modest picnic area where visitors can eat their packed lunches.

The Piazza and beyond

Designed by architect Charles Fowler, the **covered central market** (0870 780 5001, www.coventgardenmarket.co.uk) is a mix of cool and quirky shops (toy shop Eric Snook, antiques seller Nauticalia) and upmarket chains (Culpeper, Monsoon and the like). The Apple Market in the North Hall is where you'll find antique stalls on Mondays, a general market Tuesday to Friday and hand-made crafts at weekends. Jubilee Hall Market is a bit tackier, flogging novelty T-shirts and other tat.

Outside in the Piazza, usually in front of the portico of St Paul's Church, comedians, musicians and living statues perform for the amusement of tourists and families. It was under this portico that Samuel Pepys observed what is thought to have been Britain's first Punch and Judy show ('an Italian puppet play', as he described it) on 9 May 1662; fittingly, the **Punch & Judy Festival** (*see p22*) is held here on the first Sunday in October. You can also catch Punch and Judy's slapstick at the annual May Fair in St Paul's churchyard.

Every summer there are open-air operatics courtesy of the **Royal Opera**

LUNCH BOX

Also in the area: Pizza Express, Strada, Wagamama.
Café Pasta *2-4 Garrick Street, WC2E 9BH (7497 2779, www.cafepasta. co.uk).* Straightforward pasta, pizza and grills.
Christopher's *18 Wellington Street, WC2E 7DD (7240 4222, www. christophersgrill.com).* A smart, upmarket restaurant with American cuisine and hearty brunches.
Upper Deck Café *London Transport Museum, WC2E 7BB (7379 6344, www.ltmuseum.co.uk).* Enjoyable museum café. *See p237.*
Wahaca *66 Chandos Place, WC2N 4HG (7240 1883, www.wahaca.co.uk).* Delicious Mexican street food at affordable prices. *See p247.*
World Food Café *1st Floor, 14 Neal's Yard, WC2H 9DP. (7379 0298, www. worldfoodcafenealsyard.co.uk).* Homespun, tasty vegetarian platters.

House (*see p173*). The ROH itself is a beautiful space, and has an upstairs café with wonderful views over the Piazza. Guided tours give the curious a glimpse into working dressing rooms and rehearsal studios; if you have enough time to take in a performance, there are free lunchtime recitals on Mondays.

Out of the market, head towards the river and down to the Strand. In the 14th century, this was a swanky residential street that stood right on the riverbank. Gradually, the overflow of hoi polloi from Covent Garden threatened to overwhelm the narrow strip; by 1600 the wealthy folk had run away, and the Strand had a reputation for poverty and bawdiness. Sir Christopher Wren suggested the creation of a reclaimed embankment to ease congestion and house the main sewer, and by the mid-19th century the area's respectability was restored. At the Strand's eastern end is the Aldwych, a grand crescent that dates to 1905 – although the name, 'ald wic' (old settlement), has its origins in the 14th century. On its south side stands the imposing bulk of **Somerset House** (*see p66*).

Great Days Out

STATELY HOMES

Chiswick House

Burlington Lane, W4 2RP (8995 0508, www.chgt.org.uk). Turnham Green tube, then E3 bus/Hammersmith tube, then 190 bus/ Chiswick rail. **Open** *Apr* 10am-5pm daily. *May-Oct* 10am-5pm Mon-Wed, Sun. Last entry 30mins before closing. Closed Nov-Mar. *Tours* by arrangement; phone for details. **Admission** *House (EH)* (incl audio guide) £4.40; £3.70 reductions; £2.20 5-16s; free under-5s; £11 family (2+3). *Gardens* free. **Credit** MC, V. 5+

The fifth Duke of Devonshire commissioned this grand manor to sit on the site of an old Jacobean mansion. Chiswick House is one of the finest examples of neo-Palladian architecture in England and illustrious house guests have included Alexander Pope and Jonathan Swift(in more recent times, the Beatles filmed the video for *Paperback Writer* in its gardens). The house was built more as a private art gallery than a home, and exhibits aren't especially child-friendly – although eagle-eyed kids could look out for two sculptures of the Green Man and a lead Sphinx.

Extensive work on the grounds that began in 2009 has been completed and a walk through the gardens makes you feel as if you've stepped into a classical landscape painting – there are obelisks among the trees, an exquisitely domed temple, a lake and a cascading waterfall. The usual kitchen garden activities for children and the House Festival are back on this summer and the cafe has reopened in a new contemporary building with fine views over the grounds.

Buggy access. Disabled access: stairlift, toilet. Nearest picnic place: Chiswick Park. Shop.

Fenton House

3 Hampstead Grove, NW3 6RT (7435 3471/ 01494 755563 information, 01494 755572 box office, www.nationaltrust.org.uk). Hampstead tube/Hampstead Heath rail. **Open** *Late Mar* 11am-5pm Sat, Sun. *Apr-Oct* 2-5pm Wed-Fri; 11am-5pm Sat, Sun, bank hols (last entry 30mins before closing). *Tours* phone for times. **Admission** *(NT)* £6; £3 5-15s; free under-5s; £15 family (2+2). **No credit cards.** 5+

What's remarkable about this 17th-century house is how little it changed during 300 years of continuous occupation. It's best known for the impressive Benton Fletcher collection of early keyboard instruments, including spinets harpsichords, clavichords and virginals. Instruments were donated on the condition that

professional musicians be allowed to play them; check the website for details of lunchtime and evening concerts.

There is also a collection of paintings and drawings by the Camden Town Group and many fine examples of English and Continental porcelain from George Salting (who donated his amazing Chinese pottery collection to the V&A). Children particularly enjoy the Meissen Harlequins and the 'curious grotesque teapot'. Outside, they can run around the carefully tended vegetable garden, herb garden, lawns and orchard, whose 30 varieties of old English apples can be sampled on Apple Day (celebrated every year on 21 October). Occasional garden trails are available.

Buggy access. Disabled access: ramp. Nappy-changing facilities.

Guildhall

Corner of Gresham Street & Aldermanbury, EC2P 2UJ (7606 3030, 7606 3030 ext 1463 tours, www.corpoflondon.gov.uk). St Paul's tube/Bank tube/DLR/Moorgate tube/rail. **Open** *May-Sept* 9.30am-5pm daily. *Oct-Apr* 9.30am-5pm Mon-Sat. Last entry 4.30pm. Closes for functions; phone ahead to check. *Tours* by arrangement; groups of 10 or more only. **Admission** free. **Map** p318 P6. 8+

This stunning building is one of the few in the area to survive the Great Fire of London. It was built between 1411 and 1440 and is now used as the seat of local government: the Court of Common Council meets at 1pm on selected Thursdays each month in the Great Hall (visitors are welcome; phone for dates). The Hall is also open when it's not being used for official business. The impressive space has a vaulted ceiling, marble monuments, and banners and shields of 100 livery companies on the walls; every Lord Mayor since 1189 is named on the windows. Two large wooden statues of Gog and Magog, carved in 1953 to replace the pair destroyed in the Blitz, stand in the West Gallery. They represent the mythical conflict between Britons and Trojan invaders; the result of this struggle was the founding of Albion's capital city, New Troy, on whose site London is said to stand. On the north wall hangs a fascinating list of trials and grisly executions.

You can only nose round the Guildhall's enormous medieval crypt on a pre-booked group tour; tours last half an hour and are free. In the absence of an on-site café, packed lunches can be scoffed in the cloakroom area, which is equipped with a water cooler.

Buggy access. Disabled access: lift, ramp, toilet. Nappy-changing facilities. Nearest picnic place: grassy area by London Wall. Shop.

Sightseeing

Ham House

Ham Street, Ham, Richmond, Surrey TW10 7RS (8940 1950, www.nationaltrust.org.uk). Richmond tube/rail, then 371 bus. **Open** *House* Mid Feb noon-4pm Mon-Wed, Sat, Sun. Early Mar noon-4pm Sat, Sun. Mid Mar-Oct noon-4pm Mon-Wed, Sat, Sun. *Gardens* Jan-Early Feb 11am-4pm Sat, Sun. Mid Feb-Oct 11am-5pm Mon-Wed, Sat, Sun. Nov-Mid Dec 11am-5pm Sat, Sun. Closed 1 Jan, 25, 26 Dec. *Tours* Wed (pre-booking essential); phone for details. **Admission** (NT) *House & gardens* £10.40; £5.80 5-15s; free under-5s; £26.60 family (2+2). *Gardens only* £3.30; £2.10 5-15s; free under-5s; £9.25 family (2+2). **Credit** AmEx, MC, V. 5+ (house). All ages (gardens).

Ham House celebrates its 400th anniversay in 2010, so expect special events to celebrate. It is a Sleeping Beauty of a house, with very little changed since it was built and furnished in the 17th century by William Murray (whipping boy to James I) and his descendants. It sits on the river in gorgeous landscaped grounds, which include the Cherry Garden, with its central statue of Bacchus and lavender parterres, and the maze-like Wilderness, as well as the oldest thorn bush and orangery in the country. Many of the original interiors have been lavishly restored, offering a rare chance to see the bold colour schemes of the day – strong, contrasting colours in damask, velvet and satin. Television drama *Elizabeth* was filmed here, and there are extensive collections of period furniture, art and textiles.

Children tend to get more excited by Ham House's reputation as one of the most haunted buildings in Britain: ghostly visitors are said to include William's daughter, the Duchess of Lauderdale, and her pet dog. Regular family events include entertaining Ghost Tours, which are suitable for over-fives; a torch-lit adult version is also available.

Open-air theatre takes place in the garden in summer, and there are egg trails for Easter, art and craft days for the August bank holiday weekend, more spooky tours for Hallowe'en and all manner of carols, feasts and craft events for Christmas. A ferry crosses the river to Marble Hill House (*see below*) at weekends year round, and daily during the summer.

Café. Disabled access: lift, toilet. Nappy-changing facilities. Shop.

Marble Hill House

Richmond Road, Middx TW1 2NL (8892 5115, www.english-heritage.org.uk). Richmond tube/rail/33, 90, 290, H22, R70 bus. **Open** *Apr-Oct* 10am-2pm Sat; 10am-5pm Sun. Closed Nov-Mar. **Admission** (EH) £5; £4.30 reductions; £2.50 5-15s; free under-5s; £12.50 family (2+2). Price includes tour. **Credit** MC, V. 5+

In the days when Marble Hill House was constructed, Twickenham was a country retreat, fashionable for weekend salons. It's a superb Palladian villa, built in the 1720s for Henrietta Howard, mistress to King George II when he was Prince of Wales. The mansion is packed to the brim with Georgian antiques and paintings, but the star of the decorative show is the Honduran mahogany staircase, whose construction nearly sparked a war with Spain. Marble Hill House hosts special events throughout the year, including Easter trails and open-air concerts; guided tours can be taken of the house and its surrounding parkland, and there's a ferry across the Thames to Ham House (*see above*).

Café. Nearest picnic place: Marble Hill Park. Shop.

19 Princelet Street

19 Princelet Street, E1 6QH (7247 5352, www.19princeletstreet.org.uk). Aldgate East tube/Liverpool Street tube/rail. **Open** check website or phone for occasional open days. *Tours* groups by appointment. **Admission** free; donations appreciated. **Map** p319 S5. 3+

Chessington World of Adventures. *See p51.*

Sightseeing

For decades, this house was in danger of collapsing, but now it's Grade II listed and the home of Europe's only museum devoted to immigration and cultural diversity. Extensive restorations are planned, although until the £3 million funding is raised, it's quite difficult to visit the house because of its fragility. Still it's worth making an effort to experience the haunting atmosphere, rickety staircase and fascinating stories of its past inhabitants.

The house was first home to exiled Huguenot silk weavers (you can still see a big bobbin hanging above the door), then to Irish dockers. In 1869, Polish Jews converted it into an Ashkenazi synagogue; in the 20th century, it hosted English lessons for Bangladeshi women. It's also the site where Jewish scholar David Rodinsky simply disappeared one day (Iain Sinclair and Rachel Lichtenstein wrote *Rodinsky's Room* based on the story). *Buggy access. Nearest picnic place: Christ Church grounds.*

Osterley Park & House

Osterley Park, off Jersey Road, Isleworth, Middx TW7 4RB (8232 5050, www.national trust.org.uk). Osterley tube. **Open** House Mar-Oct noon-4.30pm Wed-Sun. Dec 12.30-3.30pm Sat, Sun. *Gardens* Mar-Oct 11am-5pm Wed-Sun. *Park* Jan-Mar, Nov, Dec 8am-6pm daily. Apr-Oct 8am-7.30pm daily. *Tours* by arrangement; minimum 15 people. **Admission** (NT) *House & garden* £8.80; £4.40 5-18s; free under-5s; £22 family (2+3). *Garden only* £3.85; £1.95 5-18s; free under-5s. *Park* free. **Credit** MC, V. 3+
Robert Adam remodelled the country retreat of self-made banking magnate Sir Francis Child in the 18th century. No expense was spared and the house is incredibly grand, despite its setting being decidedly more suburban these days. Mrs Child's flower garden is still delightful, and the rest of the grounds are currently being restored to their former glory.

The house was largely unchanged by Childs' descendants before being donated to the National Trust in 1949; the splendour of the state rooms alone makes the house worth a visit. Children will enjoy exploring 'below stairs' and discovering what life was like as a servant, before visiting the horses in the Tudor stables; there's also a resident spectre, said to lurk in the basement. Regular events include tours of the house, bluebell walks, outdoor performances and the annual (free) Osterley Day, full of arts and fun.
Buggy access (not when busy). Café. Disabled access: stair climber, toilet. Nappy-changing facilities. Nearest picnic place: front lawn, picnic benches in grounds. Shop.

PM Gallery & House

Walpole Park, Mattock Lane, W5 5EQ (8567 1227, www.ealing.gov.uk). Ealing Broadway tube/rail/65 bus. **Open** May-Sept 1-5pm Tue-Fri, Sun; 11am-5pm Sat. Oct-Apr 1-5pm Tue-Fri; 11am-5pm Sat. Closed bank hols. *Tours* by arrangement; phone for details. **Admission** free. Audio guide £1. **Credit** AmEx, MC, V. 5+
Visitors to Sir John Soane's Museum in Lincoln's Inn Fields (*see p79*) will know about the architect's wonderfully eccentric use of light and space. Soane built Pitzhanger Manor (pitshanger means 'wooded slope frequented by kites') as his weekend country retreat, and it is now, along with the PM Gallery, Ealing's flagship cultural centre.

Among the exhibits is the Hull Grundy Martinware pottery collection, and there's a workshop programme for all ages; special events for kids include half-term craft sessions and 'clay play'. Soane's ornamental gardens are now known as Walpole Park, Ealing Borough's rose-scented pride and joy, which hosts jazz and comedy in summer.
Buggy access. Disabled access: lift, ramp, toilet. Nappy-changing facilities. Nearest picnic place: Walpole Park.

Syon House

Syon Park, Brentford, Middx TW8 8JF (8560 0881, 8847 4730 Tropical Forest, 8847 0946 Snakes & Ladders, www.syonpark.co.uk). Gunnersbury tube/rail, then 237, 267 bus/ Kew Bridge rail. **Open** *House* mid Mar-Oct 11am-5pm Wed, Thur, Sun, bank hol Mon (last entry 4pm). *Gardens* Mar-Oct 10.30am-5pm daily. Nov-Feb 10.30am-4pm Sat, Sun. *Tours* by arrangement; phone for details. *Tropical Zoo* 10am-5.30pm daily. *Snakes & Ladders* 10am-6pm daily (last entry 5.15pm). **Admission** *House & gardens* £9; £8 reductions; £4 5-16s; free under-5s; £20 family (2+2). *Gardens only* £4.50; £3.50 5-16s; free under-4s; £10 family (2+2). *Tropical Zoo* £6.50; £5.50 3-15s; free under-3s; £22 family (2+3). *Snakes & Ladders* £5 under-2s; £6 under-5s; £7 over-5s; free over-16s. Reduced rate after 4pm. **Credit** MC, V. 5+
This turreted Tudor mansion has been the seat of the Duke of Northumberland for over 600 years and looks out over the Thames towards Kew. It was built on the site of a medieval abbey that was brutally dissolved by Henry VIII, and it was here that Henry's fifth wife Catherine Howard awaited her execution. Henry's coffin was later brought here in transit to Windsor Castle; as if by divine retribution, it mysteriously burst open during the night

and the king's remains were found being licked by dogs. It was here, too, that the doomed Lady Jane Grey reluctantly accepted the crown and became queen for nine days. In short, it's bursting with history.

The rooms, designed by Robert Adam, are positively breathtaking (John Betjeman described Syon as 'the grand architectural walk'), from the grand Roman hallway in black and white marble to the Red Drawing Room, with its crimson silk walls and Roman statues. Its magnificently-preserved grandeur has made it a popular filming location: *The Madness of King George* was filmed here, as were scenes from *Gosford Park*.

Outside, children will love the restored 19th-century Great Conservatory, with its huge iron and glass dome – and if the extensive Capability Brown-landscaped gardens aren't enough for a run around, there's also indoor adventure playground Snakes & Ladders (an extra charge applies). Then there's the London Tropical Zoo enclosure, full of endangered animals that live in or near water, such as piranhas, snakes, crocs and poison tree frogs.

A programme of family-friendly events includes demonstrations, re-enactments and after-dark walks in winter, when the woods are illuminated with dazzling light displays (check the website for details). In summer, movies are screened in the gardens; bring a picnic to consume on the lawns before the film begins. *Café. Nappy-changing facilities. Nearest picnic place: Syon House Gardens, Syon Park. Shop.*

THRILLS & CHILLS

Chessington World of Adventures

Leatherhead Road, Chessington, Surrey KT9 2NE (0870 444 7777, www.chessington.com). **Getting there** *By rail* Chessington South rail, then 71 bus or 10-min walk. *By car* J9 off M25. **Open** Check website for timetables. **Admission** (online advance price) £24; £17 3-15s; annual pass £68; £50 3-15s. Free under 1m tall. Check website for on-the-day prices & other annual passes. **Credit** AmEx, MC, V. All ages

There are two main attractions at Chessington: animals and rides. The zoo has gorillas, tigers, lions and leopards as well as smaller animals; keep an eye out for its latest residents, the zebras, antelopes and Oryxes in the new Wanyama Reserve. Chessington has taken a leaf out of London Zoo's book and introduced child-friendly animal antics presentations (2pm & 4pm). At the new Sea Life aquarium, a walk-through ocean tank offers a chance to get close

to the sharks, while the Amazonian display includes piranhas.

Many of the adventure rides are geared towards families with young children, unlike the more extreme offerings at nearby stablemate Thorpe Park (*see p55*). There's lovable Beanoland with dodgems and foam ball firing, a large soft play area for younger tots, plus an extreme games area and more challenging white-knuckle rides for older kids, like the Vampire rollercoaster and Rameses Revenge water plunge. Guides dressed up as fun characters help families on their way around. *Buggy access. Café. Car park (free). Disabled access: toilet. Nappy-changing facilities. Restaurant. Shops.*

Chislehurst Caves

Old Hill, Chislehurst, Kent BR7 5NB (8467 3264, www.chislehurstcaves.co.uk). **Getting there** *By rail* Chislehurst rail. **Open** 9am-5pm Wed-Sun. *Tours* phone for details. **Admission** £5; £3 5-15s, reductions; free under-5s. **Credit** MC, V. 8+

Twenty miles of caves sit beneath Chislehurst, carved out of the chalk by Druids, Saxons and Romans. Since then, the caves have been turned to all sorts of purposes, including an ammunition dump in World War I and a mushroom farm; during World War II, they acted as Britain's largest bomb shelter. Most of the underground scenes in the TV series *Merlin* were filmed here. The 45-minute lamplit tour covers about a mile of the tunnels; children will enjoy locating the Druid Altar, the Caves Church and the Haunted Pool. *Restaurant. Shop.*

Legoland

Winkfield Road, Windsor, Berks SL4 4AY (0870 504 0404, www.legoland.co.uk). **Getting there** *By rail* Windsor & Eton Riverside or Windsor Central rail, then shuttlebus. *By car* J3 off M3 or J6 off M4. **Open** *Mid Mar-early Nov* times may vary, check website for timetables. **Admission** *One-day ticket* £38; £28 3-15s, reductions. *Two-day ticket* £75; £55 3-15s; free under-3s. *Shuttlebus* £4.20; £2.10 3-15s, reductions. Free under-3s. **Credit** AmEx, MC, V. All ages

What immediately strikes first-time visitors to this shrine to the famous brick is the sheer size of the car park; once you're in, it's the impressive view of the park, which cascades, ride after ride, down a steep hill with Berkshire's rolling countryside in the distance. Legoland remains an incredibly popular family day out – though while it's suitable for all ages, even hard-to-

Sightseeing

please early teens, adults may occasionally struggle to see the appeal. That's largely because of the queues, which can be particularly testing for toddlers' tempers. The best advice is to come early and make a beeline for the rear of the site first, thus avoiding the worst waits.

Queues aside, there are some brilliant rides. Driving School puts six to 13s behind the wheel of whizzy electric cars, amid roundabouts, traffic lights and much confusion; there's also a scaled-down version for tots. Other star turns include the twisting Dragon rollercoaster, Miniland's scaled-down London landmarks and the Imagination Theatre – with a brand-new Clutch Powers 4D adventure show. Also new in 2010 is a pirate themed adventure playground with Pirate Falls Dynamite Drench and a live acrobatic show at its centre.

There's plenty to see while you wander from queue to queue, but those with preschool children should seize the chance to go in term time. It's also a good idea to take activities to keep the kids amused while they're waiting, and to draw up a hit list of the rides your children particularly want to try beforehand: call the day before to check your chosen attractions will be running.

Buggy access. Cafés. Disabled access: toilet. Nappy-changing facilities. Nearest picnic place: grounds. Restaurants. Shops.

London Bridge Experience

2-4 Tooley Street, SE1 2SY (0800 043 4666, www.londonbridgeexperience.com). London Bridge tube/rail. **Open** 10am-5pm Mon-Fri; 10am-6pm Sat, Sun. **Admission** £21.95; £17.95 reductions; £16.95 under-16s; free under-5s; £64.95 family (2+2). **Credit** MC, V. All ages (Bridge Experience). 11+ (London Tombs)

This won the top prize in 2009's inaugural Screamie Awards (as voted for by the public) and there's now 2,000 extra square feet of thrills to enjoy. The experience is a split-level one. The first part is a fun-for-all-the-family history lesson that engages all five senses and serves the choicest cuts from the crossing's 2,000-year history. The second takes you underground to the 'London Tombs', and frightens the pants off you. We like the first bit best, where actors appear at every turn: in a cobwebbed replica of a Victorian study, we meet the ghostly portrait of Sir John Rennie, who designed the 1831 bridge, and whose ravings are translated by a dusty butler; through heavy doors and along dank passages we're shown Boudicca's sacking of London, narrated by a bloodied Roman soldier amid disembowelled corpses. Next up is the Russell Crowe-like viking, who asks his

guests to help pull down the bridge's wooden piers. After that, we're introduced to William Wallace's ghost, and taken into a chamber of gore run by the chap in charge of heads on sticks, once proudly displayed on London Bridge. Each period involves interaction with the key players, who also include a garrulous lighterman's widow, the American who bought the bridge in 1970 (it's a myth that he thought he was buying Tower Bridge, he insists), and the Queen. It's all quite kitsch and entertaining; the shocks and horrors come downstairs in the dark and threatening Tombs, where zombie actors show little mercy.

Buggy access. Café. Disabled access: lift; toilet. Nearest picnic place: South Bank. Shop.

London Dungeon

28-34 Tooley Street, SE1 2SZ (7403 7221, www.thedungeons.com). London Bridge tube/rail. **Open** times vary, phone or check website for details. **Admission** £22.50; £20.50 reductions; £16.50 5-14s; £18.95 for registered disabled; free carers, under-5s. **Credit** AmEx, MC, V. **Map** p319 Q8. 10+

In thrillingly dark and smelly surrounds, the London Dungeon leads its visitors through the more gruesome episodes of London's history. Costumed actors bring the city's characters and disasters to life, often pretending to be one of the waxwork models and frightening kids into delighted squeals by suddenly moving. There's a gruesome section devoted to Jack the Ripper, and another for demonic 18th-century barber Sweeney Todd, another for the operating room of Tooley Street's butcher surgeon. New for 2010 is 'Bloody Mary: Killer Queen' devoted to the deaths commissioned by Henry VIII's daughter.

Guaranteed to provoke even more high-pitched exclamation is 'Labyrinth of the Lost', the largest horror mirror maze in the world. If that's not enough depravity for you, there's the Traitor Boat Ride to Hell (visitors play the part of condemned prisoners, death sentence guaranteed), and Extremis: Drop Ride to Doom, which aims, charmingly, to recreate at least part of the experience of being hanged.

The Dungeon is clearly on to a winner, judging from the length of the weekend queues outside the Victorian railway arches that are its home. There are always plenty of small children standing in line, where gorily made-up Dungeon staff work the crowds, but we'd advise against taking anyone younger than ten – our eleven-year-old tester came out rather whey-faced, but said he loved it. Tours last around 90 minutes; you can purchase fast-track tickets on the website to beat the queues.

Buggy access. Disabled access: toilet. Nappy-changing facilities. Nearest picnic place: Hay's Galleria. Shop.

Madame Tussauds

Marylebone Road, NW1 5LR (0871 894 3000, www.madame-tussauds.co.uk). Baker Street tube/13, 27, 74, 113, 159 bus. **Open** 9am-6pm daily (last entry 5.30pm). Times vary during holiday periods. **Admission** £25.54; £21.46 4-15s; free under-4s. £88.78 family (2+2 or 1+3). **Credit** AmEx, MC, V. **Map** p314 G4. **3+**

Adults may find it hard to escape the fact that they're paying dearly to stand among a bunch of static waxwork models – although Madame Tussauds works hard to ramp up the excitement. As you enter the first room, you're dazzled by paparazzi flashbulbs; starry-eyed kids can then take part in a 'Divas' routine with Amy Winehouse and Justin Timberlake. Robbie Williams, meanwhile, has a kiss sensor that activates a twinkle in his eye. New figures are constantly added – in 2010 Helen Mirren, Robert Pattinson and Steven Gerrard have joined the throng – and old favourites updated: Kylie Minogue and the Queen have been recast no less than four times. There's a *Pirates of the Caribbean* diorama in the hull of the Black Pearl, staffed by Keira, Orlando and Johnny; the World Stage hall is an interactive room split into zones for sports, culture, politics, popular music, royals and history. Holographs and touch screens add pizzazz. Nobody prevents visitors hugging the stars (or pinching their bottoms, if so inclined).

Elsewhere, the kitsch Spirit of London ride takes you through 400 years of London life in a taxi pod. Children love this, and always want to ride again to spot the historic figures around them. Below stairs lurks Scream – the Chamber of Horrors, which isn't child-friendly at all. It surrounds you with corpses and eviscerated victims of torture, with a truly terrifying 'live' experience (actors dressed up as psycho killers jump out and stalk you; unsurprisingly, it's over-12s only). Such morbid thrills chime with the work of Marie Tussaud (1761-1850), who made death masks out of wax in the French Revolution. Her cast of the mask of Marie-Jeanne du Barry, Louis XV's mistress, is the oldest work on display: it's now used as the peaceful face of the reclining, animatronic *Sleeping Beauty*. See also *p138* **Great Days Out**.

Café. Disabled access: lift, toilet. Nappy-changing facilities. Nearest picnic place: Regent's Park. Shop.

London Dungeon. *See p52.*

Sightseeing

Ripley's Believe It or Not

*1 Piccadilly Circus, London, W1J 0DA
(0203 238 0022, www.ripleyslondon.com).
Piccadilly Circus tube.* **Open** 10am-10.30pm
daily. **Admission** £21.90; £19.90 reductions;
£17.90 4-15s; free under 4s. £69.80 family
(2+2). **Credit** MC, V. All ages
Robert LeRoy Ripley opened his first
odditorium in Chicago, in 1930. He's long gone,
but the 31 museums that bear his name march
weirdly (some say wonderfully) on. The five-
floor London one has plenty of oddities to
make your eyes pop; we particularly enjoyed
the two-way gurning mirror, which has
unsuspecting visitors trying out seemingly
impossible facial contortions, unaware they're
being watched by everyone else. The
matchstick Tower Bridge fascinates children,
as do the freakshow exhibits, like two-headed
calves and shrunken skulls.

A more dizzying delight is the Topsy Turvy
Tunnel, which is like a bridge through a
kaleidoscope that has you staggering drunkenly
about while attempting to cross it. It's near
the Mirror Maze, which engendered mutiny
in the ranks when we learned you had to pay
£4.95 extra to get lost in it. The admission price
is high enough, without hidden extras, we
felt. After all, there are all sorts of free
museums in town where you can see some
pretty freaky stuff – pickled tumours in the
Hunterian (*see p91*), anyone? Still, Ripley
would no doubt say that you have to go past a
load of boring stuff in a regular museum
before meeting things that make you say 'I
don't believe it!' every time, which is what we
said when we saw Leonardo da Vinci's
Last Supper painted on a grain of rice. You'd
better believe it.

Thorpe Park

*Staines Road, Chertsey, Surrey KT16 8PN
(0871 663 1673, www.thorpepark.com).*
Getting there *By rail S*taines rail, then 950
shuttlebus. *By car* J11 or J13 off M25. **Open**
times vary, check website for timetables.
Height restrictions vary, depending on rides.
Admission £36; £22 under-12s; free under-
1m tall. £96 family (2+2). Check the website or
phone for advance bookings; allow 24hrs for
processing. **Credit** MC, V. 5+
The big thrills of Thorpe Park are mostly
designed to appeal to older children, and many
of the rides have height restrictions. That said,
parents with young, or short children will find
plenty to do at Neptune's Beach (a big paddling
and sunbathing spot), Octopus Garden (little,
friendly rides) and the delightful Mr Monkey's
Banana Ride, with its slightly sinister
commentary. The family can get together again
for a soaking in the Rumba Rapids, another
favourite of ours. Perhaps we're just wet.

Teenagers meanwhile, will love the
horrifyingly fast Stealth (standstill to 80mph
in two seconds, plus a hideous vertical drop),
and the gore of horror-themed white-knuckler,
Saw. It is quite shockingly awful, but you're a
wuss if you don't give it a go: this is, after all,
Europe's most extreme G-Force experience.
Unless you make a beeline for Saw on entering
the park at 10am, you'll have to be prepared to
queue for up to two hours to experience the
dark, blood-stained slasher movie build-up, the
initial drops in pitch blackness, the climb to the
top of the mountainous loop that has you
looking at the sky dry-mouthed while you wait
for the vertical downward rush. The track is
concave (they call it 'beyond vertical'), the
screams are in earnest and the eyes are best
kept tight shut; unsurprisingly, it's not
recommended for under-12s (you have to be
over 1.4m tall too).

In 2010, the 'Saw Alive' horror maze (with six
'live action' rooms) was opened next door,
adding a different kind of thrill.

Our favourite ride on a hot day is the
exhilarating Tidal Wave, which hits the water
at such speed that wet pants are inevitable.
It's a perfect place for adolescents to wander
free, bonding good-naturedly in the long, long
queues (coming in wet weather and on school
days is one way to avoid them). The staff, for
the most part, are young and extremely
friendly, so the atmosphere in the park is
surprisingly pleasant.

*Buggy access. Café. Disabled access: toilet.
Nappy-changing facilities. Restaurants. Shops.*

Trocadero

*Coventry Street, W1D 7DH (7439 1791,
www.londontrocadero.com). Piccadilly Circus
tube.* **Open** 10am-midnight Mon-Thur,
Sun; 10am-1am Fri, Sat. **Admission** free;
individual attractions vary. **Credit** varies.
Map p317 K7. 5+
At its heart, this pulsating indoor complex
houses a vast arcade of coin-in-the-slot video
games, simulator rides and dance machines.
The noise and disorientating lights are a fast
track to tantrums and headaches – and still
they come to spend all their pocket money.
There's a seven-screen cinema, a dodgem track,
a ten-lane bowling alley and various fast-food
outlets. The sports bar is grown-ups only.

*Buggy access. Cafés. Disabled access: lift,
toilet. Nappy-changing facilities. Nearest
picnic place: Leicester Square, Trafalgar
Square. Restaurants. Shops.*

Sightseeing

Museums & Galleries

Lots of things to discover and do.

London has a lot to thank the Victorians for. Led by Queen Victoria and her influential consort Albert, the philanthropists and activists of the day fought for enlightenment and knowledge for all. The Victorian era gave us the great trio of museums on Exhibition Road – the **V&A** (see p68), the **Science Museum** (see p92) and the **Natural History Museum** (see p87) – as well as the underground trains on which to travel to them. These great museums are constantly evolving, and there are lots of new openings to enjoy in 2010: the Darwin Centre (see p8 **Nature Watch**) at the Natural History Museum; the China and Medieval galleries at the V&A, and the revamped Wellcome Wing at the Science Museum.

You can see what life was like for Victorians in this great city at the new galleries at the **Museum of London** (see p10 **London Stories Retold**). The galleries took three years to complete, at a cost of £20 million, and the imaginative exhibits, touch screens, audio-visual intallations and exhibitions set underneath glass flooring will appeal to children's sense of fun.

Greenwich also has a new attraction at the **Old Royal Naval College**. **Discover Greenwich** (see p85) is a visitor centre with a permanent gallery telling the story of Greenwich's 500-year history. Up in Camden, the **Jewish Museum** (see p84 **The all-new Jewish Museum**) has reopened its doors after expanding into the building next door and has put a lot of thought into making its exhibits child-friendly.

New openings aside, you'll find most of the capital's museums and galleries put considerable effort into making their exhibits accessible to children. The **British Museum** (see p73) may be more than 250 years old but the extraordinary collections aren't in the least bit stuffy and the museum's trails really capture the attention of small minds. There are all kinds of fantastic activities and workshops going on at venues listed in this chapter, but bear in mind that it's usually best to book ahead. Our top tip for a successful day out is to arrive early, pack lots of snacks and avoid trying to do too much in one day.

ART & DESIGN

Camden Arts Centre

Corner of Arkwright Road & Finchley Road, NW3 6DG (7472 5500, www.camdenartscentre. org). Finchley Road tube/Finchley Road & Frognal rail. **Open** 10am-6pm Tue, Thur-Sun; 10am-9pm Wed. **Admission** free. **Credit** MC, V. 7+ (parental advisory)

Misleadingly named for grockles, as it's nowhere near Camden Town, but worth seeking out. It's a sleek contemporary arts centre hosting regular exhibitions in its three galleries, with a state-of-the-art ceramics studio attached. Half terms bring four-day courses in clay, mixed media, photography and sculpture for five to sevens and eight to 11s (£140; £100 reductions).

The café is a gem, with a spacious terrace, daily specials, hearty sandwiches, great coffee and stripey marshmallow-topped hot chocolate. *Buggy access. Café. Disabled access: lift, toilet. Nappy-changing facilities. Nearest picnic place: gallery garden. Shop.*

Design Museum

Shad Thames, SE1 2YD (7940 8790, www.designmuseum.org). Tower Hill tube/ London Bridge tube/rail/47, 100, 188 bus. **Open** 10am-5.45pm daily. **Admission** £8.50; £6.50 reductions; free under-12s. **Credit** AmEx, MC, V. **Map** p319 S9. 5+

This stylishly converted Thameside warehouse full of inspiring design is a surprisingly child-friendly sort of place: young visitors are given inside: there's no missing its bright orange premises (with flashes of take-no-prisoners pink and electric blue), which were designed by Mexican architect Ricardo Legorreta. Inexpensive, inspiring children's workshops run in half term and the summer holidays, often led by industry professionals – perfect for fledgling fashion mavens. Temporary exhibition Horrockses Fashions: Off the Peg Style in the '40s and '50s runs from July to October 2010. *Buggy access. Café. Disabled access: lift, toilet. Nearest picnic place: Bermondsey Square.*

Geffrye Museum

136 Kingsland Road, E2 8EA (7739 9893, www.geffrye-museum.org.uk). Hoxton rail/ Liverpool Street tube/rail, then 149, 242 bus/ Old Street tube/rail, then 243 bus. **Open** 10am-5pm Tue-Sat; noon-5pm Sun, bank hol Mon. **Admission** free; donations appreciated. *Almshouse* £2; £1 reductions; free under-16s. **Credit AmEx**, MC, V. 5+
Set in one of the most urban sections of London, The Geffrye Museum is a strange oasis. The rooms within the attractive 18th-century almshouses recreate interiors from different periods, from the Elizabethan era to the present day. Visitors walk past in a roped-off corridor, admiring – or deploring – the tastes and styles of the past. It's like time-travelling without the

Tardis. On the first Saturday of the month, there are free quizzes and craft activities for five to 16s, while half terms bring hands-on workshops for all ages. In summer, there's an eclectic array of garden parties and family days; kids might learn bhangra dancing, make masks or listen to a Caribbean steel band. Events often spill into the glorious gardens, so bring a picnic to eat on the grass. In winter, the Christmas Past exhibition sees each room decorated for the festive season according to its period; the museum also holds an outdoor Twelfth Night ritual, with singing, holly- and ivy-burning and a taste of traditional Twelfth Night cake for the kids (and mulled wine for grown-ups). Temporary exhibitions are housed in the second, newer, half of the museum, along with the airy, inviting restaurant. *Buggy access. Disabled access: lift, toilet. Nappy-changing facilities. Nearest picnic place: museum grounds. Restaurant. Shop.*

Guildhall Art Gallery

Guildhall Yard, off Gresham Street, EC2V 5AE (7332 3700, www.guildhall-art-gallery. org.uk). Mansion House or St Paul's tube/Bank tube/DLR/Moorgate tube/rail/8, 25, 242 bus. **Open** 10am-5pm Mon-Sat; noon-4pm Sun. **Admission** £2.50; £1 reductions; free under-16s. Free to all after 3.30pm daily, all day Fri. **Credit** (over £5) MC, V. **Map** p318 P6. 6+
Perhaps the most exciting exhibit here for children is the Roman ampitheatre that lies under the courtyard. The remains are fairly scant and only the foundations of the walls and entrance survive – but the site does an excellent job of suggesting how the amphitheatre would have looked, with staggered seats printed on a screen, dynamic illustrations of gladiators and sound effects. Up in the Main Gallery is the vast *Defeat of the Floating Batteries at Gibraltar* by John Singleton Copley, the largest painting in Britain. The City of London's gallery has some gems, with works by Constable, Reynolds and the Pre-Raphaelites, and absorbing depictions of London through the ages. In October the gallery takes part in the annual Big Draw (*see p22*), and there are pre-bookable half-term workshops; every Friday, four free tours (hourly from 12.15pm, no booking needed) take in the highlights of the collection. *Buggy access. Disabled access: toilet. Nappy-changing facilities. Nearest picnic place: Finsbury Circus.*

Hayward Gallery

Belvedere Road, SE1 8XX (7921 0813, www.southbankcentre.co.uk). Embankment tube/Waterloo tube/rail. **Open** 10am-6pm daily; call to check for late night openings

Dulwich Picture Gallery. *See p57.*

Get creative with art activities at the **Design Museum**.

a Family Trail worksheet to doodle on, while acclaimed Get Creative! sessions usually run once a month. Here, creative five- to 11-year-olds can dabble in arty activities: the monthly-changing themes range from modern millinery to furniture design and architecture. The cost is £4 per child, though participants must be accompanied by a paying adult (£8.50); fees also cover admission to the museum's current crop of exhibitions. Here from November 2010 to March 2011 is 100 Years of Fashion Illustration. *Buggy access. Café. Disabled access: lift, toilet. Nappy-changing facilities. Nearest picnic place: Butler's Wharf riverside benches. Shop.*

Dulwich Picture Gallery

Gallery Road, SE21 7AD (8693 5254, www.dulwichpicturegallery.org.uk). North Dulwich or West Dulwich rail. **Open** 10am-5pm Tue-Fri; 11am-5pm Sat, Sun, bank hol Mon. **Admission** £5; £4 reductions; free under-18s. **Credit** MC, V. 6+
This tiny gallery, built by the eccentric, energetic Sir John Soane in 1811, punches well above its weight with its outstanding collection of 17th- and 18th-century old masters. They include paintings by the likes of Rembrandt, Tiepolo, Rubens, Van Dyck and Gainsborough, while temporary exhibitions romp across the centuries. It's also a community hub of arty activity. Tuesday's Evening Art School gives 15 to 18s the chance to develop their portfolios, Wednesday's quirkily themed after-school creative sessions are

aimed at seven- to ten-year-olds, while there are six-week art courses on Thursday nights, devoted to different media (silk screen printing, paper cut-outs) for 11 to 14s; prices range from £55 and £65.

Holidays bring yet more activities, often involving making things along a seasonal theme; Art in the Garden gatherings are on Wednesdays in the summer hols and cost £2 per child. Artplay afternoons, held on the first and last Sunday of the month, invite parents and over-fours to partake in artist-led activities, from making sock puppets to designing African masks (£2; free with gallery ticket). Check online for details and fees of all courses and classes; booking is generally essential, although Art in the Garden and Artplay are drop-ins. *Buggy access. Café. Disabled access: toilet. Nappy-changing facilities. Nearest picnic place: gallery gardens. Shop.*

Fashion & Textile Museum

83 Bermondsey Street, SE1 3XF (7407 8664, www.ftmlondon.org). London Bridge tube/rail. **Open** 11am-6pm Wed-Sun. Last entry 5.15pm. **Admission** £6.50; £3.50 reductions; free under-12s. **Credit** MC, V. 8+
Founded by flamboyant British fashion designer Zandra Rhodes and now run by Newham College, this colourful museum showcases fashion, textiles and jewellery, with temporary exhibitions to supplement the permanent collection. We don't just mean colourful on the

A FAMILY COLLECTION | A NATIONAL MUSEUM | AN INTERNATIONAL TREASURE HOUSE

Free family fun...step back in time just minutes from Oxford Street

- Outstanding Old Masters
- Fabulous French art
- Perfect princely armour
- Rare Renaissance treasures
- Ravishingly refurbished state rooms
- Animated animals
- Monsters and myths
- Queens and Cavaliers
- Chivalrous Knights
- Warrior Kings

FREE entry
FREE exhibitions
FREE armour handling
FREE family trails
FREE family activities
Family multimedia tour and interactive games

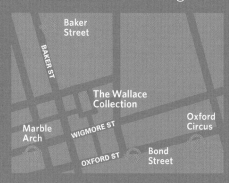

Hertford House, Manchester Square, London W1U 3BN www.wallacecollection.org

Design for living: the **Geffrye Museum**. *See p58.*

Admission £11; £5.50-£8 reductions; £4.50 12-16s; free under-12s. Prices vary; phone for details. **Credit** AmEx, MC, V. **Map** p318 M8. 7+ (parental advisory)

Brutalist beauty the Hayward was closed for four months in early 2010 for repairs and renewal. When it opened its doors on 19 June it was to show off a new site-specific exhibition featuring the work of Brazlian artist Ernesto Neto, which runs until 5 September alongside group show The New Décor. The gallery's position within the Southbank Centre makes it popular with families on a day out. The light, bright pavilion by Daniel Graham was added in 2003; children enjoy watching cartoons on the touch screens or just wandering around the visually confusing space created by curved, two-way mirrors. There are no permanent collections on display; instead, three or four major temporary exhibitions are staged through the year. *See also p30* **Great Days Out**.
Buggy access. Café. Disabled access: lift. Nappy-changing facilities. Nearest picnic place: Jubilee Gardens/riverside benches. Shop.

Kenwood House

Hampstead Lane, NW3 7JR (8348 1286, www.english-heritage.org.uk). Archway tube, then 210 bus. **Open** 11.30am-4pm daily.
Admission free. **Credit** MC, V. 5+

English Heritage runs this majestic 17th-century mansion perched at the north end of Hampstead Heath. Your children are likely to ignore the house and instead go fizzy at the great rolling expanse of green in front that leads down to the lake, where there are a couple of excellent climbing trees to be found. They'll also like hide and seek in the rhododendrons, the posh ice-creams, lunch or (especially) breakfast in the Brew House (*see p223*), and the fact that the site provides a superb jumping-off point for all things Heathly. After letting off steam, they might be persuaded inside the house to see the very decent collection of paintings: Gainsborough, Vermeer, Reynolds, Van Dyck, Hals, Turner and a great Rembrandt self-portrait.
Buggy access. Café. Disabled access: toilets. Nappy-changing facilities. Nearest picnic place: House grounds, Hampstead Heath. Restaurant.

Museum of Brands, Packaging & Advertising

2 Colville Mews, Lonsdale Road, W11 2AR (7908 0880, www.museumofbrands.com). Ladbroke Grove or Notting Hill Gate tube/ 23 bus. **Open** 10am-6pm Tue-Sat; 11am-5pm Sun. Last entry 45mins before closing.
Admission £5.80; £3.50 reductions; £2 7-16s; free under-7s; £14 family (2+2). **Credit** MC, V. **Map** p310 A6. 6+

Spanning some 200 years of brands, the vast collections in this museum cover Victorian leisure pursuits, the advent of radio, the chirpy thrift of wartime Britain and the liberal revolution of the swinging '60s. The displays,

originally collected by consumer historian Robert Opie, who started his obsession at 16 when he decided to keep a Munchies wrapper rather than throw it in the bin, are geared towards nostalgic adults, but historically minded children may be amused by the antiquated toys, magazines and comics on show – not to mention old versions of all their favourite chocolate wrappers. Temporary exhibition Political Mugs runs until 28 November 2010, looking at political intrigue over the last 200 years as depicted by souvenir mugs, jugs, tins and toys.
Buggy access. Café. Disabled access: toilet. Nappy-changing facilities. Nearest picnic place: Kensington Gardens. Shop.

National Gallery

Trafalgar Square, WC2N 5DN (7747 2885, www.nationalgallery.org.uk). Charing Cross tube/rail/24, 29, 176 bus. **Open** 10am-6pm Mon-Thur, Sat, Sun; 10am-9pm Fri. *Tours* 11.30am, 2.30pm daily. **Admission** free. *Temporary exhibitions* prices vary. *Tours* free. **Credit** MC, V. **Map** p317 K7. 5+
There are 2,300 paintings to see here, all free of charge, which makes it a good idea to 'manage' a visit if accompanied by children, lest they get overwhelmed. The gallery is great at providing ways of doing this, and the latest innovation is the Artstart Interactive Guide, which can be found in the Sainsbury Wing and the East Wing's espresso bar. Choose a preselected tour, or design one of your own then print it out. Alternatively, children can guide their parents thanks to the Teach Your Grown-ups About Art audio tour, which equips kids with a map and audio guide, then asks them to relay choice snippets to their elders. Other audio guides ask children to follow secret agents or hunt for kings and queens, learning about various paintings as they go. Seeing Things trails – designed for specific age-groups and printable from the website – also help navigate the collections, which include many a masterpiece: Turner's *The Fighting Temeraire*, Botticelli's *Venus* and Jan Van Eyck's Arnolfini Portrait among them. Pick up a floorplan at the information desk before you set off.

Family events include magic carpet storytelling sessions for under-fives on Sunday mornings, plus two-hour art workshops for five to 11s at 11am to 1pm and 2pm to 4pm; you can't book ahead, so turn up well in advance of start times (detailed on the website). The school holidays also bring a healthy spread of free activities, led by painters and sculptors.

Come lunchtime, Oliver Peyton's National Café (*see p222*) offers simple, sustaining fare to fuel the children's creativity: a boiled egg with soldiers, perhaps, or lovely creamy macaroni cheese. *See also p36* **Great Days Out**.
Buggy access. Café. Disabled access: lift, toilet. Nappy-changing facilities. Nearest picnic place: Trafalgar Square. Restaurant. Shop.

National Portrait Gallery

2 St Martin's Place, WC2H 0HE (7306 0055/ tours 7312 2483, www.npg.org.uk). Leicester Square tube/Charing Cross tube/rail/24, 29, 176 bus. **Open** 10am-6pm Mon-Wed, Sat, Sun; 10am-9pm Thur, Fri. *Tours* times vary, phone for details. **Admission** free. *Temporary exhibitions* prices vary. *Video guide* £3. *Tours* free. **Credit** AmEx, MC, V. **Map** p317 K7. 5+
Likenesses of Britain's great and good make up the NPG's tremendous collection, from Tudor royalty to modern-day actors, writers, politicians and academics. Children will particularly enjoy the gory provenance of recent acquisition *Self* by Marc Quinn, a sculpture made out of the artist's own blood. The third Saturday of the month brings free storytelling for over-threes and crafts activities for over-fives, while school-holiday workshops might range from making Regency bonnets and top hats to sketching oil-pastel portraits. *See also p36* **Great Days Out**.
Buggy access. Café. Disabled access (Orange Street entrance): lift, toilet. Nappy-changing facilities. Nearest picnic place: Leicester Square, Trafalgar Square. Restaurant. Shops.

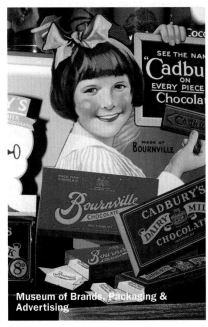

Museum of Brands, Packaging & Advertising

Sightseeing

Great Days Out
Bloomsbury

British Museum

Bloomsbury is remarkably quiet considering its central London location. Blue plaques dotted around the area's grand squares attest to its popularity with literary and arty types (before a time when they could no longer afford to live here). EM Forster, Dorothy L Sayers, Jerome K Jerome, William Morris, Dante Gabriel Rossetti, Virginia Woolf and her 'set' are just a few of the names that resided for a time within the stately Georgian townhouses around these parts. It remains a pleasantly bookish, cultural sort of place, thanks to its fine clutch of museums – headed up, of course, by the mighty British Museum – and specialist book and art supply shops.

Bloomsbury is also home to Lamb's Conduit Street, a Dickensian-looking thoroughfare that's become a bastion of independent traders. The bike shop, grocer's, bookshops and boutiques ooze character; happily, it's too compact to strike fear into shop-resistant children's souls. The perfect reward for good behaviour is just around the corner: the park, pets' corner and playground at Coram's Fields.

Welcome to the Ancient World

Step into the **British Museum** (*see p73*), and you're whisked into all sorts of weird and wonderful ancient civilisations. Pick up activity backpacks and trails from the Paul Hamlyn Library, or take a wander and prepare to be astonished. In one room, graceful Grecian youths strike nonchalant poses; in the Africa gallery on the floor below, you might find a defiantly-bristling two-headed dog named Kozo (Room 23). On the upper floor, the Egyptian mummies in rooms 62 and 63 will send a delicious thrill down your spine, as the unseeing eyes of long-dead priests and pharoahs stare back at you; the first century AD mummified cat looks far friendlier.

Don't try to cram it all into one visit – and if the kids need a break from statues and sarcophagi, head to the light-flooded Great Court. Below here, the Clore Education Centre and Ford Centre for Young Visitors host weekend and holiday activity sessions: mummy-making is an eternally popular offering.

For earnest Egyptologists, the **Petrie Museum of Egyptian Archaeology** is also close by (*see p75*). It's a dimly lit, delightfully old-fashioned sort of establishment, run by enthusiastic staff; thrillingly, you can request a torch with which to explore the murkier recesses. Peek at the skeleton in a pot, write your name in hieroglyphs, and admire the eclectic array of beads, tools, pots and textiles, displayed in rows of Victorian glass cabinets.

Have a field day

Seven acres of lawns, football pitches, sandpits, swings and slides await at **Coram's Fields** (see p112) – sheer heaven for space-starved city kids, who run circuits around the grass like giddy spring lambs. As a sign on the gate firmly states, unaccompanied adults are banned, giving parents extra peace of mind. Older kids can swoop along the flying fox or zoom down the helter-skelter while tinies potter in the sandpit or fearlessly ascend the climbing frame. Smell a certain fruity something in the air? That'll be the petting zoo – a whiffy but happy home to goats, geese, ducks, guinea pigs and other docile mini-beasts.

Bring a picnic to spread out on the grass, or eat at the on-site café. It's run by the Kipferl team, who also own a great little Austrian deli/café in Smithfield, so expect bretzels and sachertorte alongside open sarnies, hot dishes and soups.

By comparison to Coram's Fields, Bloomsbury's other squares are more sedate. Just north of Coram's, the tranquil, plane tree-shaded **St George's Gardens** (www.friendsofstgeorgesgardens. org.uk) were a burial ground in the 18th and 19th centuries. Children can decipher the crumbling inscriptions on the tombs that dot the gardens, or hunt for the final resting-place of Oliver Cromwell's granddaughter, Anna Gibson; those who like their history dark and gory may be interested to learn that this was the site of the first recorded attempt at body-snatching in 1777.

Past the uncompromising, concrete bulk of the Brunswick Centre (home to a massive Waitrose that's good for picnic provisions, along with various shops) lies **Russell Square** – a jewel among Bloomsbury's garden squares. It's a sun-dappled, quietly dignified expanse, with a

---

LUNCH BOX

Also in the area: ASK, Carluccio's Caffè, Giraffe, Hummus Bros, Pizza Express, Tas, Yo! Sushi, Wagamama.
Court Café *British Museum, Great Russell Street, WC1B 3DG (7323 8990).* A handy pit-stop for sarnies and cakes.
Fryer's Delight *19 Theobald's Road, WC1X 8SL (7405 4114).* Glorious fish and chips (some say London's finest), served in kitsch surrounds.
Garden Café at Russell Square *Russell Square Gardens, WC1B 5EH (7637 5093).* Sun yourself on the patio while scoffing ice-creams.
Kipferl *Coram's Fields, 93 Guilford Street, WC1N 1DN (www.kipferl.co.uk).* A summer-only joint offering superior light lunches and cakes, overlooking the playground; the café is closed on Mondays.
La Porchetta *33 Boswell Street, WC1N 3BP (7242 2434, www.la porchettapizzeria.co.uk).* This busy pizzeria and pasta joint doesn't stint on portion sizes.

---

water-jet fountain at the centre that cries out to be scampered through; at its northern end, the café has a lovely terrace and does a fine trade in ice-cream cornets as well as more substantial sustenance.

Find out about the foundlings

In the 18th century, Coram's Fields was the site of the Foundling Hospital. A home for abandoned and destitute children, it was established by a kindly sea captain, Thomas Coram. Though the orphanage was demolished in the 1920s, its small inhabitants – and the adults who campaigned on their behalf – are remembered at the **Foundling Museum** (see p71) on Brunswick Square, overlooking Coram's Fields. The little love tokens left by the poverty-stricken mothers who abandoned their babies at the hospital would touch the hardest of hearts: a key; a button; a scrap of poetry; letters; a hazelnut shell. Look out for special family days, when activities might include making a Victorian jumping-jack or a pop-up street scene.

Great Days Out

Orleans House Gallery

Riverside, Twickenham, Middx TW1 3DJ (8831 6000, www.richmond.gov.uk/orleans_house_gallery). St Margaret's, Richmond or Twickenham rail/33, 490, H22, R68, R70 bus. **Open** *Apr-Sept* 1-5.30pm Tue-Sat; 2-5.30pm Sun, bank hols. *Oct-Mar* 1-4.30pm Tue-Sat; 2-4.30pm Sun, bank hols. **Admission** free; donations appreciated. **Credit** MC, V. 5+
This elegant Thames-side gallery is on top form thanks to a recent Lottery cash injection, and has been selected to take part in museummaker for 2010. This is a project that teams craft makers with galleries to create new site-specific commissions. From 12 June to 26 September, weaver Eleanor Pritchard will create a fantasy banquet at Orleans House, telling the story of each guest. Outside, the woodland gardens are open until dusk. Upbeat children's workshops run year-round: the after-school Art Club caters for five- to ten-year-olds, while 10:15 entertains ten to 15s. All need to be booked via the website. The Coach House education centre hosts holiday art workshops, using the gallery's exhibitions as a starting point. The team also co-ordinates the annual summer Larks in the Park children's theatre festival (28 June-27 Aug in 2010), with performances in parks across the borough. *Buggy access. Café. Disabled access: toilet. Nappy-changing facilities. Nearest picnic place: Orleans House Gallery grounds, Marble Hill Park or riverside benches. Shop.*

Queen's House

Romney Road, SE10 9NF (8312 6565, www.nmm.ac.uk). Cutty Sark DLR/ Greenwich DLR/rail. **Open** 10am-5pm daily. Last entry 4.30pm. *Tours* times vary; call for details. **Admission** free; occasional charge for temporary exhibitions. *Tours* free. **Credit** (over £5) MC, V. 4+
The first house to be built in Britain in a consciously Classical style was designed in 1616 by Inigo Jones and lived in by successive queens. It's now home to the National Maritime Museum's art collection, which includes all sorts of pictures of naval heroes, battles, uncharted lands and stormy seascapes. For a cherry-picked selection of its treasures, explore the second-floor Art for the Nation exhibition. An exhibition on the ground floor charts the house's former life as a naval boarding school (the timetable revolved around lessons in seafaring and lashings of cocoa), while first floor galleries are devoted to the Tudors and early polar photography. On the Trail of the Stuarts is a 'detective notebook' that leads children around the building,

while a trail for younger children tests their observational skills; download them from the website before you go.
The Tulip Stairs was the first self-supporting spiral staircase in the country: while adults admire its elegant lines and wrought iron fleurs-de-lys, children are advised to keep a watchful eye out for the resident ghost. It was supposedly captured on film by a couple of Canadian visitors in 1966 as it ascended the staircase, and spotted again in 2002 by a spooked gallery assistant, who saw it vanish through a wall. A colonnade connects the building to the National Maritime Museum (*see p100*). *Buggy access. Cafés. Disabled access: lift, toilet. Nappy-changing facilities. Nearest picnic place: picnic area on grounds, Greenwich Park. Shop.*

Royal Academy of Arts

Burlington House, Piccadilly, W1J 0BD (7300 8000, www.royalacademy.org.uk). Green Park or Piccadilly Circus tube. **Open** *Temporary exhibitions* 10am-6pm Mon-Thur, Sat, Sun; 10am-10pm Fri. *John Madejski Fine Rooms* Tours only 1pm Tue; 1pm, 3pm Wed-Fri; 11.30am Sat. **Admission** *Fine Rooms* free. *Exhibitions* prices vary; free under-7s. **Credit** AmEx, DC, MC, V. **Map** p316 J7. 7+
George III established Britain's first art school in 1768. It moved to its present location at Burlington House a century later, and there's a real sense of occasion as you walk under the arches into its impressive courtyard. Works by British artists from the 18th century to the present day (Constable, Reynolds, Turner, Millais, Waterhouse, Hockney among them) are on permanent, free display in the John Madejski Fine Rooms – but the main focus is on the major temporary exhibitions. Who could forget Charles Saatchi's 1997 YBA show, Sensation? The annual Summer Exhibition, held from June to August, is incredibly popular; children will probably find the endless and unstructured rooms of work submitted by the general public overwhelming, although there are some interactive family workshops and gallery talks on offer. At other times, grab an activity sheet for 'art detectives' from reception. The fountains in the Burlington Courtyard (designed by the architects who brought us similar watery pleasures at Somerset House) provide a welcome distraction on all but the frostiest of days. *Buggy access. Café. Disabled: lift, toilet. Nappy-changing facilities. Nearest picnic place: Green Park, St James's Square. Restaurant. Shop.*

Sightseeing

South London Gallery

Saatchi Gallery

Duke Of York's HQ, Duke of York Square, King's Road, SW3 4SQ (7811 3085, www. saatchi-gallery.co.uk). Sloane Square tube. **Open** 10am-6pm daily (last admission 5.30pm). **Admission** free. 7+ (parental advisory)

After a stint in County Hall, the Saatchi moved to its current home off the King's Road in 2008, and immediately struck a resonant note with its inaugural exhibition: emerging young artists from China. The gallery's self-ascribed brief is to exhibit work by innovative, as-yet-unrecognised artists or by international artists with no real profile in this country. You'll need to do your 'suitability' homework before you go (best achieved through the Saatchi's extensive website as well as independent reviews). When you get there you'll find an open, airy, elegant set of conjoined spaces, which amount to just the right size for small legs to manage. An adventure in art – and best of all it's free. *See also p108* **Great Days Out**.

Buggy access. Disabled access: lift, toilets. Nappy-changing facilities. Nearest picnic place: Duke of York Square.

Serpentine Gallery

Kensington Gardens (near Albert Memorial), W2 3XA (7402 6075, www.serpentine gallery.org). Lancaster Gate or South Kensington tube. **Open** 10am-6pm daily. **Admission** free; donations appreciated. **Credit** AmEx, MC, V. **Map** p311 D8. 7+ (parental advisory)

Summer 2010 sees the tenth anniversary of the annual Serpentine Pavilion architectural commission, and Jean Nouvel has got the job. His design is for a dashing scarlet modernist structure that should excite the senses of all ages. The permanent gallery may be housed in an unlikely looking 1930s park building, but it maintains a high profile in the art world with a rolling two-monthly line-up of exhibitions. The bonus of a family day trip here is the gallery's location in the middle of Kensington Gardens, which means that when the fidgets set in, families can decamp straight on to the grass expanses outside the door. The events programme includes family days, artist-led drawing and painting courses, and trails relating to the current exhibitions; check the website for dates.

Buggy access. Disabled access: toilet. Nappy-changing facilities. Nearest picnic place: Hyde Park. Shop.

Somerset House & Galleries

Strand, WC2R 1LA (7845 4600, www. somersethouse.org.uk). Embankment or Temple tube/Charing Cross tube/rail. **Open** 10am-6pm daily. *Courtyard 7.30am-11pm daily. River terrace 8am-6pm daily (extended hours apply for restaurant). Embankment Galleries 10am-6pm Mon-Wed, Fri-Sun; 10am-9pm Thur. Courtauld Gallery 10am-6pm daily. Tours 1.15pm, 2.45pm Thur; 12.15pm, 1.15pm, 2.15pm, 3.15pm Sat.* **Admission** *Parts of South building, courtyard & river terrace* free.

Tours free. *Temporary exhibitions* prices vary; phone for details. **Credit** MC, V. **Map** p317 M7. 8+ (galleries), 5+(courtyard) This one-time Tudor palace became a royal residence (Elizabeth I often stayed here before she was crowned) before it was remodelled into neo-classical splendour and used as offices by various public bodies (all gone, bar the Inland Revenue). These days it houses some of the UK's finest small galleries, although children will be equally enamoured of the enchanting courtyard with its ice-rink in winter and play fountains in summer; kids love running down the ever-shifting corridors of water as the jets dance up and down. The Courtauld Gallery has a huge collection of Impressionist and post-Impressionist paintings as well as older works, which are on permanent display. It also stages temporary exhibitions throughout the year; Cezanne's Card Players runs from October 2010 until January 2011. The Embankment Galleries, which opened in April 2008, focus on photography, design, fashion and architecture. London Fashion Week will return here in 2010 after a successful debut appearance in 2009.

There are imaginative free family workshops on Saturdays for six to 12s (2-3.30pm) and occasional Studio Days for 13- to 18-year-olds, themed around the art in the galleries; these must be booked ahead and cost £15.
Buggy access. Cafés. Disabled access: lift, toilet. Nappy-changing facilities. Nearest picnic place: courtyard. Restaurant. Shops.

South London Gallery

65 Peckham Road, SE5 8UH (7703 6120, www.southlondongallery.org). Peckham Rye rail/12, 36, 171, 345 bus. **Open** noon-6pm Tue-Sun. **Admission** free. **Credit** AmEx, MC, V. 5+ (parental advisory)
A major extension of this Camberwell gallery opened in June 2010, incorporating the neighbouring Victorian house, which was converted into extra gallery space, a new café and a resident artist's flat. The gallery is known for its forward-thinking approach. In the 1990s, it was one of the main showcases for Young British Artists, giving shows to Marc Quinn, Gavin Turk and Tracey Emin; it was the first gallery to exhibit Emin's famous appliquéd tent. It remains one of the capital's foremost contemporary art galleries, with exhibitions that comprise installations, performance pieces and film, as well as paintings and sculpture. Inventive family workshops tie in with the current exhibitions: check online for details.
Buggy access. Disabled access: lift, toilet. Nappy-changing facilities. Nearest picnic place: gallery garden.

Tate Britain

Millbank, SW1P 4RG (7887 8888, www.tate.org.uk). Pimlico tube/77A, 88, C10 bus. **Open** 10am-5.50pm daily; late opening 6-10pm first Fri of mth. *Tours* 11am, noon, 2pm, 3pm Mon-Fri; noon, 3pm Sat, Sun. **Admission** free. *Temporary exhibitions* prices vary. *Tours* free. **Credit** MC, V. **Map** p317 L7. 5+ Downriver from its younger sister, Tate Britain possesses a princely collection of British fine art, sweeping from 1500 to the present day. It's an extraordinary spread, with something for everyone: from Constable's placid landscapes to Blake's apocalyptic visions; the Turner collection is magnificent. Every year, four shortlisted contenders for his namesake award (the Turner Prize) exhibit here, in a flurry of controversy and media hype. Tate Britain's temporary exhibitions are also a big draw, and children should enjoy Rude Britannia: British Comic Art, from 9 June to 5 September 2010, and the celebration of Eadweard Muybridge's early photographic explorations of moving horses and people from 8 September 2010 to 16 January 2011.

A children's discovery trail, available from the information desks, explores the 'secret' Tate, and there's a cosy family reading area in the Rotunda outside Room 17 that offers tips on getting the most out of a visit. The venerable art trolley is wheeled out at weekends and during school holidays (11am-5pm), laden with activities. Check the website for more family and kids' goings-on. When you've finished here, you can cruise swiftly to Tate Modern for another art fix, on the Damien Hirst-decorated Tate to Tate boat.
Buggy access. Café. Disabled access: lift, toilet. Nappy-changing facilities. Nearest picnic place: lawns, Riverside Gardens. Restaurant. Shop.

Tate Modern

Bankside, SE1 9TG (7887 8000, www.tate.org.uk). St Paul's tube/Blackfriars rail. **Open** 10am-6pm Mon-Thur, Sun; 10am-10pm Fri, Sat. Last entry 45mins before closing. **Admission** free. *Temporary exhibitions* prices vary. **Credit** AmEx, MC, V. **Map** p318 O7. 5+ Tate Modern isn't just a gallery, but a day out in its own right. Even getting here along the South Bank is an event. Then comes the excitement of reaching the doors of Turbine Hall via a wide dramatic slope. And once inside, the sheer scale of the gallery's major exhibition space is enough to give most children a sensory hit. This is where, each year, a large-scale, specially commissioned work is installed in the autumn and stays until April. The permanent collections are shown in four wings on Levels 3 and 5, guided by themes such as Cubism, Futurism and Vorticism, Surrealism, Abstract Expressionism and European Informal Art and Minimalism. Grand expansion plans are under way and due for completion in 2012, although the public donation pot is falling short of pre-recession expectations. Architects Herzog & de Meuron plan to create vast new exhibition and performance spaces inside the power station's old oil tanks, as well as building a new structure on the south side of gallery.

Early art appreciation is encouraged by the family activity packs available from Level 3. The Start team will help you choose which art materials, puzzles or architectural trails are suitable for your brood (available at weekends, noon-4pm, and in school hols). Family trails (free) and a kids' multimedia tour for the over fives (£4) are available anytime. On Level 5, the Bloomberg Learning Zone offers educational attractions for over-fives, including games, multimedia activities and a short film. *See also p30* **Great Days Out.**

Buggy access. Café. Disabled access: lift, toilet. Nappy-changing facilities. Nearest picnic place: grounds. Restaurant. Shops.

Vestry House Museum

Vestry Road, E17 9NH (8509 1917, www.walthamforest.gov.uk/rd/vestry-house). Walthamstow Central tube/rail. **Open** 10am-5pm Wed-Sun. *Tours* groups only, by prior arrangement. **Admission** free; donations appreciated. **No credit cards.** 6+

Vestry House became a museum in 1932, but it was once a workhouse; look out for the stone plaque above the entrance, which decrees: 'if any would not work, neither should he eat' – one to remember when the kids won't tidy their rooms. It's an engaging little museum devoted to local history. One room displays vintage toys and games; another is done up as a Victorian parlour. On the ground floor you can see a reconstructed police cell (the building served a stint as a police station in the late 19th century), complete with amusing wax figures dressed as village bobby and drunkard. You can also walk through the workhouse garden, admire a reconstructed Bremer Car (London's first petrol-driven vehicle), and learn about the housewife's lot with a display of labour-intensive domestic paraphernalia (carpet beaters, flat irons, and other antiquated devices). Temporary exhibitions run for one to two months at a time and there are family workshops every third Sunday of the month and during school holidays.

Buggy access (ground floor). Disabled access: toilet (ground floor). Nappy-changing facilities. Nearest picnic place: museum garden. Shop.

Victoria & Albert Museum

Cromwell Road, SW7 2RL (7942 2000, www.vam.ac.uk). South Kensington tube. **Open** 10am-5.45pm Mon-Thur, Sat, Sun; 10am-10pm Fri. *Tours* hourly 10.30am-3.30pm daily. **Admission** free. *Temporary exhibitions* prices vary. **Credit** AmEx, MC, V. **Map** p313 E10. 5+

This major museum is in the middle of a colossal overhaul under the umbrella name of Future Plan. Much of its incredible collection of sculpture, ceramics, textiles, jewellery and decorative arts of every description is being displayed in dramatically fresh ways. The Medieval and Renaissance Galleries opened in December 2009 and show 1,800 objects in chronological order. Phase one of the new China galleries has also opened, with its glorious new light-filled spaces and imaginative displays of unrivalled collections. Children will particularly like the pottery studio, where they can sometimes watch demonstrations. The British Galleries are particularly good for hands-on exhibits: kids can squeeze into a corset and crinoline, try on an armoured gauntlet or construct the Crystal Palace; other interactive displays are marked on the museum's floorplan with a special symbol. Family trails (designed for seven to 12s) can also be picked up from the information desk. On Saturdays and school holidays, over-fives can take their pick of various activity backpacks, then delve in to find puzzles, games and challenges linked to the displays.

There's also lots going on in the art studios and media labs at the museum's Sackler Centre. Sunday's Drop-in Design events bring all sorts of arts and crafts, from making extravagant accessories to designing crazy cups for the Mad Hatter's tea party, and there are brilliant holiday sessions. The café (*see p237*) offers high chairs, and under-tens can order half-price portions of adult mains. Give the children a run around in the grassy courtyard (they can even paddle in summer) then check out the Theatre and Performance galleries – a visual feast of costume, puppets and stage sets, which might inspire the kids to stage a show of their own back at home. *See also p102* **Great Days Out.**

Buggy access. Café. Disabled access: toilet. Nappy-changing facilities. Nearest picnic place: basement picnic room (weekends & school holidays), museum garden, Pirelli Gardens. Restaurant. Shop.

Wallace Collection

Hertford House, Manchester Square, W1U 3BN (7563 9500, www.wallacecollection.org). Bond Street tube/2, 10, 12, 30, 74, 113 bus. **Open** 10am-5pm daily. **Admission** free. **Credit** MC, V. **Map** p314 G5. 6+

Victoria & Albert Museum

Wallace Collection. *See p68.*

An important collection of 18th- and 19th-century art lies in this London townhouse, once the city residence of the Marquesses of Hertford, the Wallaces. There are paintings by great masters like Titian, Rembrandt and Velázquez as well as a series of grand, irresistibly opulent rooms showcasing Sèvres porcelain, Louis XIV and XV furnishings and other fabulously costly trinkets. The biggest draw for most youngsters, though, is the magnificent armoury; regular events invite kids to handle some of the collection's treasures, while would-be gallant champions can stagger under the weight of a replica suit of armour in the Conservation Gallery. The house oozes grandeur – but stately demeanour belies the gallery's welcoming, family-friendly approach. All sorts of trails and artist-led activity sessions help children relate to its priceless collections of paintings, porcelain and furniture, as well as weaponry, and small visitors often go home clutching their own masks, collages, hats and watercolours. Award-winning artists are often in charge of the Little Draw sessions, held on the first Sunday of the month from 1.30pm.

In the glass-roofed courtyard, which is also a sculpture garden, is an Oliver Peyton-run French brasserie; children's mains feature organic meat and fish, and there's a two-course deal for kids for £9.50. *See also p134* **Great Days Out**.

Buggy access. Disabled access: lift, toilet. Nappy-changing facilities. Nearest picnic place: courtyard benches. Restaurant. Shop.

Whitechapel Gallery

77-82 Whitechapel High Street, E1 7QX (7522 7888, www.whitechapelgallery.org). *Aldgate East tube.* **Open** 11am-6pm Tue, Wed, Fri-Sun; 11am-9pm Thur. **Admission** free. **Credit** MC, V. 5+
This East End favourite looks comfortable inside its expanded space, having appropriated the old Whitechapel Library next door. Whatever you think about the library having been relocated and renamed the Idea Store, the gallery has certainly benefited. The light and airy spaces created by the expansion are beautiful, and host a number of temporary exhibitions. Especially lovely is the Clore Creative Studio right at the top. This is where children's drawing workshops for ages ten to 16 are held on Saturdays, 11.30am-1pm (£10). Family art workshops, trails and activity packs are also available; see website for details.
Buggy access. Café. Disabled access: lift, toilet. Nappy-changing facilities. Nearest picnic place: Christ Church Spitalfields. Restaurant. Shop.

William Morris Gallery

Lloyd Park, Forest Road, E17 4PP (8527 3782, www.walthamforest.gov.uk/wmg). *Blackhorse Road tube, then 123 bus.* **Open** 10am-5pm Wed-Sun. *Tours* phone for details. **Admission** free; donations appreciated. **Credit** MC, V. 5+
William Morris was born in Walthamstow, so it's fitting that the only public gallery devoted to his considerable achievements as an artist, socialist, conservationist, craftsman and designer of all that flowery wallpaper is situated in E17. The handsome moated house was where Morris lived as a child and its galleries show a diverse range of exhibits: his satchel and coffee cup are on show alongside tiles, textiles, tapestries, furniture and glass designed by Morris and his Arts & Crafts movement contemporaries. Kids may enjoy the family trails, which encourage them to examine ceramic tile illustrations of stories like Beauty and the Beast, while activities run on the second Sunday of the month and include doll-making, book illustration, calligraphy workshops and pattern-making. During September, the gallery is at the centre of the E17 Art Trail, with displays from local artists and community groups. To the rear of the house, invisible from the road, is Lloyd Park, with its aviary, skateboard park, play areas and a moat with ducks and geese. The park recently received a £3.8 million lottery grant which should spruce things up no end.
Buggy access. Nearest picnic place: Lloyd Park. Shop.

CHILDHOOD

Foundling Museum

40 Brunswick Square, WC1N 1AZ (7841 3600, www.foundlingmuseum.org.uk). *Russell Square tube.* **Open** 10am-5pm Tue-Sat; 11am-5pm Sun. *Tours* by arrangement. **Admission** £7.50; £5 reductions; free under-16s. **Credit** MC, V. **Map** p317 L4. 3+
'Foundlings' was the affectionate name for the residents of London's Hospital for the Maintenance and Education of Exposed and Deserted Children. Founded in 1739 by retired sea captain Thomas Coram, it was largely funded by donations from the painter William Hogarth and the composer George Frideric Handel. For the next 215 years, the hospital provided education for 27,000 children who had been abandoned by their mothers.

As well as paintings by Hogarth and other artists, the museum has a second-floor room dedicated to Handel. Kids love the 'musical

Sightseeing

chairs', with hidden speakers playing excerpts from the composer's works. The best time to visit the museum is on the first Saturday of every month, when activities are laid on for children: dressing up, listening to stories, becoming a curator for the day or designing cards might feature on the agenda. Extra family fun days and storytelling sessions take place on Tuesdays and Thursdays during the school holidays. Brilliant backpacks for three to fives and five to eights can be borrowed for free at any time; they're stuffed with games, puzzles, dressing-up gear, finger puppets and more. Themes include the sea, transport and time with the foundlings. There is also a range of trails to follow.

The bright spacious café is worth visiting too. An antique tavern clock counts the hours and classical music hangs in the air… It's a peaceful place to lunch thanks to its relatively reclusive location, and the menu features innovative sandwiches, pies and salads. There's also a good range of cakes and a popular cream tea. *See also p62* **Great Days Out**.
Buggy access. Café. Disabled access: lift. Nappy-changing facilities. Nearest picnic place: Brunswick Square, Coram's Fields. Shop.

London International Gallery of Children's Art

Waterlow Park Centre, Dartmouth Park Hill, N19 5JF (7281 1111, www.ligca.org). Archway tube. **Open** 10am-4pm Fri-Sun. **Admission** free; donations appreciated. **No credit cards.** 5+
LIGCA has moved from the O2 Centre to this much nicer location in Highgate's Waterlow Park (*see p120*). The gallery celebrates the creativity of children all over the world with temporary exhibitions that change every few months. Art materials are left out for any young visitor who might want to get creative; staff also offer children's birthday parties. The gallery is manned by volunteers, so phone before setting out.
Buggy access. Disabled access: lift, toilet. Nappy-changing facilities. Nearest picnic place: Waterlow Park.

Pollock's Toy Museum

1 Scala Street (entrance on Whitfield Street), W1T 2HL (7636 3452, www.pollockstoy museum.com). Goodge Street tube. **Open** 10am-5pm Mon-Sat. **Admission** £5; £4 reductions; £2 3-16s; free under-3s. **Credit** MC, V. 5+

Light, airy spaces at the **Whitechapel Gallery**. *See p71.*

In a quiet corner of Fitzrovia, occupying two townhouses, this museum is a warren of wonderfully atmospheric rooms and creaky, narrow staircases. It's named after Benjamin Pollock, the last of the Victorian toy theatre printers: to see examples of his tiny tableaux, visit room six. Elsewhere, there are treasures gathered from nurseries across the world, from delicate china dolls to mechanical tin toys and dapper lead soldiers. Adults are more likely to appreciate the nostalgia value of the old board games and playthings, but the museum shop has child appeal, with its reproduction cardboard theatres, wind-up music boxes, animal masks and tin robots.
Nearest picnic place: Crabtree Fields, Colville Place. Shop.

Ragged School Museum

46-50 Copperfield Road, E3 4RR (8980 6405, www.raggedschoolmuseum.org.uk). Mile End tube. **Open** 10am-5pm Wed, Thur; 2-5pm 1st Sun of mth. **Admission** free; donations appreciated. **No credit cards.** 6+ (term time), 2+ (school holidays)
Thomas Barnardo arrived in London to train as a doctor in 1866. But when he came face to face with the poverty, overcrowding, disease and lack of provision for poor children to get an education, he jettisoned his plans and set up his first Ragged School. The largest of these was established here, just by Regent's Canal, ten years later. The buildings have now been converted into a fascinating museum, with gallery areas revealing what life was like in the Victorian East End. There's also a mock-up of a classroom where mock lessons – complete with slates, dunce hats and a costume-clad teacher – are staged for today's children; they're open to people of all ages on the first Sunday of the month. The 45-minute lessons start at 2.15pm and 3.30pm; book on arrival at the museum, as places are limited. In the holidays, special events run on Wednesdays and Thursdays (check the website for details). There's also a Victorian kitchen and displays on local history and industry.
Buggy access. Café. Disabled access: toilet. Nappy-changing facilities. Nearest picnic place: Mile End Park. Shop.

V&A Museum of Childhood

Cambridge Heath Road, E2 9PA (8983 5200, recorded information 8980 2415, www.vam. ac.uk/moc). Bethnal Green tube/rail/8 bus. **Open** 10am-5.45pm daily. **Admission** free. Under-12s must be accompanied by an adult. **Credit** MC, V. 1+
When this iron building was first erected here in 1872 its purpose as a museum was pretty vague.

Exhibits were mainly those left over from the Food and Animal Products collections of the Great Exhibition. Its development into the Museum of Childhood was almost an accident; when post-World War I curator Arthur Sabin noticed that many of the museum's visitors were bored-looking children, he decided to pepper the galleries with child-friendly objects and toys. These days, it's a real treasure trove. Don't miss the Front Room Gallery as you go in. Caroline Irby's thought provoking study of multicultural Britain, A Child From Everywhere (until 30 August 2010), is a collection of photos and interviews with children from just about every country across the world. The well-stocked shop and Benugo café are on the ground floor; note the 19th-century black and white mosaic floor tiles, made by female prisoners in Woking jail. The mezzanine and upper floors are configured to house the permanent collections, alongside temporary and touring exhibitions: Kids will enjoy Sit Down: Seating for Kids (until September 2010), which explores seats made especially for children from 1680 to the present day. Many of them are rather covetable. There's an irresistibly soft ride-on ladybird the size of a small dog, made by teddy-bear manufacturer Steiff in 1962, and an example of the self-assembly Spotty chair, made from laminated cardboard and popular in the '60s. An interactive exhibit that nods to the story of Goldilocks and Three Bears by asking children to try five chairs and vote for the most comfortable is little more than a distraction though.
A lot of thought has gone into making this museum child-friendly; after all, it's a tease to see so many toys and not be able to play with them. To compensate, there are activity stations in each area with Lego, stickle bricks, a sandpit, board games, rocking horses, a book corner and many other treats. In the high-ceilinged, open gallery space, the encouragement to play means the din inside is redolent of an indoor playcentre. It's not conducive to studying what's inside the cases, which is a shame for adults; some of the exhibits – like the 1780s models of a Chinese rock garden and the 1825 Viennese model theatre – merit a bit of contemplation.
Buggy access. Café. Disabled access: lift, toilet. Nappy-changing facilities. Nearest picnic place: basement, museum grounds. Shop.

ETHNOGRAPHY

British Museum

Great Russell Street, WC1B 3DG (7323 8000, 7323 8299, www.britishmuseum.org). Holborn, Russell Square or Tottenham Court Road tube.

Open *Galleries* 10am-5.30pm Mon-Wed, Sat, Sun; 10am-8.30pm Thur, Fri. *Great Court* 9am-6pm Mon-Wed, Sun; 9am-11pm Thur-Sat. *Tours* Highlights 10.30am, 1pm, 3pm daily; phone for details. *Eye Opener tours* phone for details. **Admission** free; donations appreciated. *Temporary exhibitions* prices vary. *Highlights tours* £8; £5 under-11s, reductions. *Eye Opener tours* free. **Credit** AmEx, DC, MC, V. **Map** p317 K5. 5+

The British Museum opened its doors to the public in 1759 and was free even then to 'all studious and curious persons' who wanted to take advantage of its collections. Visitors have now reached six million per year and for good reason: there's an incredible array of treasures from across the globe. Other museums would give their eye teeth for a fraction of its priceless relics, which include the Rosetta Stone, the Lewis Chessmen, the Anglo-Saxon helmet from Sutton Hoo and the Elgin Marbles. Rooms 62 and 63 of the Roxie Walker galleries are top of most children's agendas; it's here that the mummies reside, exerting an eerie spell over visitors. The Africa galleries, full of vivid colours and spooky masks, and Living & Dying – a surreal collection of tribal objects relating to death and mortality from the collection of the Wellcome Trust – are also atmospheric.

Norman Foster's two-acre covered Great Court was an inspired idea, and equals Tate Modern's Turbine Hall (*see p67*) for vast indoor spaces that children love to feel tiny in. The café at the far end is overpriced, but it's a lovely light place to sit, and no-one seems to mind if you bring a picnic.

Plans were passed in December 2009 for a large expansion of the building on its north side. A new conservation wing (much of it underground) will allow the museum's staff more opportunity to save ancient treasures, while above ground, a large new exhibition space will take the pressure off audience crushes for temporary exhibitions. Meanwhile, children can enjoy the walk-through South Africa Landscape curated by Kew Gardens on the west lawn of the museum forecourt until 10 October 2010. Journey Through The Afterlife (4 November 2010-6 March 2011), an exhibition looking at ancient Egypt's Book of the Dead, might also be a morbid hit.

Inventive and free family events run on Saturdays, ranging from Islamic tile-painting workshops to Indian dance lessons, while digital photography-based sessions are held on selected Sundays at the Samsung Digital Photography Centre. Handling sessions take place daily in various galleries and there are some fantastic trail booklets available in the Paul Hamlyn Library that help children of different ages get the best out of the museum. *See also p62* **Great Days Out**. *Buggy access. Cafés. Disabled access: lift, toilet. Nappy-changing facilities. Nearest picnic place: Russell Square. Restaurant. Shops.*

Horniman Museum

100 London Road, SE23 3PQ (8699 1872, www.horniman.ac.uk). Forest Hill rail/122, 176, 185, 312, 356, 363, P4, P13 bus. **Open** 10.30am-5.30pm daily. **Admission** free; donations appreciated. *Myths & Monsters* £5; £2.50 children; free under-3s. **Credit** MC, V. 3+

This has to be one of the most child-friendly museums in all London. The Horniman Museum was founded by Victorian tea trader Frederick John Horniman, an inveterate collector of all sorts of curios. As his worldwide travels continued, his collection grew far too large for the family home in Forest Hill; undaunted, he commissioned a new museum to contain it, which opened to the public in 1901. It's not so much what's here as how it's presented. Head straight to the Hands On Base, where there are boxes of puppets and masks to try out and all sorts of other objects to handle. The Natural History Gallery has skeletons, fossils, pickled animals, stuffed birds and insects in glass cases, presided over by an overstuffed walrus (never having seen such a beast before, the taxidermist didn't realise it ought to have thick folds of skin).

There's an aquarium, and the Nature Base, which has lots of enticing interactive exhibits about the natural world. But whatever you do, save time for the wonderful Music Gallery, where 1,600 instruments are displayed in floor-to-ceiling glass cases. What excites children are the two large, white touch-screen 'tables' in the middle of the room that enable them to choose and listen to pieces of music featuring the different instruments. Adjoining the gallery is a Hands On room, this time giving young visitors carte blanche to bash away at world instruments – including little hollow wooden frogs from South-east Asia, Tibetan singing bowls and a 'flip-flop-o-fone'. Outside, the 16-acre gardens have an animal enclosure with rabbits, goats and chickens, an elegant conservatory and a picnic spot with superb views. Until September 2010, temporary exhibition Myths and Monsters explores stories of mythical creatures from around the world.

Buggy access. Café. Disabled access: lift, toilet. Nappy-changing facilities. Nearest picnic place: museum gardens. Shop.

Petrie Museum of Egyptian Archaeology

University College London, entrance through DMS Watson Library, Malet Place, WC1E 6BT (7679 2884, www.petrie.ucl.ac.uk). Goodge Street or Warren Street tube/29, 73, 134 bus. **Open** 1-5pm Tue-Sat. Closed Easter hols. **Admission** free; donations appreciated. **No credit cards**. **Map** p317 K4. 7+

This museum was originally set up as a teaching resource for the lecturers and students of UCL. William Flinders Petrie was a professor at the University and this collection was amassed partly from his own excavations at sites around the world and partly from a large bequest from 19th-century collector Amelia Edwards. In this age of touch-screen technology and interactive bells and whistles, the museum's old-fashioned glass cabinets are practically a museum piece in their own right. Its eccentricity imbues the museum with an inimitable charm: some corners are so dimly lit, staff lend out torches. They're also endearingly keen, and happy to talk about the collection. As one chap charmingly explained to us, Amelia Edwards was 'more interested in how ordinary Egyptians lived from day to day than in bling' – which means the collections are focused on everyday minutiae such as beads, tools, amulets and clothes. Children can write their name in hieroglyphs, make a pot, or dress like an Ancient Egyptian; it's simple stuff, but great fun. The

Florence Nightingale Museum

The lady, the lamp, and her stuffed owl...

Florence Nightingale died in 1910. To mark the centenary, the Florence Nightingale Museum (*see p79*) has just reopened following a £1.4 million refurbishment. The story of The Lady with the Lamp is told afresh in three pavilions that are located in the grounds of St Thomas' Hospital on the South Bank. The new exhibits are eye-catching, with many imaginative interactive features, including an audio tour listened to on stethoscopes. Florence Nightingale's important status in Key Stage One and Two of the National Curriculum means school holidays are always busy at the museum dedicated to her life. Now the mementoes and tableaux are mounted to evoke even more strongly the field hospitals of Scutari, where nurse Nightingale first came to public attention. The details of her privileged life before then, and selfless life thereafter campaigning for health reforms, are told in a film.

Among the objects on display are her beloved, hand-reared pet owl, Athena (stuffed, and looking slightly wild of eye) and the medicine chest she took to Turkey. Trails for children are available, and art and history activities run during school holidays.

Sightseeing

skeleton in a pot, dating from around the third millenium BC, also enthralls saucer-eyed small fry, along with a mummified head and various fragmentary human remains. *See also p62* **Great Days Out**.
Buggy access. Disabled access: lift, toilet. Nearest picnic place: Gordon Square. Shop.

EMERGENCY SERVICES

London Fire Brigade Museum

Winchester House, 94A Southwark Bridge Road, SE1 0EG (8555 1200, www.london-fire.gov.uk). Borough tube/Southwark tube/rail/344 bus. **Open** by appointment 10.30am, 2pm Mon-Fri. **Admission** £3; £2 7-14s, reductions; £1 under-7s. **Credit** MC, V. **Map** p318 O9. 5+
Winchester House was where London's chief fire officers worked until 1937. Now it's a museum dedicated to the history and ongoing work of the capital's mighty Fire Brigade. Any child with a fire engine fixation will relish the chance to come here. Visits are by appointment only, which means an expert guide will take you round the collection, comprising memorabilia, photos, uniforms, paintings and equipment, showing how firefighting has changed since the Great Fire of 1666. Small children are most smitten with the shiny fire engines, ranging from an 1830s model to red and brass beauties. Although they're not allowed to touch the fire engines, kids are given fireman uniforms to try on, as well as colouring materials. Booking is essential.
Buggy access. Disabled access: toilet. Nearest picnic place: Mint Street Park. Shop.

Museum & Library of the Order of St John

St John's Gate, St John's Lane, EC1M 4DA (7324 4005, www.sja.org.uk/museum). Farringdon tube/rail/55, 63, 243 bus. **Open** (closed until Sept 2010) 10am-5pm Mon-Sat. Closed bank hol weekends. *Tours* 11am, 2.30pm Tue, Fri, Sat. **Admission** free; suggested donations for tours £5; £4 reductions. **Credit** MC, V. **Map** p318 O4. 5+
The St John Ambulance organisation has a long history of training older children in the skills of first aid. The museum devoted to the Order of St John's history has been undergoing a major Heritage Lottery-funded redevelopment and will reopen in September 2010. A double-height Link Gallery with an interactive timeline will compliment existing exhibits: bandages printed with first aid instructions, first-aid kits and archaic-looking ambulances, along with archaeological finds, armour, coins and seals dating back to the Order's earliest years. The redevelopment plans also include a children's trail and a learning space, along with a new entrance through the 16th-century gatehouse. Families can expect more children's activities once the doors are opened again, exact details of which weren't available as we went to press. Keep an eye on the website for the latest news.
Buggy access (ground floor). Disabled access: lift (limited access), toilet (ground floor). Nearest picnic place: Clerkenwell Close. Shop.

GREAT LIVES

Apsley House

149 Piccadilly, W1J 7NT (7499 5676, www.english-heritage.org.uk). Hyde Park Corner tube. **Open** *Apr-Oct* 11am-5pm Wed-Sun & bank hols. *Nov-Mar* 11am-4pm Wed-Sun. Last admission 30 mins before closing. *Tours* by arrangement. **Admission** £6 (includes audio guide if available); £5.10 reductions; £3 5-16s; free under-5s. *Joint ticket with admission to Wellington Arch* £7.40; £6.30 reductions; £3.70 5-16s; free under-5s; £18.50 family (2+3). *Tours* phone for details. **Credit** MC, V. **Map** p316 G8. 5+
This imposing mansion was once known as Number 1 London, because it was the first house visitors passed after going through the toll gates. It's still one of London's most impressive addresses, lording it over Hyde Park Corner. It was the family home of Arthur Wellesley, the first Duke of Wellington, who defeated Napoleon at Waterloo. His descendants still live in the building, but some of it has been given over to a museum about the duke, his campaigns and the fine art and precious antiques he brought back from his travels. Pieces include Canova's enormous marble statue of Napoleon in his birthday suit, as well as paintings by Rubens and Van Dyck. The anniversary of the battle of Waterloo, in June, brings a weekend of soldierly activities, and there's an action sheet families can pick up anytime.
Buggy access. Nearest picnic place: Hyde Park. Shop.

Benjamin Franklin House

36 Craven Street, WC2N 5NF (7930 9121, bookings 7925 1405, www.benjaminfranklin house.org). Embankment tube/Charing Cross tube/rail. **Open** 10.30am-5pm Mon, Wed-Sun. **Admission** £7; £5 reductions; free under-16s. *Tours* noon, 1pm, 2pm, 3.15pm, 4.15pm Mon, Wed-Sun. Booking advisable. **Credit** MC, V. **Map** p317 L7. 6+

Sightseeing

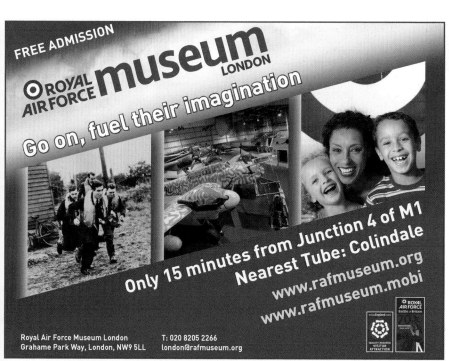

Kew Bridge Steam Museum. *See p81.*

The founding father of the United States lived just around the corner from Trafalgar Square in this 18th-century house for 16 years before the American Revolution. Here, he performed the fraught diplomatic job of 'mediating unrest' between his homeland and its colonial rulers. The house opened to the public in 2006 on Franklin's 300th birthday. It's not a museum exactly, but more of a historical experience enjoyed during guided tours led by actors who bring the history of the place to life. Projections and recorded sound recreate Franklin's London years and recount his many achievements, which include conceiving the ideas of lightning conductors, bifocal specs and fire insurance, identifying the Gulf Stream and coining enduring aphorisms such as 'early to bed and early to rise, makes a man healthy, wealthy and wise'.
Buggy access (ground floor). Nearest picnic place: Victoria Gardens, Embankment. Shop.

Charles Dickens Museum

48 Doughty Street, WC1N 2LX (7405 2127, www.dickensmuseum.com). Russell Square tube. **Open** 10am-5pm daily. **Admission** £6; £4.50 reductions; £3 5-15s; free under-5s; £15 family (2+4). **Credit** AmEx, DC, MC, V. **Map** p317 M4. 8+

Dickens wrote *Oliver Twist* and *A Christmas Carol* in this house, his home for three years. Opening in June 2010 will be an *Oliver!* The Musical exhibition, mounted in partnership with Cameron Mackintosh. Dickens has given us a vivid picture of Victorian London in his writing and the building is crammed with memorabilia and artefacts; in the basement, visitors can see a 25-minute film on Dickens's life in London. Weekly children's 'handling sessions' let young visitors write with Dickens's pen and hold various other possessions. These take place most Wednesdays, but call ahead as they are run by volunteers. There are two mini-trails for children, based on Dickens's stories, plus walking tours of Dickensian London.
Buggy access (ground floor). Nearest picnic place: Coram's Fields, Russell Square. Shop.

Dr Johnson's House

17 Gough Square, off Fleet Street, EC4A 3DE (7353 3745, www.drjohnsonshouse.org). Chancery Lane or Temple tube/Blackfriars rail. **Open** *May-Sept* 11am-5.30pm Mon-Sat. *Oct-Apr* 11am-5pm Mon-Sat. *Tours* by arrangement (groups of 10 or more).
Admission £4.50; £3.50 reductions; £1.50 under-16s; £10 family (2+ unlimited children).

Tours free, booking essential. *Evening tours* by arrangement; phone for details. **No credit cards. Map** p318 N6. 6+

Preserved in an atmospheric little square off Fleet Street is this four-storey Georgian house, which was home to Dr Samuel Johnson, author of the *Dictionary of the English Language*. He lived here with his cat, Hodge – described by his master as 'a very fine cat indeed'. Johnson fed his beloved moggie on oysters; hence the oyster shells at the foot of the bronze statue of Hodge outside the house. It's one of the few items that will really interest children, although they might enjoy trying on replica Georgian costumes in the garret or watching the ancient film playing on a loop of actors embodying the doctor and friends. There is also a children's mini guide and trail available from the front desk.

Buggy access. Nearest picnic place: Lincoln's Inn Fields. Shop.

Florence Nightingale Museum

St Thomas's Hospital, 2 Lambeth Palace Road, SE1 7EW (7620 0374, www.florence-nightingale.co.uk). Westminster tube/Waterloo tube/rail. **Open** 10am-5pm daily. **Admission** £5.80; £4.80 5-18s, reductions; free under-5s; £16 family (2+5). **Credit** AmEx, MC, V. **Map** p317 M9. 5+

After a £1.4 million development, this museum reopened in May 2010, marking the centenary of the great Lady's birth. *See p75.*

Buggy access. Disabled access: toilet. Nappy-changing facilities. Nearest picnic place: benches by hospital entrance, Archbishop's Park. Shop.

Sherlock Holmes Museum

221B Baker Street, NW1 6XE (7935 4430, www.sherlock-holmes.co.uk). Baker Street tube/74, 139, 189 bus. **Open** 9.30am-6pm daily. **Admission** £6; £4 6-16s; free under-6s. **Credit** AmEx, MC, V. **Map** p311 F4. 6+

Rarely has a fictional address had more resonance. The house is set up as if the fictional master detective and his amiable sidekick are in situ. So too, is their long-suffering landlady, Mrs Hudson, who can tell you all you need to know about the great man. Nose about Holmes's study, take a seat in his armchair by the fireplace and investigate his personal effects: the deerstalker cap, pipe, violin and magnifying glass are all present and correct. Upstairs is the room belonging to his associate, Dr Watson, while the third-floor exhibit rooms contain wax models of scenes from the stories; Holmes and his dastardly arch-enemy, Professor Moriarty, can be seen in the same room.

Nearest picnic place: Regent's Park. Shop.

Sir John Soane's Museum

13 Lincoln's Inn Fields, WC2A 3BP (7405 2107, www.soane.org). Holborn tube. **Open** 10am-5pm Tue-Sat; 10am-5pm, 6-9pm 1st Tue of mth. *Tours* 11am Sat. **Admission** free; donations appreciated. *Tours* £5; free under-16s. **Credit** MC, V. **Map** p315 M5. 7+

When Sir John Soane was Professor of Architecture at the Royal Academy, he was already opening his house and collections to students on a weekly basis. After his death in 1837 the house was turned into a museum, kept, as Soane had asked, as near to how he had left it as possible. Which is what makes this museum unique. The collections reflect his passion for an eclectic mix of artefacts and paintings, but the joy is not just in what is here, but also how Soane chose to present it; there are all sorts of ingenious nooks and crannies. It's particularly atmospheric if you visit on the first Tuesday of the month, when it stays open late and is lit by candlelight; there can be lengthy queues for admission.

The old kitchen is used for holiday workshops for children of seven and above (£15 whole day/£8 half day, book in advance): younsters learn how to make a mosaic, create a relief sculpture, paint a self-portrait and frame it, or get stuck into plaster moulding. There are also free drop-in family sessions on the third Saturday of the month (1.30-4.40pm). Children aged seven to 13 can sign up to the Young Architects Club, which meets on the first Saturday of the month. Note that buggies cannot be accommodated.

Nearest picnic place: Lincoln's Inn Fields. Shop.

LONDON & LOCAL

Bruce Castle Museum

Lordship Lane, N17 8NU (8808 8772, www.haringey.gov.uk). Wood Green tube, then 123 or 243 bus/Seven Sisters tube/rail then 123 or 243 bus/Bruce Grove rail. **Open** 1-5pm Wed-Sun. **Admission** free; donations appreciated. **No credit cards.** 4+

This splendid, Grade I-listed 16th-century mansion is a delightfully unexpected find in an otherwise unremarkable-looking suburban street. When the mansion's gardens were opened as a park, it was the first public one of its kind in Tottenham. Inside the house, displays are devoted to the history and achievements of Haringey and its residents – more interesting than you might think, as the borough was home to both madcap illustrator William Heath Robinson and Rowland Hill, the inventor of the Penny Post.

Sightseeing

The museum's Inventor Centre has numerous buttons to press and levers to pull. There are black-and-white photos dating back to the days when the area was open countryside and White Hart Lane a sleepy country track. Football fans should keep an eye out for the displays on Tottenham Hotspur and read the surprising history of Walter Tull, one of the first black football players in Britain. There are free activity sheets for kids, including a nature trail that rambles around the pleasant park outside, plus free art and craft sessions for families from 2pm to 4pm on Sundays year-round, with extra school holiday sessions. *Buggy access. Disabled access: lift, toilet. Nappy-changing facilities. Nearest picnic place: museum grounds. Shop.*

Brunel Museum

Brunel Engine House, Railway Avenue, SE16 4LF (7231 3840, www.brunel-museum.org.uk). Rotherhithe rail. **Open** 10am-5pm daily. **Admission** £2; £1 reductions; free under-16s. **No credit cards.** 5+

The Thames Tunnel, created by the Brunel father and son team Sir Marc and Isambard Kingdom, was the first underwater tunnel in the world. The Brunels worked from 1825 until 1843 to create the underwater passageway running from Rotherhithe to Wapping; young Isambard nearly drowned in the process. The story of what the Victorians hailed as 'the eighth wonder of the world' is told in this museum in the original engine house, while the tunnel itself is now used by the East London overland rail line. A major new refurbishment was completed in late 2009, giving the museum a tea-room with views over the river, an activity centre and also access to the Grand Entrance Hall for special events once a month. There's plenty for children to do, with a special wipe-clean drawing table in the award-winning sculpture garden and craft activities at weekends . There's also a popular summer play-scheme; in 2010 the kids will be helping a blacksmith to make a sundial for the new garden laid out on top of the Grand Entrance Hall roof. The giant figure of Brunel that is owned by the museum is always (and literally) a big player in the Bermondsey and Rotherhithe carnivals. *Buggy access. Café. Disabled access: toilet. Nappy-changing facilities. Nearest picnic place: museum gardens & riverbank. Shop.*

Crystal Palace Museum

Anerley Hill, SE19 2BA (8676 0700, www. crystalpalacemuseum.org.uk). Crystal Palace rail. **Open** 11am-4.30pm Sat, Sun, bank hols. **Admission** free. 7+

Housed in the old engineering school where John Logie Baird invented television, this 'exhibition of an exhibition' tells the story of the majestic, glittering glass hall that moved from Hyde Park to give this area its name. It's a friendly, if rather old-fashioned museum, with artefacts and photos in glass cases, although there are some video and audio presentations about the great glass building, which burned to the ground in November 1936. A small Logie Baird display marks the birth of home entertainment; from June 1934 the Baird Television Company occupied four studios at Crystal Palace. Note that opening hours are limited, as the museum is run by volunteers. *Buggy access. Nearest picnic place: Crystal Palace Park. Shop.*

Hackney Museum

Technology & Learning Centre, 1 Reading Lane, off Mare Street, E8 1GQ (8356 3500, www.hackney.gov.uk/museum). Hackney Central rail. **Open** 9.30am-5.30pm Tue, Wed, Fri; 9.30am-8pm Thur; 10am-5pm Sat. **Admission** free. **No credit cards.** 3+

This lively museum is a community-focused affair, with plenty to keep kids busy. Displays include exhibits on immigration in the area and a re-creation of Cooke's pie and eel shop, plus activity stations and touch-screen interactive exhibits that tie into the history of the borough. Other highlights include a re-created Saxon boat that kids can pile up with goods (the original is displayed under glass in the floor) and a section on the Matchbox car factory, founded in Hackney in 1952. Toddlers can settle into the reading corner while older kids dress up in Victorian clobber and try making matchboxes – an industry that employed countless children in Victorian times. Interactive art and role-playing workshops take place on Wednesday and Thursday afternoons, while the temporary exhibition changes every four months; until 28 August 2010 the theme is bodies. *Buggy access. Disabled access: toilet. Nappy-changing facilities. Nearest picnic place: benches in square, London Fields. Shop.*

Islington Museum

Finsbury Library, 245 St John Street, EC1V 4NB (7527 3235, www.islington.gov.uk/ museum). Angel tube/Farringdon tube/rail/153 bus. **Open** 10am-5pm Mon, Tue, Thur-Sat. **Admission** free. **No credit cards.** 5+

Islington Museum's collection sits under the Finsbury Library, where it was rehoused in purpose-built galleries in 2008, after a funding injection from the Heritage Lottery Fund. Exhibits are organised into nine themes

London Transport Museum. *See p83.*

including Wartime, Childhood and Leisure, and the displays span centuries of local history, from the days when Islington dairies provided the milk for medieval London (check out the centuries-old cow's skull) to the rise of the mighty Arsenal football club. Children will enjoy the sections on Edwardian school life, and the special activity desks and quiz screens. Call or check online for half term and summer holiday events.
Buggy access. Disabled access: lift, toilet. Nearest picnic place: Northhampton Square. Shop.

Kew Bridge Steam Museum

Green Dragon Lane, Brentford, Middx TW8 0EN (8568 4757, www.kbsm.org). Gunnersbury tube, then 237 or 267 bus/Kew Bridge rail/65, 391 bus. **Open** 11am-4pm Tue-Sun, bank hols. **Admission** (annual ticket, allows for multiple visits) £9.50; £8.50 reductions; free under-16s. Under-16s must be accompanied by an adult. **Credit** MC, V. 5+

The museum inside this Victorian riverside pumping station celebrates the golden age of steam. At weekends, selected steam engines – the pumping variety, as well as the locomotive sort – burst into life, powered by a 1920s Lancashire boiler. The fascinating Water for Life gallery saturates you with facts about the history of water supply and usage in London, including information on the spread of cholera, while Down Below takes you down the sewers to learn about the work of their creator, Joseph Bazalgette, and the whiffy world of toshers (sewer scavengers). *Thomas Wickstead*, a narrow-gauge steam locomotive, gives rides on Sundays between April and October; family activities are also held during the school and bank holidays.
Buggy access. Café (Sat, Sun). Disabled access: lift, toilet. Nappy-changing facilities. Nearest picnic place: Kew Green. Shop.

London Canal Museum

12-13 New Wharf Road, N1 9RT (7713 0836, www.canalmuseum.org.uk). King's Cross tube/rail. **Open** 10am-4.30pm Tue-Sun, bank hols. Last entry 4pm. **Admission** £3; £2 reductions; £1.50 8-15s; free under-8s. **Credit** MC, V. **Map** p315 M2. **5+**

This charming museum is housed in what was once the ice warehouse of Italian-Swiss ice-cream entrepreneur Carlo Gatti. It chronicles the history of everything canal-related, as well as exploring the once highly lucrative ice trade. Kids can clamber aboard the narrowboat, *Coronis*, and get a taste of life on the waterways; an activity corner has books and

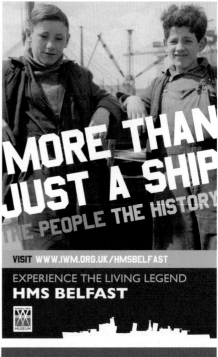

building blocks to create your own tunnel; and there's the chance to learn how to tie a sheepshank and clove hitch. Most atmospheric is the ice well, once used to store imported ice from Norway; it could be kept here for months before being delivered around London. Visitors have taken to tossing coins into the cool, dark space; extra points if you can hit the bucket. Upstairs, a life-size model horse makes convincing horsey noises in his stable, while there are four videos on canal life to watch and regular temporary exhibitions. The back of the museum leads on to Battlebridge Basin, once a grimy industrial wharf, now lined with pretty residential canal boats and converted warehouses. For those with the energy, the shopping hubs of Camden and Islington are within walking distance along Regent's Canal. *See also p122* **Great Days Out**.
Buggy access. Disabled access: lift, toilet. Nappy-changing facilities. Nearest picnic place: museum terrace, canal towpath. Shop.

London Transport Museum

The Piazza, WC2E 7BB (7379 6344, www.ltmuseum.co.uk). Covent Garden tube. **Open** 10am-6pm Mon-Thur, Sat, Sun; 11am-6pm Fri. **Admission** £10; £6-£8 reductions; free under-16s. **Credit** AmEx, MC, V. **Map** p317 L7. **2+**
Londoners are reminded every time there's a tube strike that the capital would grind to a halt without its sophisticated travel system. This much-loved museum does a sterling job of presenting a fascinating and entertaining history of transport in the capital, with 20 vehicles to explore along the way. The posters are glorious too – particularly the stylised, often wonderfully avant-garde designs of the 1920s and '30s. The museum's temporary exhibitions are usually worth making a special visit for, and until 31 March 2011, Overground Uncovered celebrates the opening of the long-awaited overground link between Dalston and south-east London. From September to December 2010, Remembering The Blitz marks the 70th anniversary of the beginning of one of the toughest periods for those on the Home Front. *See also p46* **Great Days Out**.
Buggy access. Café. Disabled access: lift, toilet. Nappy-changing facilities. Nearest picnic place: museum picnic room, Piazza. Shop.

Museum of London

150 London Wall, EC2Y 5HN (7001 9844, www.museumoflondon.org.uk). Barbican or St Paul's tube/Moorgate tube/rail. **Open** 10am-6pm daily. Last entry 5.30pm. **Admission** free. **Credit** MC, V. **Map** p318 P5. **6+**

Three years in the making, the £20 million redevelopment of the lower galleries of this excellent museum opened in May 2010. Anyone who calls themselves a Londoner should make a visit one of their top priorities. It's all massively appealing to children thanks to some highly imaginative exhibits that put interactivity and discovery at the forefront of their design. *See p10* **London Stories Retold**.
Buggy access. Café. Disabled access: lift, toilet. Nappy-changing facilities. Nearest picnic place: Barber Surgeon's Garden. Shop.

Museum of London Docklands

West India Quay, Hertsmere Road, E14 4AL (7001 9844, www.museumoflondon.org.uk/ docklands). Canary Wharf tube/West India Quay DLR. **Open** 10am-6pm daily. Last entry 5.30pm. **Admission** free. **Credit** MC, V. **4+**
The Museum of London's Docklands sister is just as fascinating as its older sibling, and since April 2010 is free for anyone to get in. It lies in a beautiful converted warehouse overlooking a large wharf and has a wealth of absorbing exhibits. Displays devoted to migration and river trade explore the history of how 'the world came to the East End', with plenty of nautical relics and atmospheric recreations. Must-sees for kids include Sailortown, a murky, full-size recreation of 18th-century Wapping (look out for the wild animal emporium), the gibbet cage (where captured pirates met their end) and the Mudlarks Gallery, crammed with interactive exhibits and with a soft play area for under-fives. The galleries on the modern history of the docks are more interesting for adults than children, but everyone can learn something from the London, Sugar & Slavery and Docklands at War exhibitions. Many of the displays come with an entertaining audio commentary, voiced by *Time Team*'s Tony Robinson.

Costumed storytelling sessions and craft workshops take place at the museum every Saturday, with extra sessions held during the school holidays. The line-up has plenty to interest younger children, including storytimes and Monday play sessions for under-fives. There's a refectory with a children's menu (one child eats free with any adult meal bought at lunchtime), but the best place to enjoy your sandwiches is out on the quayside, beneath the giant loading cranes. *See also p88* **Great Days Out**.
Buggy access. Café. Disabled access: lift, toilet. Nappy-changing facilities. Nearest picnic place: quayside benches, refectory. Restaurant. Shop.

Sightseeing

The all-new Jewish Museum

The Jewish Museum (*see p90*) has been in Camden since 1992, in a Victorian house on Albert Street, just off Parkway. In March 2010, it reopened its doors to reveal a £10 million expansion, into the building behind – a former piano workshop. The first impression is of light and space in the area that leads out from the original house, now home to the ticket and information desk and shop. The Welcome Gallery hosts a permanent exhibition designed to shoot down any pre-existing stereotypes visitors may have of the Jewish community in London today. Videos play on screen strips hanging from the ceiling and introduce us to an Indian-born grandmother, a taxi driver, an ex-army engineer and a smoked salmon manufacturer. Then it's straight to the medieval mikveh, a ritual bath found in the City of London and rehoused here, before going up the stairs.

Exhibitions have been designed with imagination and a keen desire to appeal to all ages. There's lots for children to enjoy while they learn (including various trails). In the permanent exhibition History: A British Story, they can play the Great Migration boardgame, try on some traditional wedding clothes, smell chicken soup, plait some challah bread, play Yiddish karaoke, and listen to first-hand stories of those who lived in the crowded East End. The Judaism: A Living Faith gallery exhibits beautiful ceremonial objects alongside videos of families celebrating the important annual festivals like Purim, Hanukkah and Passover. The gallery documenting the Holocaust is small and very moving, but can be avoided if parents think their children are too young to be introduced to the subject. Back downstairs is the inviting café with its bleached-wood tables and high ceilings; try a *rougalach* (like a dense croissant with chocolate between the folds), or some classic chicken soup with dumplings.

Sightseeing

Museum of Richmond

Old Town Hall, Whittaker Avenue, Richmond, Surrey TW9 1TP (8332 1141, www.museum ofrichmond.com). Richmond tube/rail. **Open** 11am-5pm Tue-Sat. **Admission** free. **No credit cards.** 4+

Leafy Richmond is an area with abundant royal connections, from the 12th-century Henry I to Elizabeth I, 400 years later; fittingly, the town's museum was opened by Queen Elizabeth II. There are permanent and temporary displays on its illustrious residents of days gone by (How The Vote Was Won: Art and Theatre for Women's Suffrage runs until September 2010), plus a gallery of work by local artists. Engaging family workshops run during the school holidays – discovering one of the beautiful painted tiles in the museum, say, before creating your own.

Buggy access. Disabled access: lift, toilet. Nearest picnic place: Richmond Green, riverside. Shop.

Old Royal Naval College & Discover Greenwich

King William Walk, SE10 9LW (8269 4747, tours 8269 4799, www.greenwichfoundation. org.uk). Cutty Sark DLR/Greenwich DLR/rail. **Open** 10am-5pm daily. *Tours* 11.30am, 2pm Mon-Sat; 2pm Sun. **Admission** free. *Tours* £5; free under-16s. **Credit** MC, V. 5+

A new £6 million development opened in March 2010 at the Old Royal Naval College. Discover Greenwich is a brand new visitor centre designed to introduce visitors to the Greenwich story before they go on and visit its individual world-famous attractions. The central exhibition space in the new centre tells 500 years of fascinating history using interactive models and some previously unseen artefacts. There's also a space for temporary exhibitions, The Clore Learning Centre, a new shop, a Tourist Information Centre, plus a new restaurant with micro brewery. In short, it's the place to come if you're planning a family day out in Greenwich and don't know quite where to start.

Sir Christopher Wren drew up the plans for the Old Royal Naval College, a show-stopping baroque masterpiece all the lovelier for its riverside location. Originally, it was a shelter for retired seamen, who were given bed and board, plus a shilling a week. In the late 19th century, the buildings were occupied by the Royal Naval College, before passing into the hands of the Greenwich Foundation. The University of Greenwich and Trinity College of Music are now in residence, but the exquisite neo-classical chapel and Painted Hall are open to the public. The hall is an outstanding feat of trompe l'oeil,

and it took 19 years to paint; see if the kids can spot the Pocahontas-like figure who represents the Americas on the Upper Hall's central ceiling panel. Check the website for seasonal events such as the Big Draw or the May Fair. *See also p114* **Great Days Out.**

Buggy access. Café. Disabled access: toilet. Nappy-changing facilities. Nearest picnic place: Naval College grounds. Restaurant. Shop.

Wimbledon Windmill Museum

Windmill Road, Wimbledon Common, SW19 5NR (8947 2825, www.wimbledonwindmill. org.uk). Wimbledon tube/rail. **Open** Apr-Oct 2-5pm Sat; 11am-5pm Sun, bank hols. School groups by appointment only. **Admission** £2; £1 under-16s, reductions.; £5 family (2+4). **No credit cards.** 5+

Wimbledon Common's windmill was built in 1817 by carpenter Charles March, at the request of locals who wanted to grind their own wheat. Having been a private residence for some years, these days it's a small museum, run by volunteers and open weekends only.

On the ground floor, there's a film about how windmills work, a display showing how the windmill was built, and a collection of woodworking tools used in its restoration. The first floor is more hands-on, with a working model of the windmill in action, the chance for children to have a go at grinding wheat with a saddle-stone or hand quern, and commentaries at the push of a button. Climbing the ladder takes you up to the tower, where you can see the sails' operating machinery turning on blusterous days. A new exhibition about modern attempts to harness wind power opened in February 2010.

Buggy access (ground floor). Nearest picnic place: Wimbledon Common. Café. Shop.

MUSIC

Handel House Museum

25 Brook Street (entrance at rear), W1K 4HB (7495 1685, www.handelhouse.org). Bond Street tube. **Open** 10am-6pm Tue, Wed, Fri, Sat; 10am-8pm Thur; noon-6pm Sun. **Admission** £5; £4.50 reductions; £2 6-16s (free Sat); free under-6s. **Credit** MC, V. **Map** p316 H6. 5+

It's odd to think that Jimi Hendrix and legendary composer George Frederic Handel lived as near neighbours in this small street, albeit centuries apart. This Georgian townhouse was Handel's home from 1723 until his death in 1759; Hendrix lived two doors down. To mark the 40th anniversary of Hendrix's death, the Handel

Sightseeing

Museum is organising an exhibition of music and memorabilia, as well as tours of the unfortunate musician's flat at no.23 during 2010. Meanwhile, the permanent collection at the Handel Museum includes paintings, letters, scores and a reproduction of his harpsichord. The house interiors have been painstakingly restored but children are encouraged to visit, with free entry on Saturdays, plus the odd family-friendly musical event (the Thursday evening recitals are aimed more at adults). The child-friendly ethos extends to trails, quizzes and activities to go with the displays.
Buggy access. Disabled access: lift, toilet. Nappy-changing facilities. Nearest picnic place: Hanover Square. Shop.

Musical Museum

399 High Street, Brentford, Middx TW8 0DU (8560 8108, www.musicalmuseum.co.uk). Kew Bridge rail. **Open** 11am-5.30pm Tue-Sun, bank hols. Last entry 4.30pm. **Admission** £8; £6.50 reductions; free under-16s. **Credit** MC, V. 5+
Children who find themselves all thumbs when it comes to music lessons will be deeply impressed by the ingenious self-playing pianos and violins on display at this museum of automatic instruments. Other exhibits include clockwork musical boxes, orchestrions (a mechanical instrument that sounds like a large ensemble), musical toys and barrel organs. Most are in working order and are demonstrated by the staff, with their functions fully explained. Upstairs is a concert hall with an orchestra pit from which a Wurlitzer console slowly rises, as it did in cinemas in the 1930s; check the online events diary for performances and films.
Buggy access. Café. Disabled access: lift, toilet. Nappy-changing facilities. Nearest picnic place: riverside. Shop.

NATURAL WORLD

Garden Museum

Church of St Mary-at-Lambeth, Lambeth Palace Road, SE1 7LB (7401 8865, www.gardenmuseum.org.uk). Lambeth North tube/Waterloo tube/rail, then 507 bus/C10, 77 bus. **Open** 10.30am-5pm daily (closed 1st Mon of mth). **Admission** £6; free-£5 reductions; free under-16s. **Credit** MC, V. **Map** p317 L10. 6+
At first glance, a museum about gardening perhaps wouldn't have obvious appeal for most children, but step into this tranquil setting – a deconsecrated church by the Thames – and it's surprising how enticing it can be. Inside, the collection of tools and gardening paraphernalia has some unexpected oddities, including a weird-looking 'vegetable lamb' (believed for centuries to be half lamb, half plant), a set of pony boots (worn by lawnmower-pulling horses to prevent their hooves from marking the grass) and a cunning, cat-shaped bird scarer.
Outside, the old graveyard has some distinguished residents: the Tradescants, a pioneering family of gardeners and botanists; Captain William Bligh, of *Bounty* fame; and half a dozen archbishops of Canterbury. The wild garden is awash with valerian, poppies, harebells and cow parsley, while the 17th-century-style knot garden is a riot of colour in summer, enclosed in neat box-hedge borders.
Buggy access. Café. Disabled access: toilet. Nappy-changing facilities. Nearest picnic place: Archbishop's Park. Shop.

Natural History Museum

Cromwell Road, SW7 5BD (7942 5000, www.nhm.ac.uk). South Kensington tube. **Open** 10am-5.50pm daily. **Admission** free; charges apply for special exhibitions. **Credit** MC, V. **Map** p313 D10. 4+
The stately façade of this venerable museum is one of London's top landmarks, and a mecca for streams of families. Inside, exhibits are split into four colour-coded zones, each with its own marvels.
The Blue Zone is the one most younger visitors make a beeline for, thanks to the famous dinosaur gallery – presided over by a scary, animatronic T-Rex. (The baby dinosaurs hatching out of their eggs are better for those of a sensitive persuasion.) In the mammals gallery, the sabre-toothed tiger skeleton also elicits a delicious shudder, while a life-size model of a blue whale quietens all but the loudest of children. The Green Zone encompasses the child-friendly and fiendishly popular Creepy Crawlies exhibit: watching leaf-cutter ants at work, exploring a termite mound and gawping at the world's longest stick insect (a twiggy, leggy 56.7cm beast) are among its attractions. Geology takes centre stage in the Red Zone, which you can access directly from the museum's Exhibition Road entrance. It's a dramatic, dark, escalator ascent through the centre of the earth. At the top you'll find the ground-shaking earthquake simulator – a reliable source of giggles (and a few shrieks of alarm). Finally, the Orange Zone comprises the wildlife garden and the new Darwin Centre buildings (*see p8* Nature Watch).
If seeing the scientists at work inspires the kids to get hands-on, take them down to the Investigate Centre in the main museum's

Sightseeing

Great Days Out
Docklands

By 2012, Canary Wharf will no longer be the tallest tower in the UK (the Shard, over at London Bridge, is set to top it by several hundred feet). In fact, by 2012, it may not even be the tallest tower in Docklands after Boris Johnson helped move plans for the slightly taller Columbus Tower forward. Until then, its flashing beacon, with the wispy plume of steam at its apex, remains the iconic symbol of this Thatcherite development. It's visible from all over London although unfortunately, (in true Thatcher style) you have to work in the building to enjoy the views.

Museum of Docklands

Docklands is the semi-official name given to the massive redevelopment of this eastern stretch of the Thames. And here on the **Isle of Dogs** (supposedly named after some royal kennels in the area), where great ships once lined up in impressive docks, there are now shiny office blocks, luxury flats and the biggest cluster of high-rise buildings in Europe. That said, a day out here makes a surprisingly pleasant family excursion – the land around the buildings is essentially a very large and well-tended garden with no traffic to worry about.

These days, the area is easily accessible from the centre of town, thanks to the Jubilee line. Visitors disembark in the sleek, cavernous Canary Wharf underground station, which was designed by Norman Foster; the area around the curved entrances has been made into a pretty Japanese garden.

But perhaps the most scenic way to travel here is by taking the **Docklands Light Railway**, or DLR (7363 9700, www.tfl.gov.uk/dlr), which zips along raised tracks and gives great views over the area. Children will be fascinated by the driverless trains and can even pretend they're in control of the train if you travel outside peak time and manage to nab seats in the glass-fronted lead carriage.

If you want to combine Canary Wharf with some more traditional sightseeing, then consider buying a Rail & River Rover ticket (£13.50, £6.75 children, free under-5s, £33 family), which allows a day's travel on the DLR with unlimited trips on the City Cruises sightseeing boats that run between Greenwich Pier, Tower, Waterloo and Westminster. But don't be too quick to leave… This centre of commerce has its tourist attractions too.

Trails and sails

With its clean lines and neat landscaping, Docklands is a bit like a model town, and children will enjoy exploring the bridges, pathways and open stretches of water.

To give some purpose to your roaming, tackle one of the three excellent walking trails (entitled Transitions, Open Spaces and Architecture & Design) and downloadable at www.canarywharf.com (click on the 'arts and events' link). The first tackles the rich history of Docklands, while the second leads you around the area's various gardens. The third has all sorts of facts about the buildings (existing and planned) and leads visitors past various artworks and sculptures that are dotted around. Our favourites are Ron Arad's red spike *Windwand* and his *Big Blue* at Westferry Circus and Lynn Chadwick's *Couple on Seat* in Cabot Square.

Emma Biggs's wonderfully intricate mosaics, embedded into the floor of Jubilee Place shopping centre, evoke the area's past ('London used to be a city of ships. A thousand vessels a week passed through the docks').

For some idea of what this city of ships once looked like, head for the thoroughly enjoyable **Museum of London Docklands** (*see p83*). Follow the bouncing bridge (it's supported on floats) from Cabot Square; the museum is in a row of converted warehouses on the edge of West India Quay. Inside, there are some fantastically evocative photographs, paintings, prints and models of the bustling docks as they would have been when this area was London's industrial heart. The museum's three jam-packed floors tell the story of the Thames, the port of London and its people, from Roman times up to the Docklands redevelopment.

Children will be rewarded for their learning when they get to the Mudlarks Gallery, with all its hands-on discovery games. It's so popular that entry is by timed ticket. There's also a great café where for every adult meal bought a child eats for free.

Great escape

If all this talk of industry and business is making the children feel old before their time, it might be the moment to grab some fresh air. A short south-bound DLR ride from Canary Wharf takes you

LUNCH BOX

Also in the area: Nando's, Wagamama, Pizza Express.

1802 *Museum In Docklands, No.1 Warehouse, Hertsmere Road, West India Key, E14 4AL (7538 2702, www.museumindocklands.org.uk).* Great food and plenty of atmosphere.

Carluccio's Caffè *Reuters Plaza, E14 5AJ (7719 1749, www.carluccios.com).* Child-friendly and reasonably priced.

Gun *27 Coldharbour, E14 9NS (7515 5222, www.thegundocklands.com).* A smart gastropub that does great chips and welcomes nippers.

Mudchute Kitchen *Mudchute Farm, Pier Street, E14 3HP (7515 5901, www.mudchutekitchen.org).* Fresh, flavoursome farm grub. *See p231.*

Smollensky's *1 Reuters Plaza, E14 5AJ (7719 0101, www.smollenskys.com).* Great steaks, popular with kids. *See p250.*

to Mudchute. Here, in the shadow of Docklands' high rises, lies **Mudchute City Farm** (*see p137*).

From Mudchute station, take the raised path past the parkland and allotments, where you can play spot-the-llama as you make your way towards the farm entrance. The closer you get, the more audible the resident ducks, chickens, pigs, goats, donkeys and horses become. Inside sprawl acres of fields and pastures; this is one of the largest city farms in Europe. If helping to feed the animals makes you a bit peckish, head for the farm's acclaimed café, Mudchute Kitchen, for a scrumptious farmhouse breakfast or slab of cake.

If animals aren't the order of the day, there's always **Island Gardens** (cross the main road from the eponymous station), with its beautiful view of Greenwich on the other side of the Thames. Cross via the spookily drippy Victorian foot tunnel that runs below the river; the attendant-operated lifts (7am-7pm Mon-Sat, 10am-5.30pm Sun) are big enough for a fleet of buggies. You're not allowed to cycle through the tunnel, though, so any bike-riders will have to dismount and push their trusty steeds.

Great Days Out

basement (open weekday afternoons and weekends; call ahead to check times). Here, seven to 14s can study specimens (some living) through a microscope, and note their findings. Temporary exhibitions are also worth keeping an eye on, like Butterfly Explorers (until 26 September 2010), which allows visitors to walk among hundreds of butterflies and witness the extraordinary stages of their metamorphosis from caterpillar to butterfly.

The museum has a restaurant, a café and a sandwich bar, and there are also indoor and outdoor picnic areas if you'd rather bring your own grub.

Since January 2010, the museum has run a monthly sleepover. Children taking part must be aged eight to 11 and accompanied by a parent (groups must be a minimum of five children and one adult, £45 per person). Night activities include a torchlit adventure around the museum, a live show about beasties, and the creation of an enormous paper and clay dinosaur. *See also p102* **Great Days Out.**

Buggy Access. Cafés. Disabled access: lift, toilet. Nappy-changing facilities. Nearest picnic place: basement picnic room, museum grounds. Restaurant.

RELIGION

Jewish Museum

129-131 Albert Street, NW1 7NB (7284 7384, www.jewishmuseum.org.uk). Camden Town tube. **Open** 10am-5pm Mon-Wed, Sun; 10am-9pm Thur; 10am-2pm Fri. **Admission** £7; free-£6 reductions; £17 family. **Credit** MC, V. 4+
The Jewish Museum was closed from late 2007 to March 2010 while it underwent an expansion into an adjoining building. The resulting galleries are impressive, with a lot of consideration given to making this an engaging museum for allcomers. *See p84* **Jewish Museum.**
Buggy access. Café. Disabled access: toilets. Nappy-changing facilities. Nearest picnic place: Regent's Park. Shop.

Museum of Methodism & John Wesley's House

Wesley's Chapel, 49 City Road, EC1Y 1AU (7253 2262, www.wesleyschapel.org.uk). Moorgate or Old Street tube/rail. **Open** 10am-4pm Mon-Wed, Fri, Sat; 10am-12.30pm, 1.45-4pm Thur; 12.30-1.45pm Sun. **Admission** free, donations appreciated. **Credit** MC, V. **Map** p319 Q4. 8+
This lovely chapel and surrounding buildings are a corner for quiet contemplation just behind the roar of traffic on City Road. It was built by John Wesley in 1778, and is known as the cathedral of world Methodism. Wesley called it 'perfectly neat but not fine', although there are many more adornments now than in his day. Down in the crypt, the museum has a permanent display charting the history of Methodism, while Hogarthian prints depict poverty, alcoholism and moral degradation in 18th-century England. Look out for lunchtime recitals making use of the chapel's organ. Wesley's neighbouring house has been restored to 18th-century simplicity; much of the furniture is of the period, although the tiny four-poster in the bedroom is reproduction, as is the curious 'chamber horse' in the study – an early form of home-gym equipment.
Buggy access. Disabled access: lift, toilet. Nappy-changing facilities. Nearest picnic place: enclosed courtyard at entrance, Bunhill Fields. Shop.

SCIENCE & MEDICINE

Alexander Fleming Laboratory Museum

St Mary's Hospital, Praed Street, W2 1NY (7886 6528, www.imperial.nhs.uk/stmarys). Paddington tube/rail/7, 15, 27, 36 bus. **Open** 10am-1pm Mon-Thur; also by appointment. Closed bank hols. **Admission** £2; £1 5-16s, reductions; free under-5s. **No credit cards.** **Map** p313 D5. 8+

Old Operating Theatre, Museum & Herb Garret

In the era of the superbug, this shrine to antibiotics is both increasingly relevant and a relic from a simpler time. Visitors explore a re-creation of the laboratory where Alexander Fleming discovered penicillin back on 3 September 1928. Exhibits and a video celebrate Fleming's life and the role of penicillin in fighting disease. Staff run tours for family and school groups; note that the museum is not accessible to the disabled.
Nearest picnic place: canalside, Hyde Park. Shop.

Hunterian Museum

Royal College of Surgeons of England, 35-43 Lincoln's Inn Fields, WC2A 3PE (7869 6560, www.rcseng.ac.uk/museums). Holborn tube. **Open** 10am-5pm Tue-Sat. **Admission** free; donations appreciated. **Credit** MC, V. **Map** p318 M6. 4+
The museum's namesake, John Hunter (1728-93) was a pioneering surgeon and anatomist, appointed physician to King George III. He amassed thousands of medical specimens; after he died, the collection was enhanced and expanded by others. The Hunterian is quite possibly the weirdest museum in all of London – and the most wonderful, some would say. Its gleaming glass cabinets are filled with row upon row of specimen jars, containing human and animal remains of every description in various states of disease and dissection:

brains, hearts, hernias, big toes, paws and jaws, all spookily suspended in formaldehyde. Children (and grown-ups) of a grisly bent will be gripped by the exhibits, but more sensitive souls and younger kids should probably steer clear.

The most famous pieces in the collection are the brain of mathematician Charles Babbage and the towering skeleton of 'Irish Giant' Charles Byrne, who stood a towering 2.2m (7ft 7in) tall in his socks. There are trails for children to complete, along with a skeleton suit to try for size and a fabric body part game; medically themed events for fives to 12s take place during school holidays, led by costumed actors (booking is essential). Free tours take place at 1pm daily.
Buggy access. Disabled access: lift, toilet. Nearest picnic place: Lincoln's Inn Fields. Shop.

Old Operating Theatre, Museum & Herb Garret

9A St Thomas's Street, SE1 9RY (7188 2679, www.thegarret.org.uk). London Bridge tube/rail. **Open** 10.30am-5pm daily. Closed 15 Dec-5 Jan. **Admission** £5.80; £4.80 reductions; £3.25 6-15s; free under-6s; £13.75 family (2+4). **No credit cards. Map** p319 Q8. 7+
This museum is a real one-off. Each step up the narrow, rickety, wooden spiral staircase leads

you further from present-day London, and towards the quiet ghosts of the past. The Herb Garret smells pungently of fennel and other herbs and contains a jumble of ghoulish exhibits packed under its dark eaves. Nineteenth-century amputation kits and terrifying obstetric implements jostle with bits of Victorians preserved in jars and early anatomical charts.

Go through a narrow antechamber to find Europe's oldest operating theatre, perched rather incongruously and incredibly inside the roof of St Thomas' Church (St Thomas' Hospital was on this site until it moved to Lambeth in 1862), where re-enactment demonstrations at 2pm every Saturday bring the traumas of pre-anaesthesia surgery gorily to life. On Saturday mornings at 11.30am there are children's workshops exploring 18th- and 19th-century medicine, while at 2pm on Sundays there are lectures about how herbs were used as drugs.

Nearest picnic place: Southwark Cathedral Gardens. Shop.

Royal London Hospital Museum

St Philip's Church, Newark Street, E1 2AA (7377 7608, www.bartsandthelondon.nhs.uk/ museums). Whitechapel tube. **Open** 10am-4.30pm Tue-Fri. **Admission** free, donations welcome. **Credit** (café) MC, V. 7+

The Royal London Museum lies in the former crypt of St Philip's Church; its entrance is down an unpreposessing side street, at the bottom of an unlikely set of steps. Inside, exhibits chronicle the history of what was once the biggest general hospital in the UK: the Royal London opened in 1740, so there's a lot of history to explore.

The museum devotes a section to each century, with special displays relating to the hospital's most famous patients and staff, including Thomas Barnardo, Florence Nightingale, John Merrick (the Elephant Man) and Edith Cavell. The development of nursing and childcare is traced through displays of starchy uniforms, and there's a forensics case with a copy of Jack the Ripper's notorious 'From Hell' letter. Most entertaining, however (and a welcome respite if you've been dragging children about all day), is the 1934 X-ray control unit that could have been created by a mad inventor from a sci-fi B-movie, and the plummily-narrated documentaries, dating from the 1930s to the '60s. These show, for example, children wearing pilot's goggles receiving doses of ultraviolet light at a time when London smog prevented the natural synthesis of vitamin D.

Buggy access. Café (in hospital). Disabled access: lift, toilet. Nappy-changing facilities (in hospital). Nearest picnic place: hospital garden. Shop.

St Bartholomew's Hospital Museum

West Smithfield, EC1A 7BE (7601 8152, www.bartsandthelondon.nhs.uk/museums). Barbican or St Paul's tube. **Open** 10am-4pm Tue-Fri. *Tours* (Church & Great Hall) 2pm Fri. **Admission** free. *Tours* £5; £4 reductions; free under-16s accompanied by adult. **No credit cards. Map** p318 O6. *12+*

The museum is located in the North Wing of this famous London hospital, an institution that's been part of the city's landscape since the 12th century. A video relates the story of the hospital's origins as a refuge for chronically sick people hoping for a miraculous cure. Audio loops give a flavour of what it was like to work here as a 13th-century sister, say, or a 15th-century apprentice surgeon. The exhibits include 19th-century watercolours and sketches of various diseases, leather lunatic restraints, a wooden head used by medical students to practise their drilling techniques on and photographs documenting the slow progress of nurses from drudges to career women. Don't miss the two huge paintings by local lad William Hogarth.

Café (in hospital). Nearest picnic place: hospital grounds.

Science Museum

Exhibition Road, SW7 2DD (0870 870 4868, www.sciencemuseum.org.uk). South Kensington tube. **Open** 10am-6pm daily. **Admission** free; charges apply for special exhibitions. **Credit** MC, V. **Map** p313 D9. *4+*

There are grand plans afoot on Exhibition Road. This venerable museum celebrated its centenary in 2009 and kicked off a period of extensive development. By 2015, there will be a new façade, a massive rooftop extension devoted to cosmology and astronomy and two new permanent galleries. But until these projects are finished, the existing attractions remain just as much fun as they've always been. No one's too young or too old to get a kick out of a visit here: the Science Musuem is a temple to scientific knowledge and discovery that welcomes inquisitive visitors of all ages. Icons of science (Stephenson's *Rocket* locomotive, Crick and Watson's DNA model) are treated with due respect, but this place couldn't be less stuffy: with its games, simulators and interactive exhibits, it feels like a giant playground.

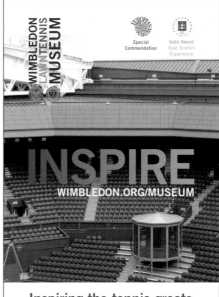

The jewel in its crown is the Launchpad, where 50 hands-on exhibits and experiments keep kids agog; here, they can make a rainbow, check out their chilly noses on the thermal imaging screen, attempt to run a radio on pedal-power or take a dizzying turn on the rotation station. It's aimed at eight to 14s, but appeals to all ages. Other areas cater to younger children: five to eights can explore the Pattern Pod, while under-sixes race around the magical, multi-sensory Garden play areas, whose marvels include computerised flowers and giant building blocks. Extra charges apply for the IMAX cinema and the third-floor motionride simulator – though both are free for members. If you're planning to eat here, the Deep Blue Café is a reliable bet (see p227). It's in the Wellcome Wing, which reopens in June 2010 after an extensive refurbishment.

As you'd expect, the museum attracts hordes of visitors during the school holidays. Book ahead if you want to catch a film, and try to arrive at Launchpad at 10am to avoid lengthy queues. Free half-hour tours on different themes are held throughout the year, while Science Night sleepovers (eight to 11s) are another big draw. It's £35 well spent, as kids get the chance to take part in hands-on science activities and explore the galleries before hunkering down for the night: you need to book well in advance, and the minimum group size is five children and one adult. During school holidays workshops and storytelling sessions are also on offer. See also p102 **Great Days Out**.
Buggy access. Cafés. Disabled access: lift, toilet. Nappy-changing facilities. Nearest picnic place: Hyde Park, museum basement and 1st floor picnic areas. Restaurant. Shop.

Wellcome Collection
183 Euston Road, NW1 2BE (7611 2222, www.wellcomecollection.org). Euston Square tube/Euston tube/rail. **Open** 10am-6pm Tue, Wed, Fri, Sat; 10am-10pm Thur; 11am-6pm Sun. **Admission** free. **Credit** MC, V. **14+** (parental advisory)
The man behind this collection was Sir Henry Wellcome, a pioneering 19th-century pharmacist, philanthropist and entrepreneur, who amassed an idiosyncratic selection of artefacts relating to the medical profession, a tiny proportion of which is displayed in the permanent Medicine Man section of the museum. Unlike many of London's medical museums, the Wellcome Collection displays its exhibits in modern, airy galleries that are well laid out and stuffed to the brim with eye-opening curios. Sensitive children might find some of the items too grisly (the vicious, bladed torture

chair; the slips of real human skin) or too saucy (Japanese sex aids, phallic amulets), but older children will get a kick out of seeing a religious mendicant's nail sole sandals, a mummified body from Peru, Napoleon's toothbrush and a lock of George III's hair.

Medicine Now presents exhibits on the themes of genomes, malaria, obesity and the body. The permanent sections are bolstered by a programme of excellent temporary exhibitions that examine various aspects of life and death. Until September 26 2010, Skin examines the importance of the body's largest organ. The events programme, suitable for teenagers, includes talks and microscopy workshops. There's also a good bookshop, and a superb Peyton & Byrne café, serving meals, fabulous cakes and a good selection of teas.
Buggy access. Café. Disabled access: lift, toilet. Nappy-changing facilities. Nearest picnic place: Gordon Square. Shop.

SPECIALIST

Bank of England Museum
Entrance on Bartholomew Lane, off Threadneedle Street, EC2R 8AH (7601 5491, cinema bookings 7601 3985, www.bankof england.co.uk/education/museum). Bank tube/DLR. **Open** 10am-5pm Mon-Fri. Closed bank hols. **Admission** free. **Credit** MC, V. **Map** p319 Q6. **5+**
Visitors walk first into Sir John Soane's beautiful 18th-century banking hall (restored to its original mahogany splendour) where the bewigged and bestockinged mannequins instantly appeal to younger visitors' imaginations. Permanent displays of notes, coins and early handwritten cheques illustrate a chronological history of banking, which is summed up in an educational film. There are lots of terribly impressive paintings, cartoons and pieces of furniture, but children will be much more excited by the everyday tools of the banking trade like calculators, weights, inkwells and the interactive foreign exchange desk.

One consistently popular exhibit is the gold bar: put a hand into a perspex case and try to lift the bar encased within. Its weight – 12.7kg (28lb) – will come as a shock to anyone who has ever fantasised about scarpering with a sack full of bullion. Activity sheets and quizzes for different age groups can be downloaded from the website before setting off, or picked up from the museum on arrival.
Buggy access. Disabled access: toilet. Nappy-changing facilities. Nearest picnic place: St Paul's Cathedral Garden. Shop.

Clink Prison Museum

1 Clink Street, SE1 9DG (7403 0900, www. clink.co.uk). London Bridge tube/rail. **Open** *June-Sept* 10am-9pm daily. *Oct-May* 10am-6pm Mon-Fri; 10am-9pm Sat, Sun. **Admission** £5; £3.50 3-15s, reductions; free under-3s; £12 family (2+2). **Credit** MC, V. **Map** p318 P8. **6+ (parental advisory)**

Borough Market and Bankside look neater and sleeker every year, but for a reminder of the area's murky past, look no further than this museum. The clinking of inmates' manacles, fetters and chains is what gave this former prison its name. In operation from 1247 until 1780, it was the place where thieves, prostitutes, debtors and – after the Reformation – priests were incarcerated. The list of allowed punishments included scourging with rods, the rack, breaking on the wheel and being crushed under heavy weights. Jailers were not paid well, so provided small creature comforts to rich inmates, at a price, and allowed whorehouse madams to carry on the trade for which they were imprisoned in return for a cut of the takings. The museum tries to recreate the atmosphere of the prison with candlelight, sawdust on the floor and moans and groans coming from the waxwork prisoners. Brave visitors can 'try on' some of the torture devices, such as a scold's bridle or ball and chains.

Children of a sensitive disposition may be scared – particularly at the entrance, where a waxwork man in a cage whimpers as you descend the stairs. *See also p30* **Great Days Out**. *Buggy access. Nearest picnic place: Southwark Cathedral Gardens. Shop.*

SPORT

London's big four – Arsenal, Chelsea, Tottenham and West Ham United – all offer stadium tours that take fans behind the scenes at their grounds. So does Wembley Stadium (*see p203*), home of the England team and host of cup finals in several sports and of major pop concerts. Arsenal and Chelsea have also made space for club museums. Largely speaking, these appeal to partisan supporters, but London's football scene has a fascinating history, and the museums have plenty to interest fans of rival teams as well.

Arsenal Museum

Northern Triangle Building, Drayton Park, N5 1BU (7619 5000, www.arsenal.com). Arsenal or Holloway Road tube/Drayton Park rail. **Open** 10am-6pm Mon-Sat; 10am-5pm Sun.

Sightseeing

Wimbledon Lawn Tennis Museum. *See p96.*

Match days 10am until 30mins before kick-off. **Admission** £6; £3 under-16s, reductions; free under-5s. *Tour & museum* £15; £8 under-16s, reductions; free under-5s. *Legends tour* £35; £18 under-16s, reductions; free under-5s. No tours match days. **Credit** MC, V. 7+

There is plenty of room for a museum in the vast Emirates Stadium. Fans will find it housed in the North Triangle building, directly opposite the north entrances. It offers a lavish celebration of all things Arsenal. Fans of the team will be thrilled by all the exhibits of course, but there's plenty to appeal to the visitor with a more general interest, particularly in the sections that deal with how the club developed. Visitors can pick up a phone to hear an account of the club's early days, initially as Dial Square FC, after its formation by workers at the Woolwich Arsenal munitions factory. The club's more recent triumphs are marked with audio-visual displays, signed shirts, medals and other memorabilia. There are also sections on the Gunners' all-conquering women's team and on the club's FA Cup and European adventures. *Buggy access. Disabled access: lift, toilet. Nearest picnic place: Finsbury Park. Shop.*

Chelsea Museum

Stamford Bridge, Fulham Road, SW6 1HS (0871 984 1955, www.chelseafc.com/tours). Fulham Broadway tube. **Open** 10.30am-4.30pm daily. *Tours* 11am, noon, 1pm, 2pm, 3pm daily. Closed match days & day before Champions League game. **Admission** £6; £4 under-16s. *Tour & museum* £15; £9 under-16s. **Credit** AmEx, MC, V. 7+

Chelsea are often mocked by other clubs for having no history, but they've still managed to put together a cracking museum. Appropriately enough, it's located in the stand that occupies what was once the club's most notorious asset, the Shed, a crumbling terrace of matchless notoriety. These days, fans have more to shout about and the museum gives pride of place to recent acquisitions, such as José Mourinho's moody overcoat. There's also plenty on the club's history of glorious inconsistency, terrible away kits and affinity with celebrity – this is probably the only museum in the country that features a photograph of Raquel Welch (in a Chelsea kit and gun holster, no less). Kids will love the two huge scale models of the ground, and the chance to see the kits belonging to icons like Frank Lampard and Didier Drogba. They can also star in their own Chelsea-themed newspaper headline. Entry comes with an excellent tour that takes in the dressing room and dug outs.

Buggy access. Café. Disabled access (call ahead): lift, toilets. Nappy-changing facilities. Nearest picnic place: Brompton Cemetery. Shop.

Lord's Cricket Ground & MCC Museum

St John's Wood Road, NW8 8QN (7616 8595, www.lords.org). St John's Wood tube/13, 46, 82, 113, 274 bus. **Open** *Tours* Apr-Oct 10am, noon, 2pm daily. Nov-Mar noon, 2pm Mon-Fri; 10am, noon, 2pm Sat, Sun. Closed some match & preparation days; phone for details. **Admission** £14; £8 5-15s, reductions; free under-5s; £37 family (2+2). **Credit** MC, V. 8+

The museum at Lord's Cricket Ground is the oldest sporting museum in the world and probably best enjoyed as part of one of the tours, which take place twice daily Monday to Friday, and three times a day at weekends. Though relatively small in size, the museum is a treasure trove of artefacts, from early bats, balls, paintings and scorecards – some going back more than 200 years – to mementoes of modern times; there is also footage of some of the best moments in cricket's history.

The must-see exhibit, of course, is the original Ashes urn. This was first presented following what a *Sporting Times* reporter called the 'death of English cricket', when the Australian tourists condemned the England side to their first ever defeat at the Oval in 1882. When England went 2-0 up in the four-match series in Australia, a group of Melbourne society women burned a bail from the top of some cricket stumps, placed the ashes inside the urn and presented them to the visiting captain.

The ground tour also offers visitors a look around the famous pavilion, its Long Room and committee rooms and, of course, the home and away dressing rooms and their balconies, as well as the media centre, the grandstand and cricket centre. Tours do not take place on match days.

Buggy access. Disabled access: toilet, lift. Nappy-changing facilities. Nearest picnic place: St John's churchyard playground. Shop.

Wimbledon Lawn Tennis Museum

All England Lawn Tennis Club, Church Road, SW19 5AE (8946 6131, www.wimbledon.org/museum). Southfields or South Wimbledon tube, then 493 bus. **Open** 10am-5pm daily. Spectators only during championships. *Tours* phone for details. **Admission** *Museum* £10; £8.75 reductions; £5.50 5-16s; free under-5s. *Museum & tour* £18; £15.75 reductions; £13 5-16s; free under-5s. **Credit** MC, V. 8+

A visit to the museum is included in a tour of the grounds. It's a high-tech shrine to all things tennis and worth a visit for anyone with even so much as a passing interest in the game. In the cinema (with 200° screens), a film of a game between Maria Sharapova and Nuria Llagostera Vives allows visitors to see each move from five different camera angles, illustrating the body science of the game. Meanwhile, in a mock up of a 1980s changing room, three-time Wimbledon champ John McEnroe (well, in hologram form at least) is waiting to take you on a tour behind the scenes and share his reminiscences.

Visitors are guided through Wimbledon's history, decade by decade, as it developed into a British sporting institution. You can also try on tennis outfits from different ages (and feel the weight difference between court outfits for men and women from 1884), test your reflexes on interactive consoles such as Reaction Station and You Are the Umpire, and listen to broadcast snippets and interviews from significant final matches. Audio and visual guides are also available. Recommended.

Buggy access. Café. Disabled access: lift, toilet. Nappy-changing facilities. Nearest picnic place: venue grounds. Shop.

World Rugby Museum, Twickenham & Twickenham Stadium

Twickenham Stadium, Rugby Road, Twickenham, Middx TW1 1DZ (8892 8877, www.rfu.com/museum). Hounslow East tube, then 281 bus/Twickenham rail. **Open** *Museum* 10am-5pm Tue-Sat; 11am-5pm Sun. Last entry 4.30pm, ticket holders only match days. *Tours* 10.30am, noon, 1.30pm, 3pm Tue-Sat; 1pm, 3pm Sun (no tours match days). **Admission** *Combined ticket* £14; £8 under-16s, reductions; free under-5s; £40 family (2+3). Advance booking advisable. **Credit** AmEx, MC, V. 7+
Fascinating for anyone interested in rugby, this museum boasts the largest collection of memorabilia in the world. With elegant presentation, it charts the history of the game from – and indeed before – William Webb Ellis famously picked up the ball and ran with it during a football game at Rugby School in 1821. Visitors learn how a proper set of rules was developed, about the split with northern clubs that led to the emergence of rugby league, and about the spread of the game throughout the country and overseas. Displays include strange-shaped early rugby balls, a jersey from the first-ever rugby international between Scotland and England in 1871, signed shirts from down the decades and a timeline of the history of the game, alongside major world developments. The upper floor has a library and temporary exhibition room. The museum is sometimes closed after match days; phone to check.

Buggy access. Disabled access: toilet. Nearest picnic place: benches around stadium. Shop.

WAR & THE ARMED FORCES

Churchill War Rooms

Clive Steps, King Charles Street, SW1A 2AQ (7930 6961, www.iwm.org.uk). St James's Park or Westminster tube/3, 12, 24, 53, 159 bus. **Open** 9.30am-6pm daily. Last entry 5pm. **Admission** £14.95; £6.50-£10.40 reductions; free under-16s (incl audio guide). **Credit** MC, V. **Map** p317 K9. 7+
Just beneath Whitehall sits a time capsule of World War II that is part of the impressive Imperial War Museum group. The nine cramped rooms of the Churchill Suite were where Britain's leaders conducted wartime business, while bombs exploded in the streets overhead. With its low ceilings and concrete bomb protection, it's an atmospheric (if slightly stifling) installation that brings the wartime period vividly to life. The map room is particularly evocative. Another, larger space in the warren of tunnels houses the multimedia Churchill Museum. Its centrepiece is a large timeline; an award-winning digital archive that chronicles every major incident of Churchill's life, from the Boer War to his long twilight as an after-dinner speaker and recipient of awards. There's also a kind of virtual peepshow of Churchill's home in Chartwell, Kent. The great man's voice, face and words come at you from all sides, and in every possible format. It's far from stiff and stuffy, and will appeal to most children – even if they end up simply playing around with all the technology. Staying here too long, though, would drive you mad: it's like being inside Winston's mind.

The temporary exhibition Undercover: Life in Churchill's Bunker opened in 2009 and has been so successful it is being extended until 2013. Family workshops linked to the exhibition will continue to take place in the school holidays; check the website for more details. There are also various Spitfire events planned for August 2010.

Buggy access. Café. Disabled access: lift, toilet. Nappy-changing facilities. Nearest picnic place: St James's Park. Shop.

Sightseeing

Firepower Royal Artillery Museum

Royal Arsenal, SE18 6ST (8855 7755, www.firepower.org.uk). Woolwich Arsenal DLR/rail. **Open** 10.30am-5pm Wed-Sun & daily during school hols. Last entry 4pm. **Admission** £5; £4.50 reductions; £2.50 5-16s; free under-5s; £12 family (2+2 or 1+3). **Credit** MC, V. 7+

Lots of kids remain fascinated by warfare, artillery and soldiers despite parents and teachers discouraging too much active celebration. Occupying a series of converted Woolwich Arsenal buildings close to the river, the Gunners Museum is dedicated to the soldiers of the Royal Artillery (not the north London Premiership team). There is a footie connection though, which is remembered in the touching introductory film in the Breech Cinema: Arsenal FC started out as Woolwich Arsenal, when a group of armaments workers had a kickabout. After the film, brace yourselves for the Field of Fire audio-visual display, where four massive screens relay archive film footage of very loud warfare (dry ice included).

Even more appealing to youngsters is the Camo Zone, where they can get their fingers on a trigger at the firing range, using sponge balls. There's also a bungee run and the chance to drive some radio-controlled tanks (activities cost £1.50 each and are supervised by friendly soldiers in fatigues). There are war game events recreating major battles with model soldiers on many weekends, so check the website for dates.

Dedicated to the gunners of the Royal Artillery: **Firepower Royal Artillery Museum**.

Sightseeing

The on-site Pit Stop Café is a reasonably priced place for rations, although if the weather's good, bring a picnic and enjoy the Thameside vista.
Buggy access. Café. Disabled access: lift, toilet. Nappy-changing facilities. Nearest picnic place: riverside. Shop.

Guards Museum

Birdcage Walk, SW1E 6HQ (7414 3271, www.theguardsmuseum.com). Victoria tube/rail. **Open** 10am-4pm daily. Last entry 3.30pm. **Admission** £4; £2 reductions; £1 ex-military; free under-16s. **Credit** (shop) AmEx, MC, V. **Map** p316 J9. 7+
This small museum is dedicated to the history of Her Majesty's five foot regiments – the Scots, Irish, Welsh, Grenadier and Coldstream Guards. It houses military relics – flags, medals, uniforms, drums and weapons – covering every campaign in the regiments' histories. Children will probably get the most out of it as a follow-up to seeing the Changing of the Guard at nearby Buckingham Palace (*see p35*). Highlights include the Grand Old Duke of York's bearskin (he commanded in peacetime, hence the nursery rhyme), plus assorted military medals, uniforms and personal effects. Worksheets for eight- to 14-year-olds add an extra dimension to a visit, and staff let kids try on bearskin hats and regimental tunics: they can have their photo taken for £5. The museum shop has an impressive collection of toy soldiers. *See also p36* **Great Days Out**.
Buggy access. Disabled access: lift. Nearest picnic place: St James's Park. Shop.

HMS Belfast

Morgan's Lane, Tooley Street, SE1 2JH (7940 6300, www.iwm.org.uk). Tower Hill tube/London Bridge tube/rail. **Open** *Mar-Oct* 10am-6pm daily. *Nov-Feb* 10am-5pm daily. Last entry 1hr before closing. **Admission** £10.70; £8.60 reductions; free under-16s. **Credit** MC, V. **Map** p319 R8. 4+
HMS *Belfast* is another member of the impressive Imperial War Museum family. The vessel itself is the only surviving large light cruiser to have served in World War II. She went on to active service in Korea, before taking on peace-keeping duties in the 1950s and '60s. *Belfast* has been preserved to reflect the different decades of her service and the various campaigns she served in.
With her nine decks, the ship is a vast playground of narrow ladders, stairs, cabins and walkways. There are guided tours, but it's just as much fun to scramble around the ship at random, from bridge to boiler room, galley, sick bay, dentist's, NAAFI canteen and mess deck; there's even an operating theatre on board. Models of sailors chatting, eating, cooking and having their teeth drilled add to the entertainment.
Drop-in family activities take place during the holidays (check the website for details), which might involve crafts, music or dance. The enjoyable, family-friendly Launch! Shipbuilding Through the Ages exhibition runs until December 2010 and thoughout August there's a Summer Stowaways Trail.
Buggy access. Café. Disabled access: toilet. Nearest picnic place: Potters Fields Park. Shop.

Household Cavalry Museum

Horse Guards, Whitehall, SW1A 2AX (7930 3070, www.householdcavalry museum.org.uk). Embankment or Westminster tube/Charing Cross tube/rail. **Open** *Mar-Sept* 10am-6pm daily. *Oct-Feb* 10am-5pm daily. **Admission** £6; £4 5-16s, reductions; free under-5s; £15 family (2+3). **Credit** MC, V. 5+
There are all sorts of curios in this museum, including a cork leg, some silver kettledrums and a deadly pistol ball. There are also, as you'd expect, lots of regimental uniforms, medals and tack. The Household Cavalry comprises the oldest and most senior regiments in the British Army and, as well as enjoying a display of their ceremonial role (detailed below) visitors can watch video diaries of serving soldiers. The museum is separated from the stables by a glass wall, so you can sometimes see the magnificent horses being rubbed down after their official duties.
The Cavalry mounts the guard on Horse Guards Parade every day at 11am (10am on Sunday): this is actually a better place to see them in action than Buckingham Palace (*see p35*), since the crowds are thinner here, and you're not held far back from the action by railings. After the old and new guards have stared each other out in the centre of the parade ground for a quarter of an hour, if you nip through to the Whitehall side, you'll catch the departing guard's hilarious dismount choreography, which involves a synchronised, firm slap of approbation on each horse's neck before the gloved troopers all swing off. During school holidays, children can settle down to listen to a story in the museum, follow detective trails or join craft workshops. *See also p36* **Great Days Out**.
Buggy access. Disabled access: toilet. Nearest picnic place: St James's Park. Shop.

Sightseeing

Imperial War Museum

Lambeth Road, SE1 6HZ (7416 5000, www.iwm.org.uk). Lambeth North tube/ Elephant & Castle tube/rail. **Open** 10am-6pm daily. **Admission** free; charges may apply for special exhibitions. **Credit** MC, V. **Map** p406 N10. 5+

Military exploits couldn't be less fashionable, but the Imperial War Museum still has an important role to play. Expecting a child to engage with the concept of a moral war might be too much to ask, but they can certainly begin to understand the effects of conflict on civilian life. Of course, there will be some guilty voyeurism too... There are guns, planes (some hanging from the ceiling), submarines, cannons, tanks and paintings of war in the main galleries. But there's far more to the museum. The collection covers conflicts, especially those involving Britain and the Commonwealth, from World War I to the present day. A clock (which was set running at midnight on 1 January 2000, when the number of lives lost during the wars of the 20th century stood at 100 million) continues to count those dying in conflicts – calculated to be two per minute.

Family-friendly temporary exhibitions include the Children's War (until February 2012), which looks at rationing, evacuation, air raids and blackouts from a child's perspective, and Horrible Histories: Terrible Trenches (until October 2010), based on Terry Deary's book about the privations of living in muddy squalor. The Ministry Of Food (until January 2011) is another favourite, showing in detail how – and what – the population of Britain was fed until rationing ended in 1954. Along with photographs, posters, original paintings, sound recordings and film footage, the displays include walk-in reconstructions of both a 1950s kitchen and an atmospheric grocer's shop that conjure up the period of shortage and frugality that resulted, impressively, in a marked improvement in child health. For the duration of the exhibition, the museum's café will serve wartime classics as well as its everyday menu. The unflinching Holocaust Exhibition, which traces the history of anti-semitism and its shameful nadir in the death camps, is not recommended for under-14s. Upstairs, Crimes Against Humanity is a minimalist space in which a film exploring genocide and ethnic violence rolls relentlessly; it's also unsuitable for under-16s.

The museum is housed in what was once the Bethlehem Royal Hospital (better known as Bedlam) on Lambeth Road, and really needs a whole day to explore. Luckily, the café is good and the grounds are perfect for a picnic, so pace yourselves. Check for one-off family-friendly events on the museum's website.

Buggy access. Café. Disabled access: lift, toilet. Nappy-changing facilities. Nearest picnic place: museum grounds. Shop.

National Army Museum

Royal Hospital Road, SW3 4HT (7730 0717, recorded information 7881 2455, www.national-army-museum.ac.uk). Sloane Square tube/11, 137, 239 bus. **Open** 10am-5.30pm daily. **Admission** free. **Credit** (shop) AmEx, MC, V. **Map** p313 F12. 3+

The history of the British Army as told by this museum will satisfy a child's love of all things gruesome (notices alert parents if there's anything unsuitable for younger children coming up). There are lots of permanent galleries as well as temporary exhibition hall the White Space, so don't try and see everything in one go. Most appealing to children will be the English Civil War helmet that they can try on; the chainmail armour they can gasp at the weight of; the immense model of the Battle of Waterloo, with 75,000 toy soldiers; and the skeleton of Napoleon's horse. The Redcoats Gallery shows how Brits conquered the world, while Nation in Arms covers both world wars, with a reconstruction of a World War I trench and a particularly good jungle area. We also liked the way we were exhorted to join the 1914 army by a virtual recruiting sergeant as soon as we stepped through the door.

The Kids' Zone and regular themed weekend events (Marching to a Different Beat on 4 and 5 September 2010, for example, where kids can take part in singalongs or drumstick workshops) have gone a long way to broadening the museum's appeal. The Kids' Zone is a free, interactive learning and play space for under-tens, with a castle and a cavalry charge of rocking horses, and opportunities to join in art activities, play board games or read; it can be booked by the hour for birthday parties. There's also a soft play area for babies. *See also p108* **Great Days Out**.

Buggy access. Café. Disabled access: lift, toilet. Nappy-changing facilities. Nearest picnic place: museum benches, Chelsea Hospital grounds. Shop.

National Maritime Museum

Romney Road, SE10 9NF (8858 4422, information 8312 6565, www.nmm.ac.uk). Cutty Sark DLR/Greenwich DLR/rail. **Open** 10am-5pm daily. **Admission** free; donations appreciated. **Credit** MC, V. 4+

As a World Heritage site, it's no wonder the attractions at Greenwich are being targeted for inclusion in the Olympic hoo-ha of 2012. The new Sammy Ofer Wing at the National

Sightseeing

HMS Belfast. *See p99.*

Great Days Out
South Kensington

During the school holidays, South Kensington is one of the most popular destinations for a family day out in London. Why? Because it's where the mighty triumverate of museums: the Science Museum, Natural History Museum and Victoria & Albert Museum reside, and millions of people trundle along the tunnel from the tube to Exhibition Road and enlightenment. Weather permitting, it's traditional to make for the green swathes of Hyde Park and Kensington Gardens after a morning's museum-strolling for a picnic. In short, South Ken's jam-packed with things to see – just don't make the mistake of trying to do it all in a day.

Dem bones

The **Natural History Museum** (*see p87*) is a big place, so start by picking up a free map from one of the information desks. Upon production of a parental credit card (a £25 refundable deposit is required), under-sevens can be kitted out with an Explorer backpack, with a pith helmet and binoculars. Themed Discovery Guides for five to 12s, meanwhile, cost a pound. Now you're all set to go.

Generations of children have stood in the lofty central hall and gazed up at the mighty diplodocus cast, which has stood here for over a century. He was a vegetarian – unlike the animatronic T-Rex. Bravado runs high in the long, snaking queue that leads to his lair, though his swishing tail, baleful eyes and low growl strike fear into the stoutest of hearts – and can be too much for smaller children.

Solace can be found in the creepy crawlies gallery, where even toddlers can tower over the mini-beasts; watching the leaf-cutting ants toiling away is strangely therapeutic. If your offspring are more in the mood for destruction, head for the Power Within gallery, devoted to volcanoes and earthquakes. Step inside the 'quake simulator, which recreates the effects of the 1995 Kobe earthquake, and prepare to be all shook up in a mocked-up supermarket.

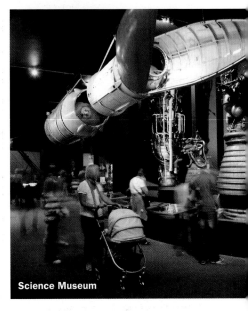

Science Museum

Not tired yet? Good, because there's plenty more to see – the gleaming new Darwin Centre for starters. Make sure you check out the programme of Nature Live talks, too; many are aimed at families, with topics ranging from carnivorous plants to bats or jungle beetles.

Super science

For an all-round top day out, it's hard to beat the **Science Museum** (*see p92*). We defy anyone to wander through the glorious free-for-all of the interactive Launchpad gallery without being tempted to pull a lever, build a bridge or blow a stupendous giant bubble. Bellowing down the 35-metre echo tube is another deeply satisying experience – and it's not often you get the chance to freeze your own shadow.

For proper explanations of why and how, children are advised to collar one of the museum's Explainers: walking, talking mines of information, clad in bright orange T-shirts.

Though there's plenty to look at, under-eights may have trouble reaching and operating the exhibits in Launchpad; they can get hands-on in the Pattern Pod (suitable for over-fives). Smaller fry can explore the Garden play zone down in the basement, donning orange waterproofs to mess about with boats and floats and constructing wobbly edifices from huge building blocks.

A right royal collection

It might seem like a less than obvious place to take the children, but that's precisely the appeal of the august **Victoria & Albert Museum** (*see p68*). Free of the swarms of marauding children, it's less hectic than the Science and Natural History museums (if you avoid the busy temporary exhibitions and concentrate on the permanent collections, that is). The galleries are dotted with oddities that hold an unexpected appeal for children: Tippoo's Tiger, a bizarre, life-size 18th-century automaton depicting a man-eating tiger in the middle of his dinner, is always a hit. Then there are the impossibly tiny miniature portraits, towering platform shoes, impassive golden deities and swashbuckling samurai swords.

Though most of the priceless pieces are safely stowed behind glass, you can poke and prod certain exhibits: pick up a map and look for the hands-on symbols. Trying a Victorian corset on for size may be best undertaken before lunch or cakes in the excellent café; you can also weave Tudor tapestries and design your own coat of arms. If you're visiting at the weekend or during the school holidays, there are imaginative arty, crafty activities – a spot of mask-making, perhaps, or creating crazy fashion accessories.

Pirate ships & pedalos

After a morning in your museum of choice, an afternoon in **Hyde Park** and **Kensington Gardens** (*see p124*) is just the job. A ten-minute walk away, over 300 acres stretch before you. Horse-riders trot briskly along Rotten Row, in-line skaters speed past, and picnic-toting families

LUNCH BOX

Also in the area: Carluccio's Caffè, Gourmet Burger Kitchen, Paul.
Café Crêperie *2 Exhibition Road, SW7 2HF (7589 8947, www. kensingtoncreperie.com).* A bustling joint that serves up made-to-order sweet and savoury crêpes, in a convenient location for the museums.
Le Pain Quotidien *15-17 Exhibition Road, SW7 2HE (7486 6154, www.lepainquotidien.co.uk).* Pricey but tasty tartines, salads, sarnies and cakes, plus child-friendly sides of houmous, guacamole and various other dips.
Lido Café *On the Serpentine, Hyde Park, W2 2UH (7706 7098).* Down-to-earth, delicious grub, served in a splendid location that has recently had a refurb.
Orangery *Kensington Palace, Kensington Gardens, W8 2UH (7376 0239, www.hrp.org.uk).* Afternoon tea and light lunches served in stunning 18th-century surrounds; there's a childrens' menu and highchairs.

hike across the grass in search of a scenic spot. Stroll up to the Serpentine, London's biggest boating lake, and take to the water in a pedalo; cheats can catch the eco-friendly solarshuttle across.

Head over to the southern side of the Serpentine for the Diana, Princess of Wales memorial fountain; sit on the edge and cool your toes, but beware the slippery Cornish granite; proper dips are best taken in the park's lido and paddling pool (*see p213*).

North of here, in Kensington Gardens, is a tribute to the princess that children will enjoy even more: the superb **Diana, Princess of Wales Memorial Playground** (*see p121*). Another draw is the famous statue of Peter Pan, on the west bank of the Long Water. It appeared on May Day morning, 1912, accompanied by a brief announcement in the *Times*: 'There is a surprise in store for the children who go to Kensington Gardens to feed the ducks in the Serpentine this morning.' Pay your respects to Peter,then head off to search for fairies in the flowerbeds.

Great Days Out

Maritime Museum is currently under construction and will include a new interactive gallery for younger visitors, among other things. Expect some upheaval in the meantime, with the outdoor play area and several galleries closed at the time of writing. Britain's seafaring heritage takes centre stage at this vibrant, appealing museum. Themed galleries address everything from the perils faced by early explorers to the slave trade. In the Ships of War gallery, doll's house owners will dream of getting their hands on the impossibly intricate model ships that were built for the Royal Navy in the 17th and 18th centuries; the *Royal George* is a beauty. In the All Hands gallery, kids can have a go at loading up a cargo ship or sending a semaphore signal, while the Bridge Gallery has a simulator where they can attempt to steer a ferry into port.

The Museum Highlights trail takes children through the galleries in search of golden mermaids, the fatal bullet hole in Nelson's blood-stained jacket and, best of all, a real-life pirate's sword, while weekends and school holidays bring a good assortment of activities to get stuck into. Up the hill, the Royal Observatory and Planetarium (*see p28*) are also part of the NMM complex. *See also p114* **Great Days Out**.
Buggy access. Café. Disabled access; lift, toilet. Nappy-changing facilities. Nearest picnic place: Greenwich Park, museum grounds. Shop.

Royal Air Force Museum Hendon
Grahame Park Way, NW9 5LL (8205 2266, www.rafmuseum.org). Colindale tube/Mill Hill Broadway rail/303 bus. **Open** 10am-6pm daily. *Tours* daily; phone for details. **Admission** free. *Tours* free. **Credit** MC, V. 3+
Hendon Airfield has existed here since 1910, hence its claim to be the birthplace of aviation in Britain. Hangers full of over 100 aircraft form the main attraction of this museum. They include a Camel, Tempest, Tiger Moth, Mosquito and Harrier – all parked at ground level or hung in dogfight poses from the rafters of the ultra-modern Milestones of Flight building. Excitingly, helicopters jut above your head as you sit in the café. Don't miss the miniature parachutists going up and down in a tube or dropping off a wire into the hands of kids eager to learn about the laws of gravity.

Plenty of other interactive games are available in the Aeronauts gallery, many in the guise of pilot aptitude tests. Only the flight simulator (over-eights only) carries an extra charge: everything else is gloriously free, so don't exhaust the kids with a full tour; you can come back as often as you like. More low-key than the

Milestones of Flight gallery are the atmospheric and dimly lit Battle of Britain building (with special exhibits in 2010 to mark the 70th anniversary of the battle's start) and the restored Grahame-White Factory.

There is plenty of lethal hardware on display, from World War II doodlebugs to modern cluster bombs and cruise missiles, so be ready to field questions about man's inhumanity to man as you walk around the galleries. Special activity days take place throughout the year, particularly on military holidays; older kids can learn the principles of rocket science, while youngsters build their own cardboard flying machines. See the website for upcoming events.

Activities for children and adults take place all year, with a cluster in the summer holidays. The ever-popular workshops (book ahead) can include activities like hot-air balloon making, rocket science, and Search and Rescue role-play. Quizzes, Pulsar Battlezone interactive laser games, face-painting, aircraft displays and giant garden games might also be on the cards.
Buggy access. Café. Disabled access: lift, toilet. Nappy-changing facilities. Nearest picnic place: on-site picnic area. Restaurant. Shop.

Winston Churchill's Britain at War Experience
64-66 Tooley Street, SE1 2TF (7403 3171, www.britainatwar.co.uk). London Bridge tube/ rail. **Open** *Apr-Oct* 10am-5pm daily. *Nov-Mar* 10am-4.30pm daily. **Admission** £12.95; £6.50 reductions; £5.50 5-15s; free under-5s; £29 family (2+2). **Credit** AmEx, MC, V. **Map** p319 Q8. 8+
This museum is small and cramped, but that's part of the point. The first excitement is the descent from the street into the museum, via an original London Underground lift. Once below, visitors are delivered straight into a mocked-up Blitz-era Underground shelter, with sounds of an air raid rumbling overhead. The convincing set includes bunks, a temporary kitchen and library, original posters and newsreel clips from the time. Other displays explore the roles of women at war, the life of evacuated children and rationing. An ex-evacuee is on hand to show you his childhood photos, there's a BBC broadcasting room and a pub, and children will enjoy trying on tin helmets and gas masks in a dressing-up corner. The visit ends in a full-size street, where a bomb has just exploded – all chillingly staged to make you think the action occurred moments before. An hour or so probably suffices for the whole place.
Buggy access. Disabled access: toilet. Nearest picnic place: Southwark Cathedral gardens. Shop.

Sightseeing

Parks & Gardens

Head for the open air.

Those who have never lived in London can't imagine how anyone can bring up children in such a large city. But Londoners have a secret... their parks are lovelier, livelier and much better equipped than the ones used by their country cousins. As well as ancient trees, well-stocked borders and beds, and landscaping to rival any rural stately home, there are often plenty of other attractions. On top of finding somewhere for the children to run wild and explore, you'll discover great cafés and restaurants – **Holland Park** (*see p116*), **St James's Park** (*see p125*), **Coram's Fields** (*see p112*); galleries – **Dulwich Park** (*see p113*), **Hyde Park** (*see p124*); zoos – **Regent's Park** (*see p124*), **Battersea Park** (*see p111*); city farms – **Crystal Palace Park** (*see p112*), **Lee Valley Park** (*see p128*); open air theatres – **Regent's Park** (*see p124*) and open air swimming pools – **Hampstead Heath** (*see p113*), **Brockwell Park** (*see p111*). What's more, most of them are free to get into.

In these pages, we've listed Royal Parks, wild urban spaces, local parks, adventure playgrounds and the surprising large open spaces reserved for Londoners by forward thinking planners over the centuries.

BOTANIC GARDENS

More botanic beauties can be found in **Chumleigh Gardens** (Burgess Park; *see p111*), the herb garden at the **Geffrye Museum** (*see p58*), **Ham House** (*see p49*), **Hampton Court Palace** (*see p40*) and **Syon House Gardens** (*see p50*).

Chelsea Physic Garden

66 Royal Hospital Road (entrance on Swan Walk), SW3 4HS (7352 5646, www.chelsea physicgarden.co.uk). Sloane Square tube/170 bus. **Open** *Apr-Oct* noon-5pm Wed-Fri; noon-6pm Sun, bank hol Mon. *Tours* times vary, phone to check. **Admission** £8; £5 5-15s, reductions; free under-5s. *Tours* free. **Credit** MC, V. **Map** p313 F12.

The Worshipful Society of Apothecaries planted this unusual garden in 1673, taking advantage of the microclimate beside the Thames. It is still a working centre for botanical research and it has the oldest rock garden in England (the 1773 construction is Grade II listed) as well as a Garden of World Medicine, a Pharmaceutical Garden and borders planted to illustrate the various plants used in perfumery and aromatherapy. The vegetable and fruit garden specialises in growing rare varieties, while the bees in the Mediterranean Garden provide honey for the shop; there's also a café

that serves light snacks and lunches (plus some evening meals during high summer). Come during the school holidays for seed-planting, pond-dipping, photography, dyeing and model-making, wildlife safaris and other earthy, outdoorsy pursuits; most are for seven to 11s, but there are some art sessions for four to sixes. *Buggy access. Café. Disabled access: toilet. Nappy-changing facilities. Shop.*

Royal Botanic Gardens (Kew Gardens)

Richmond, Surrey, TW9 3AB (8332 5655, 8940 1171 information, www.kew.org). Kew Gardens tube/rail/Kew Bridge rail/riverboat to Kew Pier. **Open** *Apr-Aug* 9.30am-6.30pm Mon-Fri; 9.30am-7.30pm Sat, Sun. *Sept-Oct* 9.30am-6pm daily. *Late Oct-early Feb* 9.30am-4.15pm daily. *Early Feb-late Mar* 9.30am-5.30pm daily. Last entry 30mins before closing. *Tours* 11am, 2pm daily. **Admission** £13; £11 reductions, late entry (after 4.45pm); free under-17s. **Credit** AmEx, MC, V.

Kew Gardens is set across 300 acres between Richmond and Kew, so don't expect to see all of its treasures in one day. These huge, world-famous gardens have numerous attractions. First stop for the little ones is the Climbers & Creepers adventure playground (where there's a new outdoor play area). Here, kids can clamber into a flower, through an illuminated blackberry tangle and dig for 'fossilised plants', while real insects buzz amid see-through habitats. This is also the base where eight- to 11-year-olds and their guardians can come for a Midnight Rambler sleepover, which offers the chance to track local wildlife and earn prizes (£40 per person, April to October; book well in advance).

Second favourite, particularly on a freezing winter's day, is the lush, tropical Palm House, where children love climbing the spiral staircases to the upper walkways, and are delighted by the discovery of the Marine Display tanks in the basement. And don't forget the outdoor Treetop Walkway, 18m (59ft) up in the air. The rest of Kew's acreage has an extraordinary array of monuments, gardens and landscapes. The famous Pagoda is one of 40 Grade II-listed structures within Kew's walls (although you can no longer climb to the top and enjoy the views), while the Minka House was originally a farmhouse outside Okazaki City in Japan. The scaled-up badger sett is brilliant fun, while the Marianne North Gallery – showing hundreds of 19th-century botanical paintings made in the field by Victorian explorers – was reopened at the end of 2009 after extensive restoration.

If you're walking around the gardens on foot, pick up a free map at the ticket office. Smaller children might prefer to ride the Kew Explorer people-mover, which plies a circular route around the gardens (£4; £1 reductions). There are cafés and restaurants dotted here and there, but on a fine day you can't beat a picnic. Summer art shows, live music and a winter ice rink in front of the Temperate House (check website for dates) make Kew a year-round treat. You can also find something of Kew at the British Museum (*see p74*) until autumn 2010, as the courtyard is transformed into a walk-through South African landscape for a few months.
Buggy access. Cafés. Disabled access: toilet. Nappy-changing facilities. Restaurants. Shop.

CEMETERIES

Abney Park Cemetery & Nature Reserve

Stoke Newington High Street, N16 0LN (7275 7557, www.abney-park.org.uk). Stoke Newington rail/73, 106, 149, 243, 276, 349 bus. **Open** *Cemetery* dawn-dusk daily. *Visitors' centre* 10am-4pm Mon-Fri. **Admission** free.
This was once the most celebrated and ornate of London's 'garden cemeteries'. Just as winsomely decayed as Highgate Cemetery but without the entry fee or Marx pilgrims, Abney Park Cemetery is a chaotic jumble of Victorian graves, trees, and blind corners. The slowly

decaying monuments – urns, angels, Celtic crosses, saints and shepherds – add romantic interest to this local nature reserve (which was Hackney's first), where birds, butterflies and bats make their home.

There's an environmental classroom at the Stoke Newington High Street entrance, which hosts free workshops for children and adults: go on a mini beast hunt, examine beetles and bugs at close quarters, or take a tree tour and learn about the hundreds of different varieties on site. The visitors' centre doubles as a shop for guides to green London and other environmentally aware literature. From the Church Street entrance path, avoid turning left if you want to steer clear of men seeking men.
Buggy access. Disabled access: toilet (visitors' centre). Shop.

Brompton Cemetery

Fulham Road, SW10 9UG (7352 1201, www.royalparks.org.uk). West Brompton tube/rail. **Open** *Summer* 8am-8pm daily. *Winter* 8am-4pm daily. **Admission** free.
With its formal layout and grand central avenue, Brompton Cemetery is managed by the Royal Parks and is a little different from its Victorian rivals. It has over 35,000 monuments to the dead, commemorating the famous and infamous, including suffragette Emmeline Pankhurst, shipping magnate Sir Samuel Cunard and boxer 'Gentleman' John Jackson, who taught Byron to box; his grave is marked by a lion. The peace and quiet is regularly disturbed by Chelsea FC's home games at neighbouring Stamford Bridge. Bond fans might also like to know that the cemetery was used as a set in *GoldenEye*.
Buggy access. Disabled access.

Highgate Cemetery

Swain's Lane, N6 6PJ (8340 1834, www. highgate-cemetery.org). Highgate tube. **Open** *East cemetery* Apr-Oct 10am-5pm Mon-Fri; 11am-5pm Sat, Sun. Nov-Mar 10am-4pm Mon-Fri; 11am-4pm Sat, Sun. *West cemetery* by tour only; phone for details. **Admission** *East cemetery* £3. *West cemetery* tours £7; £3 8-16s. **No credit cards.**
In 2009, Highgate Cemetery was upgraded to a Grade I-listed park. Not bad for somewhere that, as recently as 1981, was thoroughly neglected, with a tangle of brambles, overgrown self-sown trees and crumbling exterior walls and buildings. The cemetery is most famous for housing the grave of Karl Marx (East cemetery), and you'll often see pilgrims making their way to it through neighbouring **Waterlow Park** (*see p120*). The East Cemetery celebrates its

150th anniversary in 2010, so there will be some events to celebrate (these were unconfirmed as we went to press – see website for details).

Children love the wild wood feel of the place; thanks to its angels, shrouded urns and broken columns, this beautiful boneyard has a romantic atmosphere of ivy-covered neglect. Officially, youngsters are discouraged from visiting, unless they're coming to see the grave of a relative – but if you long to pay your respects to Marx, Mary Ann Evans (aka George Eliot), Christina Rossetti, scientist Michael Faraday, or any of the other eminent figures who now repose in the East cemetery, you can bring children along, as long as they behave well. The atmospheric West cemetery, with its Lebanon Circle Vaults, Egyptian Avenue and Terrace Catacombs, is out of bounds to casual visitors; adults and children aged eight and over can take a guided tour. Both sites close for funerals, so phone before you visit.
Buggy & disabled access (East cemetery only).

Kensal Green Cemetery

Harrow Road, W10 4RA (8969 0152, www. kensalgreen.co.uk). Kensal Green tube/rail/ 18, 23, 52, 70, 295, 316 bus. **Open** *Apr-Sept* 9am-6pm Mon-Sat; 10am-6pm Sun. *Oct-Mar* 9am-5pm Mon-Sat; 10am-5pm Sun. *All year* 10am-1pm bank hols. *Tours* 2pm Sun.
Admission free. *Tours* £5; £4 reductions.
Kensal Green Cemetary was one of London's 'Magnificent Seven' garden cemeteries. Behind an impressive neoclassical gate lie 72 acres of trees, shrubs, graves and monuments between the Grand Union Canal and Harrow Road – there's a contemporary art gallery on site too. Various 19th-century greats repose here, including Isambard Kingdom Brunel, William Thackeray, Anthony Trollope and Wilkie Collins, but the most impressive monuments are the ornate mausoleums of lesser names. There's also a Greek Revivalist chapel and mysterious catacombs, which you can visit on the two-hour guided cemetery tours that take place on Sunday afternoons (over-12s only). The annual Open Day is usually held on the first Saturday in July (check the website for details), and has a village fête atmosphere with face painting, stalls, dressing-up and a motorcade of hearses.
Buggy access. Disabled access: toilet.

Nunhead Cemetery

Entrances on Limesford Road or Linden Grove, SE15 3LP (7732 9535, www.fonc. org.uk). Nunhead rail. **Open** *Summer* 8.30am-7pm daily. *Winter* 8.30am-4pm daily. *Tours* 2pm last Sun of mth. **Admission** free.
Tours free, donations appreciated.

Royal Botanic Gardens. *See p105.*

This tumbledown vision of gothic stonework and overgrown woodland is now part nature reserve, part cemetery. A 52-acre maze of Victorian commemorative statuary with a restored chapel at its heart, it affords fine views over the city from its higher reaches. The Friends of Nunhead Cemetery run guided tours on the last Sunday of each month, while an annual open day takes place in May, bringing musical performances, face painting, plant stalls and more.
Buggy access.

CITY SPACES

Phoenix Garden

21 Stacey Street (entrance on St Giles Passage), WC2H 8DG (7379 3187, www. thephoenixgarden.ik.com). Tottenham Court Road tube. **Open** 8.30am-dusk daily.
Admission free; donations appreciated.
Map p315 K6.
A verdant oasis that's a popular spot with West End workers trying to enjoy a peaceful sandwich on warm days, Phoenix Garden is also an excellent picnic location for families out on a day trip. It lies on what was once part of an extensive leper hospital; these days, its frog-filled pond, wildlife area, quiet crooked pathways, trellises and fragmented statues come as a green and pleasant surprise, tucked as they are between bustling Shaftesbury Avenue and Charing Cross Road; the entrance is next to the playground in the garden of St Giles-in-the-Fields. Check online for advance notice of

Great Days Out
Chelsea

The arrival of Sir Thomas More in the 1520s first made Chelsea's name. This former fishing village on the banks of the Thames has been a blue chip area of residence ever since: during the 16th and 17th centuries, large mansions sprang up along the picturesque riverfront. From the late 18th until the early 20th century the area became popular with artists and writers, including Dante Gabriel Rossetti and TS Eliot.

During the 1960s the neighbourhood adopted a louche, bohemian air, with Mick Jagger and Marianne Faithfull moving into Cheyne Row and David and Angie Bowie living around the corner. By the '70s the Kings Road became a punk hangout where Vivienne Westwood and the late Malcolm McLaren held sway. Nowadays, it's only multi-millionaires like Charles Saatchi and his wife Nigella Lawson who can afford to move here, as property prices are eye-wateringly expensive.

Chelsea Physic Garden

There's no good reason why you shouldn't enjoy a bit of the high life for a day, though.

Shopping vs culture

At Sloane Square you could pop into the Royal Court, the stylish home of cutting edge theatre. Check out the website for occasional backstage tours (www.royalcourttheatre.com). Charles Saatchi and Nigella Lawson's new mansion is being built between the King's Road and Chelsea Embankment, right around the corner from the **Saatchi Gallery,** which moved here from County Hall in 2008. The gallery (see p66) holds a series of envelope pushing temporary exhibitions, many of which would appeal to children.

Next it's off up the King's Road to sample a wealth of upscale shopping opportunities. The western end – known as World's End – was once the home of Vivienne Westwood's shop at no.430, with its backwards-spinning clock. If you've walked all the way here, you deserve to rest your tired legs in Cremorne Gardens, a riverside park with uplifting views east to Old Ferry Wharf and west to exclusive Chelsea Harbour.

War – what is it good for?

The 500-year history of the British Army is told at the **National Army Museum** (see p100). Don't be put off by the rather severe modern exterior of the museum; some eccentric exhibits and displays, together with an exciting programme of family events, make this friendly museum far more entertaining than you might think.

Sure, there are a number of dry displays of regimental items – old uniforms, kit bags and the like – but there are also fascinating highlights: a model of the Battle of Waterloo, starring 75,000 toy soldiers; the skeleton of Napoleon's beloved mount, Marengo; and Florence Nightingale's lamp. Children love the more bizarre exhibits, such as the frostbitten fingers of Major 'Bronco' Lane, conqueror of Mount Everest. The Redcoats Gallery starts at Agincourt in 1415 and ends with the redcoats in the American War of Independence; Nation in Arms covers both World Wars, with reconstructions of a trench in the World at War (1914-1946) exhibition, and a D-Day landing craft. There's more military hardware, including a hands-on Challenger tank simulator, up in the Modern Army exhibition. (Note that certain exhibitions are not suitable for younger children. Faces of Battle includes previously unseen photographs and footage of Britain's faceless war wounded, displayed alongside contemporary uniform sculptures tracing their surgery, rehabilitation and recovery.)

WAACS at War looks at the role of the women who 'did their bit' for the war effort. Their roles included cooking and waiting on officers, serving as clerks, telephone operators, store-women, drivers, printers, bakers and cemetery gardeners. There is also information on the women who disguised themselves as men to go and fight.

Themed weekend events (check the website for details), which usually involve costumed interpreters and craft activities, have gone a long way to broadening the museum's appeal, as has the Kids' Zone – a free interactive learning and play space. It's the sort of place you can bring all your troops to, as its attractions include construction, reading, art activity and board-game areas tailored for under-tens, including a soft-play area for babies. It can also be booked for birthday parties.

Gardeners' world

This area is famous for its annual Flower Show, and the Chelsea Royal Hospital, just around the corner from the Army Museum, is where it's held. Also in the neighbourhood are the year-round delights of the **Chelsea Physic Garden** (see p105). The garden can be reached via Flood Street, one of the many attractive side roads branching off King's Road. The garden was set up in 1673, but the key phase of development was under Sir Hans Sloane in the 18th century. Its beds contain healing herbs and rare trees, dye plants and medicinal

LUNCH BOX

Also in the area: Pizza Express.
Benihana *77 King's Road, SW3 4NX (7376 7799, www.benihana.co.uk).* Japanese teppanyaki, with highly entertaining chefs.
Big Easy *332-334 King's Road, SW3 5UR (7352 4071, www.bigeasy.uk. com).* Cajun fare for sharing: steaks, sticky ribs, crab and the like.
Gelateria Valerie *Duke of York Square, King's Road, SW3 4LY (7730 7978).* Enticing Italian-style gelato in 24 scrumptious flavours.
Itsu *118 Draycott Avenue, SW3 3AE (7590 2400, www.itsu.com).* Polished Japanese fare.
Left Wing Café *9 Duke of York Square, SW3 4LY (7730 7094, www.patisserie-valerie.co.uk).* Part of the Patisserie Valerie cake-and-café chain.
Manicomio *85 Duke of York Square, King's Road, SW3 4LY (7730 3366, www.manicomio.co.uk).* Pasta, pizza and a shaded terrace.
National Army Museum Café *National Army Museum, Royal Hospital Road, SW3 4HT (7730 0717, www.national-army-museum.ac.uk).* Think solid, sturdy grub: meatballs, fish, chips.
Paul *134 King's Road, SW3 4X8 (7581 9611, www.paul-uk.com).* An outpost of the ever-reliable French bakery chain.

vegetables; plants are also sold. Public opening hours are restricted because this is primarily a centre for research and education. There are two deep ponds and poisonous plants, so it's not suitable for very small children, and there must be two adults for every two children under 18.

That said, the education department organises activity days for older children on interesting botanical themes over the Easter and summer holidays. Activity days should generally be pre-booked, and are suitable for seven- to 11-year-olds (although there are some for four- to six-year-olds and nine-to 13-year-olds). For a full list of dates, call 7352 5646. Educational visits and teacher-training days can also be arranged.

child-friendly events such as the agricultural show, 'grow your own' workshops and afternoon Hallowe'en and Christmas parties. *Buggy access.*

Postman's Park

Between King Edward Street & Aldersgate Street, EC1R 4JR (7374 4127, www.cityof london.gov.uk/openspaces). St Paul's tube. **Open** *Summer* 8am-7pm daily. *Winter* 8am-4pm daily. **Admission** free. **Map** p318 O6.
This park was opened in 1880, and is made up of bits of several former churchyards. It acquired its name after becoming the lunchtime favourite of postal workers from a nearby sorting office (long since demolished). The park is a lovely curio, especially for children of reading age, as it is best known for the Watts Memorial to Heroic Sacrifice. The memorial is a canopy-covered expanse of ceramic plaques, inscribed in florid Victorian style, that pay tribute to ordinary people who died trying to save others. 'Frederick Alfred Croft, Inspector, aged 31', begins one typical thumbnail drama. 'Saved a Lunatic Woman from Suicide at Woolwich Arsenal Station, But was Himself Run Over by the Train, Jan 11, 1878'. Many of the dead heroes were children, who tried to rescue drowning companions; their fates make gruesome lessons for their latter-day counterparts. In late spring, the handkerchief tree is also spectacular. *Buggy access.*

St Swithin's Garden

Oxford Court, off Cannon Street, EC4N 5AD (7374 4127, www.cityoflondon.gov.uk/ openspaces). Monument tube/Bank tube/DLR/ Cannon Street tube/rail. **Open** *Summer* 8am-7pm daily. *Winter* 8am-4pm daily. **Admission** free. **Map** p319 Q7.
This carefully tended, walled garden is the burial place of Catrin Glendwr and two of her children. Catrin was the daughter of Owain Glendwr, the fiery Welsh hero whose uprising ended bloodily in 1413. There's a memorial sculpture dedicated not only to Catrin, but to the suffering of all women and children in war. *Buggy access.*

LOCAL PARKS

Alexandra Park & Palace

Alexandra Palace Way, N22 7AY (8444 7696 park, 8365 2121 information, www.alexandra palace.com). Wood Green tube/Alexandra Palace rail/W3, 144 bus. **Open** *Park* 24hrs daily. *Palace* times vary, depending on exhibitions. **Admission** free.

Alexandra Palace was built as 'The People's Palace' in 1873, with the intent of providing affordable entertainment for all. That's still true today, although the original building burned down just 16 days after its opening. (It was speedily rebuilt, and re-opened two years later.) Inside, Ally Pally is mainly used for exhibitions, fairs and gigs, but there's also an ice-skating rink. Outside, the views over London are spectacular and almost worth the trip on their own. But there's plenty more to do than just gawp at the city below. The children's playground behind the palace is a well-equipped and wholesome place in which to take the air, with a café next to the boating lake and a skateboard park for older kids. The pitch-and-putt course is down the hill and popular with older children, and there's a farmers' market at the Hornsey Gate Entrance on Sundays (10am-3pm). The Grove is the more sheltered area of the park (between the Palace and Muswell Hill) and is very popular for family picnics; a lovely new play centre called Little Dinosaurs (*see p178*) opened here in late 2009. Annual visits from the funfair and circus are popular, as is Bonfire Night in November, which brings stunning pyrotechnics that can be seen for miles around.
Buggy access. Café. Disabled access: lift, toilet. Nappy-changing facilities (ice rink).

Phoenix Garden. See p107.

Battersea Park

SW11 4NJ (8871 7530, 8871 7539 adventure playground, www.wandsworth.gov.uk). Sloane Square tube, then 19, 137 bus/Battersea Park or Queenstown Road rail. **Open** 8am-dusk daily. **Map** p313 F13.

The land on which Battersea Park now sits was once a popular spot for duelling (the Duke of Wellington fought an abortive duel here in 1829, deliberately aiming wide of his opponent, the Earl of Winchilsea, who for his part shot his pistol into the air). The park was laid out in 1858, and was splendidly restored in 2004. Facilities range from fun water features (a boating lake, elegant fountains and a riverside promenade) to state-of-the-art sporting facilities and play areas, including a toddlers' playground and a challenging adventure playground for eight to 16s. Bikes can be hired out from London Recumbents (7498 6543; open at weekends, bank holidays and during school holidays Easter to August), there are rowing boats and a land train in July and August, and open fishing is available from mid June to mid March; for permits, call 8871 7530. Battersea Park is also home to a rich array of wildlife, and the London Wildlife Trust has nature reserves here.

The Gondola al Parco café (7978 1655) serves Italian food, with tables overlooking the boating lake and live music on summer evenings. The prettiest landmark, though, is the lofty Peace Pagoda, donated in 1985 by Japanese monks and nuns to commemorate Hiroshima Day. It stands serenely opposite the Children's Zoo (*see p140*) on the park's northern edge.
Buggy access. Café. Disabled access: toilet. Nappy-changing facilities.

Brent Lodge Park

Church Road, W7 3BL (07940 021183, www.ealing.gov.uk). Hanwell rail/E1, E2 bus. **Open** 7.30am-dusk daily. **Open** *Maze & animals* times vary, phone for details. *Indoor centre* 1.30-3pm Sat, Sun. **Admission** free. **No credit cards.**

Think of Hanwell and the Uxbridge Road springs to mind – but there is a villagey area near St Mary's Church, which includes this delightful local park. It's known locally as the Bunny Park, thanks to the rabbits that inhabit the Animal Centre, alongside sheep, goats, monkeys, mongooses, birds and reptiles. There's a café and a good playground, plus a maze with a look-out tower in its centre that was planted to mark the Millennium. The centre organises children's activity days in summer; phone the number above for details.
Buggy access. Café. Disabled access: toilet. Nappy-changing facilities.

Brockwell Park

Dulwich Road, SE24 0PA (www.brockwell park.com). Herne Hill rail. **Open** 7.30am-dusk daily. **Admission** free.

Brockwell Park was bought by London County Council in the early 19th century from various country estates, when this was still part of Surrey. They had the foresight to realise that the residents of the new housing developments in Brixton and Herne Hill would need somewhere to promenade and play in order to make it a pleasant place to live. If only all modern planners understood the same principle. Lambeth Council is currently trying to shave a chunk off the park's south-eastern corner to make way for a new road junction. Luckily, it would take more than that to spoil this lovely park. Tucked away behind the grassy slopes on the Tulse Hill side is one of south London's best playgrounds, with colour-coded sections for different age groups. There's an aerial slide and a massive sandpit; nearby are the duck ponds, with dense greenery screening out the council flats and signs with information on the coots, moorhens and tufted ducks.

There's lots to do besides, with the community greenhouses offering digging pits and planting workshops, plus a long-established BMX track and all-weather tennis courts. The beautiful walled garden is also worth seeking out. On the Herne Hill side, the 1930s lido (*see p213*) has been restored to its former pomp and is open from May to September; it's absolutely packed on sunny days. Whippersnappers (7738 6633, www.whippersnappers.org) runs kids' music classes at the lido complex year-round. The new Lido Café (*see p233*), meanwhile, is proving justifiably popular with locals.

It's a steep walk to the top of the hill, but worth it for the view north over the city. Take a breather at the late Georgian Brockwell Hall country house, now a café serving great wedges of lasagne and other pasta dishes, plus own-made cakes. The park also hosts a popular country show every July – albeit one with reggae soundtracking the vegetable competitions (*see p19*).
Buggy access. Café. Disabled access: toilet. Nappy-changing facilities.

Burgess Park

Albany Road, SE5 0RJ (7703 4275, www. southwark.gov.uk). Elephant & Castle tube/ rail, then 12, 42, 63, 68, 171, 343 bus. **Open** 24hrs daily. *Lake area* 8am-dusk daily. **Admission** free.

It's hard to believe that this was once an industrial strip beside the canal. Since the 1940s the park has grown in stages, but never with an overall plan; luckily, in an area that sorely needs

Sightseeing

Enjoying **Brockwell Park**. See p111.

community spaces, it's about to get a £6 million overhaul. Locals have asked for a cultural hub, cycle tracks, a café with outdoor seating, more benches along the old towpath and a complete renovation of the existing playground, games room and kart and bicycle track (7525 1101).

At present, most community activities are based in the Chumleigh Gardens section of the park, which is home to the Southwark Rangers Football team, a great little café with fry-ups, quiches, salads and jazz on sunny Sundays, and a thriving Peckham Sure Start scheme. Various garden styles are employed in the series of interconnecting plots; English country garden, fragrant Mediterranean, meditative Islamic and a splendid, flamboyant Caribbean garden. The Heart Garden is a fruit and vegetable patch planted, tended and harvested by people with long-term illnesses. There are also lots of community allotments.
Buggy access. Café. Disabled access: toilet.

Clissold Park
Stoke Newington Church Street, N16 5HJ (7923 3660 park ranger, www.clissoldpark. com). Stoke Newington rail/73, 149, 329, 476 bus. **Open** *7.30am-dusk daily.* **Admission** *free.*
Clissold Park isn't one of London's prettiest parks, but it's mightily popular with Stoke

Newington families, dog walkers and joggers. Although traffic is visible from most points, there's a lot to amuse children here. And with an £8.9 million lottery grant being spent on it during 2010, it's bound to get even better. The animal enclosures already have deer, rabbits, birds and goats, but there's going to be a new butterfly dome and an aviary. The lakes are to be drained and replanted.

The large playground has a good choice of activities for all ages, and is shaded by surrounding trees in summer. Younger children love scaring themselves on the wobbly bridge, while older kids favour the aerial four-way see-saw. Next to the playground, the tennis courts are home to the Hackney wing of the City Tennis Centre (7254 4235), offering family tennis evenings, coaching, junior clubs and tournaments. By early 2011, there should also be a new multi-use games area and wheels park.

The café, housed in Clissold Mansion, usually serves adequate refreshments and has a lovely terrace, but will be closed for much of 2010 for refurbishment (there's a temporary kiosk next to the playground). The annual Stokefest is held in the Park in June, and other events, like a visit from Carter's Steam Fair, take place in the summer. There's also a One O'Clock club, although it's in a rather desultory and unloved building and, at present, remains under-subscribed.
Buggy access. Café. Disabled access (not café): toilet. Nappy-changing facilities (on request).

Coram's Fields
93 Guilford Street, WC1N 1DN (7837 6138, www.coramsfields.org). Russell Square tube. **Open** *9am-dusk daily.* **Admission** *free.* **Map** p317 L4.
Thomas Coram established the Foundling Hospital for abandoned children on this spot in 1747. The building was demolished in the 1920s, and a successful campaign to set out a children's park here finally bore fruit in 1936. *See also p62* **Great Days Out.** *Buggy access. Café. Disabled access: toilet. Nappy-changing facilities.*

Crystal Palace Park
Thicket Road, SE20 8DT (8778 9496 park ranger, www.crystalpalacepark.org). Crystal Palace rail/2, 3, 63, 122, 157, 227 bus. **Open** *7.30am-dusk daily.* **Admission** *free.*
Joseph Paxton's Crystal Palace, from which this park takes its name, is long gone. The glittering glass structure, originally created to house Hyde Park's Great Exhibition of 1851, was moved here after the exhibition; in 1936, it burned down in a devastating fire. The park, though, remains – and has recently changed hands. The London

Pipe dreams

Cycle over the sewers on the Greenway track.

Who would have thought a sewage pipe could make such an interesting day out? The Greenway is a three-mile walking trail and cycleway that has been fashioned along the embankment of a large pipe that carries you-know-what from North London to the works at Beckton. It's part of the Capital Ring circular walk around London's suburbs, and the wide, bonded gravel track lifts intrepid urban explorers above the surrounding cityscape.

Great views of Canary Wharf and the Millennium Dome were already a draw, along with architectural curiosities such as the Byzantine-style, Victorian Abbey Mills Pumping Station (known as the Cathedral of Sewage). But throughout 2010, the views from this raised walkway will get ever more exciting. The Greenway skirts the Olympic Park, so walkers and cyclists can see the mass of cranes and builders at work as they construct venues for the London Olympics (*see p202* **Olympic legacy**).

In October 2009, a collection of shipping containers arrived on the banks of the Greenway. These were painted lime green and fashioned into a viewing platform, café and community art and education centre called the **View Tube**. **The Container Café** (*see p225*) is a pleasant place to sit and watch the progress down below. Bikeworks (8980 7998, www.bikeworks.org.uk) hire bikes out at £5 per hour, and also offer guided bike rides of the nearby developments.

For further details of the Capital Ring route, see www.walklondon.org.uk.

Development Agency has taken over from the local council, and has big plans for its future. It's an atmospheric place, enshrined in local folklore. A beautifully landscaped lake complex is home to Benjamin Waterhouse Hawkins' Victorian dinosaur sculptures, which caused outrage by backing up the theory of evolution, yet continue to give pleasure to kids – especially the T-Rex, who recently got a new arm (the tree he was gripping grew, and snapped off the old one). This was also the site where the Girl Guide movement was born, when a group of determined girls faced down Baden Powell at a Scout rally and demanded to join.

The LDA's plans include a review of all buildings and their current uses, so expect the museum, the National Sports Centre, café and community facilities to get a radical overhaul. Proposals also include a treetop walk, a maze and water features. The park's city farm reopened in 2008, and is still expanding its opening hours and programme of activities (*see p130*).
Buggy access. Café. Disabled access: toilet. Nappy-changing facilities.

Dulwich Park

College Road, SE21 7BQ (7525 2000, www. southwark.gov.uk). North Dulwich rail/12, 40, 176, 185, 312, P4 bus. **Open** 8am-dusk daily. **Admission** free.

It's been 120 years since Dulwich Park was landscaped on the 'Five Fields' meadows that lay here. The locals adore it, and they'll have even more to be proud of after 2010's anniversary improvements. These include an outdoor gym for anyone aged 11 and above (situated near the playground); the return of boats and pedalos on the lake (and a new boating house); and a table tennis table in the playground (bats and balls will be available to borrow free of charge from the park manager's office). Being a fan of Dulwich Park is not a new thing though; Queen Mary was a regular visitor (one of the park's four gates is named after her), and was particularly fond of the spectacular American Garden, whose rhododendrons and azaleas bloom in May. Today's visitors can also enjoy the exceptionally child-friendly Pavilion Café (*see p234*), a super playground, novelty bike hire (8299 6636, www.londonrecumbents.com) and a Barbara Hepworth sculpture, *Divided Circle Two Forms*.

The playground is one of the best in the area, with web-like climbing facilities, swings, slides and the Ability Whirl, a safe, robust roundabout that can be used by able-bodied and disabled children. A community officer runs a programme of children's activities from the Francis Peek Centre (phone for details).
Buggy access. Café. Disabled access: toilet. Nappy-changing facilities (café).

Hampstead Heath

NW5 1QR (8348 9908, www.cityoflondon. gov.uk/openspaces). Kentish Town tube/Gospel Oak or Hampstead Heath rail/214, C2, C11 bus. **Open** dawn-dusk daily. **Admission** free.

Sightseeing

Great Days Out
Greenwich

Greenwich Park

Greenwich has its own distinct identity and is a very special part of London, not least because it's where the Prime Meridian lies (every map reference point in the world is measured from here). When the Thames was the beating heart of London, Greenwich became a place of world renown, with a Royal Palace built on its slopes in the 15th century (Henry VIII and Elizabeth I were both born here). Greenwich is also famed for its maritime links, and the National Maritime Museum and Old Naval College showcase all sorts of nautical booty.

Back from the riverfront, the green swathes of Greenwich Park sweep up to the domed Royal Observatory, perched on its lofty hilltop. (Close by, a small boating lake satisfies small visitors with nautical ambitions of their own.)

So heady a mix of fresh air, beautiful architecture and educationally-improving sights is irresistible to families, who flock here for action-packed days out.

A life on the ocean wave

The best way to arrive in Greenwich is on board a Thames Clipper (www.thames clippers.com), which you can catch at Waterloo, Embankment or Blackfriers piers. You'll reach dry land by the **Cutty Sark.** This plucky little tea clipper embarked on her maiden voyage in 1869, and sailed all over the world; in 1954 she retired to Greenwich's dry docks. She's currently in the midst of a huge renovation project (which faced a severe setback when a fire broke out in May 2007), and is due to re-open in time for the Olympics. In the meantime, you can pay your respects and check the progress from a viewing platform, though there's not always an awful lot to see.

Begin the day at the new visitor centre, **Discover Greenwich** (*see p85*), which opened in March 2010 and combines a permanent exhibition on the history of Greenwich with a Tourist Information Centre and other amenities. It's a short stroll upriver, on the site of Sir Christopher Wren's **Old Royal Naval College** (*see p85*). The Baroque College is an imposing affair, set in splendid gardens. It's free to peek at the chapel and magnificent Painted Hall – though the latter's lofty depictions of allegorical scenes may not appeal to children. Weekend and school-holiday 'Tactile Tales' sessions bring the stories to life, though, with the help of a special storytelling rug. Costume-clad historical figures also pop by at weekends, so you might meet a loquacious Samuel Pepys or a 19th-century Greenwich pensioner.

Just across Romney Road, the **National Maritime Museum** (*see p100*) is a tribute to the nation's rich seafaring history, with vast collections of maritime art, maps, instruments and naval attire. Loading cargo, firing cannons and steering a ferry safely into port in the All Hands and Bridge galleries sorts out the salty sea dogs from the cack-handed landlubbers (check opening hours before you turn up). After a quick foray to see the highlights of the collection (the blood-stained jacket in which Nelson met his end, for instance, or Prince Frederick's gorgeously gilded State Barge), it's time to press on.

Toe the line

Muster your energies, then tackle the steep ascent across the park to the **Royal Observatory & Planetarium** (*see p28*). It's topped by an onion-shaped dome that houses the world's seventh largest telescope, and the mysterious-looking Time Ball – a red bobble, on top of a pole – that was first erected in 1833. Every day it rises to the top of its mast then falls at precisely 1pm; in the days before clocks and watches were common, the ships that plied the river relied on it.

After admiring the view, head for the courtyard. The Meridian Line that marks the place where the eastern and western hemispheres meet is set in the flagstones; posing for a picture with one foot on each side is de rigeur. At night, a dramatic green laser beam is projected into the sky to mark the line.

Inside, the star turns are the Weller Astronomy interactive galleries (where you can touch a four-and-a-half-million-year-old meteorite or guide a space mission) and the spectacular Planetarium. Be engulfed in dust storms on Mars or swoop over earth's polar ice caps before re-emerging, blinking, into the daylight.

The green, green grass of Greenwich

Sprawling over 183 acres, **Greenwich Park** (*see p124*) is the area's crowning glory. It's big enough to accommodate all sorts, from entwined lovers and peacefully dozing sun-worshippers to frisbee- and ball-chasing kids and families.

The boating lake is at the Greenwich end of the Park, to the left from Park Row; there's also a decent playground by the Maze Hill entrance, with storytelling

sessions, puppeteers, dance and crafts in the summer holidays. Summer Sundays also bring trumpet trios and brass bands to the bandstand, which is set towards the Blackheath end of the park: spread a picnic rug nearby and enjoy the music drifting across the grass.

The park's teeming with wildlife, too – not least the herd of red and fallow deer that roams the enclosed Wilderness area, which has hides for nosy humans dotted around its perimeter (it's in the south-eastern corner of the park). You can also take a gander at the Secret Garden Wildlife Centre, which runs wildlife-related activities and tours of the nature trail on its once-monthly drop-in days. Butterflies flit across the grassland area, and if you're lucky (and very quiet) you might hear a woodpecker at work in the trees.

For those who've forgotton their picnics, there's the lovely, hexagon-shaped **Pavilion Tea House** (*see p235*). Set amid chestnut trees, the café's outdoor tables are a heavenly spot for lunch.

Great Days Out

Hampstead Heath is less than four miles from Trafalgar Square, but up here, it's possible to believe that you are in the deepest reaches of the countryside. The 800-acre heath is as far from the manicured flowerbeds of the Royal Parks as you could hope to find. Down on Parliament Hill to the south, facilities include an imaginative playground and paddling pool, still looking spanking new after its award-winning refurb, and packed with state-of-the-art equipment designed to challenge children rather than keep them boringly safe. There's a superb One O'Clock Club, a running track and a lido down here too, though families might want to try a more adventurous swimming experience in the famous open-air swimming ponds. Also look out for the Stone of Free Speech, which was here in the 17th century and marked the place where open discussion of all subjects was permitted.

Fishing is available in six of the ponds (though you need a rod licence and a free Heath fishing permit). There are also tennis courses, bat walks, nature trails, a 'secret garden' and a wildlife pond. Clowns, magicians, musicians, storytellers and puppeteers perform in various locations throughout the year, with more appearances in summer. The Rookie Rangers wildlife club is for eight- to 12-year-olds, and meets once a week in the spring and summer holidays and once a month during term time (for information call 020 7482 7073). Check the website and local press for news of the Hampstead Heath consultation and management plan, and for details of family events. An alternative focal point is over to the north west: the listed pergola, built in the 1920s by Lord Leverhulme to join together two parts of his estate, is free to enter and fun to explore. At Golders Hill you'll find a free zoo and a pleasing butterfly house in a converted greenhouse. The Kenwood Estate, though officially part of the Heath, is run by English Heritage.
Buggy access. Cafés. Disabled access: toilet. Nappy-changing facilities.

Highbury Fields

Highbury Crescent, N5 1RR (7527 4953, www.islington.gov.uk). Highbury & Islington tube/rail/19, 30, 43, 271 bus. **Open** *Park* 24hrs. *Playground* dawn-dusk daily. **Admission** free.
Islington is a densly-packed urban area, which has two distinct sides to it. This 29-acre park is the borough's largest green space, and much needed by the families who live here. Get the children to imagine the scene when, in 1666, 200,000 Londoners fled here to escape the Great Fire. Hidden behind Highbury Pool and a series of high bushes is an unusual playground that combines old-fashioned thrills (such as a circular train requiring Flintstones-style propulsion, and an excitingly long, steep slide) with more recent additions, such as the flying fox and giant, web-like climbing frames. The outdoor tennis courts have been refurbished, and are used by the excellent Islington Tennis Centre. There's also a swimming pool, football and netball pitches and the Oasis café. A stroll across Highbury Fields takes you from busy Upper Street past imposing period terraces to Highbury Barn, a trendy enclave with several excellent food shops, restaurants and child-friendly cafés.
Buggy access. Café.

Holland Park

Ilchester Place, W8 6LU (7938 8170, www. rbkc.gov.uk). Holland Park tube/9, 27, 28, 49 bus. **Open** 8am-dusk daily. **Admission** free. **Map** p314 A9.
Holland Park is a cut above the average local park (well, what did you expect in this classy part of town?). There are so many intriguing nooks and crannies to explore that it's worth a day trip in its own right. Visitors may even have seen some pigs rooting around in the undergrowth in the early months of 2010 (used here instead of pesticides to clear scrub from the woodland areas). Children over five will want to start with the many and varied excitements on offer at the adventure playground (there's an alternative playground for under-fives too). The paths take you past formal gardens and fountains, imperious peacocks and plenty of squirrels and rabbits. Look out, too, for the open-air theatre, the peaceful Japanese Garden with a pond full of colourful koi carp, and an Ecology Centre which provides information, site maps and nets for pond-dipping. Whippersnappers (7738 6633, www.whippersnappers.org) puts on weekly musical and puppet workshops in the Youth Hostel, and the Friends of Holland Park organise holiday activities for five- to ten-year-olds. Also in the park are tennis courts, sports fields and two art spaces, the Ice House and the Orangery. Take public transport unless it's a Sunday, as parking is expensive.

Come lunchtime, there's Marco Pierre White's smart but surprisingly child-friendly Belvedere (*see p242*) for special occasions, or a smart Italian café and ice-cream kiosk for everyday treats. On sunny days though, well-to-do families from the rather chichi surrounding neighbourhoods lay out their rugs and hampers for all-day picnics.
Buggy access. Café. Disabled access: toilet. Nappy-changing facilities. Restaurant.

Sightseeing

Manor House Gardens

Old Road, SE13 5SY (8318 3986, www.
lewisham.gov.uk). Hither Green rail. **Open**
Café & park 8am-dusk daily. *House & library*
9am-7pm Mon-Fri; 9am-6pm Sat; 10am-4pm
Sun. **Admission** free.
The titular Manor House is now a thriving
public library, while its gardens have become a
pretty public park. The central lake has a
fountain in the middle and flocks of wildfowl
living in its waters, while the handsome
playground is made of natural materials and
incorporates rocks, wooden see-saws, balance
bars, climbing frames and swings. There are
also tennis courts and an area for ball games.
On one side of it is a wildlife garden; on the other
is the friendly park café, with a menu of simple,
own-made hot meals, ice-creams, drinks and
snacks. A compact farmers' market takes place
here on the first Saturday of the month.
Buggy access. Café. Disabled access: toilet.

Mile End Park

Locksley Street, E14 7EJ (7364 4147,
7093 2253 children's park, www.tower
hamlets.gov.uk). Mile End tube. **Open** 24hrs
daily. *Children's park* 10am-dusk daily.
Admission free.
This park was a long time in the making, and
it is still developing each year. The idea for
Mile End Park was first mooted in the 1940s,
but it took 50 years for the various strips to
emerge as parkland. It comprises 90 acres of
reclaimed industrial land, which runs south of
Victoria Park in a long strip alongside Regent's
Canal. For many Londoners it is the
quintessential modern urban park, divided into
dramatically different sections. The south end
of the park has a great playground, with a rope
slide, scrambling wall, complicated climbing
frame, swings and a see-saw, as well as a
dedicated area for under-fives that includes a
vast sandpit. New apparatus installed in the
playground is designed to appeal to children
with disabilities as well as to their able-bodied
playmates, with a huge, bird's nest-style swing
and a ramped bridge. A new skateboard park
arrived in 2009.
There's also the Ecology Park, with its large
climbing wall; the site-specific works and
pavilion of the Arts Park; the Terraced Garden;
the Sports Park (including Mile End Stadium);
the canalside Kirk's Place, which is good for
picnics; and an electric go-kart track.
Structured events for children expanded
during 2009 (the year of the 'Playful Park') and
now there are plenty of clubs and activities
during term time, as well as after school and in
the holidays. There's also a green-fingered club

started up in the six new children's gardens. In
the middle of the park, the café and Palm Tree
Pub provide refreshments.
Buggy access. Café. Disabled access: toilet.
Nappy-changing facilities.

Morden Hall Park

Morden Hall Road, Morden, Surrey SM4
5JD (8545 6850, www.nationaltrust.org.uk).
Morden tube. **Open** 8am-6pm daily.
Admission free.
There are rolling meadows and woodlands in this
125-acre swathe of uncommonly beautiful
National Trust parkland, which is perfect for
family picnics and cycle rides. The park sits on
the floodplain of the River Wandle, creating
marshy wetlands that shelter a whole host of
birds (look out for leggy herons and the bright
blue flash of a kingfisher), and the restored Rose
Garden is a fragrant diversion in summer.
Morden Hall itself is run as a private restaurant,
but there's the wonderful watermill to enjoy and
the Snuff Mill Environmental Centre, which runs
children's activities on the first and third Sundays
of the month. Craftspeople, furniture restorers
and artists occupy many of the old estate
buildings, and the Riverside Café (inside the old
walled Kitchen Garden) is a relaxing place to sit
back and take stock of the lovely surrounds
(there's a second hand bookshop here too).
Buggy access. Café. Disabled access: toilet.
Nappy-changing facilities. Shop.

Myatt's Fields

Cormont Road, SE5 9RA (7926 9000,
www.lambeth.gov.uk). Oval tube/Loughborough
Junction rail/P5, 36, 185, 436 bus. **Open**
7.30am-dusk daily. **Admission** free.
Myatt's Fields isn't just a park with a fabulous
new playground – it's proof that community
spirit is thriving in the depths of urban London.
Hidden between Camberwell and Brixton, these
Victorian gardens are flanked by grand
townhouses and claustrophobic estates. The area
is notorious for guns, drugs and teen pregnancy
– yet every summer, locals from both sides of the
park get together to hold the kind of fêtes that
would make a country parish proud.
The recent park refurb includes a new
playground that caters for everyone from tots to
teens. There are four kinds of swings, slides,
rockers and roundabouts, plus climbing frames,
climbing walls and mounds. The spaces under
the play frames are set up as kitchens and shop
counters; games of battleships and number
puzzles are set into the walls. A sensory trail
leads to a set of giant wooden chimes, and
the centrepiece is a spongy map of the world
that becomes a quirky play fountain each

Sightseeing

summer. There are also tennis courts, a One O'Clock Club and a brand new Green Flag Award to be proud of.
Buggy access.

Queen's Park

Kingswood Avenue, NW6 6SG (8969 5661, www.cityoflondon.gov.uk/openspaces). Queen's Park tube/rail. **Open** *7.30am-dusk daily.* **Admission** free.
Thank heavens for the philanthropy of the Victorians. This appealing park is well used by locals, and another example of the way in which a great park can transform the urban area around it. Queen's Park has a great playground with a giant sandpit, a paddling pool (being resurfaced in 2010), a small animal enclosure and patrolling wardens. At the northern end is a wild, overgrown area, where a nature trail displays pictures of the small beasts you might encounter. The café serves own-made cakes and local Disotto's ice-cream. There's also a lovely ornamental garden, a pitch-and-putt area, a pétanque pitch and six all-weather tennis courts. Children's entertainment takes place at the bandstand during the summer holidays. Each September, the annual Queen's Park Day brings fancy dress competitions, face painting, a dog show and puppetry.
Buggy access. Café. Disabled access: toilet. Nappy-changing facilities.

Ravenscourt Park

Ravenscourt Road, W6 0UL (www.lbhf.gov.uk). Ravenscourt Park tube. **Open** *7.30am-dusk daily.* **Admission** free.
This lovely local park was a little scuffed around the edges until a Friends of Ravenscourt Park association was set up in 2008. In July 2009, the park was given a Green Flag Award for the first time. Nestling between the messy bustle of Hammersmith and the quiet splendour of Chiswick, it's a hidden oasis of bucolic tranquility. The first mention of Ravenscourt Park was in the 13th century; documents record the existence of a manor house, surrounded by a moat that was fed by Stamford Brook. Disaster struck during World War II, when the house was devastated by an incendiary bomb. Only the stable block survived, and is now home to the park café. It's conveniently close to the seriously fun adventure playground (intrepid adults are often spotted commandeering the rope slide).
There's also a paddling pool, a nature trail, passable tennis courts, a bowling lawn and a pitch-and-putt course. Bonfire night is the biggest date in the diary, as enormous crowds gather to 'ooh' and 'ahh' over spectacular rockets that bathe the park in an ethereal glow. In April, the ever-popular Carter's Steam Fair rolls into the park.
Buggy access. Café. Disabled access. Nappy-changing facilities.

Southwark Park

Gomm Road, SE16 2UA (7237 1230 art gallery, www.southwark.gov.uk). Canada Water tube. **Open** *Park* 7.30am-1hr before dusk daily. *Gallery* (during exhibitions) Summer noon-6pm Wed-Sun. Winter 11am-4pm Wed-Sun. **Admission** free.
This was one of the first parks to be opened by the Metropolitan Board of Works in the 19th century. In 2001, a pretty new bandstand and a decent children's play area were added; over a decade later the whole place is still looking

Dizzy heights

Fly through the air with the greatest of ease…

What swings like a monkey, flies like a bird and can be seen in various parks in London over the summer of 2010? It could be you, as the Gorilla Circus Trapeze School takes its mobile kit out to London's green spaces during the months when the sun's supposed to shine.

The open air trapeze consists of two swings, 25 feet up in the air. Kids aged three can have a go at the Try 'n' Fly at £4 per time, while those aged six and above get tuition. The 90-minute classes have the fearless progressing from hooking their legs over their heads and hanging upside down to getting caught by an acrobat. Of course, there's a safety net below and all 'flyers' are also fitted with a belt attached to ropes, but that doesn't stop it being an adrenaline rush for all involved. Needless to say, this isn't one for kids who are scared of heights.

The schedule takes in **Ravenscourt Park** (*see above*) June 9-30 2010; **Regent's Park** (*see p124*) July 27-August 23 2010; and **The Roundhouse** (*see p176*): 26-30 August 2010. Classes must be booked in advance, but you can just show up on the day for the Try 'n' Fly sessions. For further details, call 07931 767554 or visit www.gorillacircus.com.

Getting wet in **Ravenscourt Park**.

shipshape, thanks to the efforts of the energetic Friends of Southwark Park commitee and the vandal-busting wardens.

There is plenty to encourage older children to take up sports, with an athletics track (often used by Millwall Football Club, along with the astroturf pitches) and free tennis courts. There's also a Young Friends of Southwark Park group for eight- to 14-year-olds that has started a community allotment scheme and completed a colourful mural (call 7525 2000 for details). The park also has a thriving arty scene, the hub of which is the Café Gallery Project. It holds frequent exhibitions and workshops on Saturdays and during the summer holidays, called the DIY Family Art Club; check online at www.cafegalleryprojects.com for details of the club, and the summer Children's Exhibition and winter Open Exhibition. Parkside Café & Bar, just across from the gallery, serves hot meals and sandwiches.
Buggy access. Café. Disabled access: toilet. Nappy-changing facilities (in gallery).

Thames Barrier Park

North Woolwich Road, E16 2HP (7476 3741, www.thamesbarrierpark.org.uk). Pontoon Dock DLR. **Open** 7am-dusk daily. **Admission** free.
When the Thames Barrier Park opened in 2001, it was London's first new park in half a century.

Its lush sunken gardens and undulating topiary, coupled with views over the fabulously sculptural silver fins of the Thames Barrier, means visitors don't forget the experience in a hurry.

The Barrier's visitors' centre is on the south side; the tea pavilion serves excellent coffee. A concrete and granite channel the width of a small motorway, called the Green Dock, is filled with fragrant honeysuckle and wavy yew hedges: it has superb hide-and-seek potential, with the two pedestrian bridges overhead adding an extra dimension to the game. The kids will also want to go wild at the fountain plaza, where 32 vertical jets beg to be played with. On the riverfront is the Pavilion of Remembrance, erected to remember local victims of the Blitz. The manicured, flat lawns are perfect for picnics and games; there's also a playground packed with apparatus, plus a basketball hoop and five-a-side court.

The park is fantastic for waterfowl-watching too: ducks, geese, swans and oyster catchers pick around on the gleaming mudflats, herons feed along the shore at low tide, and large numbers of teal, shelduck and cormorants enjoy the river's bounty.
Buggy access. Café. Disabled access: toilet. Nappy-changing facilities.

Victoria Park

Old Ford Road, E3 5DS (8985 1957, www.towerhamlets.gov.uk). Mile End tube/ Cambridge Heath or Hackney Wick rail/8, 26, 30, 55, 253, 277, S2 bus. **Open** 8am-dusk daily. **Admission** free.
Queen Victoria opened this park in 1845 when thousands of Eastenders signed a petition asking for a public park in the area (it's often referred to as 'The People's Park'). It was laid out by Sir James Pennethorne – a pupil of John Nash, who designed Regent's Park – and has been much loved ever since. You can see the influence of the grand master in the landscaping of this gracious green space, and by 2012 it will look even better, thanks to a lottery grant of £4.5 million being awarded in early 2010. Restoration of the Burdett-Coutts Fountain, Chinese Pagoda, Old English Garden and the stone sculpture of the Dogs of Alcibiades are planned.

With its imposing, wide carriageways, ornate lampposts and wrought-iron gates, Victoria Park is the only place out east where you can pretend you're in the countryside. There are fish in the Western Lake (you can help deplete the stock by applying for a free fishing licence); Britain's oldest model boat club convenes around the other lake, near Crown Gate East, every second Sunday. The Pools Playground,

Sightseeing

with its landscaped paddling pools, is a real favourite with all ages, and there's a fallow deer enclosure on the east side, tennis courts and a bowling green, plus football, hockey and cricket pitches. The jolly Lakeside Pavilion Café is packed to the rafters by families enjoying great organic food, sausages from Marylebone's famous Ginger Pig butchers and memorable coffee. *Buggy access. Café. Disabled access: toilet. Nappy-changing facilities.*

Wanstead Park

Entrance via Warren Road or Northumberland Avenue, E11 2LT (8508 0028, www.cityof london.gov.uk/openspaces). Wanstead tube. **Open** dawn-dusk daily. **Admission** free.

The woodlands, beautiful ponds and lakes, grassland and mown playing fields of Wanstead Park are managed alongside Epping Forest (*see p128*) by the City of London. Fishing is free here, and you can catch bream, carp, perch, tench and roach on a spot by the Ornamental Water. At the fenced-off end is a ruined grotto, built in the early 1760s, with a boathouse that's now in a photogenic state of disrepair. The other important ruin in the park is the Temple, once a fancy summerhouse; which visitors can now look around (noon-5pm Sat & Sun; phone for dates, and for details of the summer outdoor theatre, community operas and guided walks). Children will also appreciate the ball-throwing and kite-flying possibilities on the extensive grassy area between the Temple and the tea stall. The park's Wildlife Group (www.wren-group.net) is a good point of contact for animal-lovers; look out, too, for the horses being ridden around the park by members of a nearby riding school. *Buggy access. Café.*

Waterlow Park

Highgate Hill, N6 5HG (8348 8716 Lauderdale House, 8341 4807 café, www. waterlowpark.co.uk). Archway tube/143, 210, 271, W5 bus. **Open** 7.30am-dusk daily. **Admission** free.

Although Waterlow Park may be small, it's impossible to see all the boundaries at once, thanks to its being laid out on an undulating hillside. The mystery of the unknown is ever present. Once it was the garden of pretty, 16th-century Lauderdale House, but it was donated to the public by low-cost housing pioneer Sydney Waterlow as a 'garden for the gardenless'. With its majestic vistas, mature trees, formal gardens, tennis courts and beautiful seasonal planting, it's a delightful spot all year round.

Lauderdale House has a café on its west-facing terrace, and runs a year-round programme of

kids' activities that includes music, dance and drama classes, and lively children's theatre events every Saturday morning. Until recently, a small toddlers' area was the only formal playground, but a new adventure playground, built from natural materials, was opened in early 2009. Aimed at six to 13s, it can be found to the west of the lowest pond. In the old depot building, Waterlow Park Centre houses exhibitions and has an activities room available for hire. Of late, there has been talk of restoring the aviary, but a final decision has not yet been reached. *Buggy access. Café. Disabled access: toilet.*

West Ham Park

Upton Lane, E7 9PU (8472 3584, www.cityof london.gov.uk/openspaces). Stratford tube/rail/ 104, 238 bus. **Open** 7.30am-30mins before dusk daily. **Admission** free.

The City of London has been in charge of this lovely park since locals persuaded the corporation to buy what was then a private botanic garden for the public in 1874. Its ornamental gardens and established trees are glorious; as one of the few London parks to have its own plant nursery, it also has spectacular border planting. Full time park attendants make it feel safe, while the playground has plenty of colourful climbing apparatus. Highlights include a wooden prairie locomotive to clamber on, a Wendy house corner, the pre-war paddling pool, open from late May to August, and a new Wildlife Education Garden that opened in early 2010.

More unusually, some community vegetable plots have recently been established here to encourage locals to grow their own. There are 12 tennis courts (lucky locals have access to the annual tennis clinic, which is held in June), three cricket nets (Essex CCC runs free training for under-16s in July), two match-quality cricket tables, two football pitches (one all-weather), a running track and a rounders area. From late July to August, free children's events are held at the bandstand on Monday and Friday afternoons (3-4pm); a very popular bouncy castle (also free) appears on Wednesdays (noon to 5pm); and there are occasional Sunday concerts. The only thing missing is a café, though an ice-cream van takes up position near the playground from Easter to October. *Buggy access. Disabled access: toilet. Nappy-changing facilities.*

Wimbledon Common

Windmill Road, SW19 5NR (8788 7655, www.wpcc.org.uk). Putney rail, then 93 bus/85 bus. **Open** 24hrs daily. **Admission** free.

North Londoners bang on about Hampstead Heath being a slice of the countryside in the city;

south Londoners scoff and retort that Wimbledon Common is twice the size. With more than 1,000 acres of woodland, scrubland and heathland, the Common is a haven for joggers, walkers and anyone who loves the outdoors. There are cricket, football and rugby pitches, a golf course, a bog, nine ponds, and around 16 miles (over 25km) of bridleways. There's also a windmill, which is now a museum (*see p85*). The common is patrolled by rangers, on horseback and on foot, who are a mine of information about the common and nearby Putney Heath, both of which are designated SSSIs (Sites of Special Scientific Interest). They're based in the Information Centre, which also provides leaflets on the plant and animal life on the common, as well as the history of the area; it's open seven days a week. Best of all is a video microscope showing insects and other flora and fauna in minute detail; specimens are changed regularly, and you can insert your own for display. Every Saturday at 9am, there's a free park run organised by volunteers; the Wildlife Watch Club for eight- to 14-year-olds takes place on the first Sunday of the month from 10am to noon (£2).
Buggy access. Café. Disabled access: toilet. Nappy-changing facilities (café).

PLAYGROUNDS

Diana, Princess of Wales' Memorial Playground
Near Black Lion Gate, Broad Walk, Kensington Gardens, W8 2UH (7298 2117, 7298 2141 recorded information, www. royalparks.org.uk). Bayswater tube/70, 94, 148, 390 bus. **Open** Times vary, phone or check website for details. **Admission** free. Adults & over-12s must be accompanied by a child. **Map** p310 C7.
The Diana, Princess of Wales' Memorial Playground celebrated its tenth anniversary in June 2010. This commemorative play area is easily the best bit of Kensington Gardens for a child. A huge pirate ship on its own beach takes centre stage (bring buckets and spades). Beyond this lies the tepee camp: a trio of wigwams, each large enough to hold a sizeable tribe, and a tree-house encampment with walkways, ladders, slides and 'tree phones'.
The area's connection with Peter Pan creator JM Barrie is remembered in scenes from the story, etched into the glass in the Home Under the Ground. Many of the playground's attractions appeal to the senses (scented shrubs, whispering willows and bamboo are planted throughout), and much of the equipment has

been designed for use by children with special needs, including those in wheelchairs. There's also plenty of seating for parents, and unaccompanied adults aren't allowed in. A programme of free entertainment includes visits by clowns and storytelling sessions; check the website for details. The café has a good children's menu. *See also p102* **Great Days Out**. *Buggy access. Café. Disabled access: toilet. Nappy-changing facilities.*

Glamis Adventure Playground
Glamis Road, E1W 3DQ (7702 8301, www. glamisadventure.org.uk). Shadwell DLR. **Open** *Term-time* 3.15-7pm Mon (girls only); 3.15-7pm Tue-Fri; 10am-4pm Sat. *School holidays* 10am-5.30pm Mon-Fri. Times may vary, phone for details. **Admission** free.
The idea behind this community project was to create a space where children can take controlled risks while they are playing – and it must be one of the few playgrounds in the country where children are actively encouraged to build and light a bonfire. There's an amazing climbing structure, as well as swings and slides, and a vegetable garden to get grubby in. Indoor activities include arts, crafts and cooking. The playground won Adventure Playground of the Year 2007 and there's a playscheme organised during school holidays.
Buggy access. Disabled access: toilet.

Kimber Adventure Playground
King George's Park, Kimber Road, SW18 4NN (8870 2168). Earlsfield rail, then 44 or 270 bus. **Open** *Term-time* 2.30-7pm Wed-Fri; 11am-6pm Sat, Sun. *School holidays* 11am-6pm daily. **Admission** free.
Kids can swing around on monkey bars, climbing frames, big swings, tyres and ropes at this recently-refurbished adventure playground; there's also a brilliant BMX track to zoom round. (If you don't have your own BMX, you can usually hire one at the playground.) There's also a five-ramp skateboard park for those that favour four-wheeled stunts.
Buggy access. Disabled access: toilet. Shop.

Lady Allen Adventure Playground
Chivalry Road, Wandsworth Common, SW11 1HT (7228 0278, www.kids.org.uk). Clapham Junction rail. **Open** *Term-time* 10.30am-5pm Tue (under-8s only); 3-5pm Wed-Fri; 10am-noon Sat. *School holidays* 10am-noon Mon, Wed-Fri; 10am-3pm Tue. **Admission** free, donations appreciated. **No credit cards.**
The northerly tip of Wandsworth Common is home to this purpose-built playground for local children with special needs. Tuesday is for the

Sightseeing

Great Days Out
Camden

At first glance, Camden Town, especially the grubby and busy junction by the tube, seems more of a destination for adults than families. But there's plenty to interest children of all ages, including the newly expanded Jewish Museum, the funky Roundhouse, gorgeous Regent's Canal and ever popular London Zoo. Older children and teenagers, meanwhile, absolutely love the famous market, with its colourful, chaotic mix of street food vendors, stalls touting vintage clobber, cheap accessories and incense sticks, and wandering goths and punks.

On the waterfront

Children adore being by the water, even if they can't go in it. Join the Regent's Canal at **Camden Lock**, where the manually-operated twin lock is the first stopping point. It's particularly exciting if a boat happens to be coming through. The canal was built in the early 19th century to connect the Grand Union Canal at Paddington with the Thames at Limehouse, but since the 1960s has been used in the main for leisure and pleasure.

The towpath in either direction leads to some great finds; note that although it is a designated cycle route, the path is too narrow for all but the most proficient of cyclists (scooters should be fine). To the east, a decent stroll away, are the bucolic delights of **Camley Street Natural Park** (*see p125*), a small but thriving nature reserve run by the London Wildlife Trust. A little further along, just past the tunnel under York Way, in the Battlebridge basin, lies the **London Canal Museum** (*see p81*), an old-fashioned but homely shrine to life on Britain's canals; there's a children's corner and a real narrowboat to explore, along with the ice house used by enterprising ice-cream maker Carlo Gatti, who imported enormous blocks of ice from the frozen lakes of Norway.

From Camden Lock going west, families can stop off at the exclusive enclave of **Primrose Hill**, where kite flying and picnics in the park are popular pastimes and the cafés and shops have a chichi villagey feel. Carry on a little further, and you will begin to hear the strange grunts, squeals and squawks emanating from one of the capital's biggest attractions; **London Zoo** (*see p138*), a great day out in itself. The expanse of **Regent's Park** (*see p124*) is just beyond, with a very good playground at the Gloucester Gate entrance.

Camley Street Natural Park

Of course, you don't have to content yourself with merely walking alongside the water. The **London Waterbus Company** (www.londonwaterbus.co.uk) runs canal boat trips to Little Venice, where families could stop and see a performance at the **Puppet Theatre Barge** (*see p183*). If you want to go through the lock on a boat, the *Jenny Wren* goes from Walker's Quay (7485 4433, www.walkersquay.com) and heads to Little Venice on a round trip.

Market value

Camden Market is absolutely heaving at weekends (it's one of the top five tourist attractions in London – and it shows), so try to come on a quieter weekday if you don't want to lose sight of small children; most shops and stalls are open all week long. Also be aware that Camden Town tube station is exit-only on Saturday and Sunday, which means a fairly long walk up to Chalk Farm or down to Mornington Crescent for the tube if you don't want to catch the bus.

There are several different markets and hundreds of stalls to browse here, so pace yourself and be picky. Discerning shoppers tend to bypass the first market you reach after turning north from the tube station – the one at Buck Street bearing the legend 'Camden Market' – unless their party includes a teenager who is desperate for goth T-shirts, stripey tights and cheap tat.

North of the road bridge on Chalk Farm Road is the former Canal Market. Closed after a fire in February 2008, it re-opened in May 2009 with a new name, the **Canal Lock Village**, and an eclectic assortment of stalls, plus some groovy seats that look like mopeds. Alternatively, head straight for **Camden Lock Market**. Launched in 1975, this is where the whole thing began. There is a lovely open air square of stalls and shops selling good quality crafts, jewellery, textiles, alternative fashion and accessories.

The extensive **Stables Market**, just north of Camden Lock, is still undergoing redevelopment but most of the units are now filled. Small children will enjoy the large bronze statues of horses and

LUNCH BOX

Also in the area: Belgo Noord, Fresh & Wild, Pizza Express, Strada, Wagamama.
Diner *2 Jamestown Road, NW1 7BY (7485 5223, www.goodlifediner.com).* Burgers, hotdogs, fries and milkshakes delight the kids.
InSpiral *250 Camden High Street, NW1 8QS (7428 5875, www.inspiralled.net).* Kids will love the seats overlooking the canal in this quality vegan and raw food café.
Marine Ices *8 Haverstock Hill, NW3 2BL (7482 9003, www.marineices. co.uk).* A classic Italian that hasn't changed in years. *See p246.*
Tupelo Honey *27 Parkway, NW1 7PN (7284 2989, www.tupelo-honey.co.uk).* A homely café, serving solid, healthy grub and cakes.
Yum Cha *27-28 Chalk Farm Road, NW1 8AG (7482 2228).* Flawless dim sum that appeal to all ages.

workers, although parents might be scared of losing the little darlings in this warren of blind corners. There are plenty of jumbled displays of ethnic doo-dads, vintage clothes and furniture, and lots of child-friendly novelties and stalls that will intrigue older kids and teenagers. You'll also find all kinds of takeaway stands, offering foods from around the world.

Something for the grey matter

If all that browsing and spending gets a little overwhelming, you could always incorporate a bit of culture into your Camden experience. On the road north, towards Chalk Farm is the iconic **Roundhouse** (*see p176*), famed for its groundbreaking gigs in the 1960s and '70s (the Doors, Hendrix and Bowie all took to the stage here). Re-opened in 2006, it offers an avant-garde programme of music and theatre. The Roundhouse Studio also runs excellent radio, film and music workshops for teenagers in the school holidays.

South of here, just off Parkway, is the all-new **Jewish Museum** (*see p84*), which opened in March 2010 after a major refurbishment project.

Great Days Out

under-fives and their carers; the rest of the time, it's open to all under-15s (able-bodied children are welcome). Kids can dig, make dens and climb in the wild wood, or play on traditional playground equipment. Indoors there is a room for soft play, a video games room and a corner for arts and crafts. The operation is staffed by volunteers; call ahead before visiting. *Buggy access. Disabled access: toilet. Nappy-changing facilities.*

Somerford Grove Adventure Playground

Park Lane Close, Northumberland Park, N17 0HL (8808 2644, www.haringey-play.org.uk). Tottenham Hale tube/rail/Northumberland Park or White Hart Lane rail. **Open** *Term-time* 3.15-6.30pm Wed-Fri; 1-6pm Sat. *School holidays* 1-6pm Mon-Fri. **Admission** free.
Somerford Grove's features, which won it the accolade of Adventure Playground of the Year 2008, include imaginative climbing structures, den building opportunities, a stream and a pond, plus traditional play equipment. Indoor activities include arts, crafts and cooking. *Buggy access. Disabled access: toilet. Nappy-changing facilities.*

ROYAL PARKS

Bushy Park

Hampton Court Road, Hampton Court, Surrey TW12 2EJ (8979 1586, www.royalparks.org.uk). Hampton Wick, Hampton Court or Teddington Rail/111, 216, 265, 411, R68 bus. **Open** *Pedestrians* Jan-Aug, Oct, Dec 24hrs daily. Sept, Nov 8am-10.30pm daily. *Vehicle access* 6.30am-dusk daily. **Admission** free.
This is the second largest of the Royal Parks, but perhaps one of the least familiar to Londoners. It sits right next to its more famous neighbour, Hampton Court Park; its central attraction, the majestic, mile-long Chestnut Avenue, was designed by Christopher Wren as a grand driveway to Hampton Court Palace. During World War I and II, much of the park's open land was dug up to grow vegetables, and Eisenhower (who didn't fancy being in the centre of town), made his base here – hence the memorial near the Warren Plantation. The last few years have seen the park enhanced in myriad small ways, including extra planting, improved paths and the renovation of the Diana fountain, thanks to an injection of lottery cash. The Pheasantry Welcome Centre opened in August 2009 and has a café with terrace, loos and an education and community room. *Buggy access. Café. Disabled access: toilet.*

Greenwich Park

Blackheath Gate, Charlton Way, SE10 8QY (8858 2608, www.royalparks.org.uk). Cutty Sark DLR/Greenwich DLR/rail/Maze Hill rail/1, 53, 177, 180, 188, 286 bus/riverboat to Greenwich Pier. **Open** 6am-dusk daily. **Admission** free.
The oldest of the Royal Parks is part of the Greenwich World Heritage Site. It's a lovely, hilly stretch of green affording wonderful views over the Thames, to Canary Wharf and Docklands and the City of London. There's a deer park, boating lake, playground, community orchard and tennis courts. *See also p114* **Great Days Out**. *Buggy access. Cafés. Disabled access: toilet. Nappy-changing facilities.*

Hyde Park & Kensington Gardens

W2 2UH (7298 2100, www.royalparks.org.uk). Hyde Park Corner, Knightsbridge, Lancaster Gate or Marble Arch tube/2, 8, 10, 12, 23, 73, 94 bus. **Open** *Hyde Park* 5am-midnight daily. *Kensington Gardens* 6am-dusk daily. **Admission** free. **Map** p311 E7.
It's easy to forget you're slap bang in the middle of the centre of London in this grand patch of turf, which makes for a brilliant family excursion. Along with tennis courts, cafés, fountains, a lido and a boating lake, it's also home to a superb playground (*see p121*). Check online for up-and-coming events, which include some brilliant guided walks: bats, autumn leaves and tree identification are among the themes. *See also p102* **Great Days Out**. *Buggy access. Cafés. Disabled access: toilet. Nappy-changing facilities. Restaurant.*

Regent's Park

NW1 4NR (7486 7905, 7724 4069 boating lake, www.royalparks.org.uk). Baker Street, Camden Town, Great Portland Street or Regent's Park tube. **Open** 5am-dusk daily. **Admission** free. **Map** p314 G3.
This grand circular park was designed by John Nash as the Prince Regent's garden for a summer house that was never built. With its sports fields, boating lake, several playgrounds, rose garden and the star attractions of London Zoo and the Open Air Theatre within its boundaries, this is a park with something for everyone. *See also p122* **Great Days Out**. *Buggy access. Cafés. Disabled access: toilet. Nappy-changing facilities. Restaurant.*

Richmond Park

Richmond, Surrey TW10 5HS (8948 3209, www.royalparks.org.uk). Richmond tube/rail/ Norbiton rail. **Open** *Summer* 7am-dusk. *Winter* 7.30am-dusk. **Admission** free.

Go down to the woods

Leafy escapes from the Big Smoke

There's something magical about woodlands, but they are a scarce resource within urban areas, in an age where scrubland and dense plantation are seen as enemies of public safety (someone might be lurking there!). The **Woodland Trust** (www.woodlandtrust. org.uk) manages over 1,000 sites across the UK, and a significant number of them fall within the M25.

Take Ruffet & Big Wood near Purley, with its bluebells in spring and views of south London and the City, or Merry Hill near Bushey Heath – former farmland that's now a mixture of open meadows and woodland planted with native broadleaf trees (there's a young orchard here too). Then there's Joyden's Wood near Dartford, which has cycling and horse riding tracks as well as footpaths, and whose hilltop setting affords great views over London (also look out for the remains of two Iron Age Roundhouses).

The website is great for fans of the natural world, even if you don't plan a visit to one of the Woodland Trust's woods. There are endless free activity sheets to download from the site, including spotter sheets and nature trails for all seasons, crafty make-a-mask/build-a-nest/make-a-bag sheets, treasure hunt scrapbooks, woodland adventure booklets, animal track sheets and fauna-themed trump cards.

Keep an eye out for events too; there's nothing more satisfying than planting a tree, or going on a nature walk with someone who really knows their stuff.

This is the largest of London's Royal Parks; indeed, it's the biggest city park in Europe. Herds of red and fallow deer roam freely, a source of endless fascination for children. The park is also home to two shire horses called Billy and Massey and all sorts of birds and insects. Children who don't get out of town much should be taken straight to the Isabella Plantation, a tranquil woodland garden that's dotted with streams and bridges. Planted with azaleas, magnolias and rhododendrons, it's best seen in all its glory in early summer or late September.

There are plenty of places to picnic, and the park's Petersham Gate has a playground. From the top of nearby King Henry VIII's mound (the hot-tempered king had a hunting lodge here), you get a spectacular view right across London. Alternatively, you could stroll along Terrace Walk, a Victorian promenade that runs from philosopher Bertrand Russell's childhood home, Pembroke Lodge (now a licensed café, and a good lunch spot), and beyond the park to Richmond Hill. A well-kept cycle path follows the perimeter; hire kids' bikes and adult bikes with tag-alongs or kid's seats from Roehampton Gate (7581 1188). There are several good spots for kiting and lessons in power kiting are available (www.kitevibe.com). Like all the Royal Parks, Richmond hosts a summer events programme for families. For details, consult the notice at the gate lodge or check out the website. *Buggy access. Disabled access: toilet. Café. Restaurant.*

St James's Park

SW1A 2JB (7930 1793, www.royalparks. org.uk). St James's Park tube/3, 11, 12, 24, 53, 211 bus. **Open** 5am-midnight daily. **Admission** free. **Map** p317 K8.

St James's is surrounded by three palaces; Westminster (the Houses of Parliament), St James's and Buckingham. It's the park that keeps closest to its royal connections, with the Changing of the Guard and the Trooping of the Colour taking place on Horse Guards Parade. There's also a rich array of wildlife to spot, from pelicans and black swans to incredibly tame grey squirrels. The latter will eat from your hand – though watch out, as they can be vicious little critters. There's a playground up near the Buckingham Palace end, and some allotments where demonstration gardeners offer advice from May to September. *See also p36* **Great Days Out**. *Buggy access. Café. Disabled access: toilet. Nappy-changing facilities. Restaurant.*

WILDLIFE SANCTUARIES

Camley Street Natural Park

12 Camley Street, NW1 0PW (7833 2311, www.wildlondon.org.uk). King's Cross tube/ rail. **Open** 10am-5pm daily. **Admission** free. **Map** p315 L2.

Camley Street was created from an old coal yard in 1984, and a visit here is a reminder that beautiful things come in small packages. It sits

Sightseeing

on the banks of Regent's Canal, and is run by the London Wildlife Trust. It's cheering that this small oasis of wildlife has been left to flourish within the King's Cross development.

Enter the wrought iron gates and explore the winding nature trails, ponds and lovingly-tended gardens. The wood-cabin visitors' centre has nature displays and resident rabbits, plus a large, bulrushed pond full of frogs, newts and other slimy creatures that kids adore. From 10am to 3pm on Saturdays and Sundays, children can come pond-dipping and insect-hunting, assisted by park volunteers; special events for kids also run throughout the year. *Buggy access. Disabled access: toilet. Nappy-changing facilities.*

East Ham Nature Reserve

Norman Road, E6 4HN (8470 4525). East Ham tube/Beckton DLR. **Open** *call for details.* **Admission** *free.*

Managed as a nature reserve since 1977, this green spot occupies the site of the largest churchyard in London, and has three beguiling nature trails to follow. The funny little museum comprises a small room dotted with stuffed birds and mammals (all looking a little on the weary side), as well as cases of full of beetles and butterflies. *Buggy access. Disabled access: toilet.*

Greenwich Peninsula Ecology Park

Thames Path, John Harrison Way, SE10 0QZ (8293 1904, www.urbanecology.org.uk). North Greenwich tube/108, 161, 422, 472, 486 bus. **Open** *10am-5pm Wed-Sun.* **Admission** *free.*

In the middle of an urban, industrial peninsular overlooking the Thames, the Ecology Park is a pond-dipping, bird-watching paradise. The park is reserved for school visits on Mondays and Tuesdays; the rest of the week, you'll have this wetland area, with its woodland, marsh, meadowland, lakes and streams, all to yourself. *Buggy access. Disabled access: toilet. Nappy-changing facilities.*

Gunnersbury Triangle Nature Reserve

Bollo Lane, W4 5LW (8747 3881, www.wild london.org.uk). Chiswick Park tube. **Open** *Reserve 24hrs daily. Information Cabin call for details.* **Admission** *free.*

With its woodland, marsh and meadowland, this nature reserve is the scene of much ecological activity. It is run by the London Wildlife Trust and offers conservation workshops and free activities for kids. When the small information cabin is open you can pick up trail leaflets, find out about tours and hire a net for pond-dipping purposes. Bikes and dogs are not allowed. *Buggy access.*

Highgate Wood & Queen's Wood

Muswell Hill Road, N10 3JN (8444 6129, www.cityoflondon.gov.uk/openspaces). Highgate tube/43, 134, 263 bus. **Open** *7.30am-dusk daily.* **Admission** *free.*

Queen's Wood is the quieter section of this vast woodland park – originally part of the ancient Forest of Middlesex – perhaps because it offers some very steep climbs. Its dense oaks and hornbeams drown out traffic noise, giving the impression that you're rambling through a wild

Bubble fun

Summer arts events across the capital's green spaces.

Portavilion has been a feature of summer across London's parks since 2008. Its latest incarnation, 'Rosy, the ballerina', a be-ribboned pink bubble created by German art and architecture collective Raumlaborberlin, will be pirouetting around the capital's green spaces until 30 September 2010.

The portable pavilion will host a number of interactive arts events, featuring some big-name cultural institutions. The most child-friendly of these include the Big Dance event in Lloyd Park on 27 June as part of Waltham Forest Green Fair (in which Rosy will be a talking garden

of performance, music and installation); the Greenwich World Festival at **Eltham Palace** (*see p39*) on 4 July (expect a free programme of dance, music, circus and theatre); Croydon's Big Dance Bubble Festival on 9 July (where Rosy will host performances, dance jams and workshops); and Culture Bubble with the Roundhouse in **Regent's Park** (*see p124*) from 2-4 August (during which, young people aged 12-19 can sign up for different free activities such as drama, photography and spoken word). See www.upprojects.com/portavilion/ events for full details.

Epping Forest. See p128.

wood miles from the city. Listen out for the woodpeckers, whose pecking reverberates around the sun-dappled glades. There's also a deeply thrilling rope swing, if you can find it.

More popular than Queen's Wood is the flatter Highgate Wood on the other side of Muswell Hill Road, where the wide paths suit buggies and budding cyclists. Head into the less well-trodden areas for a proper adventure. For families, the centrepiece of Highgate Woods is its large, well-equipped playground, complete with sandpits, climbing equipment of various levels of difficulty and a flying fox ride that gets very busy at peak times. Great thought has gone into providing fun and challenges for the various age groups, and there's a separate area for the under-fives to call their own. The playground is pleasantly shady in summer – cooler for all concerned, as well as making hats and sun cream less of a repetitive chore. Highgate's other great asset is its café (see p235), reached by crossing the cricket pitch. The food is the usual park fare – soups, pasta dishes and cake predominate – but the quality is a cut above what you'll find elsewhere. Throughout the year, an imaginative set of activities is offered in the woods, from outdoor storytelling sessions to evening bat watches, beetle safaris and treasure hunts. Consult the website before setting out, as some events require pre-booking.
Buggy access. Café. Disabled access: toilet. Nappy-changing facilities.

Islington Ecology Centre
Gillespie Park Nature Reserve, 191 Drayton Park, N5 1PH (7527 4374, www.islington. gov.uk). Arsenal tube. **Open** *Park* 8am-dusk daily. Closed Arsenal FC weekend home matches. *Centre* 9am-4pm Mon-Fri; noon-4pm Sun. **Admission** free.

Islington is short on green spaces, but those it has have diverse identities. Ecology Centre staff at Islington's largest nature reserve are endlessly enthusiastic and helpful on the subject of all things ecological. Fashioned from derelict railway land in the 1980s, the site has woods, meadows, wetland and ponds, with the Ecology Centre forming its educational heart. The events programme includes plenty of family-orientated events, from moth evenings to craft sessions. Nature-themed workshops run in the holidays; ring for details.
Buggy access.

London Wildlife Trust Centre for Wildlife Gardening
28 Marsden Road, SE15 4EE (7252 9186, www.wildlondon.org.uk). East Dulwich rail. **Open** 10.30am-4.30pm Tue-Thur, Sun. **Admission** free.
This leafy site was once an unlovely council bus depot, until the London Wildlife Trust took it on in the late 1980s. It's now a firm favourite with green-fingered Peckham families, who head off on nature forays amid the woodland and marshland. There's a herb garden, a pond area and a nursery for plants and trees; here, locals can pick up plants for their own gardens, giving a donation to the LWT. For children, there's a play area, sandpit and parent-and-toddler group, and the visitors' centre has tanks of fish and stick insects to peep at.
Buggy access. Disabled access: toilet. Nappy-changing facilities. Shop.

Parkland Walk
NE London (Finsbury Park, Stroud Green, Crouch End, Highgate Muswell Hill) N4, N8, N6, N10 (www.parkland-walk.org.uk). Finsbury Park tube, Highgate Tube, Crouch Hill BR. **Open** 24hrs daily. **Admission** free.

Sightseeing

The longest nature reserve in London runs the length of the disused Northern Heights railway line that links Finsbury Park with Highgate, and Highgate with Alexandra Palace, cutting through the terraced backs of Stroud Green, Crouch End and Muswell Hill on the way. The path was resurfaced in spring 2009, so it's less muddy than it used to be, but retains a hint of wilderness you won't find in most of London's parks (and offers great potential for snooping into other people's gardens too).

Highgate to Finsbury Park is the longer and more interesting stretch, and a gentle downhill stroll all the way; it's also a popular cycle route that's a safe ride for kids. Just after the disused platforms of the old Crouch End Station, look out for the Spriggan climbing out of one of the arches – a quietly disconcerting sculpture by Marilyn Collins, that's said to have inspired Stephen King to write his short story 'Crouch End'.

The Parkland Walk heads into Finsbury Park at the Oxford Road Gate; straight ahead, weary walkers can seek refreshment in the café by the boating lake. Finsbury Park's fantastic playground, built with a £5 million Heritage Lottery Fund, is also close by, but kids also love the dishevelled playground halfway down the walk with its brilliant rope swings, wooden walkways and long slides down the steep bank.

WIDE OPEN SPACES

Epping Forest

Information Centre, High Beech, Loughton, Essex IG10 4AF (8508 0028, www.cityof london.gov.uk/openspaces). Loughton or Theydon Bois tube/Chingford rail. **Open** *Information Centre* Summer 11am-6pm daily. Winter 10am-3pm daily. *Forest* 24hrs daily. **Admission** free.

Epping Forest is 12 miles (19km) long and several miles across, and was saved from development by the Corporation of London in 1878. Commoners still have grazing rights and, each summer, English Longhorn cattle can be seen chewing the cud. For most visitors, it's the walking, horse riding or cycling opportunities that are the biggest draw. The forest contains Iron Age earthworks and two listed buildings – the Temple in Wanstead Park (*see p120*) and the 16th-century Queen Elizabeth's Hunting Lodge (Rangers Road, E4 7QH, 8529 6681; under-16s must be accompanied by an adult). The latter has a quiz trail, weekend craft activities and Tudor-themed dressing up; in the kitchen area, you can smell food made from 400-year-old recipes.

Work on the Branching Out Project began in August and will take five years to complete.

Using Heritage Lottery money, there are plans for a new Interpretation Centre next door to Queen Elizabeth's Hunting Lodge; an education programme; improved trails and a visitor hub to encourage visitors to go deeper into the forest.

If you're coming by public transport, be prepared for some exercise. Chingford railway station gives access to the Hunting Lodge and some lovely strolls at the south end. Loughton and Theydon Bois (Central line) are the forest's nearest tube stops, though it's a two-mile uphill walk from both. The best advice is to get a map and plan your route in advance – or take the car. At High Beech car park there's a small tea hut, as well as the Epping Forest Field Centre. *Buggy access. Disabled access: toilet. Nappy-changing facilities. Shop.*

Lee Valley Park

NE London (Hackney, Walthamstow, Waltham Abbey, Cheshunt, Broxbourne, Hoddesdon) E10-EN11 (01992 717711, www.leevalley park.org.uk). **Open** 24hrs daily. **Admission** varies; phone or check website for details.

Incredibly, this long, thin park on both sides of the River Lee stretches 26 miles from Hertfordshire all the way to the East India Dock Basin. It has a network of lakes, waterways, parks and countryside areas, and there's plenty to do. A gentle guided walk is a good way to start; the well-signposted park is ideal for picnics, walking or fishing. It's also a nature lover's paradise. Some 32 species of mammals are said to make their home in the park, along with 21 species of dragonfly. Waymarked walks, some providing easy buggy access, take you to see orchids, grasshoppers and waterlilies. The birdwatching is excellent too.

Other attractions include the Lee Valley Riding Centre (*see p207*) and Lee Valley Ice Centre (*see p210*), which offers family sessions at the weekends and during school holidays. The erstwhile Lee Valley Cycle Circuit has been handed over to the Olympic builders to become a velopark in time for 2012. Lee Valley Boat Centre (Old Nazeing Road, Broxbourne, Herts EN10 7AX, 01992 462085, www.leevalleyboats. co.uk) hires boats by the hour and organises narrowboat holidays.

The fascinating town of Waltham Abbey, which borders the park, has plenty of cafés and shops and an Augustinian abbey, founded in 1060 by King Harold. The Royal Gunpowder Mills (Beaulieu Drive, Waltham Abbey, Essex EN9 1JY, 01992 707370, www.royalgunpower mills.com) and Epping Forest (*see above*) are also just a ten-minute drive from the town. *Buggy access. Disabled access: toilet. Kiosk. Nappy-changing facilities.*

Meet the Animals

A safari in the heart of London.

London may be a dense urban city, but it actually has the most diverse range of animal species in the UK thanks to its zoos, city farms, aquariums and wetland and nature reserves. From gorillas, tigers and llamas to rare-breed pigs, cows and sheep; from scorpions, sharks and turtles to giant rabbits, parrots and Komodo dragons, they're all here. Below we list the best places to see all these amazing creatures, but it's worth looking at the **Parks & Gardens** chapter too (*see pp105-128*), as some parks also have animal enclosures.

AQUARIUMS

Horniman Museum

100 London Road, SE23 3PQ (8699 1872, www.horniman.ac.uk). Forest Hill rail/176, 185, 197, 356, P4 bus. **Open** 10.30am-5.30pm daily. **Admission** free; donations appreciated. **Credit** MC, V.

This fantastic gem of a museum (*see p74*) has an amazing aquarium, which houses hundreds of species of aquatic animals and plants across seven distinct zones. Recent additions include a very large lobster, some young seahorses and a clutch of anableps, whose more common name is the four-eyed fish (they only have two eyes but can see above and below the water simultaneously). Visitors working their way around explore the diverse nature of ecosystems from across the globe and read about the threats such fragile environments face. Ecosystems covered include British pond life, Devonshire rockpools, Fijian coral reefs, mangrove swamps and South American rainforests. The tank-viewing dens and interactive displays are always a favourite with children. The aquarium is currently conducting a specialised study of newts (which can be found in the Horniman garden's nature trail) and how their capacity for limb regeneration might be of use to human medicine. Check the website for details of events and activities.

Buggy access. Café. Disabled access: lift, toilet. Nappy-changing facilities. Nearest picnic place: museum gardens. Shop.

Sea Life London Aquarium

County Hall (riverfront entrance), Riverside Building, SE1 7PB (7967 8000, 7967 8002 tours, www.londonaquarium.co.uk). Westminster tube/Waterloo tube/rail. **Open** 10am-6pm Mon-Fri (last entry 5pm); 10am-7pm Sat, Sun (last entry 6pm). *Tours* (groups of 10 or more) phone for details. **Admission** £17.50; £16 reductions; £12.50 3-14s; free under-3s; £54 family (2+2). **Credit** MC, V. **Map** p317 M9.

Prices for entry to this popular attraction in the old riverside offices of local goverment have risen significantly again this year, despite the economic climate. However, it's hard to be churlish once inside the aquarium itself. The big draw this year is the revamped Rainforests of the World area – complete with crocodiles, poison arrow frogs and piranhas (best seen at feeding time). Woodchip underfoot is a nice atmospheric touch, making children feel as if they are embarking on a real adventure. Another favourite attraction is the Shark Walk, where a floating glass platform allows visitors to walk just above where sharks are swimming. Around the aquarium, there are hundreds of varieties of fish and sea life from all over the world, including stingrays, Californian cownose rays and sea scorpions. We particularly like the tunnel constructed from a 25-metre-long whale skeleton, beneath which visitors can view a tropical ocean of fish, coral and green turtles.

To get the best value, time your visit to coincide with feeding times (check the website for the day's schedule); the sharks are usually fed at 2.30pm. If you're pushing a buggy, enter and leave from the London Eye side; you'll avoid McDonald's and the tricky steps up to Westminster Bridge.

Buggy access. Disabled access: lift, toilet. Nappy-changing facilities. Nearest picnic place: Jubilee Gardens. Shop.

FARMS

Belmont City Farm

Mill Hill, London, NW7 1QT (8959 3308, www.belmontfarm.co.uk). Crystal Palace rail. **Open** *Mar-Oct* 8am-6pm Mon-Fri; 9am-6pm Sat, Sun. *Nov-Feb* 8am-5pm Mon-Fri; 9am-5pm Sat, Sun. **Admission** £4; free-£2 reductions.

Sightseeing

This farm in north-west London opened its doors at the end of 2009. It is home to alpacas and wallabies as well as more traditional farm animals like goats, pigs, cows and chickens. The enclosures are clearly marked with information about individual species (factsheets can also be downloaded from the website before a visit). Even the parents might learn something: that goats have square pupils rather than round ones, for example, or that it takes three times as long to digest cow's milk as goat's milk. Weekends are the best time to go for a close encounter of the furry kind; children can join in at feeding sessions between 10am and 4pm (see daily timetable on arrival) or pet the smaller animals between 11am and noon and 3pm to 4pm. At the centre of the site, the café specialises in waffles. There's a range of savoury and sweet options, with wholemeal and wheat free waffles also available. All-day breakfasts are popular with everyone, and kids get their own menu, with a drink and a main course for £3.95.

Crystal Palace Park Farm

The Croft, Ledrington Road, SE19 2BS (8778 5572, www.crystalpalaceparkfarm.co.uk). Crystal Palace rail. **Open** 10.30am-noon, 2.30-4pm Mon, Tue, Thur, Fri; noon-4pm Sat, Sun & bank hols. **Admission** free.

This farm was shut for many years, with only the animal paintings on the old stable doors left to remind park visitors of its former use. However, Crystal Palace Park Farm reopened in April 2008, much to the delight of local residents. Set within the park, it's a city farm with a small yard and paddocks with the added bonus of lovely views.

There are kune pigs, alpacas, goats, Shetland ponies and a reptile room. Children will like climbing the steep ramp to see the smaller mammals. The facility is very well used by local schools, who get guided tours with an education officer. In the afternoons, casual visitors can often handle the smaller animals, if there's a free member of staff handy. The neighbouring Capel Manor College (8778 5572,

Battersea Dogs & Cats Home
One to take home...

Petting animals in London's city farms, and observing wild creatures in its zoos and aquariums is exciting, sure, but there's nothing quite as thrilling as owning a pet. So, once the calls and clamours have reached fever pitch and the excuses have been exhausted, it's time to get serious. **Battersea Dogs and Cats Home** (4 Battersea Park Road, SW8 4AA, 7622 3626, www.battersea. org.uk) is a good place to start the search for a furry, four-legged friend, and parents don't have to promise anything beforehand, as casual visitors are as welcome as those coming

with definite plans to take an animal home (bear in mind that the adoption process can take several visits). It is 150 years since Mrs Mary Tealby opened a temporary refuge for lost and starving dogs; the home quickly became famous when the likes of Charles Dickens and Queen Victoria lent their support and patronage. A programme of events celebrates the anniversary in 2010, including a reunion of furry alumni in Battersea Park on 12 September. There's a shop and a café on site. *Battersea Dogs and Cats Home is open 1-4pm Mon-Fri; 10.30am-4pm Sat, Sun.*

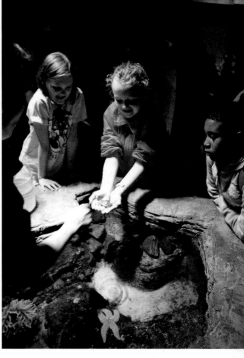

Sea Life London Aquarium. *See p129.*

www.capel.ac.uk) runs full time animal care courses for 16- to 18-year-olds. There's no café on site, but the surrounding park is perfect for leisurely family picnics.
Buggy access. Disabled access: ramp, toilet. Nappy-changing facilities. Nearest picnic place: Crystal Palace Park.

Deen City Farm & Community Garden

39 Windsor Avenue, SW19 2RR (8543 5300, www.deencityfarm.co.uk). Colliers Wood tube, then 200 bus. **Open** 10am-4.30pm Tue-Sun, bank hols. **Admission** free; donations appreciated. **No credit cards.**
This farm is a member of the Rare Breeds Survival Trust and is home to a wide range of unusual species. Set on beautiful National Trust land within the Morden Hall Park Estate, it is noticeably different from London's other city farms. The strutting white peacocks parade their spectacular feathers, often accompanied by a competitively exhibitionist turkey. Meanwhile the other animals quietly compete for visitors' attention; there are Shetland sheep, pigs, cows, ducks, chickens and geese, alpacas and a huddle of rabbits and guinea pigs that you can handle at certain times (check when you arrive). There's a generous area used for pony rides – it's £1 per ride for the under-eights on Wednesdays (noon), weekends (3pm) and school holidays –

and the sandwiches and cakes in the cheerful café are refreshingly cheap (children's lunch packs are £3.50).
Buggy access. Café. Disabled access: toilet. Nappy-changing facilities. Nearest picnic place: Morden Hall Park. Shop.

Freightliners City Farm

Paradise Park, Sheringham Road, off Liverpool Road, N7 8PF (7609 0467, www.freightlinersfarm.org.uk). Caledonian Road or Holloway Road tube/Highbury & Islington tube/rail. **Open** *Summer* 10am-4.45pm Tue-Sun, bank hols. *Winter* 10am-4pm Tue-Sun. **Admission** free; donations appreciated. **No credit cards.**
It's hard to believe that busy Holloway Road has a farm just behind it. The half-hectare site is as much community centre as working farm, with cookery lessons running in the café, volunteer bee-keeping activities and a Dad's Club on Saturday mornings. There's a weekly gardening club on Wednesdays, an Adopt an Animal scheme and a very busy timetable of events throughout the school holidays (check the website for details). You can even hold a party on the farm.
Freightliners is home to amiable cows, sheep, goats and two pigs called Tina and Tamara, as well as all kinds of poultry. The collection of animals, many of them rare breeds, is impressive. Giant Flemish rabbits are the

Mudchute City Farm. *See p137.*

biggest you'll see anywhere, while exotic cockerels with feathered feet squawk in your path. You can buy hen and duck eggs of all hues, plus seasonal, own-grown fruit, vegetables and plants. The café, built by volunteers out of green oak and straw bales, is open on Friday, Saturday and Sunday and serves homemade soup, salads, sandwiches and cakes; it offers a healthy children's menu too.

Buggy access. Café. Disabled access: toilet. Nappy-changing facilities. Nearest picnic place: farm picnic area. Shop.

Hackney City Farm

1A Goldsmiths Row, E2 8QA (7729 6381, www.hackneycityfarm.co.uk). Cambridge Heath Road rail, then 26, 48, 55 bus. **Open** 10am-4.30pm Tue-Sun, bank hols. **Admission** free; donations appreciated. **Credit** MC, V.

Rural it ain't, but this tiny, bucolic idyll is much appreciated by residents in one of the least leafy corners of London. Around the small courtyard, outbuildings house some very pretty Golden Guernsey goats, sheep, pigs, Larry the donkey, chickens, geese and ducks, along with some smaller, fluffier animals, including rabbits and guinea pigs. The larger animals get to frolic in a small field out back during the day. The farm does a healthy trade in eggs, and started pig production late in 2008 by bringing in some Tamworth pigs from Mudchute City Farm.

The inviting farm garden has raised beds full of seasonal vegetables, a plant nursery and a play area with a sandpit, wigwams and trails. Award-winning onsite café Frizzante (*see p227*) sources ingredients locally where possible and offers rustic food inspired by regional Italian cooking. It's worth checking out the noticeboard for activities aimed at children and parents; popular pottery drop-in sessions cost £5 for two hours.

Buggy access. Café. Disabled access: toilet. Nappy-changing facilities. Nearest picnic place: gardens. Shop.

Hounslow Urban Farm

A312 at Faggs Road, Feltham, Middx TW14 0LZ (8831 9658, www.hounslow.info). Hatton Cross tube, then 15min walk or 90, 285, 490 bus. **Open** *Summer* 10am-5.30pm daily (last entry 4.30pm). *Winter* 11am-4pm Sat, Sun (last entry 3pm). Times & days may vary, phone or check website for details. **Admission** £4.25-£5; £3.50-£4.25 reductions; £2.75-£3.50 2-16s; free under-2s; £12-£15 family (2+2). **No credit cards.**

London's largest community farm rears rare, endangered and historic breeds as part of a conservation programme, and offers plenty of opportunities for petting and feeding. Bags of feed are on sale at the shop, which also sells cuddly toys, peacock feathers and all manner of animal-themed souvenirs, and gives shelter to the farm's parrot and its lounge of lizards. Within its 29 acres, the farm houses British saddleback pigs, goats, ducks, Shetland ponies, alpacas, chipmunks and a recently arrived donkey. Turn up at the right time of year and you could be lucky enough to feed the orphan lambs and peek at the piglets. You can even buy a small animal – such as a rabbit or a guinea pig – and get some helpful care advice. Activities are held daily and throughout the school holidays: animal handling, scarecrow-making and pig racing might feature, with a children's entertainer on bank holiday Mondays and every Tuesday during the holidays. There is a picnic area and a shop, and a brace of new pedal tractors in the playground.

Buggy access. Shop. Disabled access: toilet. Nappy-changing facilities. Nearest picnic place: farm picnic area.

Kentish Town City Farm

1 Cressfield Close, off Grafton Road, NW5 4BN (7916 5421, www.ktcityfarm.org.uk). Chalk Farm tube/Kentish Town tube/rail/ Gospel Oak rail. **Open** 9am-5pm daily. **Admission** free; donations appreciated. **No credit cards**.

Just a short walk from Parliament Hill Fields is London's oldest city farm. The name may have changed since 1972, when it was known as Fun Art Farm, but the ethos remains the same. This was the model for London's other community led city farms, and provides much more than a chance to gawp at some livestock. The site is far larger than first appearances suggest, stretching along the back of the railway, way beyond the farmyard into fields and well-tended vegetable gardens. There's also a frog-filled pond with a dipping platform to investigate.

Livestock includes farmyard ducks, goats, pigs, horses, cows, chickens and sheep, with some rare breeds. As well as petting the animals, children can get involved with their care by mucking out (arrive by 9am), feeding them (with supervision) and taking care of the site. During the holidays, a host of activities are held in the farm centre and children's parties can be held here at weekends (hire includes use of the kitchen). Drop-in play and singsong sessions for the under-fives take place during the week, as well as after-school clubs like practical city farming, pottery and cookery classes. There's a three- year waiting list to join the Camden Pony Club, which is based here, but the Riding School offers weekend pony rides from March to September, weather permitting (1.30pm, Sat & Sun, £1). The farm welcomes school visits from all boroughs, and holds May Day celebrations, a summer horse show, an Easter egg hunt, Apple Day activities and a Christmas fair.

Buggy access. Disabled access: toilet. Nappy-changing facilities. Nearest picnic place: farm grounds.

Rich pickings: produce at **Hackney City Farm**.

Great Days Out
Marylebone

The first thing children need to learn is how to pronounce the area's name (clue: it doesn't sound like a girl's name followed by a French dog's snack). Bounded by brash, busy Oxford Street to the south and stately Regent's Park to the north, Marylebone is an affable (and affluent) little enclave. Its leafy squares, terraces of Georgian townhouses and boutique-lined high street are perfect for a leisurely stroll – particularly on Sundays, when one of London's largest farmer's markets sets up shop here.

Once the children's tolerance for shopping has worn off, Regent's Park is a hop, skip and a jump away, while for rainy days, the Wallace Collection is a little-known treasure. Kids may be unmoved by the promise of Old Masters and 18th-century porcelain, but the magnificent armoury is another matter entirely. And there's always Madame Tussaud's…

Up in arms

Entrance to the **Wallace Collection** (*see p68*), a grand, 18th-century townhouse-turned-museum, is absolutely free; inside, all sorts of treasures await. Anyone with a penchant for chivalry, derring-do and gory battles will be enraptured by the array of armour and weaponry, ranging from gold-inlaid scimitars and creepy, beak-fronted helmets to mighty cannons and gleaming suits.

Elsewhere, you can gawp at Frans Hals' *Laughing Cavalier* (sporting a magnificent moustache), marvel at Louis XV's commode and admire Catherine the Great's lovely Sèvres porcelain ice-cream cooler.

Kids can try the weighty suits of armour on for size in the Conservation Gallery, or pick up a free Warrior Kings trail – which takes you round all manner of jewel-encrusted weaponry. Visiting on the first Sunday of the month? Then prepare to

London Zoo.

get sketching at one of the Little Draw drop-in workshops. There are also armour-handling, hat-designing and watercolour painting sessions on the busy events calendar; most cost a mere £4.

Wax lyrical

If all that sounds terribly serious and you've got cash to burn, you could head down to the gaudy attractions of **Madame Tussaud's** (see p54). Where else could you have your picture taken next to Amy Winehouse, Johnny Depp and the Queen in one afternoon? Yes, when it comes down to it they're just waxwork models, but Madame Tussaud's isn't world famous by accident; a lot of effort has been put in to contextualising the figures and providing interactive excitement. The Spirit of London ride in a small version of a London taxi is our personal favourite.

Head upmarket

Marylebone is a mecca for foodies, thanks to fine food emporiums such as La Fromagerie and the Ginger Pig (both on Moxon Street), and a host of swish restaurants. More exciting to children is the vibrant **Marylebone Farmer's Market** (www.lfm.org.uk), where grown-ups can sample slivers of whiffy cheese and compare olive oils while kids eye up the slabs of home-made cake. It's held on Sunday mornings in the Cramer Street car park, which is just off the high street. If you're around on Saturday, head for the chichi **Cabbages & Frocks** (www.cabbagesandfrocks.co.uk) market, in the grounds of St Mary's Parish Church. Friendly stallholders sell jewellery and clothes alongside salamis, artisan breads and all sorts of on-the-spot little somethings to keep you going until lunch. Topped with pastel swirls of icing and covered with pretty handmade sugar flowers, Peggy's Cupcakes are irresistible.

Coming up roses

To work off your foodie excesses in the fresh air, head north for **Regent's Park** (see p124), one of London's most genteel patches of green. In early summer, the breeze is particularly fragrant, as the Inner Circle's magnificent rose gardens come into bloom. There's plenty of resident wildlife, too, particularly around the lakes (where you can take a boat out for half an hour or more). In summer, families might want to plan ahead and see a puppet show or family friendly Shakespeare at the **Open Air Theatre** (see p189), but there's always plenty of sport to watch as well, on the many pitches up on the north side.

Also at the north end of the park, the delights of the famous **London Zoo** (see p140) await. Though its entrance charges are substantial, the zoo does offer an inimitable day out. There are far too many attractions to list – though we've got a particularly soft spot for the gorillas, the tireless ants in B.U.G.S., the Komodo dragon in the reptile house, and the incredible tigers. Tons of special events run throughout the day, too, from storytelling sessions in the brilliant Animal Adventure children's zoo and play area to meet-the-spider events, to Animals in Action (where birds and small mammals perform tricks to demonstrate their evolutionary adaptations) and the classic penguins' feeding time.

LUNCH BOX

Also in the area: Ask, Carluccio's Caffè, Paul, Ping Pong, Pizza Express, Tootsies Grill, Wagamama.

Boathouse Café *The Boating Lake, Hanover Gate, Regent's Park NW1 4NU (7724 4069).* Survey the boating lake from the ample terrace at this family-friendly joint, which serves pizza, pasta and snacks.

Fishworks *89 Marylebone High Street, W1U 4QW (7935 9796, www.fishworks.co.uk).* The £5 kids' menu includes fishfingers, fish cakes and mussels, with ice-cream to follow; or there's spaghetti in tomato sauce.

Golden Hind *73 Marylebone Lane, W1U 2PN (7486 3644).* Proper fish and chips, kids' portions and a warm welcome for families.

Honest Sausage *Inner Circle, off Chester Road, Regent's Park NW1 4NU (7224 3872, www.honest sausage.com).* Bacon butties or free-range bangers, served in a bread bun or atop a heap of mash.

Great Days Out

Lee Valley Park Farms

Stubbins Hall Lane, Crooked Mile, Waltham Abbey, Essex EN9 2EF (01992 892781, www.leevalleypark.org.uk). Broxbourne or Cheshunt rail. **Open** *Mid Feb-Oct* 10am-5pm daily. Closed Nov-mid Feb. **Admission** £7; £5.60 reductions, 2-16s; free under-2s; £28 family (2+3). **Credit** MC, V.

There are actually two farms here. Hayes Hill is a traditional farm and rare-breeds centre, while Holyfield Hall is its commercial neighbour. At Hayes Hill, try persuading your children that the animals are more exciting than the pedal tractors or the new soft play feature, Bundle Barn. They can also meet Tallulah the Tamworth and Barbara the Berkshire pig, as well as some Essex pigs (a seriously endangered species). Also in residence are Ella and Evie the goats, sheep, llamas, water buffalo and chickens. In the spring, visitors are encouraged to bottle-feed the new

Junior Keeper for the Day

Buckets of meat, and steaming piles of poo… It's all in a day's work at London Zoo.

It's been a while since Johnny Morris was on the telly, but even without his anthropomorphic animal exploits on the small screen, most kids love the idea of being cheek by jowl with wild animals, especially if they can take on the responsibility of looking after them.

London Zoo has been running Keeper for the Day packages for adults for several years, and in 2010 decided it was time for the children to have a go. Junior Keeper for a Day is aimed at 11- to 15-year-olds and costs £150 (which includes the entry price of an accompanying adult). Each group of three children gets their own keeper as a guide, who will lead them through the excitement of dung-sniffing, feeding and tending to the animals. Intentionally or otherwise, the scheme drives home the amount of thought and care that goes into looking after the animals. The food preparation area is hung with giant blackboards, one for each species, listing ways in which its life can be 'enriched'. So, for instance, one hippo likes to put things on its head, so keepers are encouraged to find things it can use for this. In the tigers' enclosure, perfume is smeared on trees to stimulate the tigers, encouraging them to leave their own scent. The zoo's intention is to maintain the animals' dignity and keep them content while ensuring they retain their natural instincts. Exceptions are made of the animals used in the zoo's 'Animal in Action' performances, when the junior 'keepers' might get to meet skunks (de-stinked, with soft fur), coatis (playful mammals from Central America) and kinkajou (cute regal mammals), literally face to face. Many of these animals were pets brought to the zoo after their owners got tired of looking after them, hence their ease around humans.

London Zoo isn't the only animal institution to allow children to go behind the scenes. The Sealife London Aquarium offers Junior Aquarist Days, where children aged ten to 16 can 'work' at the aquarium (it costs £195 and lasts from 10.30am to 5.30pm). The day begins in the food preparation area where buckets of dead squid and mackerel await. Junior Aquarists then get to help feed the rays, sea turtles, sharks, and other species, and clean out their habitats.

Junior Keeper for a Day: see www.zsl.org.
Junior Aquarist for a Day: see www.sealife.co.uk.

lambs. Stroking Rex the 'therapy' rabbit is another draw – but watch out for Newton the bearded dragon.

If all this all seems a bit cosy, then go and watch the cows being milked over at Holyfield Hall (from 2.30pm daily) and learn about large-scale dairy production. There are guided tours for school parties, tractor-trailer rides and pig races at various times throughout the year (weather permitting). *Buggy access. Café. Disabled access: toilet. Nappy-changing facilities. Nearest picnic place: farm picnic areas. Shop.*

Mudchute City Farm

Pier Street, Isle of Dogs, E14 3HP (7515 5901, www.mudchute.org). Crossharbour, Mudchute or Island Gardens DLR. **Open** 9am-5pm daily. **Admission** free; donations appreciated. **No credit cards**.
Sensitive landscaping blocks out the urban sprawl on this 27-acre plot, but the looming towers of Canary Wharf leave visitors in no doubt they are still in the city. Once the kids have seen the animals, there are lots of paths through well-established woods and hedgerows to explore; wherever you roam on site, you can still hear the donkeys. Early risers can join the duck walk at 9am, and kids can handle the smaller animals (including ferrets and guinea pigs) in Pets' Corner from 9.30am to 4pm. Visitors can also help to feed the larger animals – rare breed cows, Tamworth pigs, goats, llamas and horses – which adds to the excitement. Volunteers have done quite a bit to smarten up Mudchute in the past year. There's now a bread oven in the café, and the facilities are available for hire for private parties. There's an after-school club for five- to 12-year-olds and plenty of seasonal events to enjoy. The site lends itself to picnics, but the café is too good to ignore (*see p233*). *Buggy access. Café. Disabled access: toilet. Nappy-changing facilities. Nearest picnic place: farm grounds. Shop.*

Newham City Farm

Stansfeld Road, E6 5LT (7474 4960). Royal Albert DLR/262, 300, 376 bus. **Open** 10am-5pm Tue-Sun, bank hols. **Admission** free; donations appreciated. **No credit cards**.
Newham was established in the first wave of the city farm movement in London, and has been going strong now for over 30 years. Alongside the usual farmyard poultry, sheep, pigs and goats is the largest animal on the farm: Biaze, a shire horse, who pulls a dray cart that visitors can ride in. There are also some smaller, furrier chaps (rabbits, guinea pigs and

two ferrets), a twittering house of finches and a kookaburra. The visitors' centre runs plenty of holiday activities, such as the ever-popular 'Be a Farmer for a Day' sessions (you will need to book these in advance) and various other drop-in activities. Fun Days offer the likes of sheep-shearing demonstrations and felt-making and visitors can also taste the honey produced by bees from the farm's own hives. As well as some picnic space, there's a café serving teas, coffees and light snacks. *Buggy access. Café. Disabled access: toilet. Nappy-changing facilities. Nearest picnic place: farm picnic area. Shop.*

Spitalfields City Farm

Buxton Street, off Brick Lane, E1 5AR (7247 8762, www.spitalfieldscityfarm.org). Whitechapel tube. **Open** *Summer* 10am-4.30pm Tue-Sun. *Winter* 10am-4pm Tue-Sun. **Admission** free; donations appreciated. **No credit cards**.
Just around the corner from the gleaming towers of the City is this compact community farm. There's a daily goat-milking demo, mice and rabbits for stroking, and a full complement of cows, pigs and sheep. Children can take part in workshops on dairy farming, healthy eating, sustainability and animal welfare. Outside the farmyard, there is much to see. The Ideas Garden

Making friends at **Spitalfields City Farm**.

Sightseeing

WWT Wetland Centre

is a mini gardening museum, while another small patch is being planted up as a forest.

In spring, the Wildlife Garden is gorgeous, as bluebells, snowdrops and foxgloves nod in the pungent breeze, scented by wild garlic. Keen eight- to 13-year-olds can join the Young Farmers' Club, which runs a play scheme on Saturdays from 10.30am to 3.30pm. Veg, fruit and plants are on sale, and the new raised picnic area has a fire pit for cooking. Annual events include the Sheep and Wool Fayre in May, Apple Day in October and the Christmas Fair, with donkey rides for £1.

Buggy access. Disabled access: toilet. Nappy-changing facilities. Nearest picnic place: Allen Gardens. Shop.

Surrey Docks Farm

South Wharf, Rotherhithe Street, SE16 5ET (7231 1010, www.surreydocksfarm.org.uk). Canada Water tube, then 381, C10 bus.
Open 10am-5pm Tue-Sun. **Admission** free; donations appreciated. **No credit cards.**
The area around this Rotherhithe institution has changed dramatically since the farm was dreamt up in 1975, and it's now hemmed in by the gated developments and luxury flats of Surrey Quays. Sheep, goats and chickens mooch around a central farmyard, while out in the pens there are organically reared cows, pigs, donkeys and horses, fenced in by delightful wrought-metal railings – handiwork of resident blacksmith Kevin Boy. (This is the only City Farm in London to have a working forge on the premises, which offers classes to local schoolchildren.) Kids can also learn about food production from the dairy, milking barn, bee room, orchard, herb garden and vegetable plots. The farm café got a makeover in spring 2010 and is now open daily. If the kids seem inspired, they can return on the third Saturday of every month for the Young Farmers' Club (eight- to 13-year-olds) to learn more.

Buggy access. Café. Disabled access: toilet. Nearest picnic place: riverside. Shop.

Vauxhall City Farm

165 Tyers Street, SE11 5HS (7582 4204, www.vauxhallcityfarm.info). Vauxhall tube/rail/ 2, 36, 44, 77 bus. **Open** 10.30am-4pm Wed-Sun. **Admission** free; donations appreciated. **No credit cards.**

This tiny sliver of mud and muck is Vauxhall's answer to the countryside. Many of the animals – Poppy and Pepper, a pair of Anglo-Nubian goats, plus their black Wensleydale sheep friends – inhabit a specially constructed straw-bale animal house, built by Barbara Jones in 2001, with sedums on the roof to attract bees. Start here and then wander through to the duck pond and community garden. There's no café, but you can picnic near the rabbit and chicken enclosures. The farm runs pony-riding sessions in nearby Spring Gardens for children and riders with disabilities, hosts the Ruby Rhymes under-fives singing group on Fridays, and holds classes in art, spinning, dyeing and weaving (plants for natural dyes are grown in a special garden). Facilities are fairly basic – and the chatter of the radio can spoil the bucolic feel – but, together with the slippery pathways, cloying mud and occasional dollop of horse muck, this gives a passable representation of a working farm.

Buggy access. Disabled access: toilet. Nappy-changing facilities. Nearest picnic place: Spring Gardens.

Woodlands Farm

331 Shooters Hill, Welling, Kent DA16 3RP (8319 8900, www.thewoodlandsfarmtrust.org). Falconwood rail/89, 486 bus. **Open** 9.30am-4.30pm daily. **Admission** free; donations appreciated. **No credit cards**.

Woodlands Farm and the ancient Oxleas Wood were almost flattened by the Department of Transport to make way for a motorway. Public support saved the site and in 1997 it became one of Greater London's newest city farms. The farm's ideology is based on sustainable and organic methods of producing food. As well as its livestock, it has an award-winning cottage garden, a sensory garden and a wildlife garden, not to mention orchards and meadows. Residents include noisy geese, hens, guinea pigs, a flock of sheep, Daisy the British white cow and two Vietnamese pot-bellied pigs called Doris and Iris. The farm hosts educational group visits, giving lessons on conservation, composting, farm animal care and the history of farming. From 2010, there are free monthly children's activity workshops on the first Wednesday of the month (3.30-5.30pm). Also keep an eye on the events diary to see what's in the offing. The farm also sells logs, manure, eggs and hay at good prices. Children who sign up as volunteers can help feed and muck out the animals on Saturday mornings, but must be accompanied by a carer or parent; call the farm for details.

Buggy access. Café (weekends, summer only). Nearest picnic place: farm grounds. Shop.

WETLAND RESERVES

Greenwich Peninsula Ecology Park

Thames Path, John Harrison Way, SE10 0QZ (8293 1904, www.urbanecology.org.uk). North Greenwich tube/108, 161, 422, 472, 486 bus. **Open** 10am-5pm Wed-Sun. **Admission** free.

The construction of the Blackwall Tunnel destroyed much of the area's natural marshland, but it began to creep back after the gasworks were decommissioned late last century. This patch underwent a huge regeneration project in 1997 to become a freshwater habitat for frogs, toads, newts and many species of bird. There are themed quiz trails and word searches, and children can collect the materials to make paintings, collages or sketches. Take to the hides to watch the birds without disturbing them, or borrow the necessary equipment to get up close and personal with the wildlife (the visitors' centre provides pond-dipping nets, trays, magnifiers, bug jars and binoculars). Look at the website for details of drop-in activities during the school holidays.

Buggy access. Disabled access: toilet. Nappy-changing facilities. Nearest picnic place: Southern Park.

WWT Wetland Centre

Queen Elizabeth's Walk, SW13 9WT (8409 4400, www.wwt.org.uk/london). Hammersmith tube, then 33, 72, 209 (alight at Red Lion pub) or 283 bus (Duck Bus direct to Centre). **Open** *Summer* 9.30am-6pm daily. *Winter* 9.30am-5pm daily (last entry 1hr before closing). *Tours* 11am, 2pm daily. *Feeding tours* 3pm daily. **Admission** £9.95; £7.40 reductions; £5.50 4-16s; free under-4s; £27.75 family (2+2). *Tours* free. **Credit** MC, V.

Although it's not in the middle of town, this is one of London's best family days out. Set over 104 acres, the centre is home to rare international bird species such as New Zealand's beautiful black swans and white-faced whistling ducks, while every season brings new migratory visitors, including lapwings, hobbies and ospreys. There's a bat house, plus six observation hides; the largest is the three-storey Peacock Tower, which even has a lift. There's a new 'rain' garden due to open in summer 2010, that makes the most of natural water supplies. At its centre, a pavilion (an old shipping container disguised by grass) teaches visitors to conserve water in their own gardens at home.

Sightseeing

You can take free guided tours with well-informed, friendly bird-watchers, or simply enjoy romping around the paths past the main lake, reed beds, ponds and wetland meadows. The Discovery Centre is a game attempt at recreating wetland habitats – such as mangrove swamps – indoors (fibreglass crocodiles and all), and there are various water-based games for the kids to try. Children aged three to 11 will happily ignore the birds and play for hours in the adventure playground, shooting through the water-vole tunnels, tackling the climbing walls and flying through the air on zip wires. There's a self-service restaurant with lovely views over the main lake, which offers a tempting array of edibles.

Buggy access. Café. Disabled access: lift, toilet. Nappy-changing facilities. Nearest picnic place: centre picnic areas. Shop.

ZOOS

Battersea Park Children's Zoo

Queenstown Road, Battersea Park, SW11 4NJ (7924 5826, www.batterseazoo.co.uk). Sloane Square tube, then 19, 137 bus/ Battersea Park or Queenstown Road rail/ 156, 345 bus. **Open** *Summer* 10am-5pm daily (last entry 4.30pm). *Winter* 10am-4pm daily. **Admission** £7.50; £6 3-15s; free under-2s; £25 family (2+2). **Credit** MC, V. **Map** p313 F13.

Those who find London Zoo overwhelming in terms of visitor numbers, choice of exhibits and sheer square footage may find this small riverside zoo in Battersea Park a less daunting prospect. Kids can chatter with the squirrel monkeys and brown capuchins, watch mice running around in their own doll's house and crawl down a pair of tunnels, popping up in a bubble in the meerkats' den. New Zealand kune pigs provide vocal entertainment with top-volume snorting to amuse the toddlers, and the mynah birds might have a word with you, if you're lucky. At weekends, visitors can watch the animals being fed (feeding time for meerkats and otters is 11am and 2.30pm; for monkeys it's 11am and 3pm) and get friendly with the farm animals at Barley Mo Farm at noon and 3.30pm. Look at the website for one-off themed event days. The Lemon Tree café provides basic lunch fare, and there's a pretty good playground for all ages. One warning: you have to enter and leave via the gift shop, so get your excuses ready early.

Buggy access. Café. Disabled access: toilet. Nappy-changing facilities. Nearest picnic place: zoo picnic area. Shop.

London Zoo

Outer Circle, Regent's Park, NW1 4RY (7722 3333, www.zsl.org). Baker Street or Camden Town tube, then 274 or C2 bus. **Open** *Mar-June, Sept, Oct* 10am-5.30pm daily. *July, Aug* 10am-6pm daily. *Nov-Feb* 10am-4pm daily. Last entry 1hr before closing. **Admission** (including £1.70 voluntary contribution) £19.80; £18.30 reductions; £16 3-15s; free under-3s; £65 family (2+2 or 1+3). **Credit** AmEx, MC, V. **Map** p314 G2.

Strange bird calls and flashes of brightly coloured fur can be glimpsed through the boundary netting of the perimeter fence from Regent's Park and the banks of Regent's Canal. London Zoo has revamped itself significantly over the last ten years, with animals rehoused in imaginative enclosures that follow the 'natural habitat' philosophy of zookeeping. The most exciting addition in recent years is Gorilla Kingdom, where visitors can get within a foot of three adult gorillas – albeit separated by a sheet of reinforced glass.

There's so much to do and see here that the best way to enjoy it is with an annual pass (which also gains a discount on the carousel rides and bouncy castle, and in the cafés). Staying for a couple of hours is then guilt free and allows children to get the most out of a few exhibits without museum legs setting in. Otherwise it's a dash around Into Africa, the indoor Clore Rainforest Lookout, the Meet The Monkeys walkthrough and insect extravaganza B.U.G.S., then Butterfly Paradise tunnel and the Aquarium. Between them lurk lions, tigers, hippos, camels and flamingos: all impossible to walk past quickly. Daily events include the Animals In Action display at noon, which has the audience ducking as hawks, vultures, owls and parrots soar millimetres above their heads for strategically placed titbits while a keeper relays amusing anecdotes. Better than a science lesson any day. One of our favourite attractions is Tim Hunkin's charming clock, just outside the Victorian bird house, the Blackburn Pavilion, which grinds into mechanical action every half hour.

The Children's Zoo, unveiled in Easter 2009, was designed for children by children. Here, kids can groom goats and sheep, meet the llamas, climb with coatis, explore the tunnels in the Roots Zone or listen to a story in the tipi. The Splash Zone will have parents cursing, unless they've been organised enough to bring spare clothes and shoes; you have been warned. New for 2010 are Junior Keeper for the Day events (*see p136*). *See also p134* **Great Days Out**.

Buggy access. Café. Disabled access: toilet. Nappy-changing facilities. Nearest picnic place: zoo picnic areas. Restaurant. Shop.

Activities

1000s of things to do…

1000 Great Holiday Ideas

1000 things to do in London

1000 things to do in New York

1000 things to do in London for under £10

1000 things for kids to do in the holidays

1000 things to do in Britain

From £12.99

Parties

Throw a birthday bash to remember.

Whether it's a no-expense spared extravaganza or an afternoon of pass-the-parcel and pin the tail on the donkey, good parties are all about the planning. Those aiming to impress can hire a fire engine, employ a science boffin to ensure proceedings go with a bang, or arrange an arty afternoon of jewellery-making; the options are endless. Then again, you may decide that the most memorable sort of knees-up needs nothing more than games, balloons and bunting, with a candle-topped cake at the end.

Whatever sort of party you've got in mind, and whatever your budget, there are places and people that can help. Entertainers of every stripe can hold small guests enthralled, while specialist enterprises run from eco-friendly party bag companies to a gluten-free baker's. Alternatively, professional party planners will organise the whole thing – at a price.

If the thought of rampaging, sugar-fuelled kids and accidental spillages sends a chill down your spine, there are plenty of reasonably priced halls; that extra £50 could be worth it to save your carpet. Most play centres (*see p177-179*) also offer party deals, although it's often cheaper to ignore the package and just turn up; check if their insurance allows cakes with candles.

We've focused on birthdays, but the teen-friendly companies are all great for bah and bat mitzvahs, and many entertainers also specialise in keeping tiny wedding guests amused.

ACTIVITY PARTIES
Arts & crafts

For more artistic options, *see p193*. Clapham's **Papered Parlour** (*see p195*) also offers adorable arts and crafts parties.

Arty Party
8675 7055, www.artyparty.co.uk.
A team of professional artists arrive with all the materials to make jewelled mirrors, jaunty wooden boats, towering giraffes and other crafty items in their two- to three-hour party packages. Staff are pretty undaunted by rowdy kids, having held workshops for crowds of 400 at park fun days. They charge £230 for up to 20 kids aged over four.

Jewel Party
07590 077460, www.jewelparty.co.uk.
Children as young as three return home from a Jewel Party bedecked in necklaces, rings and bracelets of their own making. Parties are themed according to the materials used, with beads and sweetie jewellery being the big favourites. Boys enjoy the Fimo clay workshops, bashing out Gothic signet rings and pirate-style necklets. The company has cannily introduced a recession-busting package of a 40-minute bracelet workshop at £75 for up to ten kids. Otherwise, standard packages start at £150 for one-and-a-half hours, with invites included.

Pottery Café
735 Fulham Road, SW6 5UL (7736 2157, www.pottery-cafe.com). Parsons Green tube/ 14, 414 bus. **Open** 11am-6pm Mon; 10am-6pm Tue-Sat; 11am-5pm Sun. **Credit** MC, V.
This café and paint-your-own studio offers children's parties for £19.95 a head. In a separate party room, kids aged seven and over can make a joyful mess painting their very own piece of pottery. It's not just mugs and plates; most popular with the kids are the beautiful money-boxes, shaped like dragons and fire-engines. The package includes invites, balloons, a party leader, sandwiches and a drink – as well as the glazed and fired results of the children's artistic endeavours. (You return a week later to collect the pieces.) You're welcome to bring your own food and cake.

Scrub up at the **Soap & Bubble Company**.

Buggy access. Café. Disabled access.
Nappy-changing facilities.
Branch 322 Richmond Road, Twickenham,
Middx TW1 2DU (8744 3000).

Soap & Bubble Company

8402 7565, www.soapandbubble.com.
Soap & Bubble arrive equipped with all the
ingredients to make soaps, chocolate lip balm,
body glitter, bubble bath and even floating
ducks. All they ask you to provide is some space
and a large table. The team will even tidy up
afterwards, leaving you with a spotless house
and a child eager to jump in the bath to test their
home-made concoctions. Two-hour parties start
at £175 for up to eight kids aged eight and above.

Cookery

For cookery lessons and workshops, *see
also p197-198* **Kids' Cookery School**
and **Munchkins**.

Cookie Crumbles

0845 601 4173, www.cookiecrumbles.net.
Kids from four to 15 prepare their own
three-course meals during these absorbing
parties. Even non-foodie children enjoy bashing
out dough and getting covered in flour while
preparing such goodies as pizza snakes and
ricotta ravioli. Two-hour parties start at
£165 for six kids, with CC providing all
ingredients and equipment; you won't have to
lift a spoon. The company also produces
birthday gift boxes, containing everything
small chefs need to bake various sweet treats.
Over the years, Cookie Crumbles' workshop
programmes have taught over 10,000 children
how to cook, so you can rest assured they
really know their onions... and sausages,
and tiramisu.

Gill's Cookery Workshop

*7 North Square, NW11 7AA (8458 2608,
www.gillscookeryworkshop.co.uk). Golders
Green tube.*
Fancy a party without piles of sausage rolls
cluttering your freezer? Gill Roberts invites your
guests to her kitchen, where for three hours they
cater their own party. Popular themes include
the American party (burgers and brownies) or
Italian pizzas and ice-cream. Kids also bake a
mini birthday cake to take home. Parties start
at £250, and are suitable for four to 16s.

Firemen

Hot Hire

07947 028899, www.hot-hire.co.uk.
Imagine the thrill as a real fire engine turns up at your party, complete with qualified fireman. Kids get to ride in the engine and try out the hose, followed by an optional disco and games (you can sound the siren if your party is on private land). Hold your party on a school night and the fire engine can meet your guests at the school gate and drive them to the venue. Packages for three- to 16-year-olds start at £99, with a free fireman's helmet for each child.

Pamper parties

Mini Makeovers

8398 0107, www.minimakeovers.com.
Girlies aged five to 15 are treated to a makeover and manicure, before rounding things off with a celebratory disco. The little ones adore being prettied up as fairies and princesses, while tweens favour Hannah Montana and *High School Musical* parties. The basic package costs £160 for eight kids, with dance classes, photoshoots and limousine hire as optional extras.

Performance

For more clubs and companies that run term-time music and drama courses, as well as staging parties, *see chapter* **Arts & Entertainment**.

Blueberry Playsongs Parties

8677 6871, www.blueberryplaysongs.co.uk.
These fun, guitar-led musical parties for one- to six-year-olds involve dancing, bubbles, party games and puppets. Packages start from £85, including 20 balloons and a gift for the birthday child. *See also p173.*

Drama Parties

0151 336 4302, www.dramaparties.com.
Parties run by the Little Actors Theatre Company give four to 14s the chance to experience a full drama workshop with a party atmosphere. Themes include murder mystery, pirates and Halloween; if the birthday boy or girl has a particular passion, you can suggest your own theme. Prices start at £130 for an hour, with invites and thank-you cards thrown in.

Funky Chicks

8302 6992, www.funky-chicks.co.uk.
Day-glo lycra-clad dancers host these disco parties that are aimed at five- to 12-year-olds. Competitions, dressing up and party games

accompany a dance class, with the birthday child taking a starring role in a final performance. You'll probably need to hire a hall to accommodate the team's acrobatic moves and body popping, and book well in advance as they are becoming very popular. Spectacular parties start at £500 for two hours.

Jigsaw

8447 4530, www.jigsaw-arts.co.uk.
This long-running stage school also offers imaginative singing, dancing (everything from ballet to cheerleading moves and hip hop) and drama parties. Jigsaw's experienced tutors will put three- to 12-year-old partygoers through their performing paces and the parties cost from £120 for one hour.

Science Boffins. *See p146.*

Activities

Kate Gielgud Acting Parties

8964 5490, www.tiddleywinks.co.uk.
Custom-written dramas that centre on the birthday child are Kate's speciality. Born with an infectious passion for drama (she's Sir John's great-niece), her parties are absorbing affairs with themes such as James/Jane Bond and classy murder mysteries. Prices start at £300 for two hours, and she arrives with scripts and costumes. Plays can be adapted for four- to 13-year-olds.

Movie Parties

7387 4341, www.movie-parties.co.uk.
Movie-mad eight to 16s get eight hours to plan, rehearse, shoot, edit and screen their own film with a team of professionals. Each child is given a DVD of the finished result to take home. Themes include *Charlie's Angels, Harry Potter* and *Pirates of the Caribbean,* using your house and local parks as the backdrop to all sorts of scenes of derring-do; finally the kids get the chance to leap over your garden fence brandishing a sword with total impunity. It costs £1,300 for a maximum of 12 guests.

Puzzles

Puzzle Party

0844 848 2822, www.happypuzzle.co.uk.
Children are divided into teams at a puzzle party, and each team works on the same challenges – although the emphasis is on completion rather than winning. Pick from giant road maps, marble runs, code-breakers, optical illusion puzzles and more. The parties work equally well at home or in a hired hall, are hosted by an entertainer, and are best for ages six and above. Call for prices.

Science & nature

Animal Magic

01323 482211, www.animal-magic.co.uk.
Lindsey Parker and her team bring a host of furry, scaly and feathered friends to parties for one- to 16-year-olds. The little ones will love holding and stroking rabbits and guinea pigs, while teens are likely to be fascinated by the geckos and snakes. Particularly popular is 'Mouse Town', a wooden construction put together by the kids, for a colony of mice to explore. Parties, starting from £95 for one hour, can be themed – *Harry Potter,* for example, might involve meeting a crew of owls, snakes and a bearded dragon. The team bring their own disinfectant to wipe up any little animal accidents.

Science Boffins

0800 019 2636, www.scienceboffins.com.
Kids' excitement levels reach a peak as mini volcanos erupt, balloons self-inflate, light goes round corners and bottles become rockets. For parents, it's pretty exciting that all experiments are guaranteed safe and mess free. Parties start at £195 for one hour, which buys you a qualified boffin who'll hold five- to 11-year-olds entranced with competitions and experiments of an educational bent.

Sport

Campaign Paintball

Old Lane, Cobham, Surrey KT11 1NH (01932 865999, www.campaignpaintball.com). Effingham Junction rail.
A short jaunt southwest of London, Campaign's site is divided into action-packed play zones. The eerily authentic Dodge City is a big hit, along with the Jungle zone and spooky Dark Tower. Packages for ten to 15s cost £24.95 per child including 300 paintballs, seven games, tuition and a barbecue lunch. The day ends with a trophy presentation.

League One Sports Academy

8446 0891, www.leagueone.co.uk.
Children's football parties (three to 12s) with a bit of basketball and cricket thrown in for good measure. The coaches keep up the party atmosphere, taking into account any varying skill levels, with the birthday child receiving a trophy to take home. Parties start at £190 for 90 minutes, and all equipment is provided. The company's headquarters are in north London, but staff will consider coming to you if you have enough space.

CAKES

Cake Store

111 Sydenham Road, SE26 5EZ (8778 4705, www.thecakestore.co.uk). Sydenham rail. **Open** 8am-5.30pm Mon-Sat. **Credit** MC, V.
This Sydenham-based cake specialist can deliver its creations to the whole of London. Colourful cakes include pirate galleons, ballet shoes, toadstools and dalmation puppies – there's nothing this bakery cannot construct from a humble vanilla sponge, it seems. Prices start at around £75 for the themed designs (generally serving 35); smaller, more traditional cakes, inscribed with a birthday message, cost considerably less.
Buggy access. Delivery service.
Disabled access.

Activities

Dodge bullets in Dodge City at **Campaign Paintball**.

League One Sports Academy.
See p146.

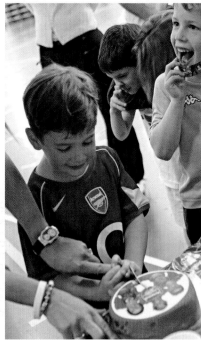

Activities

Chorak

122 High Road, N2 9ED (8365 3330). East Finchley tube/263 bus. **Open** 8am-6pm daily. **No credit cards.**
Novelty handmade birthday cakes start at £68 for a 25-35-portion job, going up to £105 for a 65-portion extravaganza. Cartoon favourites are a speciality, whether it's a picture iced onto a cake or a 3D creation leaping out at your guests. Eggless cakes are available.
Branch 229-231 Muswell Hill Broadway, N10 1DE (8815 5998).

Crumbs and Doilies

www.crumbsanddoilies.co.uk.
These days, cupcakes are de rigueur on the kids' party circuit. Gone are the squabbles over slice sizes and wilting paper plates; instead, each child can clutch their very own cake in a sticky fist. C&D are a leader in this revolution, offering six flavours and over 200 different decorations. Organic eggs, flour, lemons and vanilla are used, along with Valrhona chocolate. A dozen cupcakes will set you back £24; pastel stands on which to display them (from £10) are an optional extra. Tasting can be done at the Saturday stall at the King's Road farmer's market.

Dunn's

6 The Broadway, N8 9SN (8340 1614, www. dunns-bakery.co.uk). Finsbury Park tube/rail, then W7 bus/Crouch Hill rail/41, 91 bus. **Open** 7am-6pm Mon-Sat; 9am-5pm Sun. **Credit** MC, V.
Fruit- or sponge-based party cakes are adorned with stars like Upsy Daisy and Ben 10, or the birthday child's photograph (prices starting at £46). Older kids may enjoy the glamour of seeing themselves on the magazine cover cake (£75). A standard sponge (that's 14 servings) costs £28. *Buggy access. Delivery service. Disabled access.*

Euphorium Bakery

202 Upper Street, N1 1RQ (7704 6905, www.euphoriumbakery.com). Highbury & Islington tube/rail. **Open** 7am-10.30pm Mon-Fri; 8am-10.30pm Sat, Sun. **Credit** MC, V.
Starting from £13 for an eight-inch cake, even the basic numbers here are banana or apple flavoured, filled with berries or covered in crisp chocolate. Prices include your choice of message, which can be iced on to the cake or inscribed on a choccie plaque. A gluten-free Chocolate Lover's cake is available (£30/ten servings).
Buggy access.
Branches 79 Upper Street, N1 0NU (7288 8788) 26A Chapel Market, N1 9EN (7837 7010); 211 Haverstock Hill, NW3 4QN (7431 8944); 45 South End Road, NW3 2QB (7794 2344).

Konditor & Cook

22 Cornwall Road, SE1 8TW (7261 0456, www.konditorandcook.com). Waterloo tube/rail. **Open** 7.30am-6.30pm Mon-Fri; 8.30am-3pm Sat. **Credit** AmEx, MC, V.
Chocolate curly whirly, lemon chiffon and frosted carrot cakes are among the specialities of this famed London bakery. Dinky 'magic cakes' are perfect for parties; mini lemon fondant fancies iced with pictures or letters that can be lined up to spell out a name or birthday message. An eight-inch cake starts at £21.20, while Magic Cakes cost £37 per dozen.
Buggy access. Delivery service. Disabled access.
Branches 10 Stoney Street, SE1 9AD (7407 5100); 46 Gray's Inn Road, WC1X 8LR (7404 6300); Curzon Soho, 99 Shaftesbury Avenue, W1D 5DY (7292 1684); 30 St Mary Axe, EC3A 8BF (0845 262 3030); 63 Stanford Street, SE1 9NB (7921 9200).

Lola's Kitchen

Unit 2, Primrose Hill Workshops, Oppidans Road, NW3 3AG (7483 3394, www.lolas-kitchen.co.uk). Chalk Farm tube. **Open** for collection only, noon-5pm Mon-Sat. **Credit** MC, V.
Lola's lovely cupcakes come in a dizzying array of flavours (chocolate, coconut, peanut butter, rocky road and red velvet, to name but a few), with a seemingly endless array of decorations. The online ordering system is easy to use and purchases can be delivered or picked up. Traditionalists who like one big cake to slice can go for proper birthday cakes, adorned with mini cupcakes, or the 'showgirl' – a giant cupcake that feeds 15 (£45). Mini cupcakes start at £1 apiece, with a minimum order of 24. If you want to taste before you buy, Lola's wares are stocked in Harrods, Selfridges and various high-end delis.
Delivery service.

Margaret's Cakes of Distinction

224 Camberwell Road, SE5 0ED (7701 1940). Elephant & Castle tube/rail, then 12, 45, 68, 176 bus. **Open** 9am-5pm Mon-Sat. **No credit cards.**
Margaret takes considerable care over her pretty sponge- or madeira-based cakes, all of which can be personalised with marzipan figures. A basic birthday number starts at £25.
Buggy access. Disabled access.

Marnie Searchwell

7735 1444, www.marniesearchwell.co.uk. **No credit cards.**
Gluten-free cakes in a variety of enticing flavours are Marnie's speciality, and they

Activities

really are delectable. She tries to use organic ingredients as much as possible, from the eggs to the buttercream, and is also happy to alter recipes for those sensitive to dairy, eggs and corn. A simple, iced seven-inch cake starts at £45, with more elaborate creations starting at £70. Every cake is carefully handbaked and delivered by Marnie and her son, so do give her at least two weeks' notice. She also offers a near-impossible to resist cake of the month club.
Delivery service.

No Weird Stuff

01334 310037, www.noweirdstuff.co.uk. **Credit** MC, V.
Is it possible to have a sugar-free kids' party? This mail order company can help the miracle come to pass, with its no added sugar and gluten-free fruit cakes, which are also free from artificial flavourings and preservatives. The sweetness is achieved using xylitol, a natural sweetener derived from birch trees, while the gluten-free flour is milled on the premises to ensure there's no contamination. Cakes arrive undecorated, leaving you to add your own toppings, with prices starting from £11.99.
Mail order.

Primrose Bakery

69 Gloucester Avenue, NW1 8LD (7483 4222, www.primrosebakery.org.uk). Chalk Farm tube. **Open** 8.30am-6pm Mon-Sat; 10am-5.30pm Sun. **Credit** MC, V.
Primrose Bakery sells gorgeous cupcakes and swirly layer cakes that come in a flurry of unusual flavours, such as lime and coconut or rose (decorated with petals), as well as the more classic vanilla and chocolate offerings (which are made using 70% cocoa). Mini alphabet cupcakes forming the birthday child's name are particularly popular. Mini cupcakes start from £1.25 each, and celebration cakes are around £30.
Buggy access. Delivery service.
Branch 42 Tavistock Street, WC2E 7PB (7836 3638).

COSTUMES

If you are looking for inexpensive TV character or classic costumes (such as princesses, pirates and the like), it's worth checking out Asda, Mothercare, Argos and TK Maxx. For more toyshops and boutiques with dressing-up gear, *see p281.*

Online

J&M Toys

0113 288 7716, www.jandmtoys.co.uk.
Over 150 costumes, for children aged between three and eight are stocked by this fancy dress specialist: soldiers, brides, snowmen, firemen, pilots and many more. The fabulous astronaut all-in-one, for example, costs around £20, while the nifty nurse's uniform is a steal at just £12.95. There are also various nativity costumes – a boon for parents not gifted in the art of sewing.

Natural Nursery

01392 207243, www.naturalnursery.co.uk.
Natural Nursery sells a dinky range of ethically traded dressing-up outfits for toddlers (18 months to three years old). The range includes pretty bumble bee, ladybird, ballerina and fairy dresses, along with adorable dinosaur and dog costumes (£14.99-£19.99).

Shops

Angels

119 Shaftesbury Avenue, WC2H 8AE (7836 5678, www.fancydress.com). Leicester Square or Tottenham Court Road tube.

Open 9.30am-5.30pm Mon, Tue, Thur, Fri; 10.30am-7pm Wed. **Credit** AmEx, MC, V.
This Oscar-winning costumiers stocks some 10,000 outfits in myriad themes, catering for kids, adults and even dogs. Anakin Skywalker, Jack Sparrow, sword-waving warrior kings and sugary-hued satin princess dresses are among the offerings. Order online or pop to the shop to try before you buy. Prices start around £20. *Buggy access. Disabled access. Mail order (0845 054 8854).*

Escapade

45-46 Chalk Farm Road, NW1 8AJ (7485 7384, www.escapade.co.uk). Camden Town tube. **Open** 10am-7pm Mon-Fri; 10am-6pm Sat; noon-5pm Sun. **Credit** AmEx, MC, V.
A host of TV hero dress-ups include Ben 10, the *High School Musical* cast, Lewis Hamilton, Spongebob and the Teletubbies. The full range is available online, with a selection in Camden to try on for size. Fairies, cowboys and authentic looking astronauts are also stocked, along with nativity costumes; prices start at £10.99. Giant cardboard characters (from £26.99) can be bought to enhance your party theme, Winnie the Pooh, Daleks and a talking C-3PO among them. *Buggy access. Delivery service. Disabled access. Mail order.*

Primrose Bakery

Activities

Harlequin

254 Lee High Road, SE13 5PL (8852 0193). Hither Green or Lewisham rail/DLR/21, 261 bus. **Open** 10.30am-5pm Mon; 10am-5.30pm Tue, Thur, Fri; 10am-1pm Wed; 10am-5pm Sat. **Credit** MC, V.

Ever popular princess, knight and bandit outfits start at £9.95, with Spider-Man, Scooby Doo and Batgirl from £29.95. Harlequin also specialises in accessories, so the shop is lined with hats, boas, wigs and pompoms.

Buggy access.

Party Superstores

268 Lavender Hill, SW11 1LJ (7924 3210, www.partysuperstores.co.uk). Clapham Junction rail/39, 77, 345 bus. **Open** 9am-6pm Mon-Wed, Fri, Sat; 9am-7pm Thur; 10.30am-4.30pm Sun. **Credit** AmEx, MC, V.

All manner of fancy dress kits are supplemented by shelf upon shelf of accessories, wigs and hats (from £1.99). Superheroes are big with the boys, with full Batman regalia costing from £24.99; girls like to browse the drawers of glittery wands, tiaras and fairy wings. Over 50 different sorts of themed tableware are also stocked, while the full balloon service includes inflation and delivery.

Buggy access. Delivery service. Disabled access. Mail order.

Preposterous Presents

262 Upper Street, N1 2UQ (7226 4166, www.preposterouspresents.co.uk). Highbury & Islington tube/rail. **Open** 10am-6pm Mon-Sat; 12.30-4.30pm Sun. **Credit** MC, V.

PP specialise in putting an outfit together completely from scratch – you just have to tell them who you want to be transformed into, and they will then flit around gathering the necessary accessories and wigs until you look the part. Ready-assembled costume sets are also available, including knights, fairies and various animals (from £15); accessory kits start at £4.99. Whoopee cushions, itching powder and fake blood abound.

Buggy access. Disabled access.

ENTERTAINERS

Action Station

0870 770 2705, www.theactionstation.co.uk. Entertainers of all shapes and specialities are represented by this agency, from storytelling spacemen, spies, mermaids, cheerleaders and cowgirls to drama teachers, make-up artists, fire-eaters, jugglers and also DJs. Children of all ages are catered for, while prices start at £150 for an hour.

Get creative at the **V&A Museum of Childhood.**

Great places to party

Colour House Children's Theatre

Front seats for the delightful show, ending with the cast singing *Happy Birthday* to the guest of honour. Then the empty theatre is yours. From £75 per hour, with catering, entertainment and a mini disco all available on top. *See p185.*

Discover

A Story Builder takes the children on an hour's journey on the magical Story Trail, followed by a craft workshop in the private party room. Prices start at £6.50 per child, with great party bags and books as extras. Bring your own food. *See p172.*

Kentish Town City Farm

KT has a nice big room to hire, at £50 for two hours (they allow you setting up and cleaning time). It comes complete with a kitchen and tables – and entrance to the farm is free, for all sorts of animal encounters. *See p133.*

Little Dinosaurs

Play centres are terrific for parties. But this newcomer has something different to offer, and that's beautiful outside space in the middle of a park, where kids can get a breather from the playframe and parents can escape the noise. Charging from £3.50 per child, Little Dinosaurs offers unlimited drinks, your own host and a buffet tea. *See p178.*

London Zoo

Bring over ten kids and get 20% off your entrance fees; one adult is admitted free with every ten children. It's a marvellous day out, and one of the few zoos that can be enjoyed year round; most enclosures have indoor as well as outdoor viewing areas. *See p140.*

National Army Museum

The NAM offers children's party packages, costing from from £395-£595 for 20 children. For that, you get a private party room, food and drink, party bags, invites and an hour's exclusive use of the Kids' Zone – an interactive learning and play space for under-tens, with a castle and a cavalry charge of rocking horses. Entertainers can also be arranged, at an additional cost.

Rainforest Café

The party package is £14.95 per child for a two course meal and jam-packed activity bag. That's the same price as the usual deluxe kids meal, but with every six guests you get a free birthday cake. Insist on sitting in the upper dining room to party among the amazing animatronics. *See p245.*

V&A Museum Of Childhood

Bethnal Green's treasure trove of toys has a room that accommodates 15-20 children for weekend parties. You can throw in catering and an activity like a storytrail around the museum or some good old arts and crafts (ages four and over). The room is £100 for three hours; activities and catering are extra. *See p73.*

WWT Wetland Centre

An hour and a half's entertainment comes courtesy of your own 'explainer'; small guests are also treated to goodie bags and a picnic in the Mongolian yurt. Packages cost from £250 per party, with entrance fees to the enchanting park and wonderful playground included. *See p139.*

Activities

Ali Do Lali
0778 972 0294, www.dralidolali.co.uk.
Do Lali arrives on a magic carpet, then proceeds to thrill the assembled youngsters with fire eating, sword swallowing and magic. Toddlers particularly like his puppets and special drawing board – an illustration of the birthday child which magically comes alive. A one-hour show starts at £160. If you've booked him before, Do Lali pledges to deliver a different act whenever he returns.

Amanda
8578 0234, www.amandasactionkids.co.uk.
Bringing new meaning to the words 'high energy', Amanda whirls one- to six-year-olds through two giddy hours of dancing, music and parachute games, like a sugar-coated Su Pollard. Prices start at £140 for a party led by one of her team, but it's worth shelling out an extra £30 for Amanda herself.

Christopher Howell
7993 4544, www.christopherhowell.net/kids.htm.
A respected close-up magician, Howell puts on absorbing shows for children. An hour-long

Tutu cute **Natural Nursery**. *See p151.*

party (from £200) features magic, storytelling, balloon modelling and the chance for kids to perform various illusions. Shows are suitable for children aged four to six.

Jenty the Gentle Clown
07957 121764, www.jentythegentleclown.com.
Specialising in parties for under-threes, Jenty can also hype it up with a disco and limbo dancing for kids up to 11. Traditional games, face-painting, magic and singalongs with the banjo are all part of the fun. Jenty charges £145 for one hour, £195 for two.

Juggling John
0845 644 6659, www.jugglingjohn.com.
John has four party packages to suit different age ranges from babies to ten-year-olds, with ball juggling to amuse the tinies and fire juggling for those with older kids (and high ceilings). Magic, clowning and escapology also feature. Prices start at £185 for an hour.

Magic Mikey
0808 100 2140, www.magicmikey.co.uk.
A one-man powerhouse who thrills four to 12s with a mixture of puppetry, balloon modelling, games, magic and above all humour, Mikey also comes with a belting disco. One of his two-hour shows costs around £275.

Mel's Magic
01992 552026, www.mels-magic.co.uk.
Used to intimate gatherings as well as large crowds, Mel is adept at both mingling and performing close-up tricks as well as presenting her full show (ages three to ten), complete with a magically appearing live rabbit. You can also book her circus skills workshop, where kids of six and above can learn to unicycle, juggle and stilt-walk. Her fees start at £165 for one hour.

Merlin Entertainments
01494 479027, www.merlinents.co.uk.
Merlin is sure to represent a party host of your liking: clowns, magicians, puppeteers and DJs can be hired here, and circus skills workshops, craft parties, musical workshops and animal encounter shows can all be arranged. Staff are adept at mixing and matching performers for larger events: you could have an animal show with a break for magic in the middle, for instance. Prices start at £140 for an hour-long performance.

Mr Happy Magic
01245 426016, www.mrhappymagic.com.
Parties are packed with magic, games, puppets and an optional disco. Happy (his real name

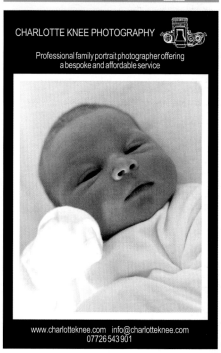

since he changed it by deed poll) is ably assisted by Charlie the Dog – beloved by his audience of three- to seven-year-olds. Two hours of silliness start at £170.

Silly Millie the Clown
7823 8329, 07939 239397, www.sillymillie theclown.co.uk.
Expect happy, giggly parties with Silly Millie's cheeky take on party games, karaoke, plate spinning and magic. Three- to nine-year-olds adore her shows, and the older children get taught a card trick or two. Millie charges from £85 per hour.

HALLS FOR HIRE

For other inspired venues, *see p153*.

Dragon Hall
17 Stukeley Street, WC2B 5LT (7404 7274, www.dragonhall.org.uk). Holborn tube.
Open 9am-10pm daily. **No credit cards.**
This central community centre has three rooms, with kitchen facilities, for hire. The airy, 200-seater main hall is £55/hr with a PA system as an optional extra. The main hall comes with tables and chairs and has a dance floor.

East Dulwich Community Centre
46 Darrell Road, SE22 9NL (8693 4411, www.eastdulwichcommunitycentre.org.uk). East Dulwich rail. **Open** 9am-11pm Sat; 11am-9pm Sun. **No credit cards.**
A sturdy hall with a kitchen, with room for 120 kids, costs from £35 an hour. There's a stage, toilets and a large playground.

Highbury Fields One & Two O'Clock Club
Bandstand, Highbury Fields, Baalbec Road, N5 1UP (7704 9337, www.islington.gov.uk). Highbury & Islington tube/rail. **Open** *Summer* noon-6pm Sat, Sun. *Winter* 10am-4pm Sat, Sun. **No credit cards.**
At weekends, you can hire this children's centre – complete with all the play equipment, a kitchen and also a private outdoor space – from £90 in the winter, and £100 in the summer.

Old Cholmeley Boy's Club
68 Boleyn Road, N16 8JG (07963 778636). Dalston Kingsland rail. **Open** 9am-6pm daily. **No credit cards.**
A quirky venue with a large main room, scattered with sofas, where 150 kids can party (£50-£70 for an afternoon). Kitchen and music facilities are available, as is a terrace.

EQUIPMENT HIRE
Play equipment

Cool Parties
0844 450 0045, www.cool-parties.co.uk.
After ten minutes on this website, you could fill your garden with bouncy castles, slides, trampolines, inflatable sumo wrestlers, a rodeo bull and a quad bike circuit. A package of soft play equipment, perfect for toddlers, starts at £95 per day, while a full inflatable obstacle course costs from £175. Cool can also provide you with more sensible gear such as marquees, staff, child-sized tables and hall hire in north and west London. Entertainment packages, including electric car parties and teddy bear making sessions start at around £15 per child.

PK Entertainments
07771 546 676, www.fairandfete.co.uk.
An entire old-fashioned funfair can be hired through PK; that includes swingboats, hoopla, roundabouts and chair-o-planes. If money's no object you can hire everything, or pick a favourite stall or two. Prices start at £100 for the coconut shy (complete with 50 nuts), with slippery poles going for £120 and swingboats for £160. The company can also provide Punch & Judy, stilt-walkers and assorted entertainers.

Marquee hire

Sunset Marquees
Unit 5, Glenville Mews, Kimber Road, SW18 4NJ (8874 4897, www.sunsetmarquees.com). Southfields tube. **Open** 8am-6pm daily. **No credit cards.**
Sunset offers marquees in all sizes, with no pegs or hammering required (some models simply pop up). That means you can erect your marquee on hard surfaces as well as grass, and the process is blissfully fuss-free. A small marquee for 15 children starts at £190 for a weekend's hire. Chairs, lighting and stages can also be provided. *Delivery & set-up service.*

Sound equipment

Capital Hire
3 Stean Street, E8 4ED (7249 6000, www. capitalhire.com). London Fields rail. **Open** 9am-6pm Mon-Sat. **Credit** MC, V.
Rob and his friendly team can loan you a two-speaker sound system with iPod mixer from £140 for a three day hire. Units with whizzy LED lighting are £40 and, if the church hall is a bit scuffed, they even hire out dancefloors from

Activities

Fork out for something special at **Escapade**. *See p151.*

Nellie Shepherd Events

50p per sq/ft. A twinkling star cloth backdrop (from £40) will transform even the dowdiest of venues into the best disco in town. *Delivery & set-up service.*

Young's Disco Centre

2 Malden Road, NW5 3HR (7485 1115, www.justadisco.co.uk). Chalk Farm tube. **Open** by appointment 9am-7pm Mon-Sat. **Credit** MC, V.

The special children's party package (sound system and disco lights) costs from £95 for 24 hours' hire. On top of that, Young's can provide DJs, bubbles, dancefloors and candyfloss machines, and prides itself on its set-up service, delivery and collection. *Delivery & set-up service.*

ORGANISERS

See also p283 **Mystical Fairies**.

Adam Ants

8959 1045, www.adamantsparties.com. Ants can sort out all kinds of party-related tasks, from providing paper plates to arranging the entertainment for the big day. Girls can arrive in style in a Cinderella coach drawn by two white shetland ponies, while boys might just want to give the bouncy castles a good bashing. Traditional sports days can also be organised. Call for prices.

Birthday Dreams

7700 2525, www.birthdaydreams.co.uk. Kinloch Castle in Islington, Birthday Dreams' spectacular venue, can be transformed into a jungle, princess palace or knight's fort for your child's party. Captivating entertainers include Safari Pete, with his animal encounters party. Castle packages start at £475, which includes a cake and full catering; there are even canapés for the parents. Party bags and waiting staff are also provided, so the entertainers can stay in character while the serious business of sandwich serving is going on. BD can also organise parties in your home, with a clean up service as extra.

Boo! Productions

7287 9090, 07768 311068, www.booparties.com. Offering breathtaking bespoke parties, Boo! can transform your venue, with every inch decorated to create a magical underwater world, a pirate ship, or even the set of the *Wizard of Oz*. The cast of actors restage your favourite tales, with themed arts and crafts, games and

audience participation; check out the video on the website. For those with less room (and cash), there are 'Entertainer in a Suitcase' packages from £170. Full venue transformation starts at £2,000, but staff can also snazz up a lounge with a backdrop and props.

Nellie Shepherd Events

01625 533247, www.childrensartparties.co.uk. The expert Shepherd and her team organise themed parties, transforming your chosen venue into a winter wonderland, fairy glade or circus then adding entertainment, face-painting and catering. Packages start at £500. You can also hire each element separately: a decorations box, say, or a themed crafts party.

Pro-Active 4 Parties & Entertainment

0845 257 5005, www.proactive4parties.co.uk. These high-octane parties focus on sports, circus skills and discos. A long list of themes includes *Gladiators*, Boot Camp, *X Factor*, Mini Olympics, *High School Musical* and the ever popular Active Mayhem, which features an array of team sports. Staff are happy to come to your home, but most of the activities require plenty of space, and walls impervious to footballs. Parties are for children aged four and above, and prices start at £200.

Twizzle Parties

8392 0860, www.twizzle.co.uk. Put your party into Twizzle's hands and you won't have to arrange a thing. From decorations, entertainment and play equipment to catering, sound equipment and venue hire, Twizzle offers a bespoke party service for one to 16s (from £165). Pick and mix from its incredibly extensive recommendations; a toddler party could feature a nursery rhyme sing-along, supervised soft play and face painting, while teens might opt for quad bikes or a session in a recording studio.

PARTYWARE & PARAPHERNALIA

Baker Ross

0844 576 8922, www.bakerross.co.uk. This online store has hundreds of ideas for craft parties and gifts, be they beady, sparkly or foamy. It also offers fun novelty balloons, no end of party bag toys and DIY decorations.

Balloonland

12 Hale Lane, NW7 3NX (8906 3302, www.the-party-shop.co.uk). Edgware tube/Mill Hill

Activities

Get out of town

Inspirational escapes within two hours of London.

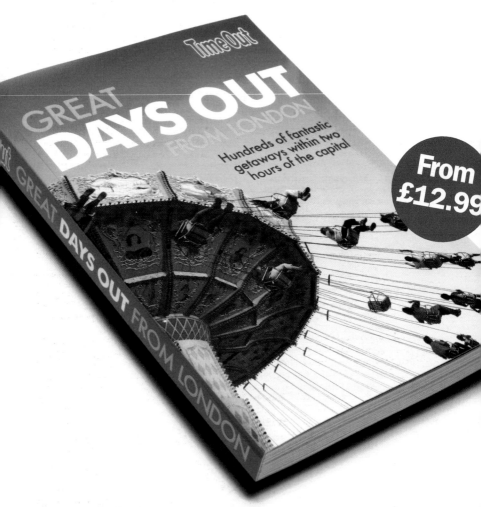

Broadway rail/221, 240 bus. **Open** 9am-5.30pm Mon-Fri; 9.30am-5.30pm Sat. **Credit** AmEx, MC, V.
Balloons come any way you want them at Balloonland. Flat or inflated, plain or shaped, latex or foil… they can even arrive singing or as part of a bouquet. Balloonland also stocks general party goods, including party bags, paper plates and tablecloths covering every TV and film theme imaginable. Balloons are available online, but you need to call the shop if you want them pre-inflated or delivered.
Buggy access. Delivery service. Disabled access. Mail order.

Circus Circus

176 Wandsworth Bridge Road, SW6 2UQ (7731 4128, www.circuscircus.co.uk). Fulham Broadway tube. **Open** 10am-6pm daily. **Credit** MC, V.
Friendly staff are happy to talk you through the enormous range of partyware, and can also help you to source caterers, venues and bouncy castle hire. Plates and decorations abound, adorned with Barbie, Peppa Pig and other heroes of the small screen. The likes of balloon arches, party games, fancy dress and pinatas complete the stock.
Buggy access. Delivery service. Disabled access. Mail order.

CYP

0870 034 0010, www.cyp.co.uk.
A dizzying array of CDs, downloads and musical games. Kids can sing along with the Fimbles, listen to CDs of fairytales or groove with the party DVDs. Many of the CDs come with free activity sheets. Prices start at £5.

Happy Green Earth

0845 388 0931, www.happygreenearth.com.
This online independent specialises in eco-friendly party bags in designs ranging from pirates to polka dots. Prices start at 10p for pink or blue candy-striped paper bags. Fillers include organic chocolate lollies and appealing wooden trinkets, such as balsa wood gliders and heart-shaped mirrors. Beeswax candles, cotton bunting and biodegradable balloons also feature.

Kidzcraft

01793 327022, www.kidzcraft.co.uk.
Click on the theme of your choice and Kidzcraft will present you with a range of crafty ideas for your very own art party. All manner of craft kits are available here, including pottery to paint and treasure chests to adorn (from £2.50). T-shirt decorating kits are another hot seller. Proud hosts can submit photos of the kids' efforts to the online gallery.

Pro-Active 4 Parties. *See p169.*

Activities

Little Cherry

01784 470570, www.littlecherry.co.uk.
Want to avoid the post-party guilt of sending bags full of plastic to the landfill? Little Cherry stocks biodegradable, compostable and recycled partyware. The recycled paper plates come in vivid colours – or your guests can eat off sialli- or palm-leaf plates. The cotton and recycled paper party bags can be bought ready-filled or empty.

Mexicolore

7622 9577, www.mexicolore.co.uk.
Mexicolore make and import authentic Mexican pinatas (made of papier-maché, not cardboard). Prices start at £20, and staff will make up custom designs to order. Fill 'em up (the traditional stuffing is sweeties) and let the kids expend all that excess energy bashing it to bits.

Non-Stop Party Shop

214-216 Kensington High Street, W8 7RG (7937 7200, www.nonstopparty.co.uk). High Street Kensington tube/10, 27, 391 bus. **Open** 9.30am-6pm Mon-Sat; 11am-5pm Sun. **Credit** AmEx, MC, V.
A great shop to browse, whether you're after cards, fancy dress and wigs or tableware and decorations. Non-Stop specialises in bespoke balloon decorations to personalise your venue; for those that just want some balloons to kick about, you can buy a pump or hire a helium cylinder. This is also one of the few London shops where you can buy fireworks year round. *Buggy access. Delivery service. Mail order.*

Party Ark

01572 748609, www.partyark.co.uk.
This user-friendly website sells partyware in TV, classic and age-specific themes. The one-click party packs have everything you need in your chosen theme in one package, so you don't have to browse. Another nice touch is the ideas panels for bewildered parents – a description of who each TV character is and what your child will expect from, say, an *Angelina Ballerina* or a *Lazy Town* party (the latter involves Daddy donning a purple catsuit). First birthdays are a speciality (celebratory sippy cups, £2.99).

Party Party

3 & 11 Southampton Road, NW5 4JS (7267 9084, www.partypartyuk.com). Chalk Farm tube/Gospel Oak rail/24 bus. **Open** 9.30am-5.30pm Mon-Sat. **Credit** MC, V.
No.3 stocks decorations and a large range of bargain balloons, while No.11 is the shop to go to for tableware and costumes. If you'd rather not leave the sofa, you can browse the entire stock online. Knowledgeable staff can talk you through the numerous balloon options; you can even bring in last year's foil numbers to be re-inflated. A lovely range of pinatas are also stocked. If you don't fancy excitable children wielding a big stick in your house, go for a 'pull' pinata, which showers the kids with sweeties once they locate the lucky ribbon. *Buggy access. Delivery service. Disabled access. Mail order.*

Party Party

9-13 Ridley Road, E8 2NP (7254 5168, www.ppshop.co.uk). Dalston Kingsland rail/ 30, 38, 56, 67, 76, 149, 236, 242, 243, 277 bus. **Open** 9am-5.30pm Mon-Thur; 9am-6.30pm Fri, Sat. **Credit** MC, V.
A stalwart of the east London party scene, Party Party has opened a second branch in Kilburn, stocking the same dizzying array of banners, fancy dress, pinatas and partyware. A massive selection of cake decorations and novelty bakeware takes centre stage, with ready-made icing (£4.29) for nervous chefs to 3D train-shaped baking pans (£14.49) for the more ambitious. Even the candles are special, with footballs, jungle characters and dinosaurs ready to grant your birthday wishes. *Buggy access. Mail order.*
Branch 206 Kilburn High Road, NW6 4JH (7624 4295).

Party Pieces

01635 201844, www.partypieces.co.uk.
Lovely tableware, party bags, decorations and CDs galore. Of particular note are the cake kits (with everything you need to create a 3D masterpiece in your kitchen) and the 'scene setters'; giant backdrops that turn your walls into Dora's jungle or a princess's ballroom. Other stock includes party game kits, candy floss and popcorn machines and some splendid invitations and thank-you cards. Filled party bags start at £1.50, and there are loads of brilliant bits and bobs for under a pound if you'd rather assemble your own.

Planet Party

8346 5432, www.planetparty.co.uk.
Beautiful partyware in classic or unusual themes, including spaceman, ballerina, bowling or sleepovers. Personalised plates, party bags and food boxes are a speciality (from 50p) with a range for twins and joint birthdays. Planet Party can also arrange your entire shindig in their Finchley venue or your home.

Arts & Entertainment

A cultural calendar that small fry can enjoy.

Even the most dignified of cultural establishments are keen to court children – who are, after all, the ticket-buying, theatre-going, gallery-visiting public of the future. If you'd assumed that places like the **Royal Opera House** (see p171) and **Wigmore Hall** (see p177) would be too grand to welcome sticky-fingered youngsters, think again.

Many galleries and museums (see pp56-104) and attractions (see pp28-55) run special events and family days year-round, with a particularly busy programme at weekends and during the school holidays. There are myriad delights on offer, with not a hint of starch and ceremony: child-friendly concerts, story sessions, meet-the-orchestra events and drop-in arts and crafts activities among them.

When it comes to theatre (see pp56-104), meanwhile, the line-up runs from endlessly innovative children's theatre companies and venues such as **Oily Cart** (see p183) and the **Unicorn Theatre** (see p190) to big-budget Christmas pantos, or crowd-pleasing touring shows based on Fifi, Angelina, Lola and co.

Children can also try their hand at all sorts of creative activities. Whether your offspring are into drama, music, cookery, art or film-making, drop-in classes, after-school clubs and longer courses abound; kids can try circus skills one day, sculpture the next. They might uncover a hidden talent for stilt-walking or a penchant for percussion – and have a whale of a time in the process.

ARTS CENTRES

Barbican Centre

Silk Street, EC2Y 8DS (box office 7638 8891, cinema 7382 7000, www.barbican.org.uk). Barbican tube/Moorgate tube/rail. **Open** *Box office* (by phone) 9am-8pm Mon-Sat; 11am-8pm Sun (in person) 9am-9pm Mon-Sat; noon-9pm Sun. **Admission** *Library* free. *Exhibitions, films, shows, workshops* phone for details. **Membership** £20-£25/yr. **Credit** AmEx, MC, V. **Map** p318 P5.
This angular, concrete art complex may look slightly forboding, but venture inside and you'll be pleasantly surprised. Maps and painted yellow lines lead confused visitors through the residential blocks that surround the centre – an intricate maze of walkways, stairs, identikit towers and split level ramps. There are some pockets of unexpected calm for everyone to enjoy: the fountains in the inner courtyard, the Waterside Café and the library, with its extensive children's section. Best of all is the conservatory, open to the public on Sunday afternoons (unless hired for a private event), where exotic palms, ferns and flowers soar towards the sky and stately koi carp patrol the ponds.
The Barbican's busy programme of cultural offerings also has plenty to appeal to small fry.

For starters, there's the excellent Saturday-morning Family Film Club, with a lively mix of movies, themed activities and monthly workshops. Screenings (£3.50-£5.50) are aimed at kids aged five to 11 and their parents; book ahead. One-off mini-seasons and special events for families also dot the Barbican's calendar, including the Animate The World! animation-fest in May and the London Children's Film Festival in November. The complex is also home to the London Symphony Orchestra (www.lso.co.uk), whose Discovery Family Concerts combine music and storytelling to great effect, with pre-concert workshops in the foyer. *Buggy access. Cafés. Disabled access: lift, toilet. Nappy-changing facilities. Restaurants. Shops.*

Rich Mix

35-47 Bethnal Green Road, E1 6LA (7613 7498, www.richmix.org.uk). Bethnal Green or Liverpool Street tube/rail. **Open** *Box office* 9.30am-9.30pm daily. **Admission** prices vary; phone for details. **Credit** MC, V.
This vast former textiles factory now houses a cross-cultural arts and media centre – with an edgy, East End flavour all of its own. There are monthly storytelling and performance poetry sessions, plus inexpensive film-making workshops for five to 12s on selected Sundays

There's plenty for youngsters to enjoy at the **Southbank Centre**.

and school holiday dates, with a maximum of ten youngsters per session. Meanwhile, Saturday and Sunday mornings bring Kids' Cine Time, with tickets at a mere £1.50 for adults or children; major Hollywood releases and animations dominate the programme. Family tickets, available before 5pm on weekdays and all day on Saturdays and Sundays are also brilliant value, while friendly parent and baby screenings take place on Monday evenings. Check online for details of the youth programme, which could encompass anything from graffiti projects to krumping and Bollywood dance classes. *Buggy access. Cafés. Disabled access: lift, toilet. Nappy-changing facilities.*

Southbank Centre

Belvedere Road, SE1 8XX (0844 847 9910, www.southbankcentre.co.uk). Embankment tube/Waterloo tube/rail. **Open** *Box office & foyer* 10am-8pm daily. *Hayward Gallery* 10am-6pm Mon-Thur, Sat, Sun; 10am-10pm Fri. **Admission** prices vary; phone for details. **Credit** AmEx, MC, V. **Map** p317 M8.
Set by the Thames, with the London Eye looming overhead, the Southbank Centre is a cultural behemoth of many parts – namely the Royal Festival Hall, the Queen Elizabeth Hall, the Hayward Gallery and the Saison Poetry Library.

It offers a heady mix of theatre, puppet shows, contemporary and classical music, circus performances, dance and art, including plenty of free events; the website has a comprehensive rundown of upcoming child-friendly offerings – which might run the gamut from classical concerts, with pieces chosen for their child appeal, to free beatboxing workshops.

Simply wandering about can be richly rewarding though – you might stumble across a weird sound sculpture, find dancers waltzing across the terrace, encounter some science buskers or catch a gospel choir in full throttle. The school holidays also mean more family activities, with treasure trails, performances, storytelling and large-scale drawing escapades, usually all free. Meanwhile, the Royal Festival Hall's music learning space, Spirit Level, includes a technology area where young people can experiment with composition and sound-making (book workshops in advance). *See also p30* **Great Days Out**.
Buggy access. Cafés. Disabled access: lift, toilet. Nappy-changing facilities. Restaurants.

Tricycle Theatre & Cinema

269 Kilburn High Road, NW6 7JR (box office 7328 1000, www.tricycle.co.uk). Kilburn tube/ Brondesbury rail. **Open** *Box office* 10am-9pm Mon-Sat; 2-8pm Sun. *Children's shows* 11.30am,

2pm Sat. *Children's films* 1pm Sat. **Tickets** *Theatre* (Sat) £5-£6; £4 reductions. *Films* (Sat) £4.50; £3.50 reductions, under-16s. **Credit** MC, V.

An art gallery, cinema and theatre in one, with its own buzzy café and bar, the Tricycle has deep local roots and a real community feel. There's a brilliant line-up of children's theatre, events and groups, from preschooler activity sessions and performances of *Goldilocks and the Three Bears* (teddies are welcome too), *Old Mother Hubbard* and the like to drama workshops and youth theatre groups for older children and teens. Half-term and holiday workshops focus on magic, theatre, circus skills and even fuzzy felt, while term-time after-school classes currently include guitar and street dance. Kids' cinema matinée screenings are at 1pm on Saturdays.

Buggy access. Disabled access: lift, toilet. Nappy-changing facilities. Restaurant.

CINEMAS

The capital is superb for cinema, catering to film buffs of all ages. As well as a wealth of kids' cinema clubs and weekend matinée screenings to choose from, children even have their own festival. The London Children's Film Festival, now in its sixth year, generally takes place in November;

its headquarters are the Barbican (*see p163*), but independent cinemas city-wide also get involved in the fun.

If you don't mind blowing the budget on the latest blockbuster screening and a bucket of absurdly-priced popcorn, go to Leicester Square. It's home to the glitzy, glossy flagships of **Vue** (0871 224 0240, www.myvue.com), the **Odeon** (0871 224 4007, www.odeon.co.uk) and the **Empire** (0871 4714 714, www.empirecinemas.co.uk). Some of the big chains also do their own version of Watch with Baby screenings, as pioneered at the **Clapham Picturehouse** (*see p167*) and now a regular feature in all Picturehouses. In addition to the cinemas below, don't forget the **Tricycle** (*see p164*).

BFI IMAX

1 Charlie Chaplin Walk, SE1 8XR (7199 6000, www.bfi.org.uk/imax). Waterloo tube/rail. **Open** *Box office* (by phone) 10.30am-7.30pm daily; (in person) from 30mins before screening. **Admission** £14; £9.75-£10.75 reductions; £9.25 3-14s; free under-3s. IMAX short films £8.50; £6.25 reductions; £5.25 4-14s; free under-4s. **Credit** MC, V.

A distinctive circular structure set in a sunken traffic island by Waterloo station houses the UK's biggest cinema screen – over 20m (65ft) high and 26m (85ft) wide. Children love donning 3D glasses to watch special effects-heavy films

BFI IMAX

Activities

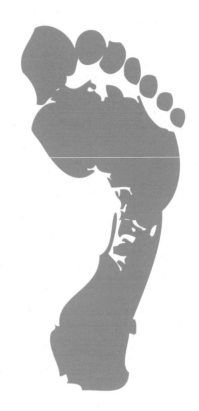

Whatever your carbon footprint, we can reduce it

For over a decade we've been leading the way in carbon offsetting and carbon management.

In that time we've purchased carbon credits from over 200 projects spread across 6 continents. We work with over 300 major commercial clients and thousands of small and medium sized businesses, which rely upon our market-leading quality assurance programme, our experience and absolute commitment to deliver the right solution for each client.

Why not give us a call?

T: London (020) 7833 6000

such as *Avatar*; it's an intense, larger-than-life experience, so avoid anything too alarming for younger children. Non-IMAX mainstream films are also shown. *See also p30* **Great Days Out**. *Bar. Buggy access. Café. Disabled access: lift, toilet. Nappy-changing facilities.*

BFI Southbank

Belvedere Road, SE1 8XT (box office 7928 3232, www.bfi.org.uk). Embankment tube/ Waterloo tube/rail. **Open** *Box office* (by phone) 11.30am-8.30pm daily; (in person) 11am-8.30pm daily. **Tickets** £5-£9 non-members; £6.40-£7.60 members; phone for children's prices. **Membership** £40/yr. **Credit** AmEx, MC, V. **Map** p317 M8.

Following a 2007 revamp, the four-screen British Film Institute (better known as the BFI) has gone from strength to strength. Check the schedule for parent and toddler showings and kids' screenings, both of which combine classic and current hits. At the monthly Fundays, activities accompany the film and the Benugo café-bar serves a special menu. Another brilliant feature is being able to watch film and television clips in the Mediatheque. *See also p30* **Great Days Out**. *Buggy access. Café. Disabled access: lift, toilet. Nappy-changing facilities. Restaurant.*

Clapham Picturehouse

76 Venn Street, SW4 0AT (0871 704 2055 , www.picturehouses.co.uk). Clapham Common tube/35, 37 bus. **Open** *Box office* (by phone) 9.30am-8.30pm daily; (in person) noon-8.30pm daily. *Kids' club activities* 11.15am, *screening* 11.45am Sat. **Tickets** £6.50-£10.50; £5-£7 reductions; £5 3-15s. *Kids' club* £3. **Membership** *Kids' club* £4/yr. **Credit** MC, V.

This much-loved local cinema was the first in London to offer parent-and-baby screenings. Big Scream! sessions for parents and under-ones still run every Thursday at 10.30am, and innovative autism-friendly screenings have also been introduced. There are Kids' Club Saturday matinées for three- to ten-year-olds, with craft workshops before the film; young members can go into the projection room and start the film as a birthday treat. *Buggy access. Café. Disabled access: toilet. Nappy-changing facilities.*

Electric Cinema

191 Portobello Road, W11 2ED (7908 9696, www.the-electric.co.uk). Ladbroke Grove or Notting Hill Gate tube/52 bus. **Open** *Box office* 9am-8.30pm Mon-Sat; 10am-9.30pm Sun. **Tickets** *Kids' club* £5-£6.50 over-3s. *Workshops* (1st Sat of month) £3. **Credit** AmEx, MC, V. **Map** p310 A7.

A far cry from your average multiplex, Notting Hill's Electric Cinema brings a touch of glamour to a trip to the flicks. Plush leather seating, footstools and tables make for a truly luxurious cinematic experience, with superior snacks to munch on; adults can quaff a glass of chilled pinot grigio or even a cocktail. There's a Saturday morning Kids' Club (10.30am), while friendly Electric Scream! shows for parents and under-ones are held at 3pm on Mondays (except bank holidays). *Buggy access. Disabled access: lift, toilet.*

Greenwich Picturehouse

180 Greenwich High Road, SE10 8NN (0871 704 2059, www.picturehouses.co.uk). Cutty Sark DLR/Greenwich rail/DLR. **Open** *Box office* (by phone) 9.30am-8.30pm daily; (in person) 11am-10pm daily. *Kids' Club activities* 11am Sat, screening 11.30am. **Tickets** £6-£10; £5.50-6.50 under-14s, reductions. *Kids' club* £4.50. **Membership** *Kids' club* £4.50/yr. **Credit** AmEx, MC, V.

Opened in 2005, the four-screen Greenwich outpost of the acclaimed Picturehouse chain has its own tapas bar. There's a children's film club on Saturday morning, suitable for fives to 15s, plus Big Scream! events at 11.30am on Wednesday and Friday. *Buggy access. Café. Disabled access: lift, toilet. Nappy-changing facilities. Restaurant.*

Phoenix

52 High Road, N2 9PJ (8444 6789, www. phoenixcinema.co.uk). East Finchley tube. **Open** *Box office* 15mins before first screening. *Kids' club* noon Sat, £2. **Tickets** £6-£9; £6 under-16s, reductions. **Credit** MC, V.

East Finchley's single-screen art deco treasure offers Bringing Up Baby screenings (normally held on Wednesdays) and Saturday-afternoon Kids' Club movies, kicking off with a hands-on activity workshop, games or a quiz and aimed at five- to eight-year-olds. The cinema can also be hired out for birthday parties; phone the cinema for details. *Buggy access. Nappy-changing facilities. Disabled access: lift, toilet.*

Rio Cinema

103-107 Kingsland High Street, E8 2PB (7241 9410, www.riocinema.co.uk). Dalston Kingsland rail/Liverpool Street tube/rail, then 67, 77, 149 bus. **Open** *Box office* (by phone) 2-8pm daily; (in person) from 30 mins before screening. *Children's screening* 4pm Tue; 11am Sat. **Tickets** £6.50-£8.50; £5 2-16s; *Children's screening* £2.50; £1.50 under-16s. **Credit** MC, V.

Activities

Baby Loves Disco

Expect an engaging mix of films at this Dalston favourite, which isn't afraid to eschew predictable Hollywood fodder in favour of more interesting smaller films and classics. Youthful members of the Saturday Morning Picture Club are given a special card to be stamped, with a free visit after ten stamps and a poster after 25 – a generous offer, considering how inexpensive tickets are. A parent-and-baby club operates on selected Tuesday and Thursday lunchtimes, with a secure place to park pushchairs, and the school holidays bring daily matinées for five- to 15-year-olds. *Buggy access. Café. Disabled access: toilet.*

Ritzy Picturehouse

Brixton Oval, Coldharbour Lane, SW2 1JG (0871 704 2065, www.picturehouses.co.uk). Brixton tube/rail. **Open** *Box office* (by phone) *9.30am-8.30pm daily. Kids' club 10.30am Sat.* **Tickets** *£6.50-£10.50; £4.50-£5 under-14s. Kids' club £3; £2 3-15s.* **Membership** *Kids' club £3/yr.* **Credit** MC, V.

Opened in 1911, this local landmark has survived numerous owners and name changes, not to mention near-demolition and dastardly redevelopment plans. Now part of the Picturehouse family, it hosts Big Scream! sessions on Fridays at 11am, open to parents with under-ones. Children as young as three can join the inexpensive Saturday Kids' Club, and there are regular autism-friendly screenings; call the box office or check online for details. There's also a laid-back café bar, with a kids' menu. *Buggy access. Café. Disabled access: lift, toilet. Nappy-changing facilities.*

Stratford East Picturehouse

Theatre Square, Salway Road, E15 1BX (0871 704 2066, www.picturehouses.co.uk). Stratford tube/rail/DLR. **Open** *Box office* (by phone) *9.30am-8.30pm daily. Kids' club 10.50am Sat.* **Tickets** *£4-£9; £4. under-15s. Kids' club £6; £3 3-10s.* **Membership** *Kids' club £4/yr.* **Credit** MC, V.

Attractions for families and children at this Picturehouse branch include a children's film club where creative activities, fun and games take place before a screening. The club is suitable for three- to ten-year-olds, and membership entitles you to attend the first film for free. *Bar. Buggy access. Disabled access: lift, toilet. Nappy-changing facilities.*

COMEDY

Comedy Club 4 Kids

Soho Theatre, 21 Dean Street, W1D 3NE (7478 0100, www.sohotheatre.com). Tottenham Court Road/Leicester Square/Oxford Circus tube. **Open** *Box office* 10am-7pm Mon-Sat. **Credit** MC, V. **Map** p315 K6.

The Soho Theatre's monthly Comedy Club 4 Kids is a winning combination of top-flight adult comedic talent and gags, without the rude bits. Well, not all the rude bits. This is aimed at children, after all, so there is a fair amount of scatologically inclined material, but nothing that would make parents blanch. It's staged along the same lines as a late-night comedy club, with the compère whipping the audience into a

Activities

heckle-inducing frenzy, before the first (often palpably nervous) comedian takes to the stage. *Bar. Buggy access. Café. Disabled access: lift, toilets. Nappy-changing facilities. Restaurant.*

DANCE

Discos & clubs

Toddlers generally embrace disco dancing with gusto – and now there are events where tinies can show their elders a move or two. Cynics might say it's a sign that children are growing up too fast while their parents can't bear to grow up at all – but a spirited burst of *We are Family* soon drowns the naysayers out.

The following events take place at various venues across town; check online to find out where the next disco will be.

Baby Loves Disco
www.babylovesdisco.co.uk.
An import from the US, BLD is thriving on these shores. Sunday-afternoon discos take place in a handful of venues, accompanied by choice 1970s and '80s tunes.

Planet Angel
www.planetangel.net.
Planet Angel's Sunday-afternoon 'Chilled' gatherings have been running in north London since 2001. It aims to create a positive, safe, social environment for children of all ages.

Whirl-Y-Gig
www.whirl-y-gig.org.uk.
This long-established collective welcomes families to its events – they're a joyous mix of carnival and alternative clubbing, with some eclectic tunes. A favourite venue for events is Jacks (7-9 Crucifix Lane, SE1 3JW). Under-18s must be accompanied by a parent, and you have to call ahead.

Tuition

For all things dance-related in the capital, including children's classes for all abilities, visit www.londondance.com.

Chisenhale Dance Space
64-84 Chisenhale Road, E3 5QZ (8981 6617, www.chisenhaledancespace.co.uk). Mile End tube. **Fees** £36/£24 2-8s, reductions; £5 11-17s youth group. **Credit** MC, V.
This Bow-based dance studio offers creative dance courses for two to eights, plus a Saturday

youth group where 11 to 17s are taught a blend of street, contemporary, jazz and creative dance. Guest choreographers from other disciplines, from ballet to Bollywood, have been known to drop in to share their wisdom. *Buggy access.*

Coconut Grove
336 Ladbroke Grove, W10 5AH (8969 8371, www.coconutgrovestudios.com). Ladbroke Grove tube. **Fees** £4.75-£9.50. **No credit cards.**
These sleek, light-filled studios in Notting Hill are busy all day and evening with a varied timetable of classes. Babies and toddlers can try out Maestro Music, where they're introduced to musical instruments and singing, or Jumping Jacks, which combines singing with movement. Classes for older children are divided by age (four to sevens; eight to 12s; 13 to 17s) and range from ballet, cheerleading and street dance to acting, jazz and musical theatre dance. *Buggy access. Cafe. Children's menu. Nappy-changing facilities. Play area.*

Dance Attic
368 North End Road, SW6 1LY (7610 2055, www.danceattic.com). Fulham Broadway tube. **Fees** £2/day; £40/6mths; £70/yr; £15/6 mths, £25/yr 13-16s. **Classes** £4-£6. *Children's ballet* £50-£62/11wk term. **Credit** MC, V.
Ballet classes for over-threes go up to Intermediate level, with RAD exams at each grade. There's also a shop stocking leotards, ballet shoes and other dance essentials. *Shop.*

Danceworks
16 Balderton Street, W1K 6TN (7629 6183, www.danceworks.net). Bond Street or Marble Arch tube. **Classes** times vary; phone for details. **Fees** *Membership* £2-£5/day; £123/year. *Classes* £4-£11/class. **Credit** AmEx, MC, V.
Six studios occupy Danceworks' stately Victorian premises, offering a vast array of adults' classes. For kids (two to 18s), there's ballet, jazz and tap, plus drop-in street dance for 11 to 16s with the Impact Youth Academy. *Buggy access. Nappy-changing facilities.*

Diddi Dance
07973 982790, www.diddidance.com.
These energetic, exuberant dance and movement classes for two to fours are tremendous fun. Free taster sessions are offered, so you can see if your little darling likes it before committing to a four or eight-week block. Dance-themed birthday parties can also be arranged.

Activities

East London Dance

Various venues around east London (8279 1050, www.eastlondondance.org). **Classes** times vary; phone for details. **Fees** free-£1. **No credit cards.**
Brazilian samba, street dance and creative, contemporary styles are favoured by this creative community. Check out the upcoming programme of free On the Move dance classes for young people. For those with all the right moves, Brink Dance is a dance company for 11 to 16s (auditions are held in September).

Greenwich Dance Agency

Borough Hall, Royal Hill, SE10 8RE (8293 9741, www.greenwichdance.org.uk). Greenwich rail. **Classes** times vary; phone for details. **Fees** *Drop-in £4 0-2s. Courses £40-£48/term 6-12s, £30-£36/term 13-20s.* **Credit** MC, V.
A packed programme has something for children of all ages, starting with relaxed drop-in classes for zero to twos. At the other end of the spectrum, 13 to 20s can work with professional choreographers, fusing multiple styles and techniques. In all age groups, the focus is on creativity and having fun.
Buggy access. Disabled access: toilet. Nappy-changing facilities.

Laban

Creekside, SE8 3DZ (8691 8600, www.laban.org). Cutty Sark DLR/Deptford rail. **Classes & fees** times & prices vary; phone for details. **Credit** MC, V.
Deptford is the slightly unlikely home to this stunning contemporary dance conservatoire, housed in an iconic, semi-translucent building designed by Herzog & de Meuron. Children's movement, contemporary dance and ballet lessons run throughout the week, though many have a sizeable waiting list. Once your child is in a class, however, the experience is fantastic; the annual Children's Show, presenting work by students aged from four to 14, showcases the kids' talents – and is packed with proud parents.
Buggy access. Disabled access: toilet. Café. Nappy-changing facilities.

Pineapple Performing Arts School

7 Langley Street, WC2H 9JA (8351 8839, www.pineapplearts.com). Covent Garden tube. **Classes** *Drop-in* 1-2pm (under-13s), 2-3pm (12-16s) Sat; 1-2pm (12-16s), 2-3pm (under-13s) Sun. *Term classes* 11am-noon (3-4s), 11am-2pm (5-12s), 2-5pm (13-17s) Sun. **Fees** £90/12wk term 3-4s; £295/12wk term over-4s; £6 drop-in session; £195 holiday course. *Trial class* £25. *Registration fee* £30-£35. **Credit** MC, V. **Map** p315 L6.

Drop-in musical, theatre, dance, ballet and street dance classes are held at these legendary Covent Garden studios every weekend; just turn up, hand over your £6 and dance. Those prepared to commit to 12-week terms can sign up for the lively Sunday School, comprising 'Pineapple Chunks' sessions for tinies, junior classes for kids and early teens, and senior classes for 13- to 17-year-olds. Intensive musical theatre and street dance courses are offered during the Easter and summer holidays.
Café.

The Place

17 Duke's Road, WC1H 9PY (box office 7121 1100, classes 7121 1090, www.theplace.org.uk). Euston tube/rail. **Classes** times vary; phone for details. **Fees** from £90-£99/11wk term; £5 discount for 2nd or subsequent class taken by same student or a sibling. **Credit** MC, V. **Map** p315 K3.
The ethos at this contemporary dance hub is that anyone can learn to dance; the centre is accessible to all ages, as well as to the disabled. There is, however, a waiting list. A steady stream of parents and kids head here on Saturdays, when classes for five- to 18-year-olds range from playful, free-form First Moves sessions to contemporary dance. More unusually, there are choreography classes for children, and all-boys 'Energiser' sessions. Shift, a company for talented 13- to 19-year-old dancers, meets twice weekly during term time to perform work by a range of choreographers; hotly-contested auditions are held every September.
Bar. Buggy access. Café. Disabled access: toilet.

Royal Academy of Dance

36 Battersea Square, SW11 3RA (7326 8000, www.rad.org.uk). Clapham Junction rail/170 bus. **Classes** times vary; phone for details. **Fees** £6-£12.50/class; £60-£154/term. **Credit** AmEx, MC, V.
The Academy's studios are a hotbed for all sorts of dance styles. Popular classes include West End jazz, tap and contemporary, with various offerings for different age groups and abilities. The ballet department accepts pupils of three and above, and there are all-boys' ballet lessons for six to nines and eight to 11s. Summer schools and workshops keep dance-mad children on their toes during school hols.
Buggy access.

Venues

See also **Chisenhale Dance Space** (*see p169*), **Laban** and **The Place** (for both, *see above*).

Royal Opera House

Bow Street, WC2E 9DD (box office 7304 4000, www.royaloperahouse.org). Covent Garden tube. **Open** *Box office* 10am-8pm Mon-Sat. *Tours* daily *(times vary, book in advance).* **Tours** £10; £9 reductions; £7 9-16s. **Credit** AmEx, MC, V. **Map** p317 L6.

Don't be daunted at the prospect of visiting one of the world's great opera houses with kids in tow: families are warmly welcomed. Inside it's bright and airy, with sumptuous costumes on display and splendid views over Covent Garden's crowds and street entertainers from the upstairs café. An engaging line-up of special events runs from puppet-making in the light-flooded Paul Hamlyn Hall to musical, magical afternoons with players from the orchestra, choreographers and composers, where everyone gets involved. Look out for child-friendly spectaculars such as *Peter and the Wolf* and *Cinderella* in 2010, and *Alice's Adventure's in Wonderland* in 2011. *See also p46* **Great Days Out**.

Buggy access. Café. Disabled access: lift, toilet. Nappy-changing facilities. Restaurant. Shop.

Sadler's Wells

Rosebery Avenue, EC1R 4TN (0844 412 4300, www.sadlerswells.com). Angel tube. **Open** *Box office* 9am-8.30pm Mon-Sat. **Credit** AmEx, MC, V.

As the epicentre of dance in London, Sadler's Wells attracts all sorts of dance superstars – including some child-friendly companies, such as the London Children's Ballet. Elsewhere in the programme, there's lots to interest older children and teenagers, including Breakin' Convention – a high-octane annual hip hop jamboree. In the adjacent Lilian Bayliss Theatre, the two-week Connect Festival is another good bet for families, mixing lively workshops with performances from dancers of all ages. The Peacock Theatre (Portugal Street, WC2A 2HT, 0844 412 4322) is a satellite venue for Sadler's Wells, with family shows every Christmas.

Bar. Buggy access. Cafés. Disabled access: lift, toilet. Nappy-changing facilities. Restaurant.

LITERATURE

Libraries

British Library

96 Euston Road, NW1 2DB (7412 7676, learning 7412 7797, www.bl.uk). Euston or King's Cross tube/rail. **Open** 9.30am-6pm Mon, Wed-Fri; 9.30am-8pm Tue; 9.30am-5pm Sat; 11am-5pm Sun, bank hols. **Credit** MC, V. **Map** p317 K3.

Activities

Perfecting the moves at **Pineapple Performing Arts School**.

Even cynical small fry can't fail to be impressed by the sheer scale of the British Library – a red brick behemoth that's home to over 150 million pieces of writing. What's more, its collection is growing at a fearsome rate: every year, the library receives a copy of everything published in the UK and Ireland, including books, newspapers, maps, magazines, prints and drawings. Its most prized treasures are on display in the dimly-lit Sir John Ritblat Gallery, including the Magna Carta, Lewis Carroll's *Alice's Adventure Under Ground* and some scribbled Beatles lyrics. Temporary exhibitions in the PACCAR Gallery are often accompanied by hands-on workshops and special events, while a smaller gallery in the entrance hall contains interactive displays on music and culture linked to the National Sound Archives.

The education department arranges regular storytelling sessions and hands-on arty workshops (carnival mask-making, perhaps, or drawing your own magnificent map) during the school holidays – see www.bl.uk/learning for details. Finally, the café is a Peyton and Byrne establishment, which means delectable treacle tarts, extravagantly-topped cupcakes and a nice line in quiches, proper sausage rolls and hot meals – at a price, mind.
Buggy access. Café. Disabled access: lift, toilet. Nappy-changing facilities. Restaurant. Shop.

Charlton House
Charlton Road, SE7 8RE (8856 3951, www. greenwich.gov.uk). Charlton rail/53, 54, 380, 422 bus. **Open** *Library* 2-7pm Mon, Thur; 9.30am-12.30pm, 1.30-5.30pm Tue, Fri; 9.30am-12.30pm, 1.30-5pm Sat. *Toy Library* (term-time only) 9.30am-12.30pm Tue, Fri (2-5s); 9.30am-12.30pm Thur (under-2s). **Admission** free. **No credit cards.**
This handsome, early 17th-century red brick mansion now houses a community centre and library. Traces of its past grandeur remain – not least the creaky oak staircase, marble fireplaces and ornate plaster ceilings. The library has a good children's section, and runs preschooler play and story sessions. Charlton Toy Library (8319 0055, www.charltontoylibrary.co.uk) is also based here, and has music and story sessions on Thursday mornings. The mulberry tree outside, dating from 1608, still bears fruit that sometimes finds its way into the crumbles, cakes and chutneys sold in the Mulberry Café. Visit at 1pm on a Friday and you'll be treated to a free concert by musicians from the Trinity College of Music, who also put on a soaring Christmas concert.
Buggy access. Café. Disabled access: lift, toilet. Nappy-changing facilities.

Idea Store
321 Whitechapel Road, E1 1BU (7364 4332, www.ideastore.co.uk). Whitechapel tube. **Open** 9am-9pm Mon-Thur; 9am-6pm Fri; 9am-5pm Sat; 11am-5pm Sun. **Credit** MC, V.
You can't miss Whitechapel's gleaming, glass-fronted Idea Store – a bold, 21st-century take on the library, built by Adjaye Associates. In addition to its book collections, it offers state-of-the-art learning and information services and an airy fourth-floor café. All sorts of groups meet here, from toddler and parent get-togethers to drop-in homework clubs – there's even a gathering for comic book and manga fans (nine to 16s). For 16 and overs, the borough's network of Idea Stores offer over 900 courses. A handful of courses are aimed at families – among them, creative dance, art and design and cookery classes for parents and children. Call or check online for dates, prices and age restrictions.
Buggy access. Café. Crèche. Disabled access: lift, toilet. Nappy-changing facilities.
Branches 1 Gladstone Place, Roman Road, E3 5ES (7364 4332); 1 Vesey Path, East India Dock Road, E14 6BT (7364 4332); Churchill Place, E14 5RB (7364 4332).

Peckham Library
122 Peckham Hill Street, SE15 5JR (7525 2000, www.southwark.gov.uk). Peckham Rye or Queen's Road rail/12, 36, 63, 171 bus. **Open** 9am-8pm Mon, Tue, Thur, Fri; 10am-8pm Wed; 10am-5pm Sat; noon-4pm Sun. **No credit cards.**
Will Alsop's unusual-looking, inverted L-shaped library plays host to a rich array of children's activities, including creative baby and toddler sessions and Sure Start and family reading groups. Mondays and Fridays bring in the Homework Club (4-7pm), while the teenage reading group's activities range far beyond literary discussions: open mic nights, creative writing workshops, debates and manga nights were on the schedule last time we dropped by. An extended programme of holiday workshops is also offered.
Buggy access. Disabled access: lift, toilet. Nappy-changing facilities.

Storytelling

Discover
1 Bridge Terrace, E15 4BG (8536 5555, www. discover.org.uk). Stratford tube/rail/DLR. **Open** *Term-time* 10am-5pm Tue-Fri; 11am-5pm Sat, Sun. *Holidays* 10am-5pm Mon-Fri; 11am-5pm Sat, Sun. **Admission** *Garden* free. *Story trail* £4; £3.50 reductions; free under-2s; £14 family (2+2). **Credit** MC, V.

opportunities for young people lie at the heart of the Roundhouse Studios, tucked below the circular hall. The eclectic workshops held here often focus on multimedia skills: filming as part of a camera crew, producing a radio show and costume design have all featured in the past, at a mere £2 a day. *See also p108* **Great Days Out**. *Bars. Buggy access. Café. Disabled access: toilet. Nappy-changing facilities.*

Royal Albert Hall

Kensington Gore, SW7 2AP (7589 8212, www.royalalberthall.com). South Kensington or Knightsbridge tube. **Open** *Box office* 9am-9pm daily. **Tickets** £5-£150. **Credit** AmEx, MC, V. **Map** p313 D9.

The 5,200-capacity rotunda, dubbed 'the nation's village hall', hosts special Family Proms during the annual BBC Proms, from July to September. The Proms Plus series, meanwhile, comprises free family events at the nearby Royal College of Music, involving musical activities and workshops that provide a bit of background on the stories behind the music. In the daytime, guided tours let you peep at the auditorium (where, if you're lucky, rehearsals may be under way for that evening's performance); one child can go free with every paying adult (£8). Note that the tour isn't suitable for under-sevens. *Bars. Buggy access. Café. Disabled access: lift, toilet. Nappy-changing facilities. Restaurants. Shop.*

Wigmore Hall

36 Wigmore Street, W1U 2BP (7935 2141, education 7258 8227, www.wigmore-hall. org.uk). Bond Street or Oxford Circus tube. **Open** *Box office* 10am-7pm daily (8.30pm on performance nights). **Tickets** £10-£30. **Credit** AmEx, MC, V. **Map** p314 H5.

With its acres of marble, wooden panelling and plush red seating, this art deco recital hall oozes grandeur. Happily, small fry are made very welcome here, thanks to a busy programme of family, community and outreach projects. The star attraction is Chamber Tots: these music and movement classes for two- to five-year-olds are immensely popular. Once-monthly family concerts, generally of specially-commissioned works, are also great fun, and suitable for five-and-overs. Regular Family Days bring more opportunities to try a spot of composing, join a junk jam, do some painting or meet the musicians and their instruments. *Bar. Buggy access. Disabled access: toilet. Nappy-changing facilities. Restaurant.*

PLAYTIME

Indoor play centres

Bramley's Big Adventure

136 Bramley Road, W10 6TJ (8960 1515, www.bramleysbig.co.uk). Latimer Road tube. **Open** *Term-time* 10am-6pm Mon-Fri; 10am-6.30pm Sat, Sun. *Holidays* 10am-6.30pm daily. **Membership** £20/yr. **Admission** *Members* £2.50 under-2s; £4 2-5s; £4.50 over-5s; free adults. *Non-members* £3.50 under-2s; £5 2-5s; £5.50 over-5s; 50p adults. **Credit** AmEx, MC, V.

Organised chaos reigns at Bramley's, tucked beneath the Westway flyover. The centrepiece is a giant three-level play frame, incorporating slides, ball pools, swings and dens, with separate areas for less rambunctious under-fives and babies. There's no time limit on play sessions, so children can play all day; free Wi-Fi lets parents catch up on work while their offspring tear about. Commendably, the café offers organic and fair trade grub; ask about children's parties, which include meals and party bags. *Buggy access (must be locked up outside). Café. Disabled access: toilet. Nappy-changing facilities.*

Discovery Planet

1st floor, Surrey Quays Shopping Centre, Redriff Road, SE16 7LL (7237 2388). Canada Water tube. **Open** 10am-6pm Mon-Sat; noon-5pm Sun. **Admission** £3.49-£4.49 under-2s; £3.99-£4.99 2-10s; free adults & babies. **Credit** (over £10) MC, V.

Filled with brightly coloured tubes, tunnels, ball ponds and slides, this huge indoor play area gives under-tens the chance to climb, slide and throw themselves about for two action-packed hours. *Buggy access. Nappy-changing facilities.*

Eddie Catz

68-70 High Street, SW15 1SF (0845 201 1268, www.eddiecatz.com). Putney Bridge tube. **Open** 9am-6pm daily. **Admission** £4.50 under 90cm; £5.50 90cm-1.55m; £1 over 1.55m; free babies under 8mths. **Credit** MC, V.

For tinies, Eddie Catz offers a soft play area and movement and music classes (for which an extra charge applies). Toddlers and older children, meanwhile, can enjoy a modestly sized adventure play frame, as well as a dressing-up area, video games and air hockey, while parents are kept sweet with newspapers and free Wi-Fi. Membership deals are available (from £65 for six months), as are birthday

Activities

parties; the Wimbledon branch also offers laser-tag parties for children aged six to 12. *Buggy access. Café. Disabled access: lift, toilet. Nappy-changing facilities. Shop.*
Branch 42 Station Road, SW19 2LP (8288 8178).

Gambado
7 Station Court, Townmead Road, SW6 2PY (7384 1635, www.gambado.com). Fulham Broadway tube/391 bus. **Open** 9.30am-6.30pm daily. **Admission** £7.45 1-2s; £9.45 3-10s; £2.50 adults; free under-1s. **Credit** MC, V.
Cheery staff and masses of things to do mean Gambado's is eternally popular, despite the hefty entry fee. Kids soon vanish into the depths of the thrilling multi-level climbing frame, which incorporates ball ponds, slides (enclosed twirly tunnels plus bumpy ones large enough for parents to join in), trampolines, assault courses and mini dodgems. Tinies get a soft-play section with big Lego bricks and face-painting. You can refuel on healthy fare at the café, and there's free internet access for the adults. At weekends, it's usually full of birthday parties.
Buggy access. Café. Disabled access: toilet. Nappy-changing facilities.

It's a Kid's Thing
279 Magdalen Road, SW18 3NZ (8739 0909, www.itsakidsthing.co.uk). Earlsfield rail. **Open** 9.30am-6pm Mon-Fri; 9am-6pm Sat, Sun. **Admission** £5 over-2s; £4 under-2s; £2 siblings. Prices of activities vary; check website for details. **Credit** MC, V.
If you find the decibel levels and commotion of bigger play centres unbearable, this sociable, small-scale outfit is a welcome alternative. Children swarm over the two-tier playzone and soft-play area while their parents look on from the café; there's a decent kids' menu, with the option to swap chips for mash, potato wedges or half a jacket potato. Grown-ups fill up on pastas, salads and panini as their offspring play; come the weekend, it's all about relaxing over an all-day fry-up and the papers. The activities schedule includes baby ballet, sing and sign and messy art; check the timetable for details of free singing and dance sessions for toddlers.
Buggy access. Café. Disabled access: toilet. Nappy-changing facilities.

Kidspace
Colonnades, 619 Purley Way, Croydon, Surrey CR0 4RQ (8686 0040, www.kidspaceadventures.com). Waddon rail/119, 289 bus. **Open** *Term-time* 10am-7pm Mon-Thur; 10am-8pm Fri; 9am-8pm Sat; 9am-7pm Sun. *Holidays* 9am-7pm Mon-Thur, Sun; 9am-8pm

Fri, Sat. **Admission** *Weekdays* £5.75; £2.75 adults; free under-1s. *Weekends & holidays* £5.95 under-3s; £8.95 over-3s; £5.50 adults. **Credit** MC, V.
This enormous indoor play centre is a cut above the competition, thanks to its towering wooden climbing frame, the Orb. Unusually, parents are allowed to explore alongside their children, zooming down the 'black hole' slide, getting lost in the labyrinth or dodging cannon fire in Thunderball City. Crazy golf, a climbing wall and cavern maze, mini go-karts and a multi-sensory play area for toddlers round off a very full family day out.
Buggy access. Café. Disabled access: lift, toilet. Nappy-changing facilities. Shop.

Kidzmania
28 Powell Road, E5 8DJ (8533 5556). Clapton rail. **Open** 10am-6pm daily. **Admission** £4.50 4-12s; £3.50 under-4s; free adults. **No credit cards.**
This indoor adventure play centre doubles up as a popular children's party venue, with its own café and full on-site catering (special party menus can be prepared). There are ball pools, climbing frames, slides and bouncy castles to entertain the troops.
Buggy access. Café. Nappy-changing facilities.

Little Dinosaurs
The Actual Workshop, The Grove, Alexandra Park, N22 7AY (8444 1338, 07957 457771, www.littledinosaurs.co.uk). Alexandra Palace rail. **Open** *May-Sept* 9.30am-6pm Mon-Fri; 10am-6pm Sat; 10am-5pm Sun. *Oct-Apr* 9.30am-5.30pm Mon-Fri; 10am-5.30pm Sat; 10am-5pm Sun. **Admission** £3.50-£4.50; adults & under 1s free. **Credit** AmEx, MC, V.
Indoor adventure play centres are loved by kids and tolerated through gritted teeth by adults in a fix on a cold or rainy day. This newcomer, though, is a thoroughly pleasant venue for all the family, whatever the weather. Inside is the usual playframe with slides, tunnels, mats and padded obstacles, but Little Dinosaurs not only has plenty of windows, it's also in the middle of a lovely park. On warmer days, the doors on two sides of this renovated building (unused and unloved by the council for many years) are thrown open to the air and guests can venture out into the generous grassy area (fenced off securely from the park), where there's a terrace with tables and chairs and toys to amuse smaller children, plus a bouncy castle. The café serves good coffee, childen's and adults' meals and snacks.
Buggy access. Café. Chidren's menu. Disabled: toilet. High chairs. Nappy-changing facilities.

Pirate's Playhouse

The Castle Climbing Centre, 271 Green Lanes, N4 2HA (8800 1771). Manor House tube, then 141, 341 bus. **Open** 10am-6pm Mon-Thur; 10am-7pm Fri-Sun. **Admission** £3.90 walkers; £2.50 crawlers; free adults & babes in arms. **Credit** MC, V.

Built as a decorative water pumping station, now a climbing centre, this distinctive Victorian castle also hosts a playframe, separate from the climbing centre itself, and filled with thrilling slides and obstacle courses. It seems small until you look up, its height providing a true challenge to clambering pre-teens; there's also a large toddler area with a spotless ball pool and soft-play puzzles. (The confined space can start to smell a bit like yesterday's socks towards the end of the day, though.) Parents can sit in comfort around the frame, or in a cosy sofa-and-magazine bedecked side room if they trust junior out of sight. Very friendly staff serve good coffee and sandwiches.
Buggy access. Café. Nappy-changing facilities.

Tumble in the Jungle

245 Wood Street, E17 3NT (0870 626 0710, www.tumbleinthejungle.co.uk). Walthamstow Central tube/Wood Street rail. **Open** 9.30am-6pm Mon, 10am-6pm Wed-Fri; Tue, Sat, Sun. **Admission** £3.50; £2.50 before 11am; £1 adults; free under 1s. **No credit cards.**

Walthamstow's indoor play centre is designed on a jungle theme, with separate areas divided by age group. There's a soft play area for babies, a small play frame for toddlers to test their muscles on, and a larger frame for older kids to run riot around. Staff provide extra entertainment and activities from time to time; look out, too, for the water sensory room, the interactive dance mats and the sports arena. As these things go, Tumble in the Jungle's admission prices are pretty reasonable, and there's a café for the adults to escape to for a bit of peace and quiet.
Buggy access. Cafe. Children's menu. Disabled: toilet. High chairs. Nappy-changing facilities.

THEATRE

Tuition

Allsorts

34 Pember Road, NW10 5LS (8969 3249, www.allsortsdrama.com). **Classes** phone for details. **Fees** £100-£180/10wk term; from £80 4-day workshop; 20% sibling discount. **Credit** MC, V.

Alumni from Allsorts have won starring roles in some big-budget flicks: Anna Popplewell (Susan in the *Chronicles of Narnia*) enrolled here at the age of six. Children (four to 18) don't need any

Acting up: fun with drama at **Lewisham Youth Theatre**. *See p180.*

Activities

previous experience to sign up for the Saturday school and holiday workshops; working in small groups, they are encouraged to take a creative approach, with role-playing and improvisation. Teachers can also arrange bespoke at-home acting tuition and drama parties.

Dramarama

8446 0891, www.dramarama.co.uk. Holiday courses: South Hampstead High School, Maresfield Gardens, NW3 5SS. Term-time classes: South Hampstead Junior School, Netherhall Gardens, NW3 5RN. Finchley Road & Frognal rail. **Fees** phone for details. **No credit cards.**
Kids of all ages and abilities can get involved in acting with Dramarama's after-school clubs, Saturday workshops and holiday courses. Three- to four-year-old thespians can become Dramatots, while older children work towards Trinity Guildhall Performance Art exams; these are recognised qualifications, the more advanced grades of which can be converted into university-entrance UCAS points. There's also a birthday party service for six to 14s, with themes ranging from mermaids to murder mysteries.

Helen O'Grady's Children's Drama Academy

01481 200250, www.helenogrady.co.uk. **Classes** times vary; phone for details. **Fees** £98/14wk term. **No credit cards.**
The academy's weekly one-hour workshops aim to build kids' self-esteem, confidence and social skills. The lower and upper primary groups (five to eights and nine to 11s, respectively) work on clear speech and fluent delivery, while the Youth Theatre (13-17s) develops more advanced dramatic techniques. A production is held at the end of the summer term. Check the website to find your nearest group.

Hoxton Hall

130 Hoxton Street, N1 6SH (7684 0060, www.hoxtonhall.co.uk). Hoxton rail. **Classes** times vary; phone for details. **Fees** £20/8wk term. **No credit cards.**
This refurbished Victorian music hall runs a vibrant after-school Youth Arts programme for seven to 19s, incorporating dance, drama and music. Children's abilities and ideas are taken seriously here, and they're given plenty of access to the hall's extensive facilities: seven- to ten-year-old musicians can compose and record their own songs in the recording studio, while the street dance group (11-17s) devises performances for the main stage with the help of professional choreographers and dancers. *Buggy access. Café.*

Lewisham Youth Theatre

Broadway Theatre, Catford Broadway, SE6 4RU (8690 3428, box office 8690 0002, www.lewishamyouththeatre.com). Catford or Catford Bridge rail/75, 181, 185, 202, 660 bus. **Classes** *Junior Youth Theatre* (8-11s,) 75 mins Wed, Sat. *Senior Youth Theatre* (15-21s) 6-8pm Mon, Thur. *ROAR! Children's Theatre* (2-11s & families) Oct-Dec 11.30am Sat. **Tickets** £4.50 (ROAR!). **Credit** (Box office) MC, V.
Lewisham Youth Theatre has forged itsself a reputation for innovation, variety and high standards. It's also stuck to its aim of making theatre accessible to all: there are no auditions, and classes and workshops are free. Most recruitment takes place in schools, but some places are allocated on a first come, first served basis. All classes work towards full productions, and there is some crossover between junior and senior groups. For details of children's theatre performances at Broadway Theatre, *see p184. Buggy access. Disabled access: toilets.*

London Bubble Theatre Company

5 Elephant Lane, SE16 4JD (7237 4434, www.londonbubble.org.uk). Bermondsey, Canada Water or Rotherhithe tube. **Open** *Box office* June-Sept 10am-6pm Mon-Fri. **Classes** phone for details. **Fees** £24-£48/12wk term. **Credit** MC, V.

Little Angel Theatre. *See p182.*

Activities

The Bubble's exemplary arts programme includes term-time theatre groups for six to eights, nine to 12s and 13-17s. There are no nail-biting auditions; all you need to take part are enthusiasm and commitment (though there may be a waiting list, as places are much in demand). Check online for details of the summer Open Performance Theatre Project, open to all ages, and the Bubble's groups in Forest Hill and Rotherhithe.

Millfield Theatre School

Silver Street, N18 1PJ (box office 8807 6680, www.millfieldtheatre.co.uk). Silver Street rail/34, 102, 144, 217, 231, W6 bus. **Open** *Box office* 10am-6pm Mon-Sat. **Classes** (4-5s) 10.30am-noon, (6-7s) 12.30-2pm, (8-14s) 11am-2pm Sun. **Fees** (4-5s, 6-7s) £100/10wk term; (8-14s) £185/10wk term. **Credit** MC, V.
Sundays at Millfield are devoted to children's theatre, with four- to 14-year-olds split into three age groups. If acting doesn't appeal, kids can enrol in all sorts of alternative classes, including ballet, tap, creative clay, manga drawing and chess. The theatre itself presents a regular calendar of musicals, comedies and drama, as well as some perky touring shows and the time-honoured Christmas panto; for 2010, it's *Jack and the Beanstalk*.
Buggy access. Disabled access: toilets.

National Youth Music Theatre

Head office: 2-4 Great Eastern Street, EC2A 3NW (7422 8290, www.nymt.org.uk). Old Street tube/rail. **Classes** phone or check website for details. **Fees** prices vary; phone for details. **No credit cards.**
The NYMT's glittering list of alumni speaks for itself, featuring the likes of Jamie Bell, Matt Lucas, Sheridan Smith and Jude Law. The company continues to audition young hopefuls for its amazing shows; check online for details of auditions and regional workshops. Stage-management opportunities appeal to those keen to work behind the scenes, while accomplished young musicians can nab orchestral roles.

Perform

Office: 49 Chalton Street, NW1 1LT (0845 400 4000, www.perform.org.uk). **Classes** phone for details. **Fees** £139/10wk term (weekday); £195/10wk term (weekends); free trials. **Credit** MC, V.
The four Cs (confidence, communication, concentration and co-ordination) are the focus at Perform – and you're never too young to start learning the basics. Story- and song-packed Mini Ps classes are aimed at three-month to three-year-olds, while sessions for four to eights and eight to 12s blend acting, singing and dancing. The website has details of venues, information

on the party service, and the latest on holiday workshops such as the all-singing, all-dancing Popstar Superstar.

Stagecoach Theatre Arts

Head office: Courthouse, Elm Grove, Walton-on-Thames, Surrey KT12 1LZ (01932 254333, www.stagecoach.co.uk). **Fees** *£315/12-13wk term (6-16s); £157.50/12-13wk term (4-7s).* **Credit** MC, V.
From humble beginnings in Surrey, this performing arts school has become a global concern, with an attendant performers' agency for young people that's the largest in the UK. The school itself has 60 branches in London alone, offering its starry-eyed young pupils a solid grounding in dance, drama and singing. Four to sixes start with half an hour's tuition in each discipline per week, which climbs to an hour for older children. Some students work towards exams in their second or subsequent year, while third-year pupils can also audition for the Stagecoach National Showcase Production, staged in London. Holiday workshops are organised too.

Sylvia Young Theatre School

Rossmore Road, NW1 6NJ (7402 0673, www.sylviayoungtheatreschool.co.uk). Baker Street tube/Marylebone tube/rail.

Classes phone for details. **Fees** *Classes £70-£92/11wk term. Summer school (10-18s) £300/wk.* **Credit** MC, V.
Thanks to the surfeit of soap stalwarts and pop stars who have honed their talents here over the years (Billie Piper, Amy Winehouse, Leona Lewis and Keeley Hawes among them), Sylvia Young's has become a household name. The full-time stage school (with around 160 pupils aged from ten to 16) and Saturday school (fours to 18s) are famously oversubscribed; there are also evening classes on Thursdays. The Easter and summer holidays bring assorted theatre and musical theatre workshops for fame-hungry eights and overs.

Puppet theatres

Little Angel Theatre

14 Dagmar Passage, off Cross Street, N1 2DN (7226 1787, www.littleangeltheatre.com). Angel tube/Highbury & Islington tube/rail, then 4, 19, 30, 43 bus. **Open** *Box office 10am-6pm Mon-Fri; 9am-4pm Sat, Sun.* **Tickets** *£6-£10.* **Credit** MC, V.
Tucked away off Cross Street, this little puppet theatre has been up and running since 1961. The setting, an old Victorian temperance hall, is charming, while the shows' themes, styles and stories are drawn from an array of cultural

Puppet Theatre Barge.

traditions. Productions are often aimed at fives and above, with occasional shows for the very young and special Baby Friendly performances, plus the odd adults-only show. The Saturday Puppet Club offers weekly sessions for various age groups; for a one-off puppet-making workshop, book a place on a family fun day. *Buggy access. Disabled access: toilet. Nappy-changing facilities. Shop.*

Puppet Theatre Barge
Opposite 35 Blomfield Road, W9 2PF (7249 6876, www.puppetbarge.com). Warwick Avenue tube. **Open** *Box office* 10am-8pm daily. **Tickets** £10; £8.50 under-16s, reductions. **Credit** AmEx, MC, V.

The fact that this diminutive theatre is afloat enchants younger visitors almost as much as the prospect of a performance. The 55-seater barge is moored on the towpath in Little Venice between November and mid July, with marionette shows at 3pm on Saturdays and Sundays and more frequent performances in the holidays. Come July, the barge floats merrily off down the Thames to perform at Richmond, with a show every day but Sunday during August, and weekend performances through September until early October. Pay attention to age recommendations, as longer shows can be tiring for little ones, and book ahead to secure seats near the front, which help children stay focused. *See also p108* **Great Days Out***.
Buggy Access.*

Touring companies

Kazzum
7539 3500, www.kazzum.org.
The Kazzum children's theatre collective has toured schools, theatres, libraries, parks and festivals with its productions, which range from playful interactive pieces to specially commissioned plays that tackle hard-hitting contemporary issues. Celebrating difference and diversity lies at the heart of its body of work.

Oily Cart
8672 6329, www.oilycart.org.uk.
Oily Cart's performances are aimed at two groups who might otherwise miss out on the magic of theatre: very young children and children with special needs. At its brilliant, multi-sensory productions, children in the audience become part of the performance, invited to explore the set and interact with the delightfully quirky performers. One previous show involved on-stage baking, making for a wonderfully fragrant auditorium (every member of the audience left with a freshly-

World of stagecraft

Teenagers with a passion for theatre are to get the chance to run a theatre company and put on a season of plays at the Theatre Royal Haymarket. Twenty 14- to 18-year-olds will be chosen to form the new company, who will then be involved in all aspects of the productions from backstage technical direction to acting, directing and producing.

Theatre director Lloyd Wood will guide the youngsters through the process, and the teens can expect lots of help and advice on what to do next. Applications should be in by 14 September 2010 and auditions will be on 19 September. For those that get accepted, fees are £250 for the term (rehearsals are every Saturday morning from 26 September).
For an application form call 7389 9662, or email alice@trh.co.uk.

baked Christmas bun); in another, toddlers tugged on ropes to start the music and lights, and pedalled away to set a Heath-Robinson-esque machine whirring into motion. Shows tour the country, but most start in London with a three- to six-week run: audience sizes are tiny, so tickets are soon snapped up by those in the know.

Quicksilver Theatre
www.quicksilvertheatre.org.
Led by its dynamic joint artistic directors, Guy Holland and Carey English, this Hackney-based children's theatre collective tours the UK with its innovative productions. The company has a firm grasp of what preschoolers enjoy ('small shows for small people in small places'), but are equally adept when it comes to producing visually striking, thought-provoking plays for older children. Creative collaborations with other companies reap rich rewards: look out for *La Di Dada*, a shadow and light show created with Indefinite Articles that's scheduled to go on tour in 2010.

Theatre Centre
7729 3066, www.theatre-centre.co.uk.
Founded in 1953 by the late Brian Way (a pioneering director, educator and writer),

Theatre Centre takes its productions to schools, theatres and festivals across the country. The company has a reputation for excellence and technical invention, and also champions up-and-coming new writers. Lisa Evans' *The Day the Waters Came*, which looks at the devastation wreaked by Hurricane Katrina, is new for 2010 and suitable for 13 and overs.

Theatre-Rites

7953 7102, www.theatre-rites.co.uk.
Theatre-Rites made its name with daring, site-specific works, starting with 1996's astounding *Houseworks*, which took over an entire house in Brixton. Staging shows in the unlikeliest of venues (a hospital ward, say, or a disused salts factory) is still a major strand of its work, but the company isn't afraid to branch out. Its shows might involve puppets, percussionists, trapeze artists and jugglers; whatever the theme, the visuals are invariably stunning. *Mischief*, an award-winning, endlessly inventive collaboration with choreographer Arthur Pita, adds dance to the mix – along with giant, bendy foam shapes and an onstage keyboard- and guitar-playing beatboxer. There are generally two to three touring productions a year, which always stop by London for a night or two.

Venues

Albany

Douglas Way, SE8 4AG (8692 4446, www.the albany.org.uk). Deptford rail/21, 36, 47, 136, 171, 177, 188, 225, 453 bus. **Open** *Box office* 9am-9pm Mon-Fri; 10am-5pm Sat; 2hrs before performance Sun. **Tickets** *Family Sunday* £5. **Credit** MC, V.
Deptford's sparky multimedia and performing arts centre retains a lively neighbourhood focus. Family Sunday events (Sept-Apr) range from specially written pieces and musical stories with sing-along songs to the jumping Baby Grooves disco; tickets cost a fiver. There's a programme of free activities for teenagers too; check the website or sign up to the Facebook group. The venue can also be hired out for parties.
Buggy access. Café. Disabled access: lift, toilet. Nappy-changing facilities.

artsdepot

5 Nether Street, N12 0GA (8369 5454, www. artsdepot.co.uk). West Finchley or Woodside Park tube. **Open** *Box office* 9am-5.30pm Mon-Fri; 10am-5.30pm Sat; noon-5.30pm Sun (later during performances). **Tickets** free-£20. **Credit** AmEx, MC, V.
This dynamic arts centre throws open its doors to children and families, offering a richly varied line-up of performances, classes and courses. Children's theatre shows take place in the 150-seat studio on Saturdays and Sundays, with a different company in residence each week.
For those that would rather take to the stage, Bright Sparks Theatre Company (eight to 12s) meets on Friday, and there are Saturday drama and story making sessions for younger children; meanwhile, artsdepot members aged from 13 to 19 can attend free playwriting and drama groups. Other offerings on the busy learning programme run the gamut from terrific messy play mornings to street dance and art classes. Innovative summer holiday activities might involve anything from turning recycled materials into artistic masterpieces to learning fast-paced dance routines to accompany the latest chart hits.
Buggy access. Café. Disabled access: lift, toilet. Nappy-changing facilities.

BAC (Battersea Arts Centre)

Lavender Hill, SW11 5TN (7223 2223, www. bac.org.uk). Clapham Common tube, then 345 bus/Clapham Junction rail/77, 77A, 156 bus. **Open** *Box office* 10am-6pm Mon-Fri; 3-6pm Sat. **Tickets** free-£15. **Credit** MC, V.
Its Victorian premises may look eminently traditional, but inside the BAC is a hotbed of ground-breaking theatre. In the past, shows have tended to be for adults, but ambitious plans are afoot to produce more work that's both for and by young people. In the meantime, 12 to 25s can join the in-house young people's theatre group, YPT. Its members often get the chance to work with the BAC's prestigious guest companies and artists (the likes of Punchdrunk and Forced Entertainment), which has resulted in some brilliantly experimental pieces. There's also an inexpensive little café, which serves simple, child-friendly grub (macaroni cheese, sausage and onion sarnies and chocolate brownie for afters).
Bar. Buggy access. Café. Disabled access: lift, toilet. Nappy-changing facilities.

Broadway Theatre

Catford Broadway, SE6 4RU (8690 0002, www.broadwaytheatre.org.uk). Catford or Catford Bridge rail/75, 181, 185, 202, 660 bus. **Open** *Box office* 10am-6pm Mon-Sat. **Tickets** £3.50-£22. **Credit** MC, V.
Sadly, this art deco theatre's Saturday-morning's ROAR! matinées are no more, but the main auditorium still hosts the rollicking Christmas pantomime and other large-scale shows. Note that there are no performances from the end of July to the beginning of September, as the entire theatre shuts down for the summer. The

Chickenshed.

acclaimed Lewisham Youth Theatre (*see p180*) is also based at the theatre, with drama groups for various ages.
Buggy access. Café. Disabled access: lift, toilet. Nappy-changing facilities.

Chickenshed

Chase Side, N14 4PE (8292 9222, www. chickenshed.org.uk). Cockfosters or Oakwood tube. **Open** *Box office* 10am-6pm Mon-Fri; 10am-5pm Sat. **Tickets** *Shows* £4-£18. *Workshops* phone for details. **Credit** MC, V.
Since its inception in 1974, Chickenshed has firmly upheld its ethos that 'everyone is welcome, and everyone is valued'. Over-fives can join the Children's Theatre group, while the Youth Theatre is open to over-13s: the waiting list is enormous, but we're assured that everyone eventually gets in. On Friday and Saturdays, colourful Tales from the Shed performances bring all sorts of stories to life for under-sevens.
Bar. Buggy access. Café. Disabled access: lift, toilet. Nappy-changing facilities. Shop.

Colour House Children's Theatre

Merton Abbey Mills, Watermill Way, SW19 2RD (8542 5511, www.colourhousetheatre. co.uk). Colliers Wood tube. **Open** *Box office* 10am-5pm daily; 1hr before show. **Shows** 2pm, 4pm Sat, Sun. **Tickets** £3.50-£9. **Credit** MC, V.

Witty, often musical renditions of classics such as *Sleeping Beauty* and *Robinson Crusoe* are the forte at this sweet little riverside venue, which has also started staging puppet shows. After-show birthday parties with a mini disco can be arranged, with front row seats for the guests and a tuneful rendition of *Happy Birthday* from the cast at the end of the performance. Call for details of children's theatre workshops and groups.
Buggy access. Disabled access: toilet. Nappy-changing facilities (in Merton Abbey Mills). Shop.

Hackney Empire

291 Mare Street, E8 1EJ (box office 8985 2424, www.hackneyempire.co.uk). Hackney Central rail/38, 106, 253, 277, D6 bus. **Open** *Box office* 10am-9pm Mon-Sat; noon-6pm Sun. *Tours* phone for times. **Tickets** prices vary; phone for details. **Tours** £10; £7 reductions. **Credit** MC, V.
This Hackney institution is up and running again after problems with funding: have a gander at the website for details of forthcoming shows. The Christmas panto for 2010 is *Jack and the Beanstalk* – and if it's anything like the barnstorming *Aladdin* of 2009, with a captivating performance from resident dame Clive Rowe and brilliantly imaginative sets, it'll be an absolute cracker.
Buggy access. Disabled access: toilet. Nappy-changing facilities.

Activities

Jackson's Lane.

Half Moon Young People's Theatre

43 White Horse Road, E1 0ND (7709 8900, www.halfmoon.org.uk). Limehouse DLR/rail. **Open** *Box office* Apr-Sept 10am-6pm Mon-Fri. Oct-Mar 10am-6pm Mon-Fri; 9.30am-4.30pm Sat. **Tickets** £5. **Credit** MC, V.

As well as staging children's theatre shows from September to April, this place also nurtures creative talent. Seven youth theatre groups give kids aged between five and 17 the chance to express themselves: there are no auditions to get in, and young people are encouraged to join in regardless of race, sex, ability or financial situation. In the holidays, there are various hands-on workshops and courses, often culminating with a performance for friends and families on the final day.

Buggy access. Disabled access: lift, toilet. Nappy-changing facilities.

HMV Hammersmith Apollo

46 Queen Caroline Street, W6 9QH (8563 3800, tickets 08448 444748, http://venues. meanfiddler.com/apollo/home). Hammersith tube. **Open** *Box office In person* from 4pm on show days. *By phone (Ticketmaster)* 24hrs daily. **Tickets** prices vary, call for details; child discount for children's show tickets. **Credit** MC, V.

Hammersmith's spacious Apollo mostly houses comedians off the telly and international music acts, but it's worth checking the listings for more family-friendly fare. The line-up for 2010 includes appearances from Australia's ever-popular kids' act the Wiggles, a family-friendly *Strictly Come Dancing* stage show and the Little Big Club, combining a number of popular television characters (Bob the Builder, Angelina Ballerina, Fifi and the Flowertots) in one big show.

Bars. Buggy access. Disabled: toilet. Nappy-changing facilities.

Jackson's Lane

269A Archway Road, N6 5AA (8341 4421, www.jacksonslane.org.uk). Highgate tube. **Open** *Box office* 10am-10pm Tue-Sat; 10am-5pm Sun. **Tickets** £5.95-£12.50. **Credit** MC, V.

A handsome red brick Gothic church conversion, Jackson's Lane is home to a 170-capacity theatre, a wonderfully atmospheric dance studio and four additional rehearsal and workshop spaces. Touring children's theatre companies take to the stage on Sundays at 2pm, while a splendid programme of children's courses includes unusual offerings such as film-making or fencing, along with tap, drama and dance for tinies with energy to burn.

Bar. Buggy access. Café. Disabled access: toilet. Nappy-changing facilities.

Lauderdale House

Highgate Hill, Waterlow Park, N6 5HG (8348 8716, www.lauderdalehouse.co.uk). Archway tube, then 143, 210, 271, W5 bus. **Open**

Box office 30mins before performance. **Tickets** £4.50; £3 reductions. **Credit** MC, V (£2 charge). Set amid ornamental gardens on the edge of peaceful Waterlow Park (*see p120*), this grand, 16th-century mansion was once home to Nell Gwynne, the mistress of Charles II. Art and photography exhibitions now occupy its stately lobby (occasionally expanding into the upper and lower galleries), but the big lure for parents is the jam-packed kids' activities programme. In term-time, most of the action takes place at weekends: Saturdays bring energetic panto-style children's shows and sing-along sessions at 10am and 11.30am, while Sunday mornings are set aside for family-friendly classical music concerts (recommended from five or six years and up). Weekday drop-in classes for preschoolers focus on music, art and movement; the programme expands in the school holidays to incorporate workshops in art, dance and drama for kids of all ages.
Buggy access. Café. Disabled access: toilet.

Lyric Hammersmith Theatre

Lyric Square, King Street, W6 0QL (0871 221 1722, www.lyric.co.uk). Hammersmith tube. **Open** *Box office* 9.30am-5.30pm Mon-Sat (until 8pm on performance days). **Tickets** children's shows £8; £6 reductions; £25 family (2+2). **Credit** MC, V.

The Lyric remains one of London's most forward-looking theatres for children's programming, largely thanks to its pioneering Creative Learning schedule. It gives 11- to 19-year-old west Londoners access to high-quality arts facilities and teaching, with an after-school club, courses and workshops. Fourteen- to 21-year-olds can also join the Lyric Young Company (£5), which yields rich returns in the shape of weekly drama classes, one-off masterclasses and the chance to audition for the company's shows.

The studio is the venue for most kids' events: top-notch weekend theatricals, school holiday workshops and preschooler specials in the week. Look out for rambunctious Messy Play workshops (£3), held after selected Saturday and Sunday shows; there are only 25 places on each, so book as early as you can. Parents can join in, or slope off to the café for brunch and a rest. The Summer Party – a free, one-day theatre festival for all the family – takes place in early July.
Buggy access. Café. Disabled access: lift, toilet. Nappy-changing facilities.

National Theatre

South Bank, SE1 9PX (box office 7452 3000, information 7452 3400, www.nationaltheatre. org.uk). Waterloo tube/rail. **Open** *Box office* 9.30am-8pm Mon-Sat. **Credit** AmEx, MC, V. **Map** p317 M8.

Activities

Shakespeare al fresco at Regent's Park's **Open Air Theatre**. *See p189.*

The National's trio of world-class theatres (the Olivier, the Lyttleton and the Cottesloe) cater mainly to grown-ups, but in the last few years there have been familiy-friendly productions of Shakespeare's *Twelfth Night* and Terry Pratchett's *Nation*, as well as stage adaptations of more obvious children's stories such as *The Cat in the Hat*. But you don't need to shell out for a ticket to have fun here. For a start, there are the free early-evening concerts held in the foyer from Monday to Saturday (and on Saturday lunchtimes), which could include anything from swirling, foot-stamping flamenco to boogie woogie piano. Another spot with plenty going on is the outdoor Theatre Square – home to the terrific Watch This Space season, which generally runs from July to mid September. Wacky street theatre performers, art installations, intrepid tightrope-walkers and puppeteers run riot on the astroturf lawn; for a full run-down of what's going on, check online.

Nurturing new talent is also part of the agenda. The New Connections programme commissions renowned playwrights and authors

Full steam ahead

A railway platform at Waterloo makes for a thrilling theatrical venue.

There's something pulling into the Eurostar platform at Waterloo this summer, and it's not a train from the Gare du Nord. Now that all trains bound for Paris leave from the shiny environs of St Pancras, there's a new performance venue in town.

York Theatre Royal put on a production of *The Railway Children* in the National Railway Museum in York in late summer 2009, and it's coming to the capital from 4 July until 4 September 2010. The action takes place on the disused platforms and tracks of the former Eurostar terminal, and the audience will sit on both sides of the performers. To adults of a certain age, E Nesbitt's story will remain inseperable from Jenny Agutter, but there's plenty for a new generation to enjoy in this story of three children whose lives change dramatically when their father is taken to prison and they move to the country.

The London show will have a new cast, but Mike Kenny's stage adaptation remains, which – coupled with Damian Cruden's direction – received high critical praise first time around for its inclusion of Nesbitt's original socialist-leaning subtext and for managing not to let a 40 tonne steam engine (which makes an uproarious entrance late in the show) upstage the rest of the performance. *The Waterloo Station Theatre, Waterloo Station, SE1 7ND (entrance near the corner of York Road & Mepham Street). (0871 297 0740, www.railwaychildren waterloo.com).*

(William Boyd, David Mamet and Anthony Horowitz have contibuted in the past) to write a new play for young performers, which schools and youth theatres nationwide can then produce. One production of each script is chosen for performance in a week-long summer festival at the National. Young actors can also join the National Theatre Young Company, made up of 13- to 19-year-old performers.

If you'd rather peek behind the scenes than take centre stage, backstage tours (£7, £6 under-18s; £13 family; not suitable for under-sevens) lead visitors into the rehearsal rooms, costume and prop workshops, dressing rooms and stages. *See also p30* **Great Days Out**. *Bars. Buggy access. Café. Disabled access: lift, toilet. Nappy-changing facilities. Restaurants. Shop.*

Nettlefold Theatre

West Norwood Library, 1 Norwood High Street, SE27 9JX (7926 8070, www.lambeth. gov.uk). West Norwood rail/2, 68, 196, 468 bus. **Open** *Box office* 9am-10pm Mon-Sat. **Tickets** £5. **Credit** MC, V.

This 200-seat theatre is built into West Norwood Library and runs one child-oriented show a month (usually on a Saturday at 2pm). Check the blog at http://nettlefoldhall.blogspot.com for details, and listings of other performances and events: a magic show was among the offerings last time we looked. *Buggy access. Disabled access: lift, toilet. Nappy-changing facilities.*

New Wimbledon Theatre

The Broadway, SW19 1QG (0870 060 6646, www.theambassadors.com/newwimbledon). Wimbledon tube/rail. **Open** *Box office* 10am-6pm Mon-Sat. **Tickets** phone for details. **Credit** AmEx, MC, V.

A steady stream of touring hits swap the bright lights of the West End for the suburban surrounds of Wimbledon to be staged at this popular theatre. A *Peppa Pig* puppet show and musical adaptation of *The Gruffalo* are among the highlights for 2010. The end-of-year pantomime is always a spectacular, no-expense-spared affair. *Bar. Buggy access. Disabled access: lift, toilet. Shop.*

Open Air Theatre

Inner Circle, Regent's Park, NW1 4NU (box office 0844 826 4242, www.openair theatre.org). Baker Street tube. **Open** *Box office* (by phone) 24hrs daily; (in person) 10am-6pm Mon-Sat Mar-Sept. **Tickets** £10-£50. **Credit** AmEx, MC, V. **Map** p314 G3.

If forecasters predict a hot summer, be sure to book ahead for the charming Open Air Theatre in Regent's Park. However old you are, there's something magical about seeing Shakespeare performed amid a leafy, rustling semi-circle of trees. The season always includes a musical and a children's play; in 2009, it was *The Tempest*, 're-imagined for everyone aged six and over', in 2010 *Macbeth*, in the same style. If rainy weather stops play, tickets will be exchanged for a later performance – subject to availability – but umbrellas, thick jumpers and blankets are always highly advisable. *Buggy access. Café. Disabled access: toilet.*

Pleasance

Carpenters Mews, North Road, N7 9EF (7609 1800, www.pleasance.co.uk). Caledonian Road tube/91, 390 bus. **Open** 10am-8pm Mon-Sat; noon-6pm Sun. **Tickets** free-£11. **Credit** MC, V.

The London arm of the famous Edinburgh Fringe venue isn't at an address that you'd stumble across by accident, but it's worth making the effort to get here. The building was once used for storing timber by the London Omnibus Company, and makes for a spacious venue. Youth theatre company Young Pleasance is based here and offers occasional workshops for local children; from September 2010, the Pleasance will also offer regular term-time drama classes for children. Check the website for family-friendly productions. *Bar. Cafe. Disabled: toilet, lift. Nappy-changing facilities.*

Polka Theatre

240 Broadway, SW19 1SB (8543 4888, www.polkatheatre.com). South Wimbledon tube/Wimbledon tube/rail, then 57, 93, 219, 493 bus. **Open** *Box office* (by phone) 9.30am-4.30pm Mon; 9.30am-5.30pm Tue-Fri; 10am-4.30pm Sat; (in person) 9.30am-4.30pm Tue-Fri; 10am-4.30pm Sat. **Tickets** £7.50-£16. **Credit** MC, V.

This children's theatre pioneer has been up and running since 1979. Daily shows are staged by touring companies in the main auditorium, while shorter works for babies and toddlers take over the Adventure Theatre once a week. There are also in-house productions, workshops and storytelling sessions for families and schools. Productions for summer 2010 include *Pirates!*, the swashbuckling story of a boy called Jim, who is kidnapped by time-travelling pirates and must escape, and *Skitterbang Island*, a musical adventure about a little girl who meets a strange creature with an unusual piece of treasure. Dramatic offerings aside, there's an appealing

Activities

little playground and wendy house, a reading corner and a cheerful café – a top place for lunch. The Polka Youth Theatre runs a number of theatre groups for different ages (three to 17s), with fees of £65 to £95 per term, while day-long workshops are a treat for children in the school holidays. There are after-school groups for three to 13s, with end-of-term performances for friends and family.

Buggy access. Café. Disabled access: lift, toilet. Nappy-changing facilities.

Shakespeare's Globe

21 New Globe Walk, SE1 9DT (7401 9919, tours 7902 1500, www.shakespeares-globe.org). Southwark or Mansion House tube/London Bridge tube/rail. **Open** *Box office* 10am-6pm daily. *Tours* May-Sept 9am-12.30pm daily. Oct-Apr 10am-5pm daily. **Tickets** £5-£35. *Tours* £10; £8.50 reductions; £6.50 5-15s; free under-5s; £25 family (2+3). **Credit** AmEx, MC, V. **Map** p318 O7.

Fidgety younger kids won't be inclined to sit – or stand – through the shows at this meticulously-reconstructed Elizabethan theatre, but older children will appreciate the atmospheric setting. Eight to 11s can also attend Childplay sessions on selected Saturdays, watching part of the play

as groundlings and taking part in themed workshops. A huge range of talks, tours and activities – many conducted by staff wearing full period costume – takes place with schools during term time, while holiday workshops and excellent seasonal events open the floor to families. *See also p30* **Great Days Out**.

Unicorn Theatre for Children

147 Tooley Street, SE1 2HZ (box office 7645 0560, www.unicorntheatre.com). London Bridge tube/rail. **Open** *Box office* 9.30am-6pm Mon-Fri; 10am-6pm Sat; noon-5pm Sun. **Tickets** £9.50-£16.50. **Credit** MC, V. **Map** p319 R9.

Set on the Southbank, this airy, modern theatre was designed in collaboration with local schoolchildren. A giant sculpture of a white unicorn rears above theatre-goers in the foyer, while performance spaces include the 300-seater Weston Theatre and more intimate Clore Theatre. Staging is often inventive: the stage set for a production of *Twelfth Night* was a living, growing garden, which happily sprouted away during the month-long run. In-house productions are accompanied by special Family Days, where everyone's encouraged to muck in with the activities and workshops; prices

Unicorn Theatre for Children.

include tickets to the show, and the chance to meet the actors afterwards. Visiting theatre companies also drop in for shorter runs, presenting all sorts of brilliant plays and puppet shows for nought to 19s.

Buggy access. Café. Disabled access: lift, toilet. Nappy-changing facilities.

Warehouse Theatre

Dingwall Road, Croydon CR0 2NF (8680 4060, www.warehousetheatre.co.uk). East Croydon rail. **Open** *Box office* 10am-5pm Mon; 10am-8.30pm Tue; 10am-10pm Wed-Fri;2-10pm Sat; 3-7pm Sun. **Tickets** £5-£12. **Credit** AmEx, DC, MC, V.

Housed in a converted Victorian cement warehouse, hidden away behind East Croydon station, the Warehouse is an unassuming gem. Theatre4Kidz shows take place on selected Saturdays, while a variety of touring shows entertain those as young as two. Croydon Young People's Theatre (CRYPT) offers a creative base for 13- to 16-year-olds; it meets 2-5pm every Saturday during term time, and puts on an annual summer show. The fee per term is a mere £12, and application forms are available online.

Bar. Buggy access. Café. Disabled access: toilet.

West End shows

As well as calling the box office to find out what ages shows are suitable for, it's a good idea to check the running length. With many musicals clocking in at two hours, the outing can turn into a frenzy of wriggling and plaintive needing-the-loo requests. If you've got young children in your party, it's probably best to avoid the West End altogether and go to a more intimate, child-specific venue in another part of town, where the plays are shorter, the house lights brighter and the bangs less likely to scare.

For two weeks in August, families can take advantage of **Kids Week** (www.kidsweek.co.uk). Run by the **Society of London Theatres** (SOLT, 7557 6700, www.officiallondon theatre.co.uk), it offers five to 16s free admission to West End shows, provided they are accompanied by a paying adult; up to two additional children can get in at half-price. Children can also go backstage, meet the stars and take part in workshops. For more on Kids Week, and information on the capital's best family-friendly shows, subscribe to the free family bulletin on the SOLT website.

Billy Elliot the Musical

Victoria Palace Theatre, Victoria Street, SW1E 5EA (0871 297 0777, www.billyelliot themusical.com). Victoria tube/rail. **Times** 7.30pm Mon-Sat. *Matinée* 2.30pm Thur, Sat. **Tickets** £17.50-£62.50. **Credit** AmEx, MC, V. **Map** p316 H10.

It would take a pretty cynical heart not to be warmed by this tale of a motherless miner's son with a passion for ballet, set to music by none other than Sir Elton John. The production (adapted from the film) contains strong language, and isn't suitable for under-eights.

Bars. Disabled access: toilet.

Flashdance

Shaftesbury Theatre, 210 Shaftesbury Avenue, WC2H 8DP (7379 5399, www.flashdancethe musical.com). Holborn or Tottenham Court Road tube. **Times** 7.30pm Mon-Thur, Sat; 8.30pm Fri. *Matinée* 5pm Fri; 3pm Sat. **Tickets** £15-£55. **Credit** AmEx, MC, V. **Map** p315 K6.

The musical based on the cult 1980s film gets its West End transfer, opening for previews in September 2010. It tells the story of Alex, an 18-year-old welder, who dances secretly at night with the dream of joining a dance academy.

Bars. Disabled access: toilet.

Grease

Piccadilly Theatre, 16 Denman Street, W1D 7DY (0844 412 6666, www.greasethe musical.co.uk). Piccadilly Circus tube. **Times** 7.30pm Mon-Thur, Sat; 8.30pm Fri. *Matinée* 3pm Sat; 5.30pm Fri. **Tickets** £15-£55. **Credit** AmEx, MC, V. **Map** p316 J6.

CBBC presenter Toby Anstis joined the cast of *Grease* as Teen Angel in January 2010. Die-hard fans certainly can't get enough of this musical – and who can blame them? The soundtrack delivers hit after hit: 'Summer Nights', 'Greased Lightnin', 'You're The One That I Want'… Just try not to sing along.

Bars. Disabled access: toilet.

Legally Blonde

Savoy Theatre, Strand, WC2R 0ET (0870 164 8787, www.legallyblondethemusical.co.uk). Charing Cross tube/rail. **Times** 7.30pm Mon-Sat. *Matinée* 2.30pm Thur; 3pm Sun. **Tickets** £20-£85. **Credit** AmEx, MC, V. **Map** p317 L7.

A highly enjoyable if somewhat daft story about the exploits of its indomitably girly, pink-loving heroine (played by Sheridan Smith) and her equally chic chihuahua, Bruiser, as the pair hit Harvard Law School in pursuit of Duncan James's Warner. It's a Broadway transfer that keeps tongue firmly in cheek.

Bars. Disabled access: toilet.

Activities

Budding trapeze artists and jugglers learn their stuff at **Circus Space**. *See p196.*

Activities

Alongside its splendid, family-friendly café (*see p237*), That Place offers a whole host of children's activities. Preschoolers can get stuck into Rucksack Music, Gymboree Gym arts, Music with Mummy and Tip Toes Dance, to name but a few of the classes, while kids of all ages are welcome to join the face-painting and pizza-baking sessions.
Buggy access. Café. Disabled access: toilet. Nappy-changing facilities.

Archaeology

Museum of London Archaeology
7410 2228, www.museumoflondon archaeology.org.uk.
Keen beans can sign up for the Museum of London's Young Archaeologists Club (YAC), which is aimed at eight to 16s. It has two branches in central London, with once-monthly meet-ups in Hackney and Rotherhithe. Activities include walking the Thames' foreshore to collect objects washed up at low tide, identifying animal bones and making mosaics, Roman-style.

Young Archaeologists Club @ UCL
Institute of Archaeology, 31-34 Gordon Square, WC1H 0PY (7679 7495, www.ucl.ac.uk/archaeology).
The Institute of Archaeology supports a children's club for eight- to 16-year-olds which meets on the third Saturday of each month, from 11am till 1pm; call first to enquire about becoming a member.

Art & crafts

All Fired Up
34 East Dulwich Road, SE22 9AX (7732 6688, www.allfiredupceramics.co.uk). East Dulwich or Peckham Rye rail. **Open** 10am-6pm Mon-Fri; 9.30am-6pm Sat; 10.30am-4.30pm Sun. **Fees** *Studio* £3/day. *Workshops & courses* phone for details. **Credit** AmEx, MC, V.
The shelves of plain white ceramics (from crockery cartoon characters to sensible plates, bowls and mugs) are crying out for colour – which kids happily apply, with varying levels of accuracy. Tables are equipped with palettes, sponges, water and brushes, while friendly staff offer tactful advice. Painted objects are glazed, fired, gift-wrapped and ready for collection in ten days. Birthday parties are run for groups of ten or more children, aged five to 15 (from £12 per head).
Buggy access.

Art 4 Fun
172 West End Lane, NW6 1SD (7794 0800, www.art4fun.com). West Hampstead tube/rail. **Open** 10am-6pm Mon, Wed-Sun; 10am-8pm Tue. **Fees** *Studio* £5.95/day. *Workshops & courses* phone for details. **Credit** AmEx, MC, V.
Children can give full rein to their artistic talents, daubing designs on to ceramics, T-shirts, tiles and flower pots. Tie-dye, mosaic-making, pottery and glass-painting are among the other options. Arty parties are a speciality, with no minimum numbers required, and there are half- and full-day school-holiday workshops for six to tens.
Buggy access. Café.

Art Yard
318 Upper Richmond Road West, SW14 7JN (8878 1336, www.artyard.co.uk). Mortlake rail/33 bus. **Classes** *Term-time* 4-5.30pm Mon, Tue, Wed, Thur. *School hols* 10am-3pm Mon-Fri. **Fees** £145/term. **Credit** MC, V.
This appealingly chaotic, colourful studio hosts after-school art clubs and school holiday courses and workshops. They might involve creating paintings, prints, collages and papier-mâché masterpieces – or even a spot of cookery.

London Brass Rubbing Centre
St Martin-in-the-Fields, Trafalgar Square, WC2N 4JJ (7766 1122, www2.stmartin-in-the-fields.org). Leicester Square tube/ Charing Cross tube/rail. **Open** 10am-6pm Mon-Wed; 10am-8pm Thur-Sat; noon-5pm Sun. **Fees** from £4.50. **Credit** MC, V. **Map** p317 L7.
The revamped London Brass Rubbing Centre is far more fun than it sounds. Enter the futuristic lift and sink beneath the pavement to the large, bright open space below that was once a series of murky vaults. Sure, there could be a few more tables for actual brass rubbing, given the vast area available, but it's a very pleasant atmosphere in which to create an artwork for the wall at home. Children can choose from the smaller replica brasses: a dragon, a decorative elephant, a unicorn, or various historical figures, including William Shakespeare. The nice people at the counter will tape the paper to the block, lend out crayons and give instruction in the gentle art of brass rubbing.

Papered Parlour
7 Prescott Place, SW4 6BS (7627 8703, www.thepaperedparlour.co.uk). Clapham Common or Clapham North tube. **Classes** *Term-time* 4.30-6pm Thur; 10am-noon Sat.

Activities

schoolkids, but throughout the holidays cookery sessions for children of three and above are offered on a bookable basis. Sessions vary in length according to what's on the menu; 'classes' run for one and a quarter hours, 'workshops' for two and a half hours and 'study days' for five hours. Fees are low, considering all ingredients are included in the price, and assisted places are available for those on low incomes. What do parents do while their offspring are whipping up dinner for all the family? They can either wait in the reception area or come back and collect their little chefs at the end of the session. *Buggy access. Disabled access.*

Munchkins
8269 1331, www.munchkinskidscooking.co.uk.
Munchkins run hands-on, jolly sessions that work wonders with fussy eaters. The team, set up by a friendly former primary school teacher, runs children's cooking courses and private classes in term time and during the holidays. It can also arrange baking or make-your-own-meal parties, with optional extras such as games and face-painting; prices start from £110 for six kids.

Recipease
48-50 St Johns Road, SW11 1PR (3006 0001, www.jamieoliver.com/recipease).
Jamie Oliver just won't let the matter of children's food rest. As if his highly publicised campaign of squeezing junk food out of schools wasn't enough, he also wants them to learn to cook from scratch at a young age. To this end, his cookery school-cum-cookshop-cum-deli-cum-advice centre for foodies in Battersea, Recipease, offers sessions for local schools and privately bookable classes for children aged eight and above (who must be accompanied by an adult). They can start with fairly simple skills like decorating biscuits and making pancakes, but can soon graduate to first lessons in 'Champion knife skills'. Children of 12 and above can join any of the Easy To Learn classes, but must also be accompanied by an adult. *Buggy access. Cafe. Disabled: toilet. High chairs. Nappy-changing facilities.*

Film & new media

For a cinema-mad child's dream birthday treat, check out Movie Parties (*see p146*).

Film Club
www.filmclub.org
Film Club aims to put movies on the (extra) curriculum by loaning films to participating

after-school film clubs, free of charge, and running specially devised film seasons. The website also contains a useful list of films, categorised by age group.

Film London
www.filmlondon.org.uk.
London's film and media agency supports projects across the capital.

Filmsteps
0870 024 2522, www.filmsteps.com.
Fast-paced five-day summer holiday film schools (£275) teach seven- to 16-year-olds the essentials of making a feature film, from planning the storyboards to operating the cameras. Thrillingly, their handiwork is premièred at a red-carpet screening, which guests are able to attend. Meanwhile, term-time Film Schools meet in Maida Vale, Belsize Park and Teddington once a week, producing everything from pop videos to film trailers; they cost £235 per term, but there are sibling discounts and scholarships.

First Light
www.firstlightmovies.com.
Funded by the UK Film Council, First Light funds film projects for five- to 18-year-olds, offering courses across the country via schools and educational groups. Its subsidiary website, www.filmstreet.co.uk, provides a bright and breezy starting point for under-12s to explore and discover filmmaking, while www.media-box.co.uk offers funding for projects involving 13- to 19-year-olds.

Mouth That Roars
23 Charlotte Road, EC2A 3PB (7729 2323, www.mouththatroars.com). Old Street tube/rail. **Open** 5-8pm Wed, Thur; noon-5pm Sun.
This east London charity offers training in video production for young people. Thirteens to 19s who live in Hackney can make a film in a day at its studio and editing suite (sessions are free and run on a drop-in basis), which also hosts weekly film screenings.

Young Film Academy
7387 4341, www.youngfilmacademy.co.uk).
Fees from £95/day; £390/4 day course.
No credit cards.
'Passion starts early' is the Young Film Academy's ethos, and its courses, workshops and movie parties aim to inspire fledgling filmmakers (seven to 18s). It's all fast-paced, hands-on stuff, whether the youngsters are making a film in a day or taking part in the Four Day Film School.

Activities

Sport & Leisure

Get fighting fit with a host of indoor and outdoor pursuits.

With the new Conservative/Lib Dem coalition government, centralised initiatives for sport in schools are bound to change. The country has to pay that deficit off somehow. But it's unlikely in this age of concern about youthful obesity and toxic childhoods that the recommendations regarding sporting activity will suggest less of it. Luckily, in London there's a wider choice of sports facilities than elsewhere in the country, and despite London's much-publicised swimming pool crisis (there aren't enough to go round, let alone train our Olympic competitors), new sports and leisure centres are, in fact, still being built; see also our box on mobile swimming pools on p214. The venues for the Olympics alone will provide a wealth of new services (*see p202* **Olympic legacy**). Oh, and don't forget all those gorgeous free green spaces listed in **Parks & Gardens** (*see pp105-128*).

There are plenty of professionals to help make exercise fun. Organisations running activity clubs for toddlers include **Tumbletots** (www.tumbletots.com) and **Crechendo** (www.crechendo.com), while local councils run affordable (often free) sports camps in the school holidays. Many independent schools host a variety of private youth sports organisations that put on intensive rugby, football, tennis and cricket coaching when term ends. These courses may be more expensive than their council-run counterparts, but they're worth the money for children who show a genuine talent for a particular sport. To find a specific course or club near you, try your council website, or contact the individual sport's governing bodies (*see p217*).

CLIMBING

Castle Climbing Centre
Green Lanes, N4 2HA (8211 7000, www.castle-climbing.co.uk). Manor House tube, 141 341 bus.
This Stoke Newington climbing centre is splendidly housed in an old Victorian water pumping station resembling a turret-topped castle. Children's classes for nine- to 14-year-olds are held on Monday and Tuesday, and during the holidays; over-14s may climb unsupervised, with parental permission, once they have passed an assessment. For private tuition, the Gecko Club (www.geckos.co.uk) is based here (£40/hr plus £10 admission). Call for details of the party service.

Mile End Climbing Wall
Haverfield Road, E3 5BE (8980 0289, www.mileendwall.org.uk). Mile End tube.
Eight- to 16-year-olds can attend beginner sessions on Friday evenings and Saturday mornings at this popular east London wall. Action-packed birthday parties for eight and aboves can be held here, and there's a busy summer holiday programme.

CRICKET

Brit Oval
Kennington, SE11 5SS (7820 5700, www.surreycricket.com). Oval tube. **Admission** *Surrey matches* £12-£102; £1-£51 under-16s. **Credit** MC, V.
Surrey's homely – but still Test-class – cricket ground here in Kennington offers an admirable youth programme.

Lord's Cricket Ground
St John's Wood Road, NW8 8QN (Middlesex 7289 1300, www.middlesexccc.com/MCC 7432 1000, www.lords.org). St John's Wood tube/13, 46, 82, 113, 274 bus. **Admission** *Middlesex matches* £10-£20; £5-£7 under-16s, reductions. **Credit** MC, V.
Even the youngest of fans will have heard of Lord's, the home ground of Middlesex and main ground for England. Tours allow visitors a glimpse behind the scenes and access to the Long Room, where a gallery depicts the great and good of the sport. Fans can also peek at the players' dressing rooms and the MCC Museum, where the Ashes urn is stored. For more details, *see p96*.

On your bike: learn road skills and gain confidence with **Bikeability**.

Playing cricket

Cricket is still associated with toffs – an image not helped by a sharp decline in cricket-playing in state schools. Various initiatives have been launched to raise the profile of the national summer sport among children and teens.

Back in 1990, a group of volunteers formed Capital Kids Cricket (www.capital kidscricket.co.uk) to promote cricket for children in the inner city; the website has a where to play section. The clubs listed below have also stepped in to promote coaching for 16s-and-unders. Try the following indoor centres:

Ken Barrington Cricket Centre
Brit Oval, Kennington, SE11 5SS (7820 5739). Oval tube.

MCC Indoor School
Lord's Cricket Ground, St John's Wood Road, NW8 8QN (7616 8612, www.lords.org/kids). St John's Wood tube/13, 46, 82, 113, 274 bus.

Middlesex County Cricket Club
East End Road, N3 2TA (8346 8020, www.middlesexccc.com). Finchley Central tube.

CYCLING

Despite the increasing popularity of cycling, British children still fall well behind their continental peers when it comes to taking the bike to school. In Britain, 90 per cent own bikes, but fewer than three per cent cycle to school. Safety is the key issue – a UK cyclist is 12 times more likely to be killed or injured than a Danish one.

In 2008, the government pledged £55 million to train pupils to ride safely. Safe Routes to Schools supports projects that encourage cycling and walking to school, by improving street design, calming traffic and linking with the 12,000 mile (19,000 kilometre) National Cycle Network. Most local authorities include Safe Routes to Schools schemes in their local transport plans. Sustrans (www.sustrans.org.uk) is the pressure group that is working to create a safer environment for cycling.

The following organisations offer more information: Bike to School Week (www.bikeforall.net); the London Cycling Campaign (www.lcc.org.uk); Go-Ride (www.go-ride.org.uk).

Bikeability

www.bikeability.org.uk.
A nationwide scheme, designed to give young cyclists the skills and confidence to ride their bikes on the roads. Kids are encouraged to achieve three levels of cycling proficiency, and can begin learning the skills as soon as they start riding a bike.

Capital Sport – Gentle Cycling

01296 631671, www.capital-sport.co.uk
Gentle cycling holidays and bike tours through London and along the River Thames. The Thames and Royalty Tour and day tours from London Bridge are ideal for families and take in palaces, royal parks and riverside cycling.

Cycle Training UK

7231 6005, www.cycletraining.co.uk.
Instructors offer individual tuition and accompanied journeys to school anywhere in Greater London. Of its participants, 81% have said they cycle more often and more confidently. The website has details of which London boroughs offer free or subsidised training.

Cycling Instructor

www.cyclinginstructor.com.
Cycling lessons in schools for adults and children. The training organisation delivers Bikeability qualifications (*see above*) too.

Herne Hill Velodrome

Burbage Road, SE24 9HE (www.hernehill velodrome.com). Herne Hill rail.
Many south London children begin their cycling careers here at the venerable home of track cycling, founded in 1892 and still going strong. The VC Londres club was set up to encourage children on to bikes, and holds weekly Friday evening sessions.

London Recumbents

7498 6543 Battersea Park, 8299 6636 Dulwich Park, www.londonrecumbents.co.uk.
London Recumbents offers an enormous range of bikes for hire and for sale at Dulwich and Battersea Parks. There are various trailer attachments, tandems and child seats to accommodate children, plus high-quality kids' bikes (including the low-lying, head-turning recumbent trikes, which kids adore).

London School of Cycling

7249 3779, www.londonschoolofcycling.co.uk.
The London School of Cycling offers private tuition for all ages and abilities, as well as cycle-maintenance workshops for beginners with small class sizes.

FOOTBALL

Playing football

Boys and girls over six can learn football skills on coaching courses, fun days and skills clinics at all of London's professional clubs, staffed by FA-qualified coaches. For venues and dates, check the club websites listed on p204 (details are generally listed on the 'Community' pages).

Elms Football School

8954 8787, www.theelms.co.uk.
The Elms in Stanmore offers Saturday and Sunday coaching, holiday courses and a school of excellence.

European Football Academy

www.footballcamps.co.uk.
Week-long residential and day camps in the UK, Ireland, Germany and Luxembourg, plus Safari camps in Zambia and Malawi. Girls, boys and teams (aged eight to 18) can attend.

Peter Hucker Soccer. *See p203.*

Olympic legacy

We're all excited about the prospect of some world-class sport in 2012, and afterwards there'll be some great new sporting facilities left for the locals. If you and the kids want to see some of these as they go up, head along to the Container Café (*see p225*) or take a bike ride along the fringes of the park on the Greenway (*see p113* **Pipe dreams**).

What Aquatics Centre
Where Olympic Park
Describe it The building was designed by Zaha Hadid, and has a distinctive wave-like roof. After the Games, it will remain a major watersports resource with a 50m competition pool and a 25m diving pool at its heart, and be open to the local community, clubs and schools. It also plans to be family-friendly, with a crèche and café and a new plaza in front of the building.

What Broxbourne White Water Centre
Where Lee Valley Regional Park
Describe it A new modernist centre set beside a 10,000 square metre lake, with two white water courses for canoeing and kayaking. After the Games, the temporary seating will be taken away, and white water rafting will join canoeing and kayaking on the slate of available activities. This is the only new venue that will be open to the public before the games in 2011.

What Eton Manor
Where Olympic Park
Describe it A new complex built on the site of the old Eton Manor Sports Club. After the Games, facilities that will remain for use by the local community include a tennis centre with four indoor and six outdoor courts, a hockey centre, and a number of five-a-side football pitches.

What Handball Arena
Where Olympic Park
Describe it The name tells you its intended use during the Games. It's not the prettiest of the proposed new builds, but after the Games it will be adapted to become a centre for indoor sports, including handball, badminton, netball and volleyball. There will also be a fitness club and café on site.

What 'Hubble Bubble' Tower
Where Olympic Park
Describe it News of Anish Kapoor's towering art sculpture cum massive slide hit the front pages on 1 April 2010. Many people thought it was an April Fool's joke, but the claim appears to be real. There really will be a mangled red form of gargantuan proportions soaring over the skyline of east London for years to come

What Olympic Stadium
Where Olympic Park
Describe it At the heart of the Olympic Park and the 2012 Olympics is the 80,000-seat Stadium. After the Games, the seating will be reduced to 25,000, but the Stadium itself will remain a centre for athletics and sporting – as well as cultural and community – events.

What Velopark
Where Olympic Park
Describe it A state-of-the-art indoor velodrome that will be developed after the Games by adding a mountain bike course and road cycle circuit. Consulting bodies will make sure that the cycling hub is suitable for all ages and abilities.

Activities

Football Academy

Langston Road, Loughton, Essex IG10 3TQ (0870 084 2111, www.footballacademyuk.com). Debden tube.
This centre has ten all-weather, floodlit, five-a-side pitches for hire. Holiday and weekend sessions are led by FA-qualified coaches under the guidance of former West Ham star John Moncur and other ex-professionals, and children's parties can be arranged.

Goals Soccer Centres

www.goalsfootball.co.uk.
There are 12 of these centres in London. Each has all-weather, floodlit pitches with junior leagues, birthday parties and coaching at weekends and school holidays.

Lambeth Dribblers

8835 9570.
Part-funded by Chelsea, this project provides free coaching for young children on the astroturf at Brixton Recreation Centre, while enabling enthusiastic dads (it's specifically aimed at fathers, not mothers) to have an enjoyable kickaround with their kids.

Little Kickers

01235 859250, www.littlekickers.co.uk.
Hugely popular classes developed by a group of FA-qualified coaches and nursery-school teachers for pre-schoolers (18 months and up) as a gentle introduction to football. The programme operates all over London.

London Football Academy

8882 9100, www.londonfootballacademy.co.uk.
Holiday courses, skill schools, birthday parties and inexpensive Saturday morning soccer school sessions in Alexandra Park.

Peter Hucker Soccer

8536 4141, www.peterhucker-soccer.com.
Former Queens Park Rangers goalkeeper Peter Hucker runs this highly rated scheme. Based in Barking and Wanstead, this organisation offers weekly pay-and-play coaching sessions, and matchplay. It can also arrange footballing parties for fives to 16s. Hucker was also responsible for founding the East London & Essex Small-Sided Soccer League (07961 867501, 01375 650833, www.eleleague.com).

Powerleague

www.powerleague.co.uk.
There are 13 Power League centres dotted around the capital, each providing all-weather, floodlit pitches. Most centres offer coaching, mini matches at weekends and during the school holidays, as well as junior leagues. If there's a birthday coming up, you can also book a pitch for a party.

Sharpshooters Football

07873 583366, www.sharpshooters football.co.uk.
Tooting Bec Common and other venues in south-west London host Sunday pay-and-play sessions for four- to 11-year-olds, plus holiday courses and footie-themed birthday parties. Talented youngsters can progress to 'Sharp Shooter Select' sessions.

South East London & Kent Youth Football League

www.selkent.org.uk.
Leagues for young players, from mini soccer for under-sevens to 11-a-sides for under-16s. The website includes a very useful 'players wanted' page, including a section on girls' football teams.

South London Special League

8319 8111, www.sl-sl.co.uk.
This league helps players with special needs to participate in football. The London FA website (www.londonfa.com) has an extensive section devoted to opportunities for children with physical and learning disabilities, and many of the community programmes run by London's professional clubs cater for special needs.

Watching football

The football season runs from August to May, and club websites include regularly updated ticket information. Ticket prices and membership packages are far too numerous to list for each club; as a rule, Premier League match seats are £30-£60 for an adult, but are reduced by up to half for kids and members (if discounts are offered) for some cup fixtures. Coca-Cola Championship and Coca-Cola League prices are around £15-£40, with reductions for children and club members.

Wembley Stadium

Wembley, HA9 OWS (0844 980 8801, www.wembleystadium.com). Wembley Park tube/Wembley Central tube/rail/Wembley Stadium rail.
The new Wembley Stadium received a considerable amount of schtick for the time it took for building works to be completed and the terrible state of its pitch once it was opened. But now it's a cracking ground that's built on an epic scale; the top tier is up in the clouds and the overhead arch is a suitably iconic replacement

Activities

for the famous twin towers. It's not even particularly difficult to get to, especially if you avoid the tube and take the overground from Marylebone – you'll be there in ten minutes; ideal for shielding the kids from the inevitable crush on the tube. You can also take excellent tours of the stadium that explore everything from the press box to the tunnel. The tours end in the royal box, where fans young and old get to brandish a very battered FA Cup to the piped cheers of the crowd, and dream of glory.

Wembley may be grand, but it can be surprisingly easy to procure a ticket for some of the less distinguished fixtures (play-off finals or non-league cup finals), or even for England games, especially friendly matches.

Barclays Premier League

Arsenal
Emirates Stadium, Ashburton Grove, N7 7AF (7619 5000, www.arsenal.com). Arsenal or Holloway Road tube.
For the club's museum, *see p95.*

Chelsea
Stamford Bridge, Fulham Road, SW6 1HS (0871 984 1955, www.chelseafc.com). Fulham Broadway tube.
For the club's museum, *see p96.*

Fulham
Craven Cottage, Stevenage Road, SW6 6HH (0870 442 1222, www.fulhamfc.com). Putney Bridge tube.
Stadium tours are available.

Tottenham Hotspur
White Hart Lane, Bill Nicholson Way, 748 High Road, N17 0AP (0844 844 0102, www. spurs.co.uk). White Hart Lane rail. **Tours** 11.30am, 2pm Mon-Fri; 10am, noon, 2.30pm non-match Sats. **Admission** *Tours* £15; £8 under-16s, reductions. **Credit** MC, V.
Book in advance for tours of pitch-side, tunnel, changing rooms, boardroom and press room. Don't turn up on spec, as they don't always run.

West Ham United
Boleyn Ground, Green Street, E13 9AZ (0871 222 2700, www.whufc.com). Upton Park tube.
Tours take place on selected Wednesdays, for which you must book in advance.

Coca-Cola Championship

Crystal Palace
Selhurst Park, Whitehorse Lane, SE25 6PU (8768 6000, www.cpfc.co.uk). Selhurst rail.

Queens Park Rangers
Loftus Road, South Africa Road, W12 7PA (08444 777 0777, www.qpr.co.uk). White City tube.

Watford
Vicarage Road, Watford, Herts WD18 0ER (0845 442 1881, www.watfordfc.com). Watford High Street rail.

Coca-Cola League

Barnet
Underhill Stadium, Barnet Lane, Herts, EN5 2DN (8441 6932, www.barnetfc.com). High Barnet tube.

Brentford
Griffin Park, Braemar Road, Brentford, Middx TW8 0NT (0845 345 6442, www.brentfordfc. premiumtv.co.uk). Brentford rail.

Charlton Athletic
The Valley, Floyd Road, SE7 8BL (0871 226 1905, www.charlton-athletic.co.uk). Charlton rail.

Leyton Orient
Matchroom Stadium, Brisbane Road, E10 5NE (0871 310 1881, www.leytonorient.com). Leyton tube.

Millwall
The Den, Zampa Road, SE16 3LN (7232 1222, www.millwallfc.co.uk). South Bermondsey rail/Surrey Quays tube.

GOLF

Golf isn't the easiest sport for kids to pick up, so the English Golf Union (*see p217*) has developed Tri-Golf for six- to 12-year-olds, and is introducing the game in primary schools. Your child can discover the basics at one of London's driving ranges; course professionals may offer lessons to develop good habits. The TopGolf system (www.topgolf.co.uk) is a point-scoring game using balls with a microchip inside. TopGolf is played at its centres in Addlestone (01932 858551), Chigwell (8500 2644) and Watford (01923 222045).

Beckenham Place Park
The Mansion, Beckenham Place Park, Beckenham, Kent BR3 5BP (8650 2292, www.glendale-golf.com). Beckenham Hill rail.

Activities

Kids can practise at this course at a reduced rate all day during the week and after 1pm at weekends. Lessons are on Saturdays at 10am (£3). It costs £10 for juniors to play a round at weekends, £8 on weekdays.

Central London Junior Golf Academy

Burntwood Lane, SW17 OAT (8871 2468, www.clgc.co.uk). Tooting Bec tube/Earlsfield rail/G1 bus.

Junior membership of the academy (£35 annual fee) gets children priority booking and a discount on after-school sessions (£75 with discount for an eight-week course) and Easter and Summer camps (£175 per week with discount for six- to eight-year-olds; £225 per week with discount for nine to 16s). Individual lessons are £20/30min and £40/hr.

KARTING & MOTOR SPORTS

Karts exceed speeds of 30mph (50kmph) and are suitable for over eights: there are two pedals (stop and go) and no gearbox to confuse the issue. These venues welcome children and can be booked for parties.

Brands Hatch

Fawkham, Longfield, Kent DA3 8NG (01474 872331, www.motorsportvision.co.uk). Swanley rail, then taxi.

The biggest motor-racing venue in the area, Brands Hatch has loads of things to do on two and four wheels, including YoungDrive!, which puts over-13s in control of a Renault Clio.

Playscape Racing

390 Streatham High Road, SW16 6HX (8677 8677, www.playscape.co.uk). Streatham rail.

Bookable for children's parties (over-eights only) or half-hour taster sessions. Enthusiasts can join the Kids' Racing Academy, on the first Saturday of each month (8.30am-1pm, £35).

MARTIAL ARTS

Training in martial arts imparts self-confidence, body awareness, assertiveness and resilience. Most local sports centres will be home to at least one martial arts club; many more are based in church halls and community centres. Try to find a club with a lively but disciplined atmosphere, and well-organised and age-appropriate teaching. Ask instructors about their

London School of Capoeira. *See p206.*

Activities

London Equestrian Centre

Lullington Garth, N12 7BP (8349 1345, www.londonridingschool.com). Mill Hill East tube. **Lessons** *Group £27/hr. Individual £25-£31/30min.*

There are 30 horses and ponies at this yard, which caters for riders of all abilities; there's even a Tiny Tots session for three-year-olds. The centre is affiliated to the Pony Club, and runs pony days and weeks in school holidays. Birthday parties are held here, and young people aged from 13 can help out at the yard in return for free rides.

Mount Mascal Stables

Vicarage Road, Bexley, Kent DA5 2AW (8300 3947, www.mountmascalstables.com). Bexley rail. **Lessons** *Group £18/50min. Individual £26/50min.*

Down in south London, this busy centre is home to 40 horses and ponies, and gives lessons to over-fives. Children's fun days (£30; for riders six years and above with some experience) allow kids to practise riding, experience stable management and play a variety of games. The centre has two indoor schools, two outdoor grass arenas and two outdoor all-weather manèges. More experienced riders can hack out in the stunning Joyden's Wood. Birthday parties for six to 12 kids can be arranged for weekends or school holidays.

Mudchute Equestrian Centre

Mudchute Park & Farm, Pier Street, E14 3HP (7515 0749, www.mudchute.org). Mudchute, Crossharbour or Island Gardens DLR/D3, D6, D7, D8 bus. **Lessons** *Group £16-£19/hr. Individual £30-£40/45min.*

This hugely popular riding school at the Mudchute City Farm *(see p137)* on the Isle of Dogs is friendly, down-to-earth and very welcoming to new riders. Lessons are some of the most reasonably priced in London, and are open to children over seven. It's a Pony Club Centre, enabling local kids who don't own a pony to study for badges and certificates, and to participate in related activities during the school holidays (gymkhanas, dressage competitions and so on).

Ross Nye's Riding Stables

8 Bathurst Mews, W2 2SB (7262 3791, www.rossnyestables.co.uk). Lancaster Gate tube. **Lessons** *Group £50/hr. Individual £60/hr.*

At the posher end of the spectrum, this stables forms the Hyde Park branch of the Pony Club; membership gives reduced prices for lessons, which take place in the park. Clients aged from six can learn to ride here.

Stag Lodge Stables

Robin Hood Gate, Richmond Park, SW15 3RS (8974 6066, www.ridinginlondon.com). East Putney tube/Putney rail, then 85 bus/Kingston rail then 85 bus. **Lessons** *Group £30-£35/hr. Individual £30/30min, £45-£60/hr.*

There are 40 or so horses and ponies (ranging from Shetlands to Irish hunters) at this stables in historic Richmond Park. Three to sevens can enjoy half-hour leading-rein rides through the park (£20-£25); jumping or flatwork lessons for all abilities take place in one of two outdoor manèges. There are pony weeks for the over-sixes in school holidays and half term (£275 for four days) – book well ahead.

Trent Park Equestrian Centre

Bramley Road, N14 4XS (8363 8630, www.trentpark.com). Oakwood tube. **Lessons** *Group £23-£30/hr. Individual £38-£42/hr.*

A caring attitude towards young riders (fours and over) and this equestrian centre's location make it a popular place to ride. Hacking is £28 per hour, Pony Days are £60 and four-day riding weeks (£220) are held in the school holidays.

Willowtree Riding Establishment

The Stables, Ronver Road, SE12 0NL (8857 6438, www.willowtreeridinglondon.co.uk). Grove Park or Lee rail. **Lessons** *Group from £10/30min, £20/hr. Individual from £20/30min, £30/hr.*

The Welsh ponies are particularly popular at this friendly yard, where children over four can learn to ride. Young and nervous riders are welcome. Lessons (flatwork only) take place in a covered, full-size indoor arena. Most teaching is at weekends and in the holidays.

Wimbledon Village Stables

24A-B High Street, SW19 5DX (8946 8579, www.wvstables.com). Wimbledon tube/rail. **Lessons** *Group £55-60/hr. Individual £75-£80/1hr.*

Although it caters mainly for adults, children are welcome at this centre, which has a small selection of quiet, safe ponies and a holiday scheme for five- to ten-year-olds (£170 for three afternoons). Riding takes place on Wimbledon Common, where the centre has two outdoor arenas for flatwork and jumping lessons. Riders must become members to ride regularly.

RUGBY UNION

A bargain compared to football. All of London clubs feature top international players, and there's never any problem

Activities

BaySixty6 Skate Park: the place to show off skating skills. *See p210*.

getting hold of tickets. The rugby season runs from September through to May.

Guinness Premiership

Harlequins

Twickenham Stoop Stadium, Langhorn Drive, Twickenham, Middx TW2 7SX (8410 6000, www.quins.co.uk). Twickenham rail. **Admission** £20-£40; £10-£40 2-16s.

Saracens

Vicarage Road, Watford, Herts WD18 0EP (01727 792800, www.saracens.com). Watford High Street rail. **Admission** £14.50-£60; £5-£15 2-16s.

National League

London Welsh

Old Deer Park, Kew Road, Richmond, Surrey TW9 2AZ (8940 2368, www.london-welsh. co.uk). Richmond tube/rail. **Admission** £12; £6 reductions; free under-16s.

SKATEBOARDING & BMX

Just as popular now as in the 1970s, skateboarding and BMX means getting fit and making friends. For details of festivals and special events look at the Skateboarders Association website (www.ukskate.org.uk). BMX became an olympic sport in 2003 – check the website of the governing body of British cycling (www.britishcycling.org.uk) for news.

BaySixty6 Skate Park

Bay 65-66, Acklam Road, W10 5YU (8969 4669, www.baysixty6.com). Ladbroke Grove tube. **Membership** free. **Prices** £6/5hrs Mon-Fri; £6/4hrs Sat, Sun; £3 beginners 10am-noon Sat, Sun.
This famous park sprawls beneath the Westway and includes a vert ramp, a medium half-pipe, a mini ramp and funboxes, grind boxes, ledges and rails aplenty. Some skaters complain about the £6 entry fee, but the high quality of the ramps goes some way to making up for it.

Cantelowes Skatepark

Cantelowes Gardens, Camden Road, NW1 (www.cantelowesskatepark.co.uk). Kentish Town tube/rail/Camden Road rail. **Open** 11am-9pm daily.
After a £1.5m makeover, this free skatepark on Camden Road reopened in 2007 and draws a devoted crowd of regulars. It has hosted qualifying rounds for the Quiksilver's Bowlriders championship for the last two years.

Harrow Skatepark

Christchurch Avenue, Wealdstone, Middx HA3 5BD (www.harrowskatepark.co.uk). Harrow & Wealdstone tube/rail.
This skatepark has a clover leaf, kidney bowls and a challenging concrete half-pipe.

Meanwhile

Meanwhile Gardens, off Great Western Road, W10 (www.mgca.f2s.com). Westbourne Park tube.
Close to the Grand Union, this community garden's skatepark features three concrete bowls of varying steepness and size, but no flatland – so it's not for wobbly beginners.

SKATING

On ice

Temporary rinks pop up all over town in winter time inside museums, galleries, parks and shopping centres.
Session times at London's permanent ice rinks vary, so call ahead before you visit; venues are generally open 10am-10pm.

Alexandra Palace Ice Rink

Alexandra Palace Way, N22 7AY (8365 4386, www.alexandrapalace.com). Wood Green tube/ Alexandra Palace rail/W3 bus.
This lofty arena runs courses for children aged five to 15 on Saturday mornings and early on weekday evenings.

Broadgate Ice Arena

Broadgate Circle, EC2A 2BQ (7505 4000 Summer, 7505 4068 Winter, www. broadgateice.co.uk). Liverpool Street tube/rail.
This compact, City-based rink is open from mid November until March, and is very child friendly. It's often less crowded than the capital's other outdoor rinks.

Lee Valley Ice Centre

Lea Bridge Road, E10 7QL (8533 3154, www.leevalleypark.org.uk). Clapton rail.
Disco nights are a big hit at this modern, well-maintained and comparatively warm rink. It's never too busy, and the ice rink is a good size. Lessons are also offered.

Michael Sobell Leisure Centre

Hornsey Road, N7 7NY (7609 2166, www. aquaterra.org). Finsbury Park tube/rail.

This small ice rink near the Holloway Road runs well-attended after-school sessions and six-week courses for children. Anyone over four is welcome; children can have ice-skating birthday parties here too, with all the necessary equipment provided. The leisure centre also offers ice hockey sessions for the over-sixes.

Queens
17 Queensway, W2 4QP (7229 0172, www.queensiceandbowl.co.uk). Bayswater or Queensway tube.
Beginners and families are nicely looked after at this well-known ice rink, which holds legendary disco nights on Fridays and Saturdays. Children's lessons cost £65 for a six-week course. Hot Belgian waffles in the café are also a big hit with kids. There's also a 12-lane Tenpin Bowling centre *(see p216)*.

Somerset House
Strand, WC2R 1LA (7845 4600, www. somersethouse.org.uk). Holborn or Temple tube.
The magnificent courtyard at Somerset House is probably London's most iconic temporary rink when it is iced over from late November until late January. Enjoy a skating session before embarking on an improving interlude in the art galleries *(see p66)*.

Streatham Ice Arena
386 Streatham High Road, SW16 6HT (8769 7771, www.streathamicearena.com). Streatham rail.
A hugely popular south London venue that offers the combined attractions of an ice rink and karting track (Playscape, *see p205*). Locals have campaigned for improvements, with particular concern for the future of the rink (Streatham has had one since 1931; see Streatham Ice Skating Action Group's website at www.sisag.org.uk. The rink offers reasonably-priced six-week courses for all ages, including classes for toddlers.

On tarmac

Citiskate (www.citiskate.co.uk) teaches hundreds of Londoners of all ages how to skate in parks, leisure centres and schools. The instructors hold qualifications from UKISA (United Kingdom Inline Skating Association); lessons are available daily.
   Citiskate's weekly Sunday Rollerstroll (www.rollerstroll.com) and Battersea Park's Easy Peasy skate on Saturday (www.easypeasyskate.com) are popular, family-friendly group skates.

SKIING & SNOWBOARDING

There are a number of dry ski slopes in the London area. Bear in mind that the minimum requirement for use is to be able to perform a controlled snowplough turn and use the ski lift.

Bromley Ski Centre
Sandy Lane, St Paul's Cray, Orpington, Kent BR5 3HY (01689 876812, www.c-v-s.co.uk/ bromleyski). St Mary Cray rail/321 bus.
There are two lifts to serve the 120m (394ft) main slope, and there's also a mogul field and nursery slope. Skiing and snowboarding taster sessions cost £18. Booking is essential.

Sandown Sports Club
More Lane, Esher, Surrey KT10 8AN (01372 467132, www.sandownsports.co.uk). Esher rail.
A big but friendly ski centre with four nursery slopes and a curving, 120m (394ft) main slope. The open practice sessions are strictly for competent skiers and snowboarders; otherwise, there are lessons for under-sevens (£27/30mins) and seven-and-overs (£49/hr). Call for details of parties, during which kids can speed down the slopes on sledges and circular 'ringos'.

Snow Centre
St Albans Hill, Hemel Hempstead, Herts, HP3 9NH (0845 258 9000, www.thesnowcentre. com) Hemel Hempstead rail then taxi.
This new snow centre in Hemel Hempstead opened in 2009 and claims to be the best and biggest in the UK. The main slope is 160m (525ft) and has two lifts, and there's also a 100m (328ft) lesson slope equipped with rope tows, as well as a snow play area for children aged two to six. There are lessons for six-and-overs and a snow school in half-term and school holidays.

Snozone
Xscape, 602 Marlborough Gate, Milton Keynes, Bucks MK9 3XS (0871 222 5670, www.snozoneuk.com). Milton Keynes Central rail.
One of the UK's largest indoor snow domes, with three slopes (in reality they're joined, so they resemble one wide slope): two of 170m (558ft) and one of 135m (443ft), with button lifts running all the way to the top. The place can feel a bit like a big fridge as it is below freezing on the slopes, but it's a good (if pricey) place to find your ski legs. Three-and-overs can also try a spot of tobogganing (under-sevens must be accompanied by a grown-up).

Activities

SWIMMING

As part of the drive towards increasing fitness for 2012, many London boroughs now provide free swimming at designated times for 16-and-unders (18-and-unders in Hackney) under the Swim4Life scheme. Children must pre-register to take part in the scheme; visit www.gll.org for a list of participating authorities.

Most local authority pools run lessons for children, plus parent-and-baby sessions to develop water confidence in those as young as three months. These are very popular, so may have long waiting lists; ask at your local pool for details. Also look out for London's mobile pools (*see p214* **Pooling resources**).

Most of the pools recommended below are open daily; phone for session times, prices and further information.

Barnet Copthall Pools
Champions Way, NW4 1PS (8457 9900, www.gll.org). Mill Hill East tube.
There are three pools and a diving area here, with coaching and clubs to join if you fancy taking the plunge.

Brentford Fountain Leisure Centre
658 Chiswick High Road, Brentford, Middx TW8 0HJ (0845 456 6675,www.hounslow. gov.uk). Gunnersbury tube/Kew Bridge rail.
A very pleasant leisure facility which has a warm, shallow teaching pool, an exciting 40m (130ft) aquaslide, underwater lighting, a flume and a wave machine.

Crystal Palace National Sports Centre
Ledrington Road, SE19 2BB (8778 0131, www.gll.org). Crystal Palace rail.
The National Sports Centre in the middle of Crystal Palace Park houses one of the capital's two 50m (160ft) Olympic-size pools; this venerable pool also has fine diving facilities (rare across the country).

Goresbrook Leisure Centre
Ripple Road, Dagenham, Essex RM9 6XW (8227 3976, www.barking-dagenham.gov.uk). Becontree tube.
The fun pool in this Dagenham leisure centre has child-friendly fountains, as well as cascades and a 60m (195ft) flume; Saturday afternoons bring pool parties. There's also a small area for proper length swimming.

Ironmonger Row Baths
1-11 Ironmonger Row, EC1V 3QF (7253 4011, www.aquaterra.org). Old Street tube/rail.
One of only three remaining Turkish baths in London. Various toys and floats come out for Saturday's family fun time, while eight to 15s can attend Super Swim sessions – a heady mix of water polo, lifesaving skills and snorkelling.

Kingfisher Leisure Centre
Fairfield Road, Kingston, Surrey, KT1 2PY (8541 4576, www.kingfisherleisurecentre.co.uk). Kingston rail.
This friendly-family centre has a teaching pool, and a main pool with a beach area and wave machine. In other words, there is a little something for everyone.

Latchmere Leisure Centre
Burns Road, SW11 5AD (7207 8004, www.dcleisurecentres.co.uk). Clapham Junction rail.
The Latchmere Leisure Centre has a decent swimming pool for those who want to swim lanes. There's also a teaching pool and a beach area, with a wave machine and slide that will appeal to children.

Leyton Leisure Lagoon
763 High Road, E10 5AB (8558 8858, www.gll.org). Leyton tube/69, 97 bus.
This east London pool has various flume, slides, fountains, rapids and cascades to liven up swimming sessions.

Pavilion Leisure Centre
Kentish Way, Bromley, Kent BR1 3EF (8313 9911, www.bromleymytime.org.uk). Bromley South rail.
Large leisure pool with shallows, flumes and a wave machine, lane swimming and a separate toddlers' pool.

Queen Mother Sports Centre
223 Vauxhall Bridge Road, SW1V 1EL (7630 5522, www.courtneys.co.uk). Victoria tube/rail.
The three terrific pools in this refurbished centre mean it's always popular with schoolkids; birthday parties can also be celebrated here.

Spa at Beckenham
24 Beckenham Road, Beckenham, Kent BR3 4PF (8650 0233, www.bromleymytime.org.uk). Clock House rail.
An award-winning leisure centre with loads of sports facilities, two swimming pools, the Space Zone soft-play area for children and a crèche for younger ones.

Activities

Swim outside all year round at **Hampton Heated Open Air Pool**. *See p214.*

Tottenham Green Leisure Centre
*1 Philip Lane, N15 4JA (8489 5322,
www.haringey.gov.uk). Seven Sisters tube/rail.*
This perennially popular leisure centre has lane
swimming and diving in the main pool, and
waves and slides in the 'beach pool'.

Waterfront Leisure Centre
*Woolwich High Street, SE18 6DL (8317 5000,
www.gll.org). Woolwich Arsenal rail/96, 177 bus.*
Greenwich borough's flagship centre. Four
pools, six slides, waves, rapids and a water
'volcano' keep the crowds happy.

Open-air swimming

London's outdoor pools (lidos) are in a
mixed state. Some are in terminal decline,
while others have been reopened after
expensive refurbs. For full details of
London's outdoor pools (and to join the
campaign to reopen those that have
closed), visit www.lidos.org.uk.

Brockwell Lido
*Brockwell Park, Dulwich Road, SE24 0PA
(7274 3088, www.brockwell-lido.co.uk). Herne
Hill rail.* **Open** May-Sept, check website for
times. **Admission** check website for details.

Rescued from the dead, this wonderful 1930s
lido has been transformed by a Heritage Lottery
Fund grant. Whippersnappers runs a brilliant
range of classes at the pool, from babies' and
toddlers' drop-in sessions to kathak dance
classes for five to sevens and circus skills,
acrobatics and street dance for older kids. The
café was reopened in 2009, and has proved a hit
with local families.

Finchley Lido
*Great North Leisure Park, Chaplin Square,
High Road, North Finchley, N12 0GL (8343
9830, www.gll.org). East Finchley tube.* **Open**
check website. **Admission** check website.
There are two indoor pools here, but it's the
outdoor pool and sun terrace that make it such
a draw for locals in the summer.

Hampstead Heath Swimming Ponds & Parliament Hill Lido
*7332 3505, www.cityoflondon.gov.uk.
Lido: Parliament Hill Fields, Gordon
House Road, NW5 1LP. Gospel Oak rail.
Men & women's ponds: Millfield Lane,
N6. Gospel Oak rail.
Mixed pond: East Heath Road, NW3.
Hampstead Heath rail.* **Open** check website
for times. **Admission** *Lido* £4.30; £2.70

Pooling resources

In September 2009, Mayor Boris Johnson pledged £7.5 million to help Londoners learn to swim. The Make a Splash programme takes two mobile pools to various destinations around London, and offers free lessons for children of all ages.

The temporary pools arrive at each site in a van; the flatpacked galvanised steel panels are fixed into a ground-level framework on site. Once the 12-metre by six-metre panels are secure, in goes the water and hey presto, there's a swimming pool that wasn't there yesterday. Clever stuff. The pools will move three times a year, in line with school term dates. The idea is that you should be a resident of one of the hosting boroughs to take advantage of the free lessons (and should be a non-swimmer when you start), but people have been known to cross borders.

Children are divided into age groups for lessons. Parents must be in the pool with children for the three months to three years and four- to five-year-old classes, while six- to ten-year-olds and 11s and overs go unaccompanied. The pools will be in Greenwich and Camden until the end of July 2010 and will then move to different, as yet unconfirmed, sites in September. Check the website for exact locations.

Make a Splash: 07786 984012, www.makeasplashlondon.org.

reductions; £12.80 family (2+2). *Ponds* £2; £1 reductions. Season tickets and early/late entry discounts available.

Hampstead's wonderfully atmospheric pools are reserved for children of eight and above; under-15s must be supervised. The unheated, Grade II-listed lido is thronged with families on sunny afternoons, and also has a paddling pool.

Hampton Heated Open Air Pool
High Street, Hampton, Middx TW12 2ST (8255 1116, www.hamptonpool.co.uk). Hampton rail. **Open** times vary according to season so check website **Admission** £5.60 weekends; £4.60 weekdays; £3.70 reductions; £2.90 children (4-15); £15.50 family (2 +3).

The water is heated to 28° at this pool, and when the sun's shining it's hard to beat. There's a shallow learner pool for babies and toddlers, and group and private swimming lessons are offered. The complex is open all year round.

London Fields Lido
London Fields Westside, E8 3EU (7254 9038, www.gll.org). London Fields rail/26, 48, 55, 106, 236 bus. **Open** call for details. **Admission** £4.15; £2.50 under-16s.

Another recently resurrected lido. Hackney Council reopened this 50m (164ft) pool in autumn 2006. The water's heated to 25°, and there are two on-site cafés at which to refuel.

Oasis Sports Centre
32 Endell Street, WC2H 9AG (7831 1804, www.gll.org). Tottenham Court Road tube. **Open** 7.30am-9pm Mon-Wed, Fri; 7.30am-8.30pm Thur; 9.30am-5.30pm Sat, Sun. **Admission** £3.90; £1.40 5-16s; free under-5s.

This excellent 28m (90ft) outdoor pool is open all year round, and is particularly appealing on winter days, when steam rises from the surface (if you can persuade the kids to brave the chilly dash from the changing rooms). Families should beware visiting at lunchtimes or after work, when stressed media types descend in force.

Pools on the Park
Old Deer Park, Twickenham Road, Richmond, Surrey TW9 2SF (8940 0561, www.spring health.net). Richmond rail. **Open** 6.30am-7.45pm Mon; 6.30am-10pm Tue; 6.30am-9pm Wed, Thur; 6.30am-8.30pm Fri; 8am-5.45pm Sat; 7am-5.45pm Sun. **Admission** £4.10; £1.70-£3.25 reductions; free under-5s. Prices may vary during peak season.

This well-maintained sports complex inside the picturesque Old Deer Park features a 33m (110ft) heated outdoor pool, and one the same size and temperature inside.

Activities

Serpentine Lido

Hyde Park, W2 2UH (7706 3422, www. serpentinelido.com). Knightsbridge or South Kensington tube. **Open** *May* 10am-6pm Sat, Sun. *June-mid Sept* 10am-6pm daily. **Admission** £4; £1-£3 reductions.

Right in the centre of town, this picturesque freshwater pool and its paddling pool are a London institution, exerting a siren song to hot, stressed-out parents and their offspring on sticky summer's days.

Tooting Bec Lido

Tooting Bec Road, SW16 1RU (8871 7198, www.wandsworth.gov.uk). Streatham rail. **Open** *late May-Aug* 6am-7.30pm daily. *Sept* 6am-4.30pm daily. *Oct-late May* 7am-2pm daily (club members only). **Admission** £4.75; £3.16 reductions, under-16s; free under-5s.

At 94m (308ft) by 25m (82ft), this art deco beauty is the second-largest open-air pool in Europe. Understandably, it's immensely popular with locals, and has a paddling pool for splash-happy toddlers.

TENNIS

Tennis is working hard to break out of its white middle-class straitjacket. Tennis for Free (TFF) is a campaign to give free access to Britain's 33,000 public courts to increase participation in tennis nationwide. It's aimed to help all ages, regardless of ability, background, race and financial circumstance. To learn more about the scheme, visit www.tennisforfree.com, type in your borough and check availability.

Holiday tennis courses at Easter and in the summer can be found in most London boroughs, but need booking well ahead: keep an eye on council websites and contact your local sports development team for details. The Lawn Tennis Association (www.lta.org.uk) publishes free guides giving contacts for private clubs and public courts listed by borough or county, along with contact details for local development officers; it also holds details of tennis holidays available.

Hackney City Tennis Clubs

Clissold Park Mansion House, Stoke Newington Church Street, N16 9HJ (7254 4235, www.hackneycitytennisclubs.co.uk). Stoke Newington rail/73 bus. **Open** *Mar* 10am-5.30pm Mon-Fri; 9am-5.30pm Sat, Sun. *Apr-Sept* 10am-7.30pm Mon-Fri; 9am-7.30pm Sat, Sun. *Oct, Nov* 10am-4.30pm Mon-Fri; 9am-4.30pm Sat, Sun. *Dec-Feb* 10am-3.30pm Mon-Fri; 9am-3.30pm Sat, Sun. **Court hire** £5.50/hr; £2.50 under-16s (10am-5pm Mon-Fri). Phone to check availability.

Part of a nationwide LTA programme to make inner-city tennis facilities cheaper to use and easier to find, this is Britain's first City Tennis Club (with courts in Clissold Park, London Fields and Millfields). Sessions for three- to 16-year-olds are offered during term time (one hour per week costs from £25 for five weeks of lessons), with free racquets and balls; holiday courses are also available. There are additional CTCs in Highbury Fields (Islington) and Eltham Park South (Greenwich).

David Lloyd Leisure

0870 888 3015, www.davidlloydleisure.co.uk. All David Lloyd centres are family-friendly, if not exactly cheap, and the courts and equipment are excellent. Check out the website or phone for your nearest venue.

Islington Tennis Centre

Market Road, N7 9PL (7700 1370, www.aquaterra.org). Caledonian Road tube. **Open** 7am-11pm Mon-Thur; 7am-10pm Fri; 8am-10pm Sat, Sun. **Court hire** *Non-members* Indoor £20/hr; £9/hr 5-16s. Outdoor £9/hr; £4.40/hr 5-16s.

Developed under the LTA's Indoor Tennis Initiative, the centre offers subsidised coaching. It also runs half-hour coaching sessions for three- to five-year-olds.

Redbridge Sports & Leisure Centre

Forest Road, Barkingside, Essex IG6 3HD (8498 1000, www.rslonline.co.uk). Fairlop tube. **Open** 6.30am-11pm Mon-Fri; 8am-9pm Sat; 8am-10pm Sun. **Court hire** prices vary; phone for details.

An independent charitable trust runs this outstanding sports centre. There are eight indoor and 18 outdoor courts to use as a member or 'pay as you play'. There are holiday activities for six- to 14-year-olds, 'fun play' sessions and a short tennis club for under-eights.

Sutton Tennis Academy

Rose Hill Recreation Ground, Rose Hill, Sutton, Surrey SM1 3HH (8641 6611, www.sjtc.org). Morden tube/Sutton Common rail. **Open** 6.30am-11pm Mon-Fri; 7am-9pm Sat, Sun. **Court hire** *Indoor* £20; £15 under-18s. *Outdoor* £8; £6 under-18s. *Clay* £13; £11 under-18s.

Frenchman Erich Dochterman, who has taught various ATP and WTA-ranked players, is head

Activities

coach at this acclaimed tennis school. There are residential courses for players seeking professional status and a scholarship scheme linked to Cheam High School. Children can be steeped in tennis culture from the age of three with Tiny Tots classes, mini tennis and holiday programmes. Facilities include six red clay, ten acrylic and 11 indoor courts.

Westway Tennis Centre

1 Crowthorne Road, W10 6RP (8969 0992, www.westway.org). Latimer Road tube. **Open** 8am-10pm Mon-Fri; 8am-8pm Sat; 10am-10pm Sun. **Court hire** *Indoor* £16-£22.50; £10-£16 4-18s. *Outdoor* £8-£9; £5-£7 4-18s.

The Westway, another product of the LTA's Indoor Tennis Initiative, follows a similar model to Islington (*see p215*): it's excellent for subsidised coaching and courses, short tennis and transitional tennis. There are eight indoor and four outdoor clay courts for kids to play on.

TENPIN BOWLING

Tenpin bowling has become the evening pursuit of choice for many a hip Londoner, but families get a look-in during the daytime. Many centres have ramps, bumpers and lightweight balls to make things easier for small children.

Admission to the following centres averages around £6 per game, including the hire of soft-soled bowling shoes. Phone for details of children's party packages.

Acton Tenpin

Royale Leisure Park, Western Avenue, W3 0PA (0871 873 3150, www.tenpin.co.uk). Park Royal tube. **Open** noon-1am Mon-Thur; noon-2am Fri; 10am-2am Sat; 10am-12.30am Sun. **Credit** MC, V.

1st Bowling Lewisham

11-29 Belmont Hill, SE13 5AU (0870 118 3021). Lewisham rail/DLR. **Open** noon-11pm Mon, Thur; 10am-11pm Tue, Wed, Fri-Sun. **Credit** MC, V.

Funland

Trocadero Centre, 1 Piccadilly Circus, W1D 7DH (7292 3642, www.funland.co.uk). Piccadilly Circus tube. **Open** 10am-midnight Mon-Wed, Sun; noon-1am Thur-Sat. **Credit** MC, V.

Hollywood Bowl Finchley

Great North Leisure Park, Chaplin Square, off Finchley High Road, N12 0GL (8446 6667, www.hollywoodbowl.co.uk). *East Finchley tube, then 263 bus.* **Open** 10am-midnight Mon-Thur, Sun; 10am-1am Fri, Sat. **Credit** MC, V.

Hollywood Bowl Surrey Quays

Mast Leisure Park, Teredo Street, SE16 7LW (7237 3773, www.hollywoodbowl.co.uk). Canada Water DLR. **Open** 10am-11.30pm Mon-Thur, Sun; 10am-midnight Fri, Sat. **Credit** MC, V.

Queens

17 Queensway, W2 4QP (7229 0172, www.queensiceandbowl.co.uk). Bayswater or Queensway tube. **Open** 10am-11.30pm daily. **Credit** MC, V.

Rowans Tenpin Bowl

10 Stroud Green Road, N4 2DF (8800 1950, www.rowans.co.uk). Finsbury Park tube/rail. **Open** 10.30am-12.30am Mon-Thur, Sun; 10.30am-2.30am Fri, Sat. **Credit** MC, V.

London Palace Superbowl

Elephant & Castle Shopping Centre, 2 Elephant & Castle, SE1 6TE (7252 6677, www.palacesuperbowl.com). Elephant & Castle tube. **Open** 11am-11pm daily. **Credit** MC, V.

WATERSPORTS

London is a river city, so there are plenty of opportunities to take to the water in canoes, dinghies or rowing boats and meander down the Thames. It's also worth checking out the city's many reservoirs.

Ahoy Centre

Borthwick Street, SE8 3JY (8691 7606, www.ahoy.org.uk). Deptford rail/Cutty Sark DLR.

This is the place to come for sailing, rowing and (for older children and teens) powerboating on the Thames, and in Surrey and Victoria Docks. Members help run the centre, which keeps prices down and fosters a community spirit.

BTYC Sailsports

Birchen Grove, NW9 8SA (8205 0017, www.btycsailsports.org.uk). Neasden or Wembley Park tube/rail.

Dinghy sailing, windsurfing, basic training and RYA courses on the Welsh Harp reservoir.

Canalside Activity Centre

Canal Close, W10 5AY (8968 4500, www.rbkc. gov.uk). Ladbroke Grove tube/Kensal Rise rail/ 52, 70, 295 bus.

The glossy black woodwork, soaring ceilings and red leather seating in this grown-up dining room might seem off-putting, but families looking for a treat are well catered for. Children get their own menu, which includes mini macaroni cheese, burger and chips and chicken and steamed broccoli, but would probably be far happier with an ice-cream sundae (something of a speciality here), especially the absurdly extravagant National Catastrophe. Adults can choose from classic brasserie mains like steamed sea bass with braised fennel and grown-up burger and chips, or opt for one of the charcuterie or cheese platters. It's a great place to get away from the tourist throngs for a while. *Buggy access. Disabled access: toilet. High chairs. Children's menu (£4.50-£6). Nappy-changing facilities.*

Tate Modern Café: Level 2

2nd Floor, Tate Modern, Sumner Street, SE1 9TG (7401 5014, www.tate.org.uk). Southwark tube/London Bridge tube/rail/Blackfriars rail. **Meals served** 10am-5.30pm Mon-Thur, Sun; 10am-9.30pm Fri; 10am-7.30pm Sat **Main courses** £6.95-£10.50. **Credit** AmEx, MC, V.
It's no wonder Tate Modern is a popular venue for a family day out – and a recent winner of the Time Out Best Family Restaurant award. With a morning of artistic appreciation in the bag, it's a relaxed spot to settle for a delicious meal and an enthusiastic welcome. Kids can choose soup, salad or garlic bread to start, followed by fresh fish fingers, pasta bolognese or macaroni cheese, then ice-cream, jelly or fruit salad. And there's a good deal for families: for every adult main course ordered, a child's main course is free. Floor-to-ceiling windows framing the Thames provide passing entertainment, but there are also art and literacy activities on the kids' menus to keep idle hands busy. It's top-quality food, with an emphasis on quality over quantity; ingredients are carefully sourced and seasonal wherever possible. Get here by 12.30pm at the latest if you want to be led straight to a table. *Buggy access. Children's set menu (£5.10 11am-3pm daily). Disabled access: lift, toilet. High chairs. Nappy-changing facilities.*

CAFÉS

Blue Mountain

18 Northcross Road, SE22 9EU (8299 6953, www.bluemo.co.uk). East Dulwich tube. **Meals served** 8am-6pm Mon-Sat; 9am-6pm Sun. **Main courses** £4.50-£8. **Credit** AmEx, MC, V.
Blue Mountain was already an East Dulwich institution long before the arrival of Bugaboos

and loft conversions, and it continues to draw the crowds with its quality all-day breakfasts and calorific cake selection. The perennial bestseller is the Full Monty: herby butcher's sausage, bacon, beans, portobello mushroom, grilled tomato, chunky toast, a choice of eggs and a cup of tea. Interesting lunchtime specials include the likes of jerk chicken (£7.95), herby salmon and haddock fish (£6.85) and a burger. The funky mosaic patio, made by local artists, is a sunny spot to observe the bustle of Northcross Road (particularly its Saturday market), and is packed with families and freelancers during the week. Long the envy of neighbouring up-and-coming enclaves such as Honor Oak, Blue Mountain now has a branch in Sydenham. *Buggy access. Children's menu (£2.45-£3.65). Disabled access: toilet. High chairs. Nappy-changing facilities. Toys.*
Branch 260 Kirkdale, SE26 4RG (8659 6016).

Brew House

Kenwood, Hampstead Lane, NW3 7JR (8341 5384, www.companyofcooks.com). Bus 210, 214. **Meals served** Oct-Mar 9am-dusk daily. *Apr-Sept* 9am-6pm daily (7.30pm on concert nights). **Main courses** £6.95-£11.95. **Credit** MC, V.
The Brew House is a self-service café run by Company of Cooks in the wonderful setting of Kenwood House (*see p60*). It would be hard to find a more picturesque, sheltered terrace on which to sit and dine in the sunshine. Breakfasts are hearty, with huge sausages, scrambled eggs, good bacon, field mushrooms and tomatoes; on bright weekend mornings, be here by 10am to stake out a table. For lunch, there's a choice of quiche and salad, a generous meat dish or soup with various accompaniments. Children can have smaller portions of the day's dishes, or a bowl of macaroni cheese that's enough to fill an adult. The queuing system takes a while to get used to, and at busy times the hot food service can seem interminably slow. Somehow, none of this matters once the food is on the table – and it's impossible to come away and not feel as if you've had lunch in the countryside. *Buggy access. Children's menu (£2.75-£4). Disabled access: toilet. High chairs. Nappy-changing facilities. Tables outdoors (50, garden). Takeaway service.*

Café On The Rye

Strakers Road, SE15 3UA (8693 9431, www.cafeontherye.co.uk). Peckham Rye rail. **Meals served** 9am-5.30pm daily. **Main courses** £3.50-£7. **No credit cards.**

From the moment this café opened in late 2007 it has done a roaring trade. Tactically positioned next to the One O'Clock Club, it's the perfect location for parents who have just had a hectic swing-pushing workout. The food is wholesome, organic and delicious, ranging from full breakfasts to toasted ciabatta stuffed with camembert, mushrooms, lemon and thyme, classic English sandwiches such as ham and tomato, and Angus beefburgers with caramelised onion, bulgar wheat and salad – and don't overlook the sweets and sticky cakes. The Just 4 Kids menu has the likes of scrambled eggs and beans on toast. The architecture is pretty tasty too: the circular wooden frontage faces the vast green expanse of Peckham Rye, and there are chairs to sit on outside and enjoy the scenery on fine days. On the day we visited, though, most of the under-fives were too busy rolling down the nearby grassy slope to take in the view.
Buggy access. Children's menu (£2.50-£3.75). Crayons. Disabled access: toilet. High chairs. Nappy-changing facilities. Tables outdoors (7, park; 16, garden). Takeaway service. Toys.

Café Provencal
2-6 Half Moon Lane (7978 9228, www.cafe prov.co.uk). Herne Hill rail or Brixton tube/rail then 37 bus. **Meals served** 10am-10pm daily. **Main courses** £8-£15. **Credit** MC, V.

Cosy up at **Café Provencal**.

The bright yellow signage with its large jaunty writing somehow suggests there's fun to be had inside this Herne Hill local. And it's true, the café actively encourages families with its cache of children's books and toys for the amusement of smaller customers. The setting is informal, and children love the cosy corner with battered green armchairs, a kidney shaped coffee table and a squidgy footstool. Staff are friendly and efficient and all-day breakfasts are a popular choice at lunchtime. There's also a choice of ciabattas, omelettes and specials, some with a Moroccan theme. Prices aren't what you'd call rock bottom, but you could always just come in for coffee and home-made cakes if the main courses stretch the budget.
Buggy access. Children's menu (£2-£4). Disabled access. High chairs. Nappy-changing facilities. Tables outdoors (2, pavement). Takeaway service. Toys.

Cibo
Mamas & Papas, 256-258 Regent Street, W1B 3AF (01484 438476, www.mamas andpapas.com). Oxford Circus tube. **Meals served** 10am-8pm Mon-Wed, Fri; 10am-9pm Thur; 9am-8pm Sat; noon-6pm Sun. **Main courses** £6.75-£9.95. **Set dinner** (4-7.30pm Mon-Fri) £9.95 3 courses. **Credit** MC, V. **Map** p314 J6.
Carefully tailored to the needs of pregnant women and small children, this café provides a peaceful haven from the West End tourist overload outside. Set at the back of the first floor of the flagship Mamas & Papas store, there's plenty of space for buggies and a very warm welcome from the predominantly Italian staff. Food is generally healthy and appealing. The breakfast section offers chive omelette with smoked salmon served on brown bread, along with lunchtime smoothies, antipasti plates, bruschettas, salads and hot meals. Children's dishes include organic burgers and fries, organic salmon fish cake and ketchup, pasta dishes and ice-cream.
Buggy access. Children's menu (£3.75-£4.75). High chairs. Nappy-changing facilities. Takeaway service. Toys.

Coffee & Crayons
915 Fulham Road, SW6 5HU (3080 1050, www.coffeeandcrayons.co.uk). Putney Bridge tube. **Meals served** 8am-6pm daily. **Main courses** £2.65-£7.95. **Credit** MC, V.
If you want to entertain your children with a clear conscience, this is definitely the place. Coffee & Crayons banks with the Co-op and uses organic and fair trade produce where possible. As the name suggests, this light, funky café

Consumer

caters for both the thirsty parent and their artistic offspring, with a range of hot drinks and smoothies upstairs and a supervised, arts and crafts-focused playroom downstairs where children can unleash their inner Picasso (there's a charge, but you can stay as long as you like). There are also regular organised events, ranging from dressing-up and music sessions to fairy school. For those simply interested in refuelling, there are snacks and pastries: the pies come highly recommended. There's plenty of room to park your buggies inside; if you can trust your toddlers not to make a beeline for the King's Road with your credit card, there are seats out front too.

Buggy access. Children's menu (£1.50-£4.25). Disabled access: toilet. High chairs. Nappy-changing facilities. Play area (£4.50 10mths-9yrs; £3.50 under 10mths). Tables outdoors (4, pavement). Takeaway service.

Common Ground

Wandsworth Common, off Dorlcote Road, SW18 3RT (8874 9386). Wandsworth Common rail. **Meals served** 9am-5.15pm Mon-Fri; 9am-5.30pm Sat, Sun. **Main courses** £3.50-£9. **Credit** MC, V.

Who needs fancy decor when the views from the window are so glorious? With cricket pitches on one side and a pristine bowling green on the other, this former lodge building keeps things simple. There are wooden floors and wooden tables in the conservatory, a generous patio with tables outside, and a cosier room with sofas and buckets of toys where parent and toddler groups meet on weekdays. The food is tastier than its simple presentation might suggest, with a children's menu that includes home-made chicken goujons or locally made sausages served with mash or chips and broccoli or peas. There are also simple sandwiches and tasty cakes.

Buggy access. Children's menu (£2.25-£4.50). High chairs. Nappy-changing facilities. Play area. Takeaway service.

Container Café

The View Tube, the Greenway, Marshgate Lane, E15 2PJ (07702 125081, www.the viewtube.co.uk). Pudding Mill Lane DLR. **Meals served** 9am-5pm Mon-Fri; 10am-6pm Sat, Sun. **Main courses** £3.50-£8. **Credit** AmEX, MC, V.

The Container Café is on the ground floor of the View Tube, a new (opened in 2009) community centre opposite the Olympic Park on the Greenway walking and cycling route. You can't miss the View Tube – it's made out of old shipping containers and painted

Mad about mushrooms

Children like nothing better than picking their own food from the great outdoors. Vegetables that would normally be greeted with desperate groans suddenly become exciting and delicious. Most exhilarating of all is wild food, because it's also essentially a treasure hunt. Fungi To Be With is run by Andy Overall, who turned his back on the music business (his band Blue Zoo made it on to *Top of the Pops* in the 1980s) to concentrate on mushrooms. During spring, summer and autumn, Overall leads forays and workshops in the wild corners of London's green spaces (Hampstead Heath, Epping Forest and Wimbledon Common). A mushroom hunt isn't just about the end result either; it's a good way of getting children to go on a whinge- free walk and improve their skills of observation into the bargain. The sheer diversity of the species will surprise the adults as much as the kids, and you'll just have to trust the little'uns not to use their new-found knowledge of the poisonous varieties to do away with their siblings. Forays begin at 10am and end at 2pm so bring a picnic to supplement the fungi finds. Forays cost £20 for adults (£15 concessions) and children go free. Look at the website for dates. Prebooking is essential (8458 0652/ www.fungitobewith.org).

Consumer

Perfect pizza

You can't beat a pizza, hot from the oven – but which of the city's chains are best for families? We've chosen a few chains and listed the good and bad points about each.

ASK

160-162 Victoria Street, SW1E 5LB (7630 8228, www.askcentral.co.uk). Victoria tube/rail. **Meals served** noon-11pm Mon-Sat; noon-10pm Sun. **Main courses** £6.25-£14. **Credit** AmEx, MC, V.
While it rarely wows with its cooking, there is plenty to like about ASK, including the amiable staff, comfy furnishings and attention to detail (such as proper chilled glasses for Peroni). Adults who don't fancy one of the 14 pizzas can opt for pasta, risottos and salads; the so-so desserts aren't really worth saving room for.
Total number of branches 22.
What's in it for the kids? The £5.95 kids' menu comes with colouring-in and wax crayons and gives sprogs a choice of ten pastas and pizzas, garlic bread, salad and a scoop of ice-cream or a banana split.
Buggy access. Children's set meal (£5.95). Disabled access. Crayons. High chairs. Nappy-changing facilities. Takeaway service.

Pizza Express

Benbow House, 24 New Globe Walk, SE1 9DS (7401 3977, www.pizzaexpress.com). London Bridge tube/rail. **Meals served** noon-11pm Mon-Thur; noon-midnight Fri, Sat; noon-10.30pm Sun. **Main courses** £6.20-£12. **Credit** AmEx, DC, MC, V.
Pizza Express now offers five different styles of pizza – regular, Romana (thinner, crisper bases), Leggera (less calories, salad on top) and posh, rectangular Theo Randall numbers and new Francesco Mazzei dishes. And guess what? The cheaper Fiorentinas, Diavolos and American Hots you've been ordering for years taste just as good as the new models. This chain is pretty reliable, though quality does vary with individual staff and you can get the odd soggy base, stingy topping or overcooked pizza.
Total number of branches 122.
What's in it for the kids? The Piccolo menu offers three courses for £6.10, with pasta options including bolognese,

a creamy version of napoletana and carbonara with mushrooms. A choice of sundaes and a cup of Bambinoccino finish things off in style. Plum organic baby food (£1) is also available. Staff are friendly enough, but waiting times during busy periods can mean little feet get itchy.
Buggy access. Children's set meal (£6.10). Crayons. Disabled access (ground floor): toilet. High chairs. Nappy-changing facilities. Tables outdoors (12, riverside). Takeaway service.

Pizza Paradiso

61 The Cut, SE1 8LL (7261 1221, www.pizzaparadiso.co.uk). Southwark tube/Waterloo tube/rail. **Meals served** noon-midnight Mon-Sat; noon-11pm Sun. **Main courses** £6.10-£17.95. **Credit** AmEx, MC, V.
There's a friendly, neighbourhood trattoria vibe to this small family chain. Kids will be happy with dough balls and starter-sized portions of spaghetti napoletana, bolognese or carbonara. Some of the pasta is homemade, including the gnocchi and filled ravioli. As well as pizzas, there are meat and fish dishes (salmon with pink peppercorn sauce, veal scallopine) and specials for those happy to spend more. The own-made ice-cream is terrific.
Total number of branches 4.
What's in it for the kids? Staff will discount a quid off some pasta dishes sold in child sizes.
Buggy access. High chairs. Tables outdoors (6, pavement). Takeaway service.

La Porchetta

74-77 Chalk Farm Road, NW1 8AN (7267 6822). Chalk Farm tube. **Lunch served** noon-3pm Mon-Fri. **Dinner served** 6-11pm Mon-Sat. **Main courses** £5.90-£11.50. **Credit** MC, V.
Portions are vast: pizzas threaten to fall off the plates, which in turn threaten to fall off the tiny tables, so consider sharing. A lengthy menu takes in all the classic pizza toppings; alternatively, there are good-looking bowls of pasta and meat and fish dishes. On our last visit, pizzas were undercooked at the centre, though the toppings tasted fine. We liked frutti di mare and messicana (Italian sausage and

chilli). No-nonsense black-clad Italian staff work the room, but getting their attention can be difficult during peak times.
Total number of branches 6.
What's in it for the kids? Children can order a half portion of pasta at a reduced price, or share one of the huge pizzas.
Buggy access. High chairs. Takeaway service.

Prezzo

17 Hertford Street, W1J 7RS (7499 4690, www.prezzoplc.co.uk). Green Park or Hyde Park Corner tube. **Meals served** noon-11.30pm Mon-Sat; noon-11pm Sun.
Main courses £6.50-£11.50. **Credit** AmEx, MC, V.
There's nothing very Italian about the dark oak panelling and moody lighting in the Mayfair branch of this chain. The pizzas aren't especially Italian either. Still, prices are keen for such a swish location near to Hyde Park. There's a selection of salads, meat dishes and risottos too; puds can be disappointing for the price.
Total number of branches 18.
What's in it for the kids? Staff perk up when children are around, and serve the kids' menu with panache: garlic bread, a choice of three pizzas/pastas, ice-cream and squash, and an activity pack too.
Buggy access. Children's set meal (£4.95). High chairs. Takeaway service.

Strada

29 Kensington High Street, W8 (7938 4648, www.strada.co.uk). High Street Kensington tube. **Meals served** 11.30am-11pm Mon-Sat; 11.30am-10.30pm Sun.
Main courses £6.95-£16.50. **Credit** AmEx, MC, V.
Strada's pizzas range from a simple margherita to more complex offerings, like the formaggio di capra (goat's cheese, walnuts, balsamic onions, celery cress, tomato sauce and mozzarella). There's five-or-so of everything else: salads, pasta, risotto, fish and meat dishes. Desserts (*panettone al forno, torta della nonna*) come with excellent ice-cream. We love that Strada puts free chilled, bottled and filtered water on every table.
Total number of branches 28.
What's in it for the kids? Not all branches offer the kids' menu, so check ahead. Where it is available, children can choose between spaghetti pomodoro, penne bolognese, pizza margherita and grilled chicken, with pannacotta or ice-cream for pudding, plus a soft drink.
Buggy access. Children's set meal (£5.50). Disabled access. High chairs. Takeaway service.

Zizzi

73-75 Strand, WC2R 0DE (7240 1717, www.zizzi.co.uk). Covent Garden or Embankment tube/Charing Cross tube/rail. **Meals served** noon-11.30pm Mon-Sat; noon-11pm Sun. **Main courses** £6.25-£11.95. **Credit** AmEx, DC, MC, V.
Ingredients on the main menu at Zizzi (buffalo milk ricotta, santos tomatoes, cotta ham) suggest thoughtful sourcing not readily apparent at other chains, while the Bambini menu offers three courses for a mere £5.95. You can check each dish online for allergen and dietary information. Service sometimes slips, though.
Total number of branches 25.
What's in it for the kids? The kids' menu offers breadsticks, a choice of seven pizzas and pasta dishes, then ice-cream.
Buggy access. Children's set meal (£5.95). Disabled access: toilet. High chairs. Nappy-changing facilities. Takeaway service.

Consumer

one of the legendary breakfasts, so it's worth arriving early before dishes sell out. Kids tend to plump for the no-nonsense, populist pasta dishes such as spaghetti bolognese or macaroni cheese; for afters, there are incredibly good home-made ice-creams and cakes. Babies with forgetful mums can purloin a tube or two of Ella's Kitchen purée from the shelves. The welcome is warm and the atmosphere delightfully laid-back. The only downside is having to order at the till, where there's invariably a queue. Still, for a café with so much to offer, including outside seating for warm days, it would be churlish to complain. *Buggy access. Children's menu (£2.25-£4.25). Disabled access: toilet. High chairs. Nappy-changing facilities. Tables outdoors (12, garden). Takeaway service.*

Garden Café

Inner Circle, Regent's Park, NW1 4NU (7935 5729, www.thegardencafe.co.uk). Baker Street or Regent's Park tube. **Oct-Apr Breakfast served** 9-11am, **lunch served** noon-4pm daily. *May-Sept* **Breakfast served** 9-11am, **lunch served** noon-4pm, **dinner served** 5-8pm daily. **Main courses** £8.50-£12.50. **Credit** MC, V.
On a sunny day, the rose garden in Regent's Park is the most lovely place to sit and watch the world go by – if you can find a free table at the Garden Café, that is – not always the most straightforward task. The food, courtesy of Company of Cooks, is a cut above the average, although a touch on the pricey side. Classics such as risotto are given imaginative touches like using barley instead of rice, and more snack-like dishes like chicken with aioli and red onion marmalade on focaccia are also served. Children are offered a limited menu, but it's home-made and topped off by ice-creams from north London's legendary purveyor of glacé, Marine Ices.
Buggy access. Children's set meal (£6). Disabled access: toilet. Nappy-changing facilities. Tables outdoors (40, park).

Golders Hill Park Refreshment House

North End Way, NW3 7HD (8455 8010). Golders Green or Hampstead tube/210, 268 bus. **Meals served** *Summer* 9am-6.30pm daily. *Winter* 9am-dusk daily. **Main courses** £6-£8. **Credit** (over £10) MC, V.
There has been a tearoom here since the 19th century. Sadly, the old building was demolished after being damaged in World War II, but the pavilion-style café that stands here now is a lovely place to sit and eat; there are views over

the well-manicured park from indoors and outdoors on the large south-facing terrace, where elderly Jewish local residents talk like they're in a Woody Allen movie, *sans* New York accent. The food is on an Italian theme, with assorted tasty, own-made pasta dishes, risottos and salads. The own-made ice-cream, available in 20 flavours, is very good (also sold from the kiosk at the side of the building in summer), as is the coffee.
Buggy access. Children's menu (£4-£5.95). Disabled access: toilet. High chairs. Nappy-changing facilities. Tables outdoors (25, terrace). Takeaway service.

Gracelands

118 College Road, NW10 5HD (8964 9161, www.gracelandscafe.com). Kensal Green tube. **Meals served** 8.30am-5pm Mon-Fri; 9am-5pm Sat; 9.30am-3pm Sun. **Main courses** £3.95-£11.95. **Credit** MC, V.
A homely if somewhat chaotic local cafe that's extremely popular with families. The all-day breakfast menu, lunchtime specials, cakes and pastries are made with attention to detail and there's a great salad bar that's full of dishes put together with imagination and love. The menu changes fairly often, but be warned, the pasta portions are on the large side and can put off even the most enthusiatic eater, so order one to share. A play area inside the café with toys and books, as well as the fantasic resource of Gracelands Yard next door (which offers workshops for children like sewing clubs, yoga classes, baby music sessions and Mini Picasso art classes), means this airy, family-focused café is always packed. All in all, a great local treasure – but one that knows it's got a captive market.
Buggy access. Children's set meal (£3.50). High chairs. Nappy-changing facilities. Play area. Tables outdoors (4, pavement; 12, garden). Takeaway service. Toys.

Hummingbird Bakery

47 Old Brompton Road, SW7 3JP (7584 0055, www.hummingbirdbakery.com). South Kensington tube. **Open** 10.30am-7pm daily. **Credit** AmEx, MC, V.
After braving the crowds of yummy mummies with kiddies on a sugar high, settle down among tasteful shades of pink and brown in the small café, or nab one of the coveted outdoor tables. American-style sweets are the order of the day, with cupcakes being the star attraction. Get to this chichi South Ken bakery early to avoid the frustrating queues and spotty service or, better yet, take one for the road.
Buggy access. Tables outdoors (4, pavement). Takeaway service.

Branches 133 Portobello Road, W11 2DY (7229 6446); 155A Wardour Street, WF 8WG (7434 3003).

Inn The Park

St James's Park, SW1A 2BJ (7451 9999, www.innthepark.com). St James's Park or Westminster tube. **Meals served** *Summer* 8am-10pm Mon-Fri; 9am-9.30pm Sat; 9am-6pm Sun. *Winter* 8am-5pm Mon-Fri; 9am-5pm Sat, Sun. **Main courses** £14.50-£20.50. **Credit** MC, V. **Map** p317 K8.

The setting for Oliver Peyton's timber-clad, glass-fronted posh park café couldn't be more idyllic. The tables on the terrace overlook St James's Park and the picturesque Duck Island; even the indoor tables have lovely views, thanks to floor-to-ceiling windows. Most families usually head straight to the self-service area, as the restaurant is pricey (there is a children's menu, but it'll set you back £7.50 and doesn't include dessert); more modestly priced self-service offerings include soups, sandwiches, pies and cakes. If it's a special occasion, you can book a summer barbecue for a party (minimum 25 people).

Buggy access. Children's menu (£7.50). Disabled access: toilet. High chairs. Nappy-changing facilities. Tables outdoors (40, patio). Takeaway service.

Lido

Serpentine Lido, Hyde Park, W2 2UH (7706 7098, www.companyofcooks.com). Hyde Park or Knightsbridge tube. **Meals served** *Jan, Feb, Nov, Dec* 8am-4pm daily. *Mar, Oct* 8am-5pm daily. *Apr* 8am-6pm daily. *May* 8am-7.30pm daily. *June* 8am-8pm daily. *July, Aug* 8am-9pm daily. *Sept* 8am-7pm daily. **Main courses** £7.50-£12.50. **Credit** MC, V.

This lakeside café was refurbished and taken over by everyone's favourite London park caterers, Company of Cooks, in spring 2010 – they also run the Brew House at Kenwood House (*p60*) and the Garden Café in Regent's Park (*see p230*). Families flock here for the relaxed atmosphere, huge terrace (seats 300), and views over the Serpentine. There are highchairs and a decent baby change area, and newspapers, should the grown ups get any snatched moments of peace. The menu veers from simple retro (knickerbocker glory, calamari) to hot dishes with a bit more ambition (steak with béarnaise sauce and salad, lobster rolls), and there's a short but functional kids' menu featuring burgers, pizza and fishfingers, accompanied by chips. Lido is licensed, so parents can go continental with lunch, or even brazen it out with a breakfast cocktail. For those in the mood for a dip before or after refreshments, the Lido and paddling pool – open May to September – is just next door.

Grab the cup cakes at the **Hummingbird Bakery** before they all go.

London
Captured

Buggy access. Children's menu (£4.50). Disabled access: toilet. High chairs. Nappy-changing facilities. Takeaway service.

Lido Café

Brockwell Lido, Dulwich Road, SE24 0PA (7274 3088, www.thelidocafe.co.uk). Herne Hill rail or Brixton tube/rail then 37 bus. **Meals served** 7.30am-6pm Mon, Tue; 7.30am-11pm Wed-Fri; 9am-11pm Sat; 9am-6pm Sun. **Main courses** £8.50-£13. **Credit** MC, V.

The Lido Café in Brockwell Park opened at the end of summer 2009 and you don't have to go swimming to enjoy its lovely setting, relaxed atmosphere and well-executed comfort food. The simple decor makes the most of the stylish 1930s interior, with large windows overlooking the pool area. Outside, from spring to autumn, the café opens a large seating area on the terrace – fenced off from the pool itself – with a hut selling barbecued food and salads, fresh juices and real fruit lollies. Inside, the children's menu features favourites like macaroni cheese, tomato pasta and burger and chips, and there are toys and books to keep little ones amused. For more structured fun, Whippersnappers run regular bookable and drop-in toddler groups in a room left of the main entrance of the Lido (see website for details: www.whippersnappers.org). The café is open all year round but gets very busy during pool-season (May-October) with hardy swimmers wrapped in towels trying to rid themselves of goosebumps. Free wi-fi and strong (Union) coffee makes it popular with the home-working crowd too.

Buggy access. Children's menu (£4). Disabled access: toilet. High chairs. Nappy-changing facilities. Toys.

Mudchute Kitchen

Mudchute Park & Farm, Pier Street, E14 3HP (7515 5901, www.mudchutekitchen.org). Mudchute DLR/D6, D7, D8 bus. **Meals served** 9am-4pm Tue-Sun. **Main courses** £3.50-£8.50. **Credit** MC, V.

This lovely spot in the middle of Mudchute City Farm *(see p137)* is well used by locals. Inside, the wax tablecloths and toys give the spacious hut a homely air. Outside, children love to sit in the large courtyard and watch the horses nodding their heads over the stable doors. The fresh, seasonal menu isn't extensive, but it's all own-made. The menu usually features a few hot dishes (Moroccan meatballs, lentil soup or pasta with mushrooms and cream, for example), and there's an all-day breakfast menu. Children might turn their noses up at Mudchute's version of baked beans on toast (made with butter beans and homemade tomato sauce), but grown-ups will be seriously impressed. The cakes are a highlight; poppy seed and ginger are both moist and delicious, while the delectable carrot cake is worth the trip alone. Wash it down with a very strong cup of coffee before heading off to look at the animals.

Buggy access. Children's menu (£2.50-£3.50). Disabled access: toilet. High chairs. Nappy-changing facilities. Tables outdoors (15, courtyard). Takeaway service.

Parlour

167 Stoke Newington Church Street, N16 0UL (7923 0654). Stoke Newington rail/bus 73. **Meals served** 8am-6.30pm daily. **Main courses** £2.25-£4.40. **Credit** MC, V.

This Stokey café specialises in gluten-, wheat- and dairy-free grub for hungry people of all ages. A wide selection of fillings are available on various different breads, or inside jacket potatoes. Freshly squeezed juices and fruit smoothies are a healthy and delicious option, and the own-made waffles a real treat – especially when they come slathered with banana, toffee and whipped cream. Relaxed, friendly staff and shabby-but-almost-chic decor complement the rustic food. There is a shady courtyard and a playroom stacked full of toys, books and games.

Fuel up at **Inn the Park**. *See p231.*

Consumer

Buggy access. Disabled access. High chairs. Nappy- changing facilities. Play area.Tables outdoors (3, garden). Takeaway service. Toys.

Pavilion Café, Dulwich

Dulwich Park, off College Road, SE21 7BQ (8299 1383, www.pavilioncafedulwich.co.uk). North Dulwich or West Dulwich rail. **Meals served** *Summer* 9am-6.30pm daily. *Winter* 9am-4pm daily. **Main courses** £3.50-£6.95. **Credit cards** MC, V.

Busy on weekdays and positively heaving at weekends, this is the park café by which all others should be judged. The well-balanced menu has serious child appeal, offering grilled chicken, penne pasta, Scotch beefburgers, chunky chips and sandwiches. There's also organic baby food, Innocent smoothies and garishly coloured ice drinks, plus raisins, crisps, fruit and crayons (obviously not for eating). For afters, there's ice-cream – also sold through a side hatch in summer. Daily specials for grown-ups are overshadowed by the all-day breakfasts of top-quality sausages and bacon, free-range eggs and chunky toast (white or wholemeal). Food is sourced locally (Borough Market for veg, William Rose for meat and Moxon's for fish), cakes are home-made and, where possible, food is prepared fresh on site. As well as serving great food, the café has also become a social hub, providing information on local events, a colourful play corner, baby changing facilities and clean toilets, and bird food for feeding the ducks; it can also cater for birthday parties. Outdoor tables offer verdant views in summer; in winter, it's a cosy spot to warm up over a hot chocolate (with a shot of rum for the grown-ups). If you don't like children, you may want to give this place a wide berth; if you have some of your own, it's a lifesaver.

Buggy access. Children's menu (£1.50-£3.95). Disabled access: toilet. High chairs. Nappy- changing facilities. Play area. Tables outdoors (12, terrace). Takeaway service.

Pavilion Café, Victoria Park

Victoria Park, Crown Gate West, E9 7DE (8980 0030, www.the-pavilion-cafe.com). Mile End tube then 277 or 425 bus. **Meals served** 8.30am-5pm daily. **Main courses** £4-£8. **No credit cards.**

On a sunny day, Victoria Park's lakeside pavilion soon gets overrun with babies and buggies. But not just because it's a convenient stopping place after a trip to feed the ducks. The lovely glass rotunda houses a mishmash of tables made from old wooden cable drums and Victorian school chairs, but there's nothing random about the food. Delicious dishes are

Mudchute Kitchen. *See p233.*

written up on blackboard walls; classier palates will be delighted with the likes of eggs benedict with spinach, or roast beef with potato salad, watercress and anchovy mayo. The ingredients are all well sourced (Ginger Pig meats, Monmouth coffees) and, wherever possible, organic. Fortunately, there are more seats next to the lake, so it's worth taking your coffee and cake (moreish brownies, lemon drizzle) and heading for a park bench.
Buggy access. Children's menu (£2-£4). Disabled access: toilet. High chairs. Nappy-changing facilities. Tables outdoors (15, park). Takeaway service.

Pavilion Café, Highgate
Highgate Woods, Muswell Hill Road, N10 3JN (8444 4777). Highgate tube. **Meals served** 9am-1hr before park closing daily. **Main courses** £6-£10. **Credit** AmEx, MC, V.
Set in a clearing amid the trees, the Pavilion Café's leafy setting makes it a firm favourite with families. Whatever the time of day, week or year, there's sure to be buggies in evidence. Indoor space is limited to seven tables, but a covered area provides shade in summer and shelter in winter. Open-air outdoor tables are in ready supply, and are completely enclosed by bushes and a fence – ideal for letting the kids have a wander while the adults order coffees. While the main menu is Mediterranean-influenced, the children's dishes are more straightforward: burger and chips and pasta are the favourites. Save room for pudding: the ice-cream is very good indeed, as is the warm, densely moist brownie. On our last visit, the chef came round with samples of a lemon polenta cake that he'd just taken out of the oven. Service is presided over by the ever-attentive head waiter, whose charm puts a twinkle in local mums' eyes.
Buggy access. Children's set meal (£3.75-£3.95). Crayons. Disabled access: toilet. High chairs. Nappy-changing facilities. Tables outdoors (30, garden). Takeaway service.

Pavilion Tea House
Greenwich Park, Blackheath Gate, SE10 8QY (8858 9695, www.companyofcooks.com). Blackheath rail/Greenwich rail/DLR. **Meals served** *Summer* 9am-5.30pm Mon-Fri; 9am-6pm Sat, Sun. *Winter* 9am-4pm daily. **Main courses** £4.95-£6.60. **Credit** MC, V.
You are best off visiting this hexagonal park café during the week; at weekends, the painfully slow service means the queue is always enormous. The menu is full of appealingly hearty fare, with meaty specials, generously filled sandwiches and a good value

Pavilion Café, Highgate

all-day breakfast menu. It's licensed, so you can wash your lunch down with a glass of wine. Options for children include pasta dishes and baked beans on toast, but limited indoor space means parents are requested to leave pushchairs outside. If you're not too full after the large main courses, the own-made cakes are very good.
Buggy access. Children's menu (£2.25-£3.50). Disabled access: toilet. High chairs. Nappy-changing facilities. Tables outdoors (15, patio).

Petitou
63 Choumert Road, SE15 4AR (7639 2613). Peckham Rye rail. **Meals served** 9am-5.30pm Mon-Sat; 10am-5.30pm Sun. **Main courses** £4.35-£6.95. **Credit** AmEx, MC, V.
This charming local café serves up solid, wholesome fare, overlaid with an appealing dash of nostalgia. Located at the leafier end of Peckham, it attracts an arty crowd alongside the bourgeois buggy wielders. All-day breakfasts range from childhood favourites such as scrambled egg, English muffins and toast with peanut butter or marmalade to (love 'em or hate 'em) cheesy marmite crumpets. Salads and quiches are made from locally sourced ingredients, cakes are homely, juices are freshly squeezed, herbal teas plentiful, and almost

everything is prefixed with 'organic'. The furniture is a junk shop pot-pourri, with an old-fashioned coat stand and mismatched wooden chairs. Community notices and posters for local events cover the walls, while the radio hums Classic FM. The relaxed atmosphere, cheery interior and shady front patio make this a perfect lunch spot for families.
Buggy access. High chairs. Tables outdoors (4, pavement).

Ragged Canteen

Beaconsfield, 22 Newport Street, SE11 6AY (7582 6465, www.beaconsfield.ltd.uk). Lambeth North tube. **Meals served** 11am-4pm Tue-Sun. **Main courses** £3-£5.30. **No credit cards.**
The café at this former Victorian Ragged School, now a contemporary art venue, is not, on the face of it, an attractive prospect for weary parents with kids in tow. First, you need to buzz your way in through a side street door behind the railway tracks, then negotiate two small flights of steps and a narrow doorway to get to a basement space with a flagstone floor, white walls, arty flyers and little else. The friendliness of the staff soon makes up for the stark interior, though. A box of toys and colouring-in pads are available, with free Wi-Fi and weekend papers for adults. The healthy eating credentials can't

be faulted either, with seasonal vegetarian dishes such as South African sweet potato stew or spinach daal with yogurt and salad, along with fair trade teas and home-baked cakes, all at reasonable prices. Good food, without the Giraffe-style gaiety (*see p222*).
Buggy access. Crayons. Disabled access (call ahead): toilets. High chairs. Nappy-changing facilities. Toys.

S&M Café

4-6 Essex Road, N1 8LN (7359 5361, www.sandmcafe.co.uk). Angel tube/19, 38 bus. **Meals served** 7.30am-11pm daily. **Main courses** £6.95-£9.50. **Credit** AmEx, MC, V.
Original Italian caff trappings have been preserved here, from the steel-edged laminated tables to the magnificent art deco façade. The retro look may appeal to adults, but there's plenty here for children to enjoy too, and the ambience is welcoming and relaxed. As well as the eponymous sausage and mash – available in various varieties – there are sides such as Heinz baked beans and cauliflower cheese, and a down-to-earth breakfast menu featuring the likes of beans on toast and boiled eggs with toast soldiers (there's an all-day breakfast, too, including just about everything). Other mains such as fish cakes and meat pies round out the choices, and there's even toad in the hole.

Head behind the tracks and down the basement stairs to get to the **Ragged Canteen**.

Buggy access. Children's set meal (£3.95). Crayons. High chairs. Nappy-changing facilities. Takeaway service. Toys.
Branches throughout town.

That Place on the Corner
1-3 Green Lanes, N16 9BS (7704 0079, www.thatplaceonthecorner.co.uk). Highbury & Islington tube/rail/Canonbury rail/21, 73, 141, 276, 341, 476 bus. **Meals served** 9.30am-6.30pm Mon-Thur; 9.30am-8pm Fri; 9.30am-8.30pm Sat; 9.30am-6pm Sun. **Main courses** £4.85-£9.50. **Credit** MC, V.

Run by two local mothers, this light-flooded café on the corner of Newington Green is very popular with the N16 buggy set. And it's easy to see why. TPOTC is a rare refuge in London where parents have no worries about annoying their table neighbours – adults aren't allowed in unless they're with a child. There's a buggy park by the door and an inviting play corner with brightly coloured cushions, a well-stocked book shelf and a large dressing-up cupboard. The tiny 'creativity room' has now been taken over by the kitchen, so the daily music, arts and crafts sessions are held in the main café – a definite improvement. The children's menu is a run-down of old favourites like sausage and mash, pasta, pizza (kids can put the toppings on themselves), burgers and cottage pie, all home-made and served with a portion of veg. Babies are also catered for with a daily organic vegetable purée, available in different textures for those with and without teeth. From grown-ups there are cakes and good coffee.

Buggy access. Children's menu (£2.90-£5.50). Crayons. Disabled access: toilet. High chairs. Nappy-changing facilities. Play area.

Tide Tables
2 The Archways, Riverside, Richmond, Surrey TW9 1TH (8948 8285, www.tide tablescafe.com). Richmond tube/rail. **Meals served** 9am-6pm daily. **Main courses** £2.70-£6.50. **Credit** MC, V.

Nestled inside the last archway under Richmond Bridge before it spans the Thames, this café's biggest draw is its location. On fine-weather days, customers sip organic coffee out on the gravelled terrace while overlooking the river. It is patronised by pumped-up joggers stopping by for an energy drink as well as more laid-back dog-walkers; parents, meanwhile, praise its toddler-friendly outdoor space and welcoming attitude to children. New mothers also flock here in droves, attracted by the comfy sofas and wholehearted support of breastfeeding. Offering toothsome vegetarian fare with a North African influence, as well as the usual pastries and muffins, the menu rates highly in terms of nutrition and variety. Regulars are treated like old friends, while newcomers are charmed by the affable owners.

Buggy access. Children's menu (£2.70). Disabled access. High chairs. Takeaway service.

Upper Deck
London Transport Museum, The Piazza, WC2E 7BB (7598 1356, www.ltmuseum. co.uk). Covent Garden tube. **Meals served** 10am-6pm Mon-Sat; 10am-5pm Sun. **Main courses** £3.10-£8. **Credit** AmEx, MC, V. **Map** p317 L7.

Situated on an airy mezzanine floor above the London Transport Museum's entrance and shop, this is definitely a rare place to sit and watch goings-on down below and out in Covent Garden's piazza. Kids will also be mesmerised by the huge set of traffic lights suspended from the ceiling. Buggies are parked on arrival and highchairs magically appear, courtesy of the incredibly accommodating staff. Children can have a half-price, half-portion version of most of the adult meals, which include burger and chips, beans on toast, pasta, panini and soup. (Adults will also appreciate the good-looking cocktail menu.) You don't have to be visiting the museum (*see p83*) to dine here.

Buggy access. Disabled access: lift, toilet. High chairs. Nappy-changing facilities.

V&A Café
Victoria & Albert Museum, Cromwell Road, SW7 2RL (7942 2000, www.vam.ac.uk). South Kensington tube. **Meals served** 10am-5.15pm Mon-Thur, Sat, Sun; 10am-9.30pm Fri. **Main courses** £6-£10. **Credit** MC, V.

Lined with glittering tiles, the V&A's main café is like a giant jewellery box, with two quieter, smaller rooms to each side. Even kids that aren't impressed by the baroque tiling will probably like the huge ball chandeliers – especially if they're given a little something from the luscious cake selection. A three-layered chocolate sponge with marbled icing, perhaps? And there's a good selection of savouries too, with a hot food counter serving crispy roasts (from pork and apple to pesto-drizzled aubergine) and an adventurous sandwich bar. Kids' portions (for the under-tens) are available from both counters for £4.95, it's buggy-friendly and high chairs are provided. As a good-weather option, there are tables outside in the peaceful red sandstone courtyard; fountains bubble in the shallow lake at the centre.

Buggy access. Disabled access: toilet. High chairs. Nappy-changing facilities.

Consumer

CHINESE

Dragon Castle

100 Walworth Road, SE17 1JL (7277 3388, www.dragoncastle.eu). Elephant & Castle tube/rail. **Meals served** noon-11.30pm Mon-Sat; 11.30am-10.30pm Sun. **Main courses** £5.50-£25. **Set meals** £15.80-£34.80 per person (min two) 2-3 courses. **Credit** AmEx. MC, V.

Residents of this unloved corner of south London, around Elephant & Castle, are over the moon about this vast, barn-like restaurant. Dragon Castle is a commendable attempt to re-create an authentic Hong Kong dining experience, complete with carp ponds, gilt dragons and a menu that runs to duck tongues and poached eels. It's a real treat to come for dim sum in the daytime, as these savoury

Get the scoop

Don't miss **Marine Ices** (*see p246*), the gelateria/Italian caff that has been fattening up Chalk Farm residents since the 1920s.

Gelateria Danieli

16 Brewers Lane, Richmond, Surrey TW9 1HH (8439 9807, www.gelateria danieli.com). Richmond tube/rail. **Open** *Summer* 10am-10pm daily. *Winter* 10am-6pm daily. Times may vary, phone to check. **Ice-cream** £2/scoop. **Credit** MC, V.
Squeezed into a narrow shopping arcade, marked at one end by two jolly guardsmen standing to attention outside a chocolate shop, this small gelateria dishes out superior sorbets and ice-creams to be savoured around Richmond Green. Wooden floorboards and a couple of chairs inside make it cosy in winter but rather cramped in summer, when queues stretch out of the door. When they're not rushed off their feet, friendly staff invite you to try before you buy.
Buggy access. Takeaway service.
Branches Bentalls Centre, Wood Street, Kingston-upon-Thames, Surrey KT1 1TX (8141 5098); 47 Queenstown Road, SW8 3RG (7720 5784, open summer only).

Gelato Mio

138 Holland Park Avenue, W11 4UE (7727 4117, www.gelatomio.co.uk). Holland Park tube. **Open** 7.30am-10pm Mon-Wed, Sun; 8.30am-11pm Fri, Sat; 9am-10pm Sun. **Ice-cream** £2.50/scoop. **Credit** MC, V.
Still only in its third summer, this stylish, orange-hued parlour already has three branches. The welcome is enthusiastic and typically Italian. Customers may be invited to have a taste before choosing; last time we were here we plumped for a gorgeous strawberry sorbet with sharp

fruity flavours. There's seating inside; alternatively, take your ice to nearby Holland Park (*see p116*). The ever-changing menu may include nocciola (hazelnut), stracciatella (chocolate chip) and arrancia (orange sorbet).
Buggy access. Delivery service. Tables outdoors (2, pavement). Takeaway service.
Branch 45 Villiers Street, WC2N 6NE (7930 5961); 37 Pembridge Road, W11 3HG (7727 0194).

Gelateria Valerie

9 Duke of York Square, SW3 4LY (7730 7978, www.patisserie-valerie.co.uk). Sloane Square tube. **Open** 8am-7pm Mon-Sat; 10am-7pm Sun. **Ice-cream** £1.75/scoop. **Credit** AmEx, MC, V.
A cone's throw away from the Saatchi Gallery, this glass-walled branch of the ever-expanding Valerie chain is a shining island in the heart of Chelsea's prime retail site. There's plenty of outside seating looking over the fountains in summer, while stools lining the glass shop front are perfect for a spot of people watching. Rum baba, wild berry yoghurt and the alarmingly coloured banana blue are among the flavours.
Buggy access. Disabled access. Tables outdoors (20, Duke of York Square). Takeaway service.
Branches throughout town.

Morelli's Gelato Counter

Harrods Food Hall, 87-135 Brompton Road, SW1X 7XL (7893 8959, www. morellisgelato.com). Knightsbridge tube. **Open** 9am-9pm Mon-Sat; noon-6pm Sun. **Ice-cream** £3.95/scoop. **Credit** AmEx, MC, V.
From its beginnings in a 1930s seaside art deco premises (the original branch in

morsels will really appeal to children. We loved the simple, steamed corn-fed chicken in a lightly spicy root ginger stock, and an enormous serving of glossy, green morning glory in XO chilli sauce. Service runs from bossy-boots to nice-as-pie, but it's all pretty much on the ball.

Buggy access. Disabled access: toilet. High chairs. Takeaway service.

Joy King Lau

3 Leicester Street, WC2H 7BL (7437 1132, www.joykinglau.com). Leicester Square or Piccadilly Circus tube. **Dim sum served** noon-5pm Mon-Sat; 11am-5pm Sun. **Meals served** noon-11.30pm Mon-Sat; 11.30am-10.30pm Sun. **Main courses** £4.60-£20. **Set meal** £10-£35 per person (minimum 2). **Credit** AmEx, MC, V. **Map** p317 K7.

Broadstairs is still trading), Morelli's has expanded into Harrods and Selfridges. Done out in Italian marble, the Harrods concession is a smart affair. But its the ice-cream that counts. Twenty flavours of freshly made gelato are served daily from an almost endless repertoire; sundaes range from the classic to the exotic, like a Thai sundae, with papaya, mango, coconut and dragonfruit. Takeaway service.

Branch Selfridges, 400 Oxford Street, W1A 1AB (0800 123 400).

Oddono's

14 Bute Street, SW7 3EX (7052 0732, www.oddonos.com). South Kensington tube. **Open** 11am-11pm Mon-Thur, Sun; 11am-midnight Fri, Sat. **Ice-cream** £2/scoop. **Credit** AmEx, MC, V.

With its minimalist interior and retro seating, this place is all about quality; the focus is on premium ingredients and classic flavours. Even on a grey day, regulars troop in for their fix of vaniglia, made from Madagascan vanilla pods. The pistachio was brilliant, with generous sprinkles of the namesake nut.

Buggy access. Disabled access. Takeaway service. Tables outdoors (3, pavement). **Branches** Selfridges, 400 Oxford Street, W1A 1AB (020-7318 3344); Whiteleys, 151 Queensway, W2 4YN (020 7792 6023).

Parlour

1st floor, Fortnum & Mason, 181 Piccadilly, W1J 9FA (7734 8040, www. fortnumandmason.com). Picadilly Circus tube. **Open** 10am-7.30pm Mon-Sat; noon-5pm Sun. **Ice-cream** £3/scoop. **Credit** AmEx, MC, V.

Decorated in ice-cream pastels, there's a definite sense of occasion about the Parlour. Pricey but gorgeous adult sundaes (£12) are matched by children's versions for £8: Tots Knickerbocker Glory has vanilla, strawberry and shortbread ice-creams with raspberries, pineapple, raspberry coulis and whipped cream. Children's cornets come with two kinds of ice-cream.

Buggy access. Disabled access: toilet. Takeaway service.

Scoop

40 Shorts Gardens, WC2H 9AB (7240 7086, www.scoopgelato.com). Covent Garden tube. **Open** 11.30am-9.30pm daily. Times vary, phone to check. **Ice-cream** £2.50/scoop. **Credit** MC, V.

A required stop if you're out and about in Covent Garden. One very generous dollop of intensely dark chocolate ice-cream spilled over the sides of the cone, and required some hastily-executed licking. Sugar-, gluten- and milk-free varieties are available for the diet conscious, and the daily baked pastries are worth a visit alone. Look out for summer events promoting unusual ingredients.

Buggy access. Delivery service. Takeaway service.

Consumer

The atmosphere is always family-friendly in this ground-floor dining room, which tries to offset a lack of natural light with lime and pink wall panels. Its menu is comprehensive, but Joy King Lau is best known for the dim sum, which draws a high proportion of Chinese punters. Tender squid rings in mild curry sauce, juicy char sui croquettes and prawn and chive dumplings will delight the more adventurous youngster. The sweet dim sum is just as good; feather-light hot sponge cake (butter ma-lai ko) and crisp, deep fried custard buns are among the highlights. *Buggy access. Disabled access. High chairs. Takeaway service.*

Royal China

30 Westferry Circus, E14 8RR (7719 0888, www.royalchinagroup.co.uk). Canary Wharf tube/DLR/Westferry DLR. **Dim sum served** noon-4.45pm daily. **Meals served** noon-11pm Mon-Thur; noon-11.30pm Fri, Sat; 11am-10pm Sun. **Dim sum** £2.65-£4.20. **Main courses** £7-£50. **Set meal** £30-£38 per person (minimum 2). **Credit** AmEx, DC, MC, V.
Royal China remains consistently dependable for its good-quality cooking and especially excellent dim sum, and the fact that this branch overlooks the Thames makes it a good choice for families visiting Docklands for the day. Staff glide discreetly among guests, providing recommendations and ensuring smooth service. We were delighted by unctuous braised pork belly with preserved cabbage, silky steamed cod with dried yellow bean sauce and a perfect dish of Chinese broccoli in ginger juice. A vast menu means there's something to appeal to all tastes.
Booster seats. Buggy access. Disabled access: toilet. Nappy-changing facilities. Tables outdoors (23, terrace). Takeaway service.
Branches 24-26 Baker Street, W1U 7AB (7487 4688); 13 Queensway, W2 4QJ (7221 2535); 805 Fulham Road, SW6 5HE (7731 0081).

FISH

Belgo Noord

72 Chalk Farm Road, NW1 8AN (7267 0718, www.belgo-restaurants.com). Chalk Farm tube. **Lunch served** noon-5pm daily. **Dinner served** 5-11pm Mon-Thur; 5-11.30pm Fri, Sat; 5-10.30pm Sun. **Main courses** £9.25-£16.95. **Set lunch** £6.95 1 course. **Credit** AmEx, MC, V.
Beer, mussels and chips made this chain famous, but if it seems a strange choice of venue for children, read on. The menu also includes a decent array of alternatives. The sausage with

stoemp mash, beer-basted rotisserie chicken or Hoegaarden beer battered haddock and frites reflect the prominent Belgian theme – as do the staff, who are quirkily dressed in traditional Trappist monks' habits. Food is served in cool, industrial surroundings with an open kitchen; noisy but cheerful. The other great reason to bring children here is that they qualify for a free two-course menu when an adult orders a main from the à la carte menu. Helpful, speedy service means you can be in and out of the door in under an hour, but the kids' menu has plenty of puzzles and colouring if parents prefer to linger.
Buggy access. Crayons. Children's menu (free). High chairs. Nappy-changing facilities. Tables outside (4, pavement).
Branches 90 Earlham Street, WC2H 9LJ (7813 2233). 44-48 Clapham High Street, SW4 7UR (7720 1118). 67 Kingsway, WC2B 6TD (7242 7469).

fish!

Cathedral Street, SE1 9AL (7407 3803, www.fishkitchen.com). London Bridge tube/rail. **Meals served** 11.30am-11pm Mon-Thur; noon-11pm Fri, Sat; noon-10.30pm Sun. **Main courses** £9.95-£26.95. **Credit** AmEx, MC, V. **Map** p317 M8.
This smart glass pavilion overlooking Borough Market and Southwark Cathedral doesn't look especially family-friendly from the outside, especially on weekdays when it's full of suits and well-heeled tourists. Nonetheless, staff are very welcoming to the high-chair set and the acoustic racket inside means a tantrum would go unnoticed. And after all, what child doesn't like fish and chips? Adults can choose from the extensive fish list and decide whether they want it steamed or grilled, or indulge in a comfortingly rich fish pie or classic cod or haddock and chips. The mushy peas are among the finest we've ever tasted. Families on a budget will prefer to get takeaway fish and chips from the kiosk to the side of the restaurant for half the price.
Buggy access. Children's set meal (£6.95). Crayons. Disabled access: toilet. High chairs. Nappy-changing facilities. Tables outdoors (30, terrace). Takeaway service.
Branch fish! kitchen 58 Coombe Road, Kingston-upon-Thames, Surrey KT2 7AF (8546 2886); fish! kitchen 170 Upper Richmond Road West, SW14 8AW (8878 1040).

North Sea Fish Restaurant

7-8 Leigh Street, WC1H 9EW (7387 5892, www.northseafishrestaurant.co.uk). Russell Square tube/Euston or King's Cross tube/rail/68, 168 bus. **Lunch served** noon-2.30pm, **dinner served** 5.30-10.30pm

Mon-Sat. **Main courses** £8.95-£19.95.
Credit MC, V. **Map** p315 L3/4.
This traditional fish and chip restaurant is quite
a grown-up sort of place (single malt whiskies
line up along the counter, while grilled sea bass
features on the menu) but staff are cheerful and
there are plenty of fried goodies to satisfy the
nippers. Forget the bigger portions altogether:
you will find 'normal' sized battered cod or
haddock with chips easily big enough to share.
Buggy access. Disabled access. High chairs.
Takeaway service.

Olley's
65-69 Norwood Road, SE24 9AA (8671 8259,
www.olleys.info). Herne Hill rail/3, 68 bus.
Lunch served noon-3pm, **dinner served**
5-10.30pm Tue-Sat; 5-9.30pm Sun. **Main**
courses £12.45-£18.45. **Set lunch** £7 1
course. **Credit** AmEx, MC, V.
The best chippy in south London is famous for
its specials. The Cilla Black Experience involves
haddock and chips with interesting sides. The
Guy Dimond Experience (named after *Time Out*
magazine's food critic) is battered lemon sole
fillet with chips and a lemon wedge. Olley's has
always been one for diversification; there are
various exotic varieties of fish on offer, which
can be steamed or grilled for batter-phobes.
High chairs are clingfilm-wrapped (!) for each
use so your child won't be picking up the last
kid's peas. The children's menu consists mainly
of the usual 'nuggets and chips' options, but
there are also calamares and prawns. The staff
will also bring small portions of the steamed

dishes on request. The creamy mushy peas are
among the best in London, and the chips also
deserve a mention, being blanched before frying.
Buggy access. Children's menu (£4-£4.50).
Crayons. Disabled access: toilet. High chairs.
Tables outdoors (12, pavement). Nappy-
changing facilities. Takeaway service.

Rock & Sole Plaice
47 Endell Street, WC2H 9AJ (7836 3785).
Covent Garden or Leicester Square tube.
Meals served 11.30am-10.30pm Mon-Sat;
noon-9.30pm Sun. **Main courses** £10-£13.
Credit MC, V. **Map** p315 L6.
Tourists in search of classic British cuisine and
nearby office workers needing comfort food
seek out this small corner chippy, near Covent
Garden. The plaice is good and juicy, but order
the less popular rock and you'll get it fried to
order. Seaside setting and newspaper wrapping
aside, this is fish and chips the way it ought to
be. It's best for families with older children,
unless it's warm enough to eat outside, as the
restaurant doesn't have high chairs and there's
very little space for pushchairs.
Tables outdoors (7, pavement).
Takeaway service.

Toff's
38 Muswell Hill Broadway, N10 3RT (8883
8656, www.toffsfish.co.uk). Highgate tube,
then 43, 134 bus. **Meals served** 11.30am-
10pm Mon-Sat. **Main courses** £8.95-£22.
Set lunch £8.95 1 course. **Credit** AmEx,
DC, MC, V.

Stein's. See p244.

Dice with spice at **Tamarind**. *See p244.*

At frying time, there's always a long queue of customers at this acclaimed Muswell Hill chippy (note the unusually high number of certificates and accolades on the door, collected over the past 40-odd years). Behind the bustling takeaway counter at the front, through a pair of saloon-style swing doors (which children love), the restaurant offers more serenity. Toff's large choice of fish can be ordered in plain or matzo-meal batter, or grilled for a healthier alternative – a rarity in most chippies. There's also a well-executed children's menu featuring proper fish and own-made chips. If you can squeeze anything else in, there are salads (tomato and red onion, olive-topped coleslaw, Greek), soups, deep-fried camembert and traditional British puds, served in veritable ponds of custard. *Buggy access. Children's menu (£3.50-£4.50). Crayons. Disabled access: toilets. High chairs. Takeaway service.*

FRENCH

Belvedere

Holland House, off Abbotsbury Road, in Holland Park, W8 6LU (7602 1238, www.whitestarline.org.uk). Holland Park tube. **Lunch served** noon-2.15pm Mon-Sat; noon-2.30pm Sun. **Dinner served** 6-10.30pm Mon-Sat. **Main courses** £12-£25. **Set meal** (Sat, Sun) £24.95 3 courses. **Credit** AmEx, MC, V.

This art deco gem in the middle of the park is run by Marco Pierre White. With its white tablecloths, leather chairs and smart period features, it certainly doesn't look very child friendly at first glance. But looks can be deceptive; staff couldn't be more welcoming, and this is a superb place to have a special family lunch with the grandparents, especially on a Sunday when the three-course set menu and pianist attract lots of families with young children in tow. There's no designated children's menu, but the chef will whip up a range of child-friendly classics (pasta, sausage and mash, meat and vegetables without the rich sauces) at a reduced price on request. With the park and adventure playground just outside, it's a family day out that everyone will remember. *Buggy access. Disabled access (ground floor, call ahead). High chairs. Tables outdoors (5, terrace).*

Le Cercle

1 Wilbraham Place, SW1X 9AE (7901 9999, www.lecercle.co.uk). Sloane Square tube. **Lunch served** noon-3pm, **dinner served** 6-11pm Tue-Sat. **Set lunch** £15 3 dishes, £19.50 4 dishes. **Set dinner** (6-7pm) £17.50 3 dishes, £21.50 4 dishes. **Tapas** £6-£16. **Credit** AmEx, MC, V.

Shh… Whisper it… A child eats free if accompanying an adult dining from the a la carte menu at lunchtime. The under-12s can tuck into five small tapas-style courses gratis, although they should be of the more gastronomically adventurous persuasion to get the most out of it. The menu is divided into sections: végétal, marin, fermier (that's meat), plaisirs, fromagerie and gourmandises (puddings). Each small dish is delicious, vividly coloured and intensely flavoured, satisfying through variety rather than quantity. White asparagus veloute with pea ice-cream can be matched with yellow fin tuna and crispy melting pork with bearnaise sauce, a couple more savoury dishes, and a pud of chocolate fondant and ginger ice-cream, say. Le Cercle is part of the Gascon family of restaurants, and the entrance, on a side road off Sloane Street, is easily missed. But word of mouth provides the cavernous basement restaurant with a steady stream of customers. A point worth noting is that there are no high chairs, so it's not great for toddlers. *Buggy access. Disabled access: lift, toilet. Children's menu (free Tue-Sat lunch).*

Roussillon

16 St Barnabas Street, SW1W 8PE (7730 5550, www.roussillon.co.uk). Sloane Square tube. **Lunch served** noon-2.30pm Mon-Fri. **Dinner served** 6.30-10.30pm Mon-Sat. **Set lunch** £35 3 courses incl half bottle wine. **Set dinner** £60 3 courses. **Set meal** £65-£78 8 course tasting menu. **Credit** AmEx, MC, V.
What is there to appeal to children at this upmarket French restaurant in SW1? Mini gourmands get their very own tasting menu – if you could only pose as a minor, it would be a very cheap way of sampling six small but perfectly formed courses for £20. Ho hum. Roussillon assumes that children shouldn't be patronised with nursery classics, and sets young foodies off on a journey of gastronomic discovery full of taste and sensation. After all, why shouldn't they sample the delights of scallops, truffle ravioli and smoked eel? Restaurant critics rave about it, and no wonder; the food is sublime, the service solicitous and the decor subdued. The restaurant manages to maintain the air of a friendly- family local (although you'd have to be very well-heeled to actually live around here) and is a welcoming place to begin an introduction of the delights of French cuisine.
Buggy access. Children's set meal (£20 lunch).

GASTROPUBS

Clissold Arms

115 Fortis Green, N2 9HR (8444 4224). East Finchley tube. **Open** noon-11pm Mon-Thur; noon-midnight Fri, Sat; noon-10.30pm Sun.

Lunch served noon-4.30pm Mon-Thur; noon-4pm Fri, Sat. **Dinner served** 6-10pm Mon-Sat. **Meals served** noon-9pm Sun. **Main courses** £11-£18.95. **Credit** MC, V.
Muswell Hill definitely needed a great gastropub like this. The decor could be more characterful, but the staff are friendly and enthusiastic, so it's no surprise that the Clissold has become a huge hit with local families. Our favourite is the Sunday roast with Yorkshire puddings for all, and the puddings aren't bad either. It's refreshing to find a pub that's comfortable with children, but recognises that parents want a treat too – and one where the pint pullers have been trained in the fine art of proper pouring.
Buggy access. Disabled access: toilet. High chairs. Nappy-changing facilities. Tables outdoors (15, terrace; 25, garden).

Lansdowne

90 Gloucester Avenue, NW1 8HX (7483 0409, www.thelansdownepub.co.uk). Chalk Farm tube. **Open** noon-11pm Mon-Sat; noon-10.30pm Sun. **Lunch served** noon-3pm Mon-Fri; 12.30-3.30pm Sat, Sun. **Dinner served** 6-10pm Mon-Sat; 6-9.30pm Sun. **Main courses** £9.50-£16.50. **Credit** MC, V.
This pleasant pub in the middle of Primrose Hill is always heaving with families in the downstairs bar (customers wanting a more polished experience can make their way upstairs to the dining room). Happily, it hasn't sacrificed its 'local pub' vibe in favour of gastro pomp, though it has all the requisite features; the decor is tasteful, if a little worn at the edges, and food takes pride of place with a huge blackboard chalked up with the day's menu. The additional pizza menu makes an appealing, child-friendly alternative to the more expensive gastro fare. Adults can choose from six or seven starters encompassing an array of salads, seafood and soups. Service can be somewhat slow on occasions, but with the pub's cheerful vibe you won't mind hanging round a little longer than usual before heading off for a bracing walk or kite-flying foray.
Buggy access. Disabled access: toilet. High chairs. Tables outdoors (8, pavement). Takeaway service.

Prince Regent

69 Dulwich Road, SE24 0NJ (7274 1567, www.theprinceregent.co.uk). Brixton tube/rail/ Herne Hill rail. **Open** noon-11pm Mon-Thur; noon-midnight Fri, Sat; noon-10.30pm Sun. **Lunch served** noon-3pm Mon-Sat; noon-5pm Sun. **Dinner served** 7-10pm Mon-Sat; 6-9pm Sun. **Main courses** £8.85-£16. **Credit** MC, V.

Consumer

At weekends, the downstairs of this friendly pub, with its elegant original features, is bouncing with toddlers. Especially on Sundays, when the locally (in)famous 'family lunch' can get a bit wild. There's plenty of space to park prams by the tables, a selection of games and books lying around, and an excellent beer selection for the adults. There's no child-specific menu, but the chef is willing to serve up items from the excellent brunch menu (eggs, smoked salmon, bacon), or small portions of selected gastro classics, such as sausage and mash or fish and chips. The puddings are worth saving room for, and children love the playful presentation, quality ice-creams and custard. The atmosphere here is as warm as the welcome; parties without children are led upstairs to escape. Note that children must be out by 7pm.
Buggy access. Disabled access: toilet. High chairs. Nappy-changing facilities. Tables outdoors (12, terrace).

Stein's
Richmond Towpath, rear of 55 Petersham Road, Richmond, Surrey TW10 6UX (8948 8189, www.stein-s.com). Richmond tube/rail. **Meals served** *Summer* noon-10pm Mon-Fri; 11am-10pm Sat, Sun. *Winter* noon-6pm Sat, Sun. Times vary depending on weather, call to check. **Main courses** £7.90-£14.90. **Set lunch** (noon-4pm Mon-Fri) £5.99 1 course incl soft drink. **Credit** MC, V.
Stein's is an unusual proposition; a riverside Bavarian beer garden with impressive views over Richmond Bridge and Richmond Hill. Customers sit outdoors on the long tables with bench seating, having picked up their food from the timber-clad kiosk. There's no indoor seating, but gas heaters provide warmth on chilly days. Watch those clouds though; at the slightest sign of rain, Stein's closes. The menu is 100% German, with wursts (sausages) at its core, but there are other Bavarian specialities like roasted pork shoulder with dumplings and pork meatloaf. *Bratkartoffeln* – potatoes sautéed with bacon, onion and spices – is a good choice for children: simple, own-made comfort food. The kitchen also rustles up some mean breakfasts and a vast array of strudel desserts. As you might expect, German beer flows freely and the Almdudler, an apple-flavoured herbal lemonade from Austria, is lovely. There is a safe, small area where under-fives can play and the picturesque, enclosed riverside location means families love it.
Buggy access. Crayons. Disabled access. High chairs. Nappy-changing facilities. Play area. Tables outdoors (28, towpath). Takeaway service.

INDIAN

Masala Zone
80 Upper Street, N1 0NU (7359 3399, www.masalazone.com). Angel tube. **Lunch served** 12.30-3pm, **dinner served** 5.30-11pm Mon-Fri. **Meals served** 12.30-11pm Sat; 12.30-10.30pm Sun. **Main courses** £7.30-£8.90. **Thalis** £8.15-£9. **Credit** MC, V.
Bright and breezy premises, with mural-daubed walls and a laid-back buzz, make Masala Zone an appealing pit-stop for families. The kitchen draws its influences from across India, with a focus on zesty street snacks: adventurous kids will enjoy sampling chickpea purée-stuffed dahi puri, crunchy chicken samosas and spicy *aloo tikki chat* – chilli-laced potato cakes, served with yoghurt and chutney. Thalis are another draw; steel platters of little bowls, filled with different dishes; the scaled-down versions on the kids' menu are great value. Curries, spicy burgers and chilli-flecked noodles complete the menu.
Buggy access. Children's set meal (£4.40). Disabled access. High chairs. Takeaway service. **Branches** throughout town.

Tamarind
20-22 Queen Street, W1J 5PR (7629 3561, www.tamarindrestaurant.com). Green Park tube. **Lunch served** noon-2.45pm Mon-Fri, Sun. **Dinner served** 5.30-11pm Mon-Sat; 6-10.45pm Sun. **Main courses** £12.95-£24.75. **Set lunch** £14.95 2 courses, £18.95 3 courses. **Set dinner** (5.30-6.45pm, 10.30-11pm) £25 3 courses. **Credit** AmEx, DC, MC, V.
Serving the cuisine of north-west India, Tamarind offers an attractive Sunday lunch deal. Under-tens can eat from a three-course tasting menu for free, if they're with two or more adults eating from the main menu. Starters include spiced potato cakes and Indian style fish fingers; for mains, there's grilled chicken, monkfish, or paneer in masala sauce, served with veg and rice. Pudding is ice-cream with fruit. The open kitchen means kids can watch the chefs working with the Tandoor oven. Note that children must be out by 7pm.
Buggy access. Children's set meal (£12.50, free under-10s, Sun lunch). High chairs. Takeaway service.

INTERNATIONAL

Ottolenghi
287 Upper Street, N1 2TZ (7288 1454, www.ottolenghi.co.uk). Angel tube/Highbury & Islington tube/rail. **Meals served**

Consumer

Bodean's. *See p248.*

8am-11pm Mon-Sat; 9am-7pm Sun. **Main courses** £9.70-£14.90. **Credit** AmEx, MC, V. A long communal table dominates this white deli-style space, all the better to frame the fabulously colourful food; tables à deux line either side. Ottolenghi's cooked breakfasts are among the best in town and there's also granola and pastries. Counter salads, which double as eat-in starters or takeaways, are a vibrantly hued riot of fresh ingredients. Children will love the display of extravagant cakes piled up in the window, but be prepared to bat away pleas to try absolutely everything. To make a meal, the menu suggests ordering three of the starter-sized dishes per person, but a robust adult appetite requires at least four.
Buggy access. Disabled access. High chairs. Tables outdoors (2, pavement). Takeaway service.
Branches 63 Ledbury Road, W11 2AD (7727 1121); 1 Holland Street, W8 4NA (7937 0003); 13 Motcomb Street, SW1X 8LB (7823 2707).

Rainforest Café
20 Shaftesbury Avenue, W1D 7EU (7434 3111, www.therainforestcafe.co.uk). Piccadilly Circus tube. **Meals served** noon-10pm Mon-Fri; 11.30am-8pm Sat; 11.30am-10pm Sun. **Main courses** £12.95-£19.50. **Credit** AmEx, MC, V. **Map** p317 K7.

This jungle-themed basement restaurant, populated by animatronic wildlife, is the closest thing to Disneyland in London. It's hideously expensive, but worth it for the experience. The unchallenging global menu of meze, pasta, seafood, ribs, steaks and burgers is nothing out of the ordinary, although it does offer organic sausages, organic salmon and pasta for children alongside the more predictable burgers, goujons and pizza. Children's set meals comprise two courses; puddings are a range of extremely sweet and sticky bowlfuls. It's worth paying an extra £3 for the Adventure Meal, as it comes with a fantastic gift pack with mask, purse, stationery and sticker book. Score a table upstairs to sit amid the fish, elephants and gorillas; downstairs has far fewer animals and is far less thrilling for the children. Take a camera with a flash as it's incredibly dark inside. Bookings are not accepted.
Buggy access. Children's set meal (£11.95). Crayons. Entertainment: face painting, weekends & hols. High chairs. Nappy-changing facilities.

ITALIAN

Carluccio's Caffè
Reuters Plaza, E14 5AJ (7719 1749, www.carluccios.com). Canary Wharf tube/DLR. **Meals served** 7am-11.30pm

Mon-Fri; 9am-11.30pm Sat; 10am-10.30pm Sun. **Main courses** £6.95-£13.95. **Credit** AmEx, MC, V. **Map** p314 J6.

Carluccio's understands that children want something to happen as soon as they sit down. And lo and behold; grissini, a soft drink and some paper and crayons appear at the table. The clattering acoustics common to most branches isn't exactly soothing, but the warmth of the service, tasty grub and shelves of aspirational deli items keep enticing the customers back. This branch is popular with the office folk of Docklands, but the waiters save a bit of extra twinkle and charm for babies. Children can choose from a selection of pasta shapes and sauces, or there's chicken and potatoes, stuffed ravioli and lasagne. To finish, the little darlings get an individual tub of Carluccio's Italian ice-cream. *Buggy access. Children's set meal (£5.95). Crayons. Disabled access: toilet. High chairs. Nappy-changing facilities. Tables outdoors (25, piazza). Takeaway service.* **Branches** throughout town.

Marco Polo

Eastfields Avenue, SW18 1LP (8874 7007, www.marcopolo.uk.net). East Putney tube/ Wandsworth Town rail. **Open** noon-11pm Mon-Thur; noon-11.30pm Fri, Sat; noon-10.30pm Sun. **Main courses** £7.50-£21.50. **Set lunch** £9.95 1 course, £11.95 2 courses. **Credit** MC, V.

There's a fine range of dishes to appeal to adults at this modish eaterie, which has undergone a recent refurbishment. Children, meanwhile, love the £5.50 pasta dishes and large, pleasantly thin pizzas, with a bowl of ice-cream to follow. A useful patch of grass beside the numerous outdoor tables means children can stretch their legs with impunity. No wonder it's packed out by Wandsworth family groups all year round. *Buggy access. Children's menu (£5.50-£6.95). Disabled access. High chairs. Tables outdoors (100, terrace). Takeaway service.*

Marine Ices

8 Haverstock Hill, NW3 2BL (7482 9003, www.marineices.co.uk). Chalk Farm tube/ 31 bus. **Lunch served** noon-3pm, **dinner served** 6-11pm Tue-Fri. **Meals served** noon-11pm Sat; noon-10pm Sun. **Main courses** £6.50-£13.60. **Credit** MC, V.

Family-run and fiercely popular, Marine Ices is little changed since it opened in 1928. This retro ice-cream parlour has a slightly strange aquatic theme, but that doesn't stop it being a great place to bring your children for a takeaway or eat-in ice-cream, or for a good-value Italian meal. Service is no frills but friendly, and the food is simple. Pizzas are the best option – huge crispy bases, heaped with toppings, that spill over the edge of your plate. Pasta is decent too; diners select a pasta shape, then choose a sauce to match. House specials are tempting

Haché. *See p249.*

Consumer

(home-made Neopolitan fennel sausage with red wine, tomato and lentil sauce, for instance), as are the meat and seafood options, but it's worth saving yourself for pudding. There's a splendid selection of ice-creams, from toffee crunch to maple walnut, along with a choice of fruity sorbets. The location is handy for the Roundhouse and Camden Market (*see p122* **Great Days Out**).
Buggy access. Disabled access. High chairs. Takeaway service.

JAPANESE

Benihana
100 Avenue Road, NW3 3HF (7586 9508, www.benihana.co.uk). Swiss Cottage tube. **Lunch served** noon-3pm daily. **Dinner served** 5.30-10.30pm Mon-Sat; 5-10pm Sun. **Set lunch** £11-£19. **Set dinner** £21-£54. **Credit** AmEx, MC, V.
The key to this Japanese restaurant chain's popularity with families isn't crayons and toys – it's making the food itself entertaining. All hot dishes are prepared on a teppan, a hot plate that sits centre stage at each table. And what a stage it is; here, cooking is theatre. First, there's an explosion of fire as the teppan is cleaned. Our chef started with an onion, which soon became a volcano and then a steam train. The rice was a beating heart. The chicken was a caterpillar. The salt and pepper pots did somersaults around our heads before landing on the top of the chef's hat. And all that with accompanying jokes: 'Watch this butterfly' said the chef, as he catapulted some butter on to the grill. Butter. Fly. Geddit? It's a natty way of charging a lot for what's essentially a pretty average stir fry, but the kids will be talking about it for weeks afterwards. On a Sunday lunchtime, they'll also go home with balloon animals made by the resident clown.
Buggy access. Children's menu (£9.50-£13.50). Entertainment: clown Sun lunch. High chairs. Takeaway service.
Branches 37 Sackville Street, W1S 3DQ (7494 2525); 77 King's Road, SW3 4NX (7376 7799).

Yo! Sushi
The Brunswick, WC1N 1AE (7833 1884, www.yosushi.com). Russell Square tube. **Meals served** noon-11pm Mon-Sat; noon-10.30pm Sun. **Dishes** £1.70-£5. **Credit** AmEx, MC, V.
Children adore watching Japanese delicacies gliding round on Yo! Sushi's conveyor belt. The deal is simple: they grab 'em and you pay for

'em, according to the item's price code. Purists may quibble at the food's authenticity, but eating here is an event as much as a meal. There's plenty for vegetarians as well as raw fish fans, and you can also order hot food (grilled chicken or salmon, and various rice or noodle dishes).
Buggy access. Delivery service. Disabled access: toilet. Nappy-changing facilities. Takeaway service.
Branches throughout town.

MEXICAN

Wahaca
66 Chandos Place, WC2N 4HG (7240 1883, www.wahaca.co.uk). Covent Garden or Leicester Square tube. **Meals served** noon-11pm Mon-Sat; noon-10.30pm Sun. **Main courses** £6.50-£9.50. **Credit** AmEx, MC, V.
Children often want a meal earlier in the day than adults, and in this case that's no bad thing; at peak times, Wahaca invariably has queues snaking out of the door. Get here at noon or at 5pm, however, and you should be shown straight to a table. The surroundings are cheerful and colourful, the staff knowledgeable and friendly. There's no children's menu as such, but ordering is easy, thanks to a range of street-food options – tacos, tostadas and quesadillas – that come in small portions at reasonable prices. Puddings include doughnuts with chocolate sauce, ice-cream and mango sorbet.
Buggy access. Disabled access: toilet. High chairs. Nappy-changing facilities.
Branches Southern Terrace, Westfield Shopping Centre, W12 7GB (8749 4517); 40 Canada Square, E14 5FW (7516 9145).

MODERN EUROPEAN

Ambassador
55 Exmouth Market, EC1R 4QL (7837 0009, www.theambassadorcafe.co.uk). Angel tube/ Farringdon tube/rail/19, 38 bus. **Breakfast/ lunch served** 9am-3pm Mon-Fri; 11am-3.30pm Sat, Sun. **Dinner served** 6-11pm Mon-Sat. **Main courses** £9.50-£17. **Set meal** (noon-2.30pm, 6-11pm Mon-Fri) £10-£15 2 courses, £15-£20 3 courses. **Credit** AmEx, MC, V.
The food takes centre stage at this quietly accomplished brasserie, with its understated decor and easy-going charm. Leisurely weekend brunches are particularly popular with families; parents ponder the papers while kids concentrate on the colouring books. The

Consumer

children's menu is a one-dish affair (generally fish and chips, with a chocolate and banana milkshake to wash it down), but there's plenty to tempt them on the main brunch menu too, from waffles with caramel bananas to scrambled eggs on sourdough toast. The kitchen are also happy to cook up child-sized versions of mains wherever possible, at half the menu price. In summer, tables spread on to the street – a traffic-free thoroughfare that's perfect for people-watching.
Buggy access. Children's menu (£1.50-£3.50 Sat, Sun brunch). Crayons. High chairs. Tables outdoors (10, pavement). Toys.

Bumpkin
209 Westbourne Park Road, W11 1EA (7243 9818, www.bumpkinuk.com). Westbourne Park tube. **Meals served** 11am-11pm daily. **Credit** MC, V.
Downstairs, the setting is country chic with distressed wood furniture and mismatched chairs – though it's clear the look came from a design studio rather than second-hand shops. Wooden crates, sheaves of wheat and miscellaneous sacks nestling under the butcher's block waiter station are a little twee, but the overall effect is as cosy as a country kitchen and has a welcoming, convivial feel. The daily changing menu is seasonal and modern, with many ingredients sourced in the UK. There's something to suit all ages and palates, from comforting macaroni cheese to excellent ribeye steak with béarnaise sauce. There's a more sedate dining room upstairs for special occasions.
Buggy access. Crayons. Disabled access: toilet. High chairs. Nappy-changing facilities.
Branch 102 Old Brompton Road, SW7 3RD (7341 0802).

NORTH AMERICAN

Big Easy
332-334 King's Road, SW3 5UR (7352 4071, www.bigeasy.uk.com). Sloane Square tube, then 11, 19, 22 bus. **Meals served** noon-11.15pm Mon-Thur, Sun; noon-12.15am Fri, Sat. **Main courses** £8.85-£32.50. **Set lunch** (noon-5pm Mon-Fri) £9.95 2 courses. **Credit** AmEx, MC, V. **Map** p313 E12.
The children's menu at this somewhat raucous restaurant offers the likes of burgers, hot dogs and chicken dippers, all served with chips and a drink (ice-cream sodas, fresh fruit juices, milk). Avoid dining here in the evening with small children, as the after-work crowd packs it out. The draw for adults consists of huge, tender

steaks, enormous, juicy burgers, vast seafood platters and racks of ribs. Alaskan king crab and lobster are house specialities and side dishes are carefully done.
Buggy access. Children's menu (£7.95). Crayons. Disabled access. High chairs. Tables outdoors (3, pavement). Takeaway service.

Bodean's
10 Poland Street, W1F 8PZ (7287 7575, www.bodeansbbq.com). Oxford Circus or Piccadilly Circus tube. **Lunch served** noon-3pm, **dinner served** 5.30-11pm Mon-Fri. **Meals served** noon-11pm Sat; noon-10.30pm Sun. **Main courses** £8-£16. **Credit** MC, V.
The main event here is barbecued meat, served in large portions; Bodean's 'signature' dish is a mighty rack (or a half rack for wusses) of baby back ribs. In addition there are steaks, burgers and fiery chicken wings. It's obviously not a vegetarian-oriented sort of place, although the sweet baked beans and fries are good. Children eat free between noon and 5pm at the weekend when accompanied by an adult; options include barbecue chicken breast or slices of smoked beef, turkey or ham with fries or mash, with ice-cream to follow. At other times, the children's menu costs £5. Big screens showing sporting fixtures can make conversation tricky, but staff do thoughtful things like bringing jugs of iced tap water without being asked, and giving extra scoops of ice-cream to older siblings, which make us feel warm about this place.
Buggy access. Children's menu (£5, free noon-5pm daily). High chairs. Nappy-changing facilities. Takeaway service.
Branches throughout town.

Gourmet Burger Kitchen
44 Northcote Road, SW11 1NZ (7228 3309, www.gbk.co.uk). Clapham Junction rail. **Meals served** noon-11pm Mon-Fri; 11am-11pm Sat; 11am-10pm Sun. **Main courses** £6.10-£9.95. **Credit** MC, V.
Burgers at this chain are highly reliable, and smaller versions (beef, chicken, puy lentil) are offered for children and customers watching their waistlines. While everyone has their favourites, superior classics like chilli or blue cheese tend to be the most satisfying. Organic buffalo burgers from Laverstoke Park Farm are a welcome addition to the menu; there's also a decent choice for vegetarians (aubergine and goat's cheese, felafel and more) .
Buggy access. Children's menu (£3.45-£3.95). Disabled access. High chairs. Tables outdoors (4, pavement). Takeaway service.
Branches throughout town.

Mix it up with meze at **Gallipoli Again**. *See p252.*

Haché

24 Inverness Street, NW1 7HJ (7485 9100,
www.hacheburgers.com). Camden Town tube.
Meals served noon-10.30pm Mon-Sat; noon-
10pm Sun. **Main courses** £5.95-£12.95.
Credit AmEx, MC, V.

Any gourmet burger bar should be able to
shine on basic burgers, and Haché truly excels.
The portions are large and the meat first-rate,
with good-quality extra toppings (flavoursome
bacon dry-cured in brine, proper cheese, and
huge mushrooms). It looks a cut above your
average gourmet burger joint too, with art
on the walls and muted lighting; nonetheless,
it's also warmly welcoming to children. There's
a wide range of burgers to choose between,
from beef, duck, lamb and venison to a welcome
vegetarian selection; chips, meanwhile, can
be frites-style, skinny or fat. Decent crêpes have

recently been added to the dessert options,
but the brownies are the thing to have.
High chairs. Takeaway service.
Branch 329-331 Fulham Road, SW10 9QL
(7823 3515).

Hard Rock Café

150 Old Park Lane, W1K 1QR (7629 0382,
www.hardrock.com). Hyde Park Corner tube.
Meals served 11.30am-12.30am Mon-Thur,
Sun; 11am-1am Fri, Sat. **Main courses** £9.95-
£15.95. **Credit** AmEx, MC, V. **Map** p316 H8.

Music blasts at impressive levels and rock
memorabilia covers the walls at this famous
themed chain restaurant, which is more suitable
for older children and teenagers than anyone
arriving in a buggy. Hamburgers and sides are
the order of the day, piled high on plates carried
by waitresses in teeny-tiny uniforms. Also on the

menu are classic salads, barbecue dishes and nachos. Fortunately, all this noise doesn't mask the fact that the food is pretty darn good. Burgers are satisfyingly juicy, nachos gooey, salads a decent size and the ice-cream sundaes excellent. Further attractions include face painting at certain times, a children's menu with pizza, pasta and burgers, and occasional themed activities. *Buggy access. Children's set meal (£6.95). Crayons. Disabled access: toilet. Entertainment: face painting (check website). High chairs. Nappy-changing facilities. Tables outdoors (10, terrace).*

Lucky 7

127 Westbourne Park Road, W2 5QL (7727 6771, www.lucky7london.co.uk). Royal Oak or Westbourne Park tube. **Meals served** noon-10am Mon; 10am-10pm Tue-Thur; 9am-11pm fri, Sat; 9am-10pm Sun. **Main courses** £4.75-£12.95. **Credit** MC, V.
Tom Conran's cosy American diner and neighbourhood hang-out is one for families with older children to enjoy. The green booths and tin ceiling are effortlessly stylish, the vibe laidback as staff banter with the regulars. Although there are a few salads and sandwiches on the menu, the choice is basically between breakfasts and burgers. There's no kids' menu, but pretty much everything will appeal to youngsters, from buttermilk pancakes or huevos rancheros to the various burger options. With shakes, coke floats, ice-creams and home-made pecan pie on offer too, what's not to like about this place? *Takeaway service.*

Planet Hollywood

57-60 Haymarket, SW1Y 4QX (7437 7639, www.planethollywoodlondon.com). Piccadilly Circus tube. **Meals served** 11.30am-midnight daily. **Main courses** £9.45-£21.95. **Credit** AmEx, DC, MC, V. **Map** p317 K7.
Movie memorabilia floor to ceiling, swinging klieg lights (just like in LA) and blasting film soundtracks might be overstimulating for tinies, but older children love it. The food is everything they approve of too; burgers, rôtisserie chicken, fajitas and steaks, accompanied by fries and washed down with shakes and pop. *Booking advisable. Buggy access. Children's menu (£8-.95). Crayons. Disabled access: toilet. Entertainment: DJs Mon-Fri dinner; all day Sat, Sun, school hols. High chairs. Nappy-changing facilities.*

Smollensky's on the Strand

105 Strand, WC2R 0AA (7497 2101, www.smollenskys.com). Embankment tube/Charing Cross tube/rail. **Meals served** noon-11pm

Mon-Thur; noon-1am Fri, Sat; noon-10pm Sun. **Main courses** £9.95-£23.95. **Credit** AmEx, MC, V. **Map** p317 L7.
Between noon and 3pm every Saturday and Sunday lunchtime, this basement steakhouse basically becomes a rather modern, food-based playgroup. There's a TV and Playstation at children's disposal and entertainment courtesy of a clown or magician. The menu is full of simple, sturdy ribstickers, with an emphasis on steaks – which arrive with good chips and a choice of sauces. The children's menu is divided into two sections: one category for under-sevens (who are

Try *phô* at **Sông Quê Café**. *See p252.*

deemed only to want fried food – burgers, chicken and fish – bar one vegetarian pasta dish) and one for 'mini adults' (who are treated to the likes of steak or jambalaya). Mains can be variable, but we've no complaints about the puds: moreish chocolate mousse and memorable Mississippi mud pie. If your children don't like noise, it may be best to take them elsewhere. *Booking advisable. Children's menu (£3.95-£7.95). Crayons. Entertainment: clown, magician, noon-3pm Sat, Sun. High chairs. Nappy-changing facilities.* **Branch** 1 Reuters Plaza, E14 5AG (7719 0101).

TGI Friday's
6 Bedford Street, WC2E 9HZ (7379 0585, www.tgifridays.co.uk). Covent Garden or Embankment tube/Charing Cross tube/rail. **Meals served** 11am-11.30pm Mon-Thur; 11am-midnight Fri, Sat; noon-11pm Sun. **Main courses** £8.29-£17.99. **Credit** AmEx, MC, V. **Map** p317 L7.
We would recommend lunchtime visits at this busy Covent Garden branch of TGI Friday's, as the bar gets very crowded in the evenings. The immensely cheery, overwhelmingly child-friendly staff here hand out balloons and activity packs to children, who are chatted to sweetly and even entertained on certain days (see the website for details). The food is varied, with an emphasis on sticky barbecues and tasty Tex-Mex dishes as well as the inevitable burgers and fries. The children's menu has all the fried regulars too, but side dishes can be exchanged for healthier options – crudités, corn on the cob or vegetables. All that good will be undone at the pudding stage, when dirt and worm pie (for chocolate and fudge fiends), sundaes and cheesecakes are the order of the day. Free Heinz baby food is provided for babes of four to ten months accompanying a dining adult. *Buggy access. Children's set meal (£2.99-£4.99). Crayons. Disabled access: lift, toilet. Entertainment: face painting Sat, Sun lunch. High chairs. Nappy-changing facilities.* **Branches** throughout town.

ORIENTAL

Wagamama
11 Jamestown Road, NW1 7BW (7428 0800, www.wagamama.com). Camden tube. **Meals served** noon-11pm Mon-Sat; noon-10pm Sun. **Main courses** £6.65-£12.75. **Credit** AmEx, DC, MC, V.
This popular chain continues to provide tasty and wholesome oriental fast food at a fair price. The Camden branch is particularly good

for families as there is plenty of space to accommodate buggies. There's something to appeal to everyone among the noodle and rice dishes; children will also love the chicken katsu (chicken breast fried in breadcrumbs) with dipping sauce and the gyoza (steamed then grilled dumplings). Developments in recent years include unusually flavoured desserts such as tamarind and chilli pavlova. To drink there's saké, juices and free green tea. *Buggy access. Children's menu (£2.85-£4.35). Crayons. Disabled access: toilet. High chairs. Nappy-changing facilities. Takeaway service.* **Branches** throughout town.

PORTUGUESE

Nando's
57-59 Goodge Street, W1T 1TH (7637 0708, www.nandos.com). Goodge Street tube. **Meals served** 11.30am-11pm Mon-Thur; 11.30am-11.30pm Fri, Sat; 11.30am-10.30pm Sun. **Main courses** £5.80-£10.60. **Credit** AmEx, MC, V.
For a quick, straightforward meal with children this chain smacks the Burger Kings of this world clear out the water. The appeal of Portuguese-inspired Nando's lies in its simplicity, lack of ceremony and keen prices. With proper wooden tables and chairs and a menu that centres around freshly grilled chicken, it's not quite a fast food restaurant – but it's not a million miles away (meal deals, bottomless refills on drinks and a super-casual vibe). Chicken served with spicy peri peri sauce of varying degrees of fierceness is the mainstay, and it's worth sticking to – grilled halves and quarters are crisp skinned and juicy inside, while sides dishes (flavoursome corn on the cob, thick cut, slightly school canteen-style chips) make for a filling, decent value meal. Vegetarian options (halloumi and roast portobello mushroom wraps, say, or bean burgers) are also available, and tasty enough. Staff on our last visit were chirpy and efficient. *Buggy access. Children's set meal (£4.15). Disabled access: toilet. Crayons. High chairs. Nappy-changing facilities. Tables outdoors (1, pavement).*

THAI

Blue Elephant
4-6 Fulham Broadway, SW6 1AA (7385 6595, www.blueelephant.com). Fulham Broadway tube. **Lunch served** noon-2.30pm Mon-Sat; noon & 2.30pm Sun. **Dinner served** 7-11.30pm Mon-Thur; 6.30-11.30pm Fri; 6-11.30pm Sat; 6.30-10.30pm Sun.

Consumer

Main courses £11.90-£28. **Set buffet** (Sun lunch) £30; £15 under-11s. **Credit** AmEx, DC, MC, V.

Smiling staff are dressed in traditional costume and welcome diners into an unusual setting. With its palms, topiary, ponds full of koi carp, waterfalls and walkways, it's not difficult to see why this restaurant is so popular with well-off local families. Adults may be disappointed that the kitchen tempers the authentic Thai fieriness, but it's good for the little ones. Even the fussiest eater usually succumbs to the platter of classic starters (mostly deep-fried offerings such as spring rolls). The extensive menu, featuring all the mainstays of Thai cuisine as well as lesser known dishes, offers several set options that are good for those on a budget. Families flock here on Sunday lunchtimes, when children eat for half price and are entertained by face painters (note that there are two sittings).

Booking advisable (Sun lunch). Buggy access. Delivery service. Disabled access: toilet. Entertainment: face painting Sun lunch. High chairs. Nappy-changing facilities. Takeaway service.

TURKISH

Gallipoli Again

120 Upper Street, N1 1QP (7226 8099, www.cafegallipoli.com). Angel tube/Essex Road rail. **Meals served** noon-11pm Mon-Thur; 10.30am-midnight Fri, Sat; 10.30am-11pm Sun. **Main courses** £6.95-£10.95. **Credit** MC, V.

The infectious party atmosphere and Turkish decor appeals to the children, while adults love the reasonable pricing. The long, narrow restaurant has a rosy glow and a throbbing beat, and is generally packed with diners sharing delicious bowls of food. Chewy pide bread with mixed meze is a good bet for starters (everyone loves to dip), while falafel, kofte and filling moussaka make for appealing mains. Staff in silver-monogrammed black shirts are extremely graceful considering how busy they are.

Buggy access. Crayons. High chairs. Tables outdoors (8, garden; 2, pavement). Takeaway service.

Branches Gallipoli Café Bistro, 102 Upper Street, N1 1QN (7359 0630); Gallipoli Bazaar, 107 Upper Street, N1 1QN (7226 5333).

Mangal II

4 Stoke Newington Road, N16 8BH (7254 7888, www.mangal2.com). Dalston Kingsland rail/76, 149, 243 bus. **Meals served** noon-1am Mon-Thur, Sun; noon-2am Fri, Sat. **Main courses** £8.45-£15.99. **Credit** MC, V.

The grilled meats and fish here are superb, which accounts for Mangal II's huge popularity with families of all nationalities. It also helps that the service is so friendly and efficient. For mains, the adana kebab (alternating patties of minced lamb and slices of aubergine grilled on a skewer) is excellent; and children in particular will relish the grilled chicken and pide and saç bread.

Buggy access. High chairs. Takeaway service.

Tas

22 Bloomsbury Street, WC1B 3QJ (7637 4555, www.tasrestaurant.com). Tottenham Court Road tube. **Meals served** noon-11.30pm daily. **Main courses** £6.95-£12.45. **Set meze** £8.65-£18.95 per person (minimum 2). **Credit** AmEx, MC, V.

Much of the menu will appeal to little ones at this cheerfully busy eaterie near the British Museum, from meze favourites such as houmous and piping-hot borek (little filo parcels, stuffed with feta cheese) to pasta with tomato sauce. For adults, there are almost 40 mezes, then a comprehensive choice of fish and rice dishes, pasta and casseroles, in addition to the expected grills. Even the fussiest of eaters will find something they're happy to order, and staff are adept at dealing with family groups.

Buggy access. Disabled access: toilet. High chairs. Tables outdoors (14, pavement). **Branches** throughout town.

VIETNAMESE

Sông Quê Café

134 Kingsland Road, E2 8DY (7613 3222). Hoxton rail. **Lunch served** noon-3pm, **dinner served** 5.30-11pm Mon-Sat. **Meals served** 11am-11pm Sun. **Main courses** £5-£8 **Credit** MC, V.

Eternally popular (and invariably packed), Song Quê is a large, bustling, canteen-style Vietnamese restaurant on the corner of Kingsland Road and Pearson Street. The menu is mind-bogglingly vast, but children are generally happy with steaming bowls of *phô* (noodle soup) or the delicately-fashioned rice paper rolls stuffed with prawns, vegetables or chicken; orders are hastily scrawled on the paper tablecloth, and appear with astonishing alacrity. Devotees consider the rich, fragrant beef *phô* the best in the city; the little parcels of beef wrapped in betel leaves are also deliciously moreish.

Buggy access. High chairs. Takeaway service.

Shopping

Where to buy what you need, from prams to party bags.

London's shopping scene has everything a parent could possibly want and need – if you know where to look. From sensible school shoes and essential baby gear to pink tulle tutus and gorgeous handmade toys, the city's throng of shops is guaranteed to deliver.

Even the most shopping-averse child needs no cajoling to visit **Hamleys** (*see p281*), or to see Santa at **Harrods** (*see below*); even when more mundane clothes- and shoe-shopping are on the agenda, though, savvier establishments are adept at keeping children sweet with well-stocked toy boxes, face-painting and colouring tables.

Along with big-name favourites such as **John Lewis** (*see p254*) and the usual chain stores, the city is well provided with independents, selling wooden toys, hand-knitted bootees, sprigged cotton frocks and hip international childrenswear labels. It's hard to resist the nostalgic appeal of shops like **Honeyjam** (*see p282*), **Olive Loves Alfie** (*see p269*) and **Aravore Babies** (*see p266*).

The city's smaller bookshops also do a sterling job, with cosy chairs to curl up on, regular visits from children's authors, and good old-fashioned storytelling sessions; drop into somewhere like **Tales on Moon Lane** (*see p259*) or the **Children's Bookshop** (*see p259*) and you won't be leaving again in a hurry.

ALL-ROUNDERS

Blue Daisy

13 South End Road, NW3 2PT (7681 4144, www.blue-daisy.com). Belsize Park tube/ Hampstead Heath rail. **Open** 9.30am-6pm Mon-Fri; 10am-6pm Sat. **Credit** AmEx, MC, V.
When you first walk in to this baby boutique, it can seem as if there's not much here. But look a little closer and the minimalist presentation hides a wealth of great products to make parenting just that bit easier and more stylish. The shop stocks prams, toys, slings, organic lotions, nappies and changing accessories, clothes, potties, plastic crockery and a lot more besides. The layout has been thoughtfully designed with a play alcove for small children and a nappy changing room, while the generous floor space means it's also easy bringing buggies inside. *Buggy access. Mail order. Nappy-changing facilities. Play area.*

Born

168 Stoke Newington Church Street, N16 0JL (7249 5069, www.borndirect.com). Bus 73, 393, 476. **Open** 9.30am-5pm Tue-Fri; 9.30am-5.30pm Sat; noon-5pm Sun. **Credit** MC, V.
Natural, organic and fair trade pregnancy products, baby equipment and clothes fill the shelves at Born, from babygros and cotton nappies to sturdy scooters (fashioned from sustainable rubberwood) and brightly-painted toys. Practical gear includes Ergo's organic cotton baby carrier and sleek buggies from the likes of Phil & Teds and Bugaboo, alongside chemical-free toiletries and baby wipes and the shop's own brand of pregnancy massage oils. The shop is a joy to visit with children in tow: there's ample space to play, and a sofa for breastfeeding mothers. *Buggy access. Delivery service. Disabled access: ramp. Mail order. Nappy-changing facilities. Play area.*

Harrods

87-135 Brompton Road, SW1X 7XL (7730 1234, www.harrods.com). Knightsbridge tube. **Open** 10am-8pm Mon-Sat; 11.30am-6pm Sun. **Credit** AmEx, DC, MC, V. **Map** p313 F9.
The fourth floor is the one to head for at Harrods, with room after room devoted to uniforms, party frocks, nursery gear, books and babygros. Toy Kingdom (7225 6781) is a child's dream come true, with its jolly demonstrators and immense range of toys. Clothes begin with beautiful babywear, including ranges from Christian Dior and Roberto Cavalli, and go through ultra-smart tweedy garb from the Harrods label (think proper winter coats with velvet collars and silk and tulle party dresses).

Couture childrenswear includes mini togs by Burberry, Missoni, Miss Blumarine, Ralph Lauren and Armani; Bunny London's exquisitely embellished dresses are also sold here. Footwear is by One Small Step One Giant Leap (*see p277*). There's face-painting, haircutting and lots of interactive fun in the holidays and at special events and launches, and children will also enjoy exploring the whole store, including the gigantic food halls. The nursery department carries all the famous pram and buggy, cot, bed and high chair brands.

Spoilt for choice
Hampstead

Shopping in Hampstead is like browsing in a very exclusive market town. But although money practically oozes out of the brickwork up here, the area manages to retain something of the bohemian, creative community that has lived here for generations. Play spot the actor as you take a stroll down Flask Walk, with its old world charm, and let the shopping begin.

Mystical Fairies (*see p282*) is sheer heaven for those who like anything pink, sparkly and otherworldly. Pregnant women may miss the Hampstead branch of Formes, now closed – although the stylish and somewhat cheaper **Séraphine** (*see p276*), just north of the tube, affords some consolation.

For children needing to be shod, it would be hard to find a better shoe shop than the small but very well stocked **Cubs** (*see p277*) on Heath Street. Down Rosslyn Hill is toy shop **Happy Returns** (*see p282*) which caters for parties and presents for zero to fives. And at a lower gradient still, on South End Green near the Royal Free Hospital, there's the fantastic **Blue Daisy** (*see p253*), which stocks just about every accessory a baby or its parent could possibly want.

The kids will love the special reading room at **Daunt Books** (*see p259*); once you've picked up a linen bag full of literary goodies, the whole family can head to neighbouring Hampstead Heath to let off some steam.

Buggy access. Café. Car park. Delivery service. Disabled access: lift, toilet. Hairdressing. Mail order. Nappy-changing facilities.

Igloo
300 Upper Street, N1 2TU (7354 7300, www.iglookids.co.uk). Angel tube/Highbury & Islington tube/rail. **Open** 10am-6.30pm Mon-Wed; 10am-7pm Thur; 9.30am-6.30pm Fri, Sat; 11am-5.30pm Sun. **Credit** AmEx, MC, V.
Quirky toys, clothes and accessories, often from lesser-known labels, have made Igloo a mecca for chic north London parents. The premises are small but well-stocked, with shelves of toys reaching to the ceiling – an enticing mix of sticker books, puppet-making kits, puzzles and skipping ropes, along with pedal cars, tipis and trikes. Racks of clothes cater for newborns to ten-year-olds, with a stellar selection of labels (fresh floral prints from Room Seven and hand-smocked frocks from I Love Gorgeous). The shoe corner has plenty of seating and some top-notch brands (Start-rite, Crocs, Camper, Angelus and Naturino, alongside some nifty dinosaur and bee wellies). All bases are covered: there's a mirrored parlour for children's haircuts, a drawing table and a gift-wrapping service.
Buggy access. Delivery service. Disabled access. Hairdressing. Mail order.
Branches 80 St John's Wood High Street, NW8 7SH (7483 2332); 227 King's Road, SW3 5EJ (7352 4572).

John Lewis
278-306 Oxford Street, W1A 1EX (7629 7711, www.johnlewis.co.uk). Bond Street or Oxford Circus tube. **Open** 9.30am-8pm Mon-Wed, Fri; 9.30am-9pm Thur; 9.30am-7pm Sat; noon-6pm Sun. **Credit** AmEx, DC, MC, V. **Map** p314 H6.
John Lewis is always a dependable port of call. Follow the stream of parents heading up to the fourth floor, dedicated to all things child-related, and take advantage of its knowledgeable staff and good service. As an all-rounder it's hard to beat, stocking everything from toys to school uniforms, clothes and sportswear, as well as nursery furniture and essentials; the down-to-earth buying-for-baby advice is a lifesaver for bemused first-time parents, and there's a free car-seat fitting advisory service. The toy department overflows with of-the-moment toys, educational games and old classics. But the real jewel in the store's crown is its shoe department (Clarks, Start-rite, Kangaroo, Timberland), with its orderly computerised ticketing system and computer games, CBeebies on the telly and free face-painting sessions to keep children happy in the pre-September peak.

There's plenty to fascinate young visitors at **Harrods**. *See p253.*

Consumer

Buggy access. Cafés. Delivery service. Disabled access: lift, toilet. Mail order. Nappy-changing facilities.
Branches Brent Cross Shopping Centre, NW4 3FL (8202 6535); Wood Street, Kingston, Surrey KT1 1TE (8547 3000).

JoJo Maman Bébé

68 & 72 Northcote Road, SW11 6QL (7228 0322 maternity, 7223 8510 baby & children, www.jojomamanbebe.co.uk). Clapham Junction rail. **Open** 9.30am-5.30pm Mon-Sat; 11am-5pm Sun. **Credit** MC, V.
Launched in 1993 as an inexpensive maternity and babywear company, JoJo has expanded into a sizeable empire. While it's still primarily a catalogue-based retailer, a network of boutiques has sprung up across London, displaying some of its vast stock of clothes, equipment and furniture. Its own-label clothing lines are relaxed and affordable, with everything from maternity bras, yoga wraps and workwear for expectant mothers to swim nappies, stripy all-in-ones and dungarees for kids. The company adheres to a strong ethical code – a spirit exemplified by the organic cotton sleepsuits and the Polartec fleeces, made from recycled plastic bottles. JoJo also supports the Nema Foundation, which runs community projects in Mozambique.
Buggy access. Delivery service. Disabled access. Mail order. Nappy-changing facilities.

Branches 101 Westbourne Grove, W2 4UW (7727 3578); 3 Ashbourne Parade, 1259 Finchley Road, NW11 0AD (8731 8961); 82 Turnham Green Terrace, W4 1QN (8994 0379); 6 Lordship Lane, SE22 8HN (8693 2123); 30 Putney Exchange, Putney High Street, SW15 1TW (8780 5165).

Little White Company

90 Marylebone High Street, W1U 4QZ (7486 7550, www.thewhitecompany.com). Baker Street or Bond Street tube. **Open** 10am-6pm Mon-Sat; 11am-5pm Sun. **Credit** AmEx, MC, V. **Map** p314 G5.
All is calm, orderly and impossibly pretty at the Little White Company. Snowy cotton soft furnishings and crisp bedlinen are neatly arrayed alongside sweetly traditional nightwear and clothes (little smocks with matching bloomers and seersucker gingham pyjamas epitomise the LWC look), and there's an attractive range of white-painted nursery furniture. Not everything's white, of course; striped towelling beach hoodies in fuchsia and navy, floral quilts and lengths of pastel-hued bunting add a splash of colour. Prices are reasonable considering the quality, with demure linen/cotton summer dresses starting at around £20.
Buggy access. Delivery service. Mail order.
Branch 261 Pavillion Road, SW1X 0BP (7881 0783).

Mamas & Papas

256-258 Regent Street, W1B 3AF (0845 268 2000, www.mamasandpapas.co.uk). Oxford Circus tube. **Open** 10am-8pm Mon-Wed, Fri; 10am-9pm Thur; 9am-8pm Sat; noon-6pm Sun. **Credit** AmEx, MC, V. **Map** p314 J6.

Amid the chaos of Regent Street, the flagship outpost for this buggy brand is a spacious, air-conditioned oasis. There are large changing rooms for bump and buggy manoeuvres, and assistants are at hand to advise on sartorial matters. As well as inexpensive baby clothes, maternity fashion and lingerie, there's a dizzying array of Mamas & Papas prams, pushchairs and car seats – the company's stock in trade. The first floor, meanwhile, is devoted to interiors, with a series of 'dream nursery' rooms displaying cots, changing tables, wardrobes and storage systems in all shapes and sizes. The first-floor Cibo café serves nutritious own-made fare for mothers-to-be and a straightforward children's menu.

Buggy access. Café. Delivery Service. Mail order. Nappy-changing facilities.

Branches Brent Cross Shopping Centre, NW4 3FL (0845 268 2000); Level 1, Westfield Shopping Centre, W12 7GF (0845 268 2000). Tandem Shopping Centre, SW19 2NX (0845 268 2000).

Mini Kin

22 Broadway Parade, N8 9DE (8341 6898). Finsbury Park tube/rail, then W7 bus. **Open** 9.30am-5.30pm Mon-Sat; 10.30am-4.30pm Sun. **Credit** MC, V.

Small but perfectly formed, Mini Kin combines a modishly stocked children's clothing boutique with a hairdressing salon. An impeccably chic array of clothes includes the unusual colours and pretty patterns of Imps & Elfs, frothy frocks from Noa Noa and nautical stripes from Bonnie Baby, and there are fragrant salves, creams, oils and lotions courtesy of Burt's Bees, Green People and Earth Friendly Baby. Out back there is the hairdressing salon, decorated to look like a mythical forest with trailing ivy and branches; animal-painted chairs and charming staff conspire to coax recalcitrant tots into the hotseat. Haircuts start at £10.95.

Buggy access. Disabled access. Hairdressing. Nappy-changing facilities. Play area.

Mothercare

526-528 Oxford Street, W1C 1LW (0845 365 0515, www.mothercare.com). Marble Arch tube. **Open** 10am-8pm Mon-Sat; noon-6pm Sun. **Credit** AmEx, MC, V. **Map** p314 G6.

Two floors house all manner of baby-related paraphernalia. It's great for bulk-buy basics such as muslins and plain rompers, and the maternity wear section often yields some good value, unexpected finds.

Buggy access. Delivery service. Disabled access: lift, toilet. Mail order. Nappy-changing facilities.

Branches throughout town.

Pure Baby

208 Fulham Road, SW10 9PJ (7751 5544, www.purebaby.co.uk). Fulham Broadway or South Kensington tube, then 14, 414 bus. **Open** 10am-6.30pm Mon-Wed, Fri, Sat; 10am-7pm Thur; 11am-5pm Sun. **Credit** AmEx, MC, V.

Located in a strategic spot near Chelsea & Westminster Hospital's Maternity Unit, Pure Baby is as smart and sleek as its well-heeled clientele. Cashmere playsuits and bootees, Bugaboo prams and organic cotton swaddling blankets are among the goodies on offer.

Buggy access. Delivery service. Disabled Access.

Soup Dragon

27 Topsfield Parade, Tottenham Lane, N8 8PT (8348 0224, www.soup-dragon.co.uk). Finsbury Park tube/rail, then W7 bus. **Open** 9.30am-6pm Mon-Sat; 11am-5pm Sun. **Credit** AmEx, MC, V.

This cavernous grotto of a shop is piled high with colourful clothes and toys. It's an excellent spot to pick up imaginative but relatively inexpensive kids' clothes; the own-brand striped knits are great value. For lovers of bold prints, there are vibrant designs from Danish labels Katvig and Minymo, while the Kidorable in the Rain range is fun and practical. In addition to the everyday clothes, there's a great selection of party wear and fancy dress. On the toy front, dollhouses, castles, farms and pirate ships fire up children's imaginations; there's also a dinky mini kitchen play area where kids can bang pots and pans about. Sign up to the mailing list for details of the regular warehouse sales.

Buggy access. Disabled access. Mail order. Play area.

Branch 106 Lordship Lane, SE22 8HF (8693 5575).

EDUCATIONAL

Books

Several toy shops (*see pp281-84*) also stock children's picture books.

Big Green Bookshop

Unit 1, Brampton Park Road, N22 6BG (8881 6767, www.biggreenbookshop.com).

Turnpike Lane or Wood Green tube.
Open 9am-6pm Mon, Tue, Thur-Sat;
10.30am-6pm Wed; noon-5pm Sun.
Credit AmEx, MC, V.
Opened in 2008, this friendly local bookshop has
developed a reputation for it excellent children's
section. Young readers can relax here with their
favourite tome and writers pop in to read and
talk to the children, too.
Buggy access. Mail order.

Bookseller Crow on the Hill
*50 Westow Street, SE19 3AF (8771 8831,
www.booksellercrow.com). Gypsy Hill rail.*
Open 10am-7pm Mon-Fri; 9.30am-6.30pm
Sat; 11am-5pm Sun. **Credit** AmEx, MC, V.
A laid-back place to while away an afternoon,
with a wealth of books for children and grown-
ups. All of the classics are present and correct,
and there's a splendid selection of picture books.
Buggy access. Mail order. Play area.

Clothes & toys on the web

CLOTHES

www.alexandalexa.com
If it's stylish, it's stocked here, from
classics such as Cacharel to hip newcomers
like Japanese brand Muchacha.

www.belleanddean.co.uk
Distinctive, etching-style animal drawings
adorn the organic cotton sleepsuits, tank
tops and T-shirts; prices are a steal.

www.dandystar.com
Dandy eschews brash, lurid slogan Ts in
favour of sweet, '70s-style designs with
an appealingly worn-in, vintage look.

www.littlefashiongallery.com
Labels on this cult kid's fashion site
range from Paul & Joe and Little Marc to
lesser-known names: check out Swedish
brand Mini Rodini's guitar-print Ts.

www.nippaz.com
One of the original purveyors of edgy,
motto-print T-shirts.

www.noaddedsugar.co.uk
Once best known for its bold slogan prints,
No Added Sugar now offers more subtle
lines: the ruffled, floral dresses are lovely.

www.nordickids.co.uk
Some of the best childrenswear in the
world hails from Scandinavia. Check out
the cream of the crop, with Plastisock,
Mini Rodini, Smafolk and more.

www.snuglo.com
Lisa Quinn's range is typified by hip,
grown-up colours and bold type: 'I want
chips, chocolate and cake' is a best-seller.

TOYS

www.brightminds.co.uk
Sparky ideas that make learning fun, from
flowering magic gardens to 'explosive
experiment' kits and slime laboratories.

www.bumpto3.com
Traditional toys (baby walkers, first bike,
mini easels) and fun newcomers – like
the ingenious build-your-own saxoflute.

www.gltc.co.uk
Everything from simple flower-pressing kits
and bubble-makers to spectacular galleon-
shaped climbing frames and toy kitchens.

www.ladybirdprints.com
Choose an image from Ladybird Books'
archive and order it as a print or canvas;
Peter and Jane peering from a wigwam or
the cover of *Ned the Lonely Donkey* are
perfect for nostalgia-tinged nurseries.

www.lapinandme.co.uk
Lapin & Me sells the sweetest toys we've
ever seen: tin tea sets, colour-in sticker
sets and reprinted '40s storybooks.

www.larkmade.com
A small but sweet range of fair trade gifts
and soft toys, including quirky cupcake-
and doughnut-shaped knitted rattles.

www.ptolemytoys.co.uk
Fabulous toys, baby products, dressing-up
clothes and educational goodies.

www.sparrowkids.co.uk
Gorgeous felt kits for crafty children
aged five and up: patterns range from
bird-shaped bags to rocket pencil cases.

Consumer

Bookworm

1177 Finchley Road, NW11 0AA (8201 9811, www.thebookworm.uk.com). Golders Green tube. **Open** 9.30am-5.30pm Mon-Sat; 10am-1.30pm Sun. **Credit** MC, V.

The shelves at this independent children's bookshop are packed with treasures. Storytelling sessions for under-fives take place on Tuesdays and Thursdays (2pm) when badges and stickers are handed out, while author visits give children the chance to meet their literary heroes and heroines.

Buggy access. Disabled access. Mail order.

Children's Bookshop

29 Fortis Green Road, N10 3HP (8444 5500, www.childrensbookshoplondon.com). Highgate tube, then 43, 134 bus. **Open** 9.15am-5.45pm Mon-Sat; 11am-4pm Sun. **Credit** AmEx, MC, V.

Clued-up staff and peaceful surrounds make this a relaxing place to pick up some new reading material. There's a children's corner with child-sized chairs and picture books at floor level, plus Thursday morning storytelling sessions for preschoolers, kicking off at 11am. Other book-related events, including regular author signings, are publicised in the shop's quarterly newsletter.

Buggy access. Mail order.

Daunt Books

51 South End Road, NW3 2QB (7794 8206, www.dauntbooks.co.uk). Belsize Park tube/ Hampstead Heath rail. **Open** 9am-6pm Mon-Sat; 11am-6pm Sun. **Credit** MC, V.

There's a cosy, welcoming reading room for children in the back of this branch of the well-loved independent, with seats where adults can read to children without fear of disturbing other customers. The room is cheerily decorated with fields and farm animals and has a good shelf of books. Just outside is the children's book section, which offers a very good choice of titles for all ages.

Buggy access. Mail order. Play area.

Branches 193 Haverstock Hill, NW3 4QL (7794 8206); 83 Marylebone High Street, W1U 4QW (7224 2295); 112-114 Holland Park Avenue, W11 4UA (7727 7022); 158-164 Fulham Road, SW10 9PR (7373 4997).

Golden Treasury

29 Replingham Road, SW18 5LT (8333 0167, www.thegoldentreasury.co.uk). Southfields tube. **Open** 9.30am-6pm Mon-Fri; 9.30am-5.30pm Sat; 10.30am-4.30pm Sun. **Credit** MC, V.

The sprawling premises of this brilliant children's bookshop house a host of titles, from books on pregnancy to teen fiction. In the unlikely event that you can't find what you're after, staff are happy to order it in. There's also an excellent programme of author events; past luminaries include Judith Kerr (*The Tiger Who Came to Tea*) and Emma Chichester Clarke (*Blue Kangaroo*).

Buggy access. Mail order. Play area.

Lion & Unicorn

19 King Street, Richmond, Surrey TW9 1ND (8940 0483, www.lionunicornbooks.co.uk). Richmond tube/rail. **Open** 9.30am-5.30pm Mon-Fri; 9.30am-6pm Sat; 11am-5pm Sun. **Credit** MC, V.

Opened in 1977 (the late, great Roald Dahl was the guest of honour), this venerable bookshop has kept up with the times. 'The Roar', its quarterly online newsletter, is invaluable for book reviews and details of signings and special events. Staff are happy to advise on the diverse stock crammed into every nook and cranny.

Buggy access. Mail order.

Owl Bookshop

209 Kentish Town Road, NW5 2JU (7485 7793). Kentish Town tube. **Open** 9.30am-6pm Mon-Sat; noon-5pm Sun. **Credit** AmEx, MC, V.

A colourful collection of children's books take pride of place in the window at this tranquil independent bookshop; inside, titles are sorted by age and interest. The shop also hosts readings by local children's authors; for details, sign up to the mailing list.

Buggy access. Mail order.

Tales on Moon Lane

25 Half Moon Lane, SE24 9JU (7274 5759, www.talesonmoonlane.co.uk). Herne Hill rail/3, 37, 68 bus. **Open** 9am-5.45pm Mon-Fri; 9.30am-6pm Sat; 10.30am-4.30pm Sun. **Credit** MC, V.

Beloved by local families, this award-winning children's bookshop is a delight. Bright, airy premises and enthusiastic staff encourage long visits, as does the wide range of books. The storytelling sessions are very popular (turn up early for a place on the sofa), and there's the odd puppet show. Check online for author events.

Buggy access. Mail order.

Victoria Park Books

174 Victoria Park Road, E9 7HD (8986 1124, www.victoriaparkbooks.co.uk). London Fields rail then 277 bus. **Open** 10am-5.30pm Tue-Sun. **Credit** MC, V.

With its book club, wall of book reviews from schoolchildren and popular patio area, this place oozes community spirit. Books are categorised

by look and feel as well as content – there's a section for interactive titles, and children can get their hands on cloth, bath and buggy books. Other stock is divided into user-friendly sections: history, art, dinosaurs, reference, a Ladybird corner and more. Teenagers and adults are also catered for. Authors visit regularly and there are drop-in story sessions at 11am on Fridays.
Buggy access. Mail order. Play area.

Educational toys & games

Education Interactive
10 Staplehurst Road, SE13 5NB (8318 6380, www.education-interactive.co.uk). Hither Green rail. **Open** *9.30am-1.30pm Mon-Fri (by appointment weekday afternoons).* **Credit** AmEx, MC, V.
As its name suggests, this place specialises in toys and games to expand the grey matter. Polydron building blocks and Times Table Lotto are among the artfully educational offerings.
Buggy access. Mail order.

Fun Learning
Bentall Centre, Clarence Street, Kingston-upon-Thames, Surrey KT1 1TP (8974 8900, www.funlearning.co.uk). Kingston rail. **Open** *9am-6pm Mon-Wed, Fri, Sat; 9am-8pm Thur; 11am-5pm Sun.* **Credit** MC, V.
You're encouraged to try before you buy at this independent retailer, which sells all manner of puzzles, computer games, art and craft activities and science experiment sets. It's a wonderful place for unusual Christmas presents (a paint-your-own chair, say), but there are affordable pocket money items too, ranging from balloon-making gunk kits to hatching dinosaur eggs.
Buggy access. Disabled access. Mail order.
Branch Brent Cross Shopping Centre, NW4 3FP (8203 1473).

Musical instruments

Chappell of Bond Street
152-160 Wardour Street, W1F 8YA (7432 4400, www.chappellofbondstreet.co.uk). Oxford Circus or Tottenham Court Road tube. **Open** *9.30am-6pm Mon-Fri; 10am-5.30pm Sat.* **Credit** AmEx, MC, V. **Map** p314 J6.
Chappell's three-storey premises showcase a gleaming array of instruments. It's a Yamaha piano and keyboard specialist. Some of the instruments (typically flutes, saxes, clarinets and trumpets) may be available on a rent-to-buy scheme, but quarter- and half-size instruments must be purchased.
Buggy access. Delivery service. Mail order.

Dot's
132 St Pancras Way, NW1 9NB (7482 5424, www.dotsonline.co.uk). Camden Town tube/ Camden Road rail. **Open** *9am-5.30pm Mon-Sat.* **Credit** AmEx, MC, V.
Run by an experienced music teacher, Dot's is a wonderfully friendly establishment. The shop sells new instruments – mostly stringed and wind, from recorders to violins – along with sheet music and books. There's a rent-to-buy scheme too. Check the website for tuition and second-hand instruments.
Mail order. Repair service.

Dulwich Music Shop
9 Upland Road, SE22 9EE (8693 1477, www.dulwichmusic.com). East Dulwich rail/ 40, 185, P13 bus. **Open** *9.30am-5.30pm Mon, Tue, Thur-Sat.* **Credit** AmEx, MC, V.
A vast array of stringed, woodwind and brass instruments are stocked here, with hire and buy-back options available too. Accessories and classical sheet music are also sold, and there's a repairs service.
Buggy access. Mail order. Repair service.

Northcote Music
155C Northcote Road, SW11 6QB (7228 0074). Clapham Junction rail, then 319 bus. **Open** *10.30am-6pm Mon-Fri; 10am-5pm Sat.* **Credit** MC, V.
This friendly little music shop is tucked away next to QT Toys, somehow squeezing string, percussion and wind instruments (which you can rent or buy) into the tiny space, as well as brass and digital equipment. In the remaining space are the music books and sheet music, some of which are appropriate for younger children (including nursery rhymes for the piano and group sing-along pieces). It's deservedly popular, so try to avoid the after school rush.
Buggy access. Delivery service. Mail order. Repair service.

Robert Morley
34 Engate Street, SE13 7HA (8318 5838, www.morleypianos.com). Lewisham DLR/rail. **Open** *9.30am-5pm Mon-Sat.* **Credit** MC, V.
To see if a child is serious about playing the piano, Morley's will hire one out, charging £250 for initial payment and delivery, then a monthly charge starting from £30. If, after a year, the child is still piano-friendly, you can buy it and get half the rental payments off the price, plus the delivery charge. Morley's also builds early keyboards such as clavichords, harpsichords and virginals.
Buggy access. Delivery service.

Consumer

LET'S FILL THIS TOWN WITH YOUNG ARTISTS

VISIT CASS ART ISLINGTON KENSINGTON OR HAMPSTEAD WITH YOUR KIDS AND GET A KID'S ACTIVITY BOOK inc. BAG AND PENCILS

FREE*

CASS ART KIDS

CASS ART ISLINGTON FLAGSHIP STORE
66-67 COLEBROOKE ROW, LONDON N1 8AB
220 KENSINGTON HIGH STREET W8
58-62 HEATH STREET NW3 (OPENING SEPT 2010)
WWW.CASSART.CO.UK

*FREE ACTIVITY BOOK & BAG WHEN YOU SPEND A MINIMUM OF £5 INSTORE. OFFER ONLY
AVAILABLE TO 3-12 YEAR OLD KIDS IN STORE. 1 BAG PER KID. TERMS AND CONDITIONS APPLY

EQUIPMENT & ACCESSORIES

Gifts

Bob & Blossom
140 Columbia Road, E2 7RG (7739 4737, www.bobandblossom.com). Old Street tube/rail/ 55 bus. **Open** 9am-3pm Sun. **Credit** MC, V.
Despites its restricted opening hours (coinciding with Sunday's famous flower market), B&B does a roaring trade in crochet-knit toys, retro spinning tops and wooden Noah's Ark sets. The boutique also sells the brand's trademark T-shirts, hats and sleepsuits, boldly emblazoned with cheeky mottos.
Buggy access. Mail order.

Cachao
140 Regents Park Road, NW1 8XL (7483 4422, www.cachaotoycafe.com). Chalk Farm tube. **Open** 8.30am-6pm daily. **Credit** AmEx, MC, V.
This shop-cum-café stocks Hello Kitty, Sylvanian Families, Ravensburger, Toby Tiger, Crayola goods and more. It's a slightly odd set up, with stock covering the walls of the café upstairs, making it a little tricky to browse – and sitting in the café with kids is asking for pester trouble. But there's also a downstairs room (albeit reached by a cramped staircase, and scented with cooking odours from the kitchen below).

Finnesse Lifestyle
453 Roman Road, E3 5LX (8983 9286, www.finnesselifestyle.com). Bethnal Green tube, then 8 bus. **Open** 9.30am-6pm Mon-Sat. **Credit** AmEx, MC, V.
Alongside its collections of organic and fair trade womenswear, accessories and home furnishings, Finnesse has an interesting selection of children's clothes and toys from around the world. Marimekko, Hug and Organics for Kids are among the labels; Pia Wallen's snug little felted slippers would make a lovely gift for a newborn.
Buggy access. Mail order.

Goody Gumdrops
128 Crouch Hill, N8 9DY (8340 3484, www.goodygumdrops.co.uk). Finsbury Park tube/rail then W7 bus/Crouch Hill rail. **Open** 10am-5.30pm Mon-Sat; 11.30am-4.30pm Sun. **Credit** MC, V.
Decorated with shiny stars, this shop stocks a mixture of mainstream and quirky toys and clothes for all ages. It's great for contemporary

Victoria Park Books. *See p259.*

crafts, such as the Buttonbag range of sew your own toys, and for beautiful gifts. Clothes includes puffy fairy dresses and more stylish offerings from Ellie & Olla and Albetta. There's a large table in the middle, stacked with tins of pocket money buys, and a drop-in story corner on Friday mornings.
Buggy access.

Green Baby
345 Upper Street, N1 0PD (7359 7037, www.greenbaby.co.uk). Angel tube/Highbury & Islington tube/rail. **Open** 9.30am-5.30pm Mon-Fri; 10am-5pm Sat; 11am-5pm Sun. **Credit** MC, V.
Eco-friendly basics are Green Baby's forte, with adorable organic cotton playsuits for summer babies and long, striped baby gowns for winter, made by a community project in India. The company also sells organic sheets, strokably soft pastel-hued sheepskins, washable nappies, Tripp Trapp high chairs, pop-up baby beds, Huggababy slings and the ever-reliable Baby Björn Active Carrier. Nappy balms and baby lotions based on pure lanolin, sweet almond oil and cocoa butter occupy the remaining space. Anything too bulky to fit in the shop can be ordered from the website or catalogue.
Delivery service. Mail order (0870 240 6894).

Branches 5 Elgin Crescent, W11 2JA (7792 8140); 52 Greenwich Church Street, SE10 9BL (8858 6690).

O Baby

126 Fortis Green Road, N10 3DU (8444 8742). Highgate tube, then 43, 134 bus. **Open** 9.30am-5.30pm Mon-Sat. **Credit** AmEx, MC, V.
This small shop sells fair trade and organic bedding, toys and clothes for babies and toddlers, natural skincare products and runs a baby list service.
Buggy access.

Semmalina-Starbags

225 Ebury Street, SW1W 8UT (7730 9333, www.starbags.info). Sloane Square tube. **Open** 9.30am-5.30pm Mon-Sat. **Credit** MC, V.
Semmalina-Starbags specialises in bespoke party bags. Wrapped in crackling cellophane and garlanded with bright ribbons, the bags can be filled with all sorts of trinkets – from the neon-lit sweetie selection to bubbles, potty putty, bouncy balls, hair bobbles, stationery and more.
Delivery service. Mail order.

So Tiny London

64 Great Titchfield Street, W1W 7QH (7636 2501, www.showroom64.com). Oxford Circus tube. **Open** 11am-6pm Mon-Fri. **Credit** AmEx, MC, V.
There are beautiful presents for newborns to be unearthed at this compact shop, ranging from Bonnie Baby's sumptuous cashmere cardies to tongue-in-cheek Rolling Stones and Led Zeppelin babygros. Tiny Mary Jane sock sets and knitted bonnets cater to more traditional tastes. The selection of new baby cards is also excellent, with some lovely hand-printed designs. Clothes sizes go up to age eight; don't miss the sale rail, which offers generous reductions.
Buggy access. Mail order. Nappy-changing facilities.

Bikes

Chamberlaine Cycles

75-77 Kentish Town Road, NW1 8NY (7485 4488, www.chamberlainecycles.co.uk). Camden Town tube. **Open** 8.30am-6pm Mon-Sat. **Credit** AmEx, MC, V.
Outside, ranks of gleaming, polished bicycles line the pavement; inside there are even more to choose from, along with baby seats, trailer bikes, lights and the all-important locks.
Buggy access. Delivery service. Disabled access. Mail order. Repair service.

D2 Leisure

143 Stoke Newington Road, N16 8BP (7254 3380, www.d2leisuregroup.co.uk). Rectory Road rail/67, 76, 149, 243 bus. **Open** 9am-5.30pm Mon-Fri; 9am-5pm Sat. **Credit** MC, V.
The bike shop formerly known as Daycock's has a great range of cycles in the kids' showroom, though staff are not always overly helpful. Most bikes can be ordered online via the website.
Buggy access. Disabled access. Mail order.
Repair service.
Branches 201-203 Roman Road, E2 0QY (8980 4966); 70-72 Loampit Vale, SE13 7SN (8297 0225).

Edwardes

221-225 Camberwell Road, SE5 0HG (7703 3676). Elephant & Castle tube, then 12, 68, 176, P3 bus. **Open** 8.30am-6pm Mon-Sat. **Credit** AmEx, MC, V.
A reliable general bike shop, Edwardes also stocks mounts for two to 12s (brands include Pro Bike, Bronx and Giant) and accessories such as bike seats, helmets, trailers and tag-alongs.
Buggy access. Delivery service. Disabled access. Mail order. Repair service.

Two Wheels Good

143 Crouch Hill, N8 9QH (8340 4284, www.twowheelsgood.co.uk). Finsbury Park tube/rail, then W7 bus. **Open** 8.30am-6pm Mon-Fri; 9am-6pm Sat; 11am-5pm Sun. **Credit** AmEx, MC, V.
Although there isn't a wide range of children's bikes, the incredibly friendly and helpful staff are more than happy to offer recommendations on bikes you can order in from the Gary Fisher and Trek websites.
Buggy access. Disabled access. Mail order.
Repair service.
Branch 165 Stoke Newington Church Street, N16 0UL (7249 2200).

Prams & accessories

See also p253-57.

Babyworld

239 Munster Road, SW6 6BT (7386 1904). Fulham Broadway tube, then 211, 295 bus. **Open** 10am-6pm Mon-Wed, Fri; 10am-5.30pm Sat. **Credit** AmEx, MC, V.
The premises may look small, but Babyworld crams lots in. Specialising in essential equipment for zero to fours, its stock includes stairgates, prams, pushchairs, high chairs, breast pumps and toys from brands such as Medela, Tomy, Maclaren, Bugaboo and Mountain Buggy.
Buggy access. Mail order.

Consumer

Pram Shop

57 Chepstow Road, W2 5BP (7313 9969, www.thepramshopnottinghill.co.uk). Notting Hill Gate tube, then 28, 328 bus. **Open** 10am-6pm Mon-Sat. **Credit** MC, V.

Staff really know their stuff at the Pram Shop – a major distributor for Sweden's Emmaljunga brand, alongside Bugaboo, Phil & Teds and Mountain Buggy. Accessories such as foot muffs, rain covers and transport bags are also sold, along with Start-rite shoes.
Buggy access. Delivery service.

Rub a Dub Dub

15 Park Road, N8 8TE (8342 9898). Finsbury Park tube/rail then W7 bus. **Open** 10am-6pm Mon- Sat; noon-4pm Sun. **Credit** MC, V.

All the biggest brands are present and correct at this well-stocked shop, from playfully-hued Bugaboos to more rugged Mountain Buggy, Out 'N' About and Phil & Teds three-wheelers. Along with Tripp-Trapp high chairs, travel cots, muslins and UV-protecting pushchair covers, there are fun mouse, tiger and ladybird shaped Wheelybugs for whizzing round the house, and plenty of toys. Eco-friendly nappy brands include Bambo and Nature Babycare, and there's a sweet-smelling array of chemical-free babywipes.
Buggy access. Delivery service. Disabled access. Nappy-changing facilities. Play area.

The nursery

Aspace

140 Chiswick High Road, W4 1PU (8994 5814, www.aspaceuk.com). Turnham Green tube. **Open** 10am-6pm Mon-Sat; 11am-5pm Sun. **Credit** AmEx, MC, V.

The understated range at Aspace includes children's beds of every description, from white-painted four posters to solid oak bunks. Handsome wardrobes, sturdy chests of drawers, and tasteful soft furnishings – mattresses, quilts, throws, curtains and cushions – round off the collection.
Buggy access. Delivery service. Mail order (0845 872 2400).

Blue Almonds

79 Walton Street, SW3 2HP (7584 8038, www.bluealmonds.co.uk). South Kensington tube. **Open** 10am-6pm Mon-Fri; 10.30am-5pm Sat. **Credit** MC, V.

The wooden nursery furniture in this old-fashioned shop – catering for a typical Kensington clientele – is prolifically painted with flowers, butterflies and sailing boats. Tartin et Chocolat blankets and cuddly toys are all soft and sweet, while the cool African print range makes a refreshing change if you're tired of conventional pastels.
Buggy access. Delivery service. Mail order.

Chic Shack

77 Lower Richmond Road, SW15 1ET (8785 7777, www.chicshack.net). Putney Bridge tube, then 14, 22 bus. **Open** 10.30am-5pm Mon-Sat. **Credit** MC, V.

Inspired by 18th-century French and Swedish antiques, Chic Shack's largely white-painted furniture and soft furnishings are delightfully elegant. Pretty without being sickly-sweet, the range includes cots, chests, toy boxes, wardrobes and pastel-pink or blue floral- and stripe-upholstered chairs.
Buggy access. Delivery service.

Dragons of Walton Street

23 Walton Street, SW3 2HX (7589 3795, www.dragonsofwaltonstreet.com). Knightsbridge or South Kensington tube. **Open** 9.30am-5.30pm Mon-Fri; 10am-5pm Sat. **Credit** AmEx, MC, V. **Map** p313 E10.

This Walton Street landmark has spawned a host of imitations. Its wooden furniture is hand-painted with bunnies and boats, soldiers and fairies; alternatively, you can come up with your own design. Beatrix Potter and Paddington Bear lampshades and bedspreads are in abundance, and handsome traditional toys are also stocked.
Buggy access. Delivery service. Mail order.

Natural Mat Company

99 Talbot Road, W11 2AT (7985 0474, www.naturalmat.com). Ladbroke Grove tube. **Open** 9am-6pm Mon-Fri; 10am-4pm Sat. **Credit** MC, V. **Map** p310 A5.

Behind a window hung with prints of children's illustrations is a range of solid nursery furniture, with a choice of organic mattresses and bedding. Knowledgeable staff can help you decide between the different materials; organic coir, latex straight from a rubber tree and mohair for mattresses, along with goose down and lambswool-stuffed cot bed covers and duvets. There are also baby jumpers in soft lambswool, cashmere blankets and cotton Breton-striped babygros.
Buggy access. Delivery service. Mail order.

Nursery Window

83 Walton Street, SW3 2HP (7581 3358, www.nurserywindow.co.uk). Knightsbridge or South Kensington tube. **Open** 10am-6pm Mon-Sat. **Credit** AmEx, MC, V. **Map** p313 E10.

This supremely traditional nursery shop stocks beautifully made wooden cots and cribs, and all the blankets and quilts you could ever need.

Olive Loves Alfie. *See p269.*

Toy libraries

As the recession stretches into the new decade, it's time to think about our children's need for new toys. Is it imperative that they own a new addition to their collection, or is it actually just as fun to borrow something for a few weeks (saving much valued storage space at home at the same time)? There are lots of good reasons to visit a toy library and saving money and space at home are just two of them. Toy libraries tend to stock specialist and educational toys, games and puzzles and lend them for up to six weeks at a time. But they're not just a lending facility and usually provide drop-in play sessions for the local community into the bargain. Membership rules vary from library to library but fees are always kept low. They are usually run by volunteers (often local parents) who can offer advice about individual toys as well as more general tips on the importance of play. What's not to like? Toy libraries are cheap, promote sharing, provide stimulating play, and are usually a good way of meeting other local families. For a list of toy libraries in your area contact the National Association of Toy & Leisure Libraries (7428 2288, www.natll.org.uk).

Prints are nostalgic and romantic, and despite the dry-clean only label, Sue Hill's cashmere knits are lovely. Waffle blankets with pink or blue satin trim are a fail-safe buy for any new arrival. *Buggy access. Delivery service. Mail order.*

FASHION

Amaia
14 Cale Street, SW3 3QU (7590 0999, www.amaia-kids.com). Sloane Square or South Kensington tube. **Open** 10am-6pm Mon-Sat. **Credit** MC, V. **Map** p313 E11.
There's an appealingly nostalgic feel to the baby clothes and childrenswear at Amaia, from the knitted all-in-ones and T-bar shoes to the ruffled cotton sundresses. Boys' clothes are equally classic, with cotton shorts, cords and linen shirts – no brash slogans or scratchy synthetics here. Prices are middling to expensive; expect to pay upwards of £50 for a little girl's day dress. *Buggy access. Mail order.*

Aravore Babies
31 Park Road, N8 8TE (8347 5752, www.aravore-babies.com). Highgate tube/ Crouch Hill rail/41, 91, W5, W7 bus. **Open** 10am-5.30pm Mon-Sat; noon-4.pm Sun. **Credit** AmEx, MC, V.
This luxury brand for babies and under-fives has some covetable pieces, all made from fairly-traded organic cotton and super-soft merino wool. At its small shop, gorgeous hand-knitted coats, dresses, bootees and dungarees nestle alongside delicate shawls and cot blankets. It also stocks other like-minded brands such as Bamboo Baby, Lille Barn, Tatty Bumpkin and the Erbaviva skincare range. *Buggy access. Mail order.*

Biff
41-43 Dulwich Village, SE21 7BN (8299 0911, www.biffkids.co.uk). North Dulwich rail/P4 bus. **Open** 9.30am-5.30pm Mon-Fri; 10am-6pm Sat. **Credit** AmEx, MC, V.
Occupying two shops, with a café next door, Biff has become a hub for local mummies. At No.41 there's an enormous selection of shoes from the likes of Lelli Kelly, Converse, Crocs, Geox and Start-rite, and an equally broad range of clothing brands for boys and girls aged all the way from two to 16. Labels include Catamini, Pepe Jeans, Powell & Craft, Bench, Roxy, Tartin et Chocolat, Quiksilver and Noa Noa. Next door caters to smaller fry, with baby gifts, Grobags, first shoes, swimwear and clothes for two-and-unders. *Buggy access. Disabled access. Mail order. Play area.*

Consumer

Bonpoint

15 Sloane Street, SW1X 9NB (7235 1441, www.bonpoint.com). Knightsbridge tube. **Open** 10am-6pm Mon-Sat. **Credit** AmEx, MC, V. **Map** p313 F9.

Describing itself as a 'French childrenswear couture house', Bonpoint brings Gallic panache and exquisite workmanship to the world of children's fashion. Charming bloomers, sundresses, linen shorts and jumpers are hard to resist, though the hefty price tags may make you think twice; the fragrant, well-heeled regulars don't bat an eyelid, *naturellement*. *Buggy access. Mail order.*
Branches 256 Brompton Road, SW3 2AS (3263 5057); 197 Westbourne Grove, W11 2SE (7792 2515).

Burberry Children

199 Westbourne Grove, W11 2SB (7221 3688, www.burberry.com). Notting Hill Gate tube. **Open** 10am-6pm Mon-Sat; noon-6pm Sun. **Credit** AmEx, MC, V.

This airy, glamorous flagship store on Westbourne Grove houses clothes with the same unusual twists on British classics offered by the adult Burberry line, only in miniature. The range goes from three months to 12 years, with a separate special occasion collection which features girls' skirts with gold-mesh petticoats and smart blazers for boys. With their immaculate detailing and signature checked lining, the macs are hardest on parental credit cards, costing around £260 depending on age. T-shirts, bags and shoes are less expensive, but you'll struggle to find much for under £30. *Buggy access. Mail order. Nappy-changing facilities. Play area.*

Caramel Baby & Child

77 Ledbury Road, W11 2AG (7727 0906, www.caramel-shop.co.uk). Notting Hill Gate or Westbourne Park tube. **Open** 10am-6pm Mon-Sat; noon-5pm Sun. **Credit** AmEx, MC, V. **Map** p310 A6.

Caramel's clothing range (0-12s), designed by Eva Karayiannis, is wonderfully idiosyncratic and effortlessly chic. Ribbon-strap floral sundresses, crisp smocks and beautifully-cut woollen coats have serious fashion appeal. As you might expect, it's not cheap; check washing instructions, too, as some pieces are made from silk or cashmere. A small selection of vintage-inspired toys are displayed downstairs, and there's a hair salon (book ahead). *Buggy access. Hairdressing. Mail order.*
Branches 259 Pavillion Road, SW1X 0BP (7730 2564); 291 Brompton Road, SW3 2DY (7589 7001).

Frère Jacques

121 Stoke Newington Church Street, N16 0UH (7249 5655). Finsbury Park tube/rail, then 106 bus/73, 393, 476 bus. **Open** 11am-6pm Tue-Sat; 11am-5pm Sun. **Credit** AmEx, MC, V.

Giving equal weight to boys' and girls' clothes (zero to eights), this place is a great little all-rounder. The emphasis is on stylish and durable design, with shelves of classic clothes from the likes of Petit Bateau and Danish label Minymo. Colourful animal-themed mackintoshes and brightly patterned wellies from Kidorable are big sellers, along with quality shoes from Pedi Ped, Robeez and Superfit. *Buggy access.*

Jakss

469 Roman Road, E3 5LX (8981 2233, www.jakss.co.uk). Bethnal Green tube, then 8 bus. **Open** 10am-5.30pm Tue-Sat. **Credit** AmEx, MC, V.

Founded in 1977, Jakss is a treasure trove of children's designer togs, ranging from all-in-ones for newborns to cutting-edge looks for 16-year-olds. The list of labels is endless: Ralph Lauren, Armani, Jottum, Burberry, DKNY, CP Company, Oilily and Stone Island fill the rails, along with children's and adult's Birkenstocks. *Buggy access. Mail order.*

Jolie à Pied

82 Lordship Lane, SE22 8HF (8693 4509). East Dulwich rail. **Open** 10am-6pm Mon-Sat. **Credit** MC, V.

Jolie à Pied has rebranded itself recently on more utilitarian lines, with Hunter wellies and hard-wearing Converse and Camper lines taking prominence in the windows. Pretty shoes are all very well, but children will jump in puddles and climb trees in anything they happen to have on, so footwear may as well be up to the task. *Buggy access.*

Notsobig

31A Highgate High Street, N6 5JT (8340 4455). Archway or Highgate tube. **Open** 10am-6pm Mon-Sat; 11am-5pm Sun. **Credit** MC, V.

An eclectic blend of labels and designers makes Notsobig's shelves a pleasure to peruse. Swishy party dresses from I Love Gorgeous and Cacherel rub shoulders with cool casuals from American Outfitters and hip Parisian label Eva & Oli; look out, too, for Little Linens' light, airy shirts and trousers. Dressing-up clothes from Bandicoot Lapin, tulle-skirted tutus sourced from Los Angeles, hand-made jewellery and a sterling selection of shoes round off the stock. *Buggy access. Delivery service. Mail order.*

Consumer

Petit Aimé

Spoilt for choice
Notting Hill

The leafy streets of Ladbroke Grove and Notting Hill are the original stamping ground of the yummy mummies and their offspring. Here, organic cotton-clad babies recline in expensive three-wheelers while their parents stroll around the shops; the streets leading off Portobello Road are sprinkled with brilliant boutiques and specialist shops, stocking all the smartest brands alongside trendsetting lesser-known labels.

For stylish children's clothing, there's no end of choice; start at the Ladbroke Grove (and cheaper) end of Portobello Road with **Sasti** (*see p270*) for hardwearing, 1970s-inspired designs. Girls will adore the romantic day dresses and party frocks at **I Love Gorgeous** (*see p272*), made from deliciously floaty fabrics; to ensure your child doesn't look out of place on the Riviera, **Petit Aimé** (*see below*) stocks the best French childrenswear designers.

Their Nibs (*see p270*) also continues to enchant both parents and children with its vintage-inspired designs and quirky prints; pirate-printed shirts and pyjamas for the chaps, and a sweet fairy design for girls.

Old-fashioned toys and games can be found at the charming **Honeyjam** (*see p282*) on Portobello Road, run by two fabulously fashionable friends. If you're in need of a more substantial set of wheels than its chunky wooden cars and pull-along animals, the **Pram Shop** (*see p264*) is the best place to go for considered advice and top of the range baby transport options.

Oh Baby London

162 Brick Lane, E1 6RU (7247 4949, www.ohbabylondon.com). Shoreditch High Street rail. **Open** 10am-6pm daily. **Credit** AmEx, MC, V.

Oh Baby's cute, cheeky and colourful own brand baby and kids' clothes are all the rage in east London and beyond. Choose from bodyvests and bright T-shirts with slogans like 'The Future Is Mine' and 'I'm a Long Term Investment' to dresses and playsuits in bright prints.
Buggy access, Delivery Service, Mail order.

Olive Loves Alfie

84 Stoke Newington Church Street, N16 0AP (7241 4212, www.oliveloves alfie.co.uk). Finsbury Park tube/rail then 106 bus/73, 393, 476 bus. **Open** 9.30am-6pm Mon; 10am-6pm Tue-Sun. **Credit** AmEx, MC, V.

This design-led boutique stocks an inspired mix of clothing for children of all ages. Gorgeous and reasonably priced, its collection is full of nautical stripes, bright paisley patterns and bold, graphic prints. Pieces by hugely popular Scandinavian designer Katvig fly out of the shop, as do Dandy Star's soft, 1970s-style Ts. Artfully arranged gifts and toys include painted wooden animals, hand-knitted cuddly toys and a washing line strung with hats; mothers-to-be will love the comfy cotton kimonos and organic bath products.
Buggy access. Mail order.

Petit Aimé

34 Ledbury Road, W11 2AB (7221 3123, www.aimelondon.com). Notting Hill Gate tube. **Open** 10am-6.30pm Mon-Sat. **Credit** AmEx, MC, V. **Map** p310 A6.

An offshoot of the acclaimed womenswear boutique next door, owned by French-Cambodian sisters Val and Vanda Heng-Vong, this white-painted boutique dresses newborns to 12-year-olds with the crème de la crème of Gallic labels: Isabel Marant, BonTon, Aymara and Antik Batik among them. Kitsch blankets, cushions and brightly coloured bedspreads from Petit Pan are a great way to liven up a nursery, and the hand-knitted rabbits will enchant younger children.
Mail order.

Quackers

155D Northcote Road, SW11 6QB (7978 4235). Clapham Junction rail, then 319 bus. **Open** 9.30am-5.30pm Mon-Fri; 10am-5.30pm Sat. **Credit** MC, V.

Kids can root through the box of toys while their parents browse the rails. There's a healthy crop of Danish designers to choose from: Minymo, Molo Kids, Phister & Philina and Louie Louis among them. Modish little cotton dresses and tiered skirts by Hilly Chrisp are superb summer buys, and there are playfully printed Hatley raincoats for autumn showers.

Consumer

Toys include floppy favourites by Moulin Roty and attractive wooden pull-alongs and trikes. *Buggy access.*

Rachel Riley

82 Marylebone High Street, W1U 4QW (7935 8345, www.rachelriley.com). Baker Street or Bond Street tube. **Open** 10am-6.30pm Mon-Sat; 10am-5.30pm Sun. **Credit** AmEx, MC, V. **Map** p314 G5.

There's a wonderfully wholesome, 1950s feel to Rachel Riley's designs, handmade in her atelier in the Loire Valley. Cherry-print poplin frocks, beruffled bloomers and pleated pinafores are traditional without being stuffy; for the chaps, there are anchor- and aeroplane-print shirts and dapper striped pyjamas. *Buggy access. Delivery service. Mail order.* **Branch** 14 Pont Street, SW1X 9EN (7259 5969).

Ralph Lauren Children's Store

143 New Bond Street, W1S 2TP (7535 4600, www.polo.com). Bond Street tube. **Open** 10am-6pm Mon-Wed, Fri, Sat; 10am-7pm Thur; noon-5pm Sun. **Credit** AmEx, MC, V. **Map** p314 H6.

Ralph Lauren's beautifully made but eye-wateringly expensive outfits are displayed in suitably stately surrounds (mahogany panelling, sepia prints and strategically arranged rocking horses). There's more to the brand than polo shirts: the baby dresses and cashmere cable-knit cardigans, in particular, are gorgeously pretty. *Delivery service. Mail order.* **Branch** 139-141 Fulham Road, SW3 6FD (7761 0310).

Sasti

8 Portobello Green Arcade, 281 Portobello Road, W10 5TZ (8960 1125, www.sasti.co.uk). Ladbroke Grove tube. **Open** 10am-6pm Mon-Sat. **Credit** MC, V.

Bold designs and colours ensure Sasti's clothes stand out from the crowd, whether you're buying cowboy-meets-Indian jeans with tan fringing down the side or a leopard-print all-in-one. Everything is made in the UK, and prices are competitive, starting at around £12 for fleeces and long-sleeved T-shirts. The kitsch accessories also make great presents for cool kids. *Buggy access. Delivery service. Mail order. Nappy-changing facilities. Play area.*

Selfridges

400 Oxford Street, W1A 1AB (0800 123400, www.selfridges.com). Bond Street tube. **Open** 9.30am-8pm Mon-Wed, Sat; 9.30am-9pm Thur, Fri; noon-6pm Sun. **Credit** AmEx, DC, MC, V. **Map** p314 G6.

The sprawling third floor is chock-full of well known children's brands to browse through – predominantly clothes, although there are a few toy ranges (including Hello Kitty and V Tech). All the major designers are represented, including Armani, Dior, D&G, Chloé, Little Marc and Tommy Hilfiger. Sonia Rykiel's range for girls features bright pink dresses with attached fabric flowers; for boys, John Galliano's jeans, khaki jackets and print T-shirts have lots of attitude. Slightly cheaper, and a favourite with fashionista parents, French brand Finger in the Nose's range includes rock 'n' roll essentials such as bootcut jeans and acid wash T-shirts. There's also a large shoe department, featuring Step2wo, and fancy dress costumes. Although there is no specific play space, there's plenty of room for children to run around; look out, too, for seasonal events such as Easter egg hunts. *Buggy access. Cafés. Delivery service. Disabled access: lift, toilet. Mail order. Nappy-changing facilities.*

Their Nibs

214 Kensington Park Road, W11 1NR (7221 4263, www.theirnibs.com). Ladbroke Grove or Notting Hill Gate tube. **Open** 10am-6pm Mon-Sat; noon-5pm Sun. **Credit** AmEx, MC, V.

Their Nibs is known for its whimsical, distinctive designs, featuring 1950s-esque prints and unusual colours. Signature prints include a toadstool fairy pattern for girls' blouses and dresses, and a pirate design for boys' shirts. More elaborate party frocks cost up to £55, but there's plenty that's a good deal cheaper; the raincoats go for £20. The vintage emporium at the back includes dollhouses, clothes and prams, and there's a small range of Stokke cribs and high chairs. Kids can play with the blackboard, mini-kitchen and books or have a haircut while you browse. *Buggy access. Hairdressing. Mail order. Play area.* **Branch** 79 Chamberlayne Road, NW10 3ND (8964 8444).

Three Potato Four

Alliance House, Newington Green, N16 9QH (7704 2228, www.threepotatofour.co.uk). Canonbury rail/73 bus. **Open** 10am-5.30pm Mon-Fri; 9.30am-6pm Sat; 11am-5pm Sun. **Credit** MC, V.

Overlooking Newington Green, this colourful boutique's clothing collection includes vibrant pieces by Dutch designer Kik Kid. There are gifts galore, too: shelves of books, old-fashioned toys and Science Museum games. A fairly reasonably priced children's hair salon

occupies a corner of the shop, and there are a couple of train tracks to keep the little ones occupied while you shop.
Buggy access. Disabled access. Hairdressing. Nappy-changing facilities. Play area.

Trotters

34 King's Road, SW3 4UD (7259 9620, www.trotters.co.uk). Sloane Square tube. **Open** 9am-7pm Mon-Sat; 10am-6.30pm Sun. **Credit** AmEx, MC, V. **Map** p313 F11.
With clothes, toys, accessories, toiletries, shoes and books, Trotters is a one-stop shop for beleagured parents. Exclusive designs from the Chelsea Clothing Company include Liberty-print dresses and nicely-cut smocks, while boys look shipshape in Petit Breton's stripy tops and cotton shorts. There's a hairdressing station with a big fish tank to distract the littl'uns during their fringe trim; first-timers get a certificate and a lock of hair for fond parents to treasure. Stocked with Converse, Pom d'Api and Startrites, the shoe section also gives out 'first shoe' certificates. Other useful bits and bobs include organic sunscreens, insulated lunchboxes and Nitty Gritty headlice treatments.
Buggy access. Delivery service. Hairdressing. Mail order.
Branches 127 Kensington High Street, W8 5SF (7937 9373); 86 Northcote Road, SW11 6QN (7585 0572); 84 Turnham Green Terrace, W4 1QN (8742 1195).

Others

Catimini

52A South Molton Street, W1K 1SE (7629 8099, www.catimini.com). Bond Street tube. **Open** 10am-6.30pm Mon-Wed, Fri, Sat; 10am-7pm Thur; 11am-5pm Sun. **Credit** AmEx, MC, V. **Map** p314 H6.
Startlingly bright colours and vibrant patterns are Catimini's signature style, with crocheted cardigans, patchwork cotton separates, sweet baggy shorts and striped T-shirts.
Buggy access. Disabled Access. Mail order. Play area.
Branch 33C King's Road, SW3 4LX (7824 8897).

Felix & Lilys

3 Camden Passage, N1 8EA (7424 5423, www.felixandlilys.com). Angel tube. **Open** 10am-6pm Mon-Sat; 11am-5pm Sun. **Credit** MC, V.
This tucked-away boutique sells colourful designer togs for babies and children, including some chic Scandinavian brands (Ej Sikke Lej, IdaT and Katvig), plus old favourites like Bob

Spoilt for choice
Crouch End

This bohemian, middle-class and family friendly neighbourhood has oddly been the home of a number of fantasy authors. Even Stephen King has visited; in his short story 'Crouch End', the area acts as an inter-dimensional portal. Meanwhile, a great range of independent toy and clothing shops encourages children to use their imaginations and to enter into their own fantasy worlds.

The original, happy, hippy, infant all-rounder **Soup Dragon** (*see p257*) continues to enchant children with its range of dollshouses, pirate ships and castles. Girls will love **Goody Gumdrops** (*see p262*), both for its tempting pocket-money purchases and stylish clothes. For gorgeous gifts, bohemian **Aravore Babies** (*see p266*) sells organic and handcrafted items such as sweet little linen dresses with crochet trims.

For the best pram and buggy advice in the area, head to **Rub a Dub Dub** (*see p264*) and pick up all the other child essentials you need at the same time. Finally, feet can be properly fitted into comfy shoes at **Red Shoes** (*see p278*) and wayward hair groomed to perfection at **Mini Kin** (*see p257*).

Goody Gumdrops

& Blossom and Toby Tiger. Look out, too, for the quirky Ella & Otto sleeping bags. Toys include wooden food and pull-along pals, along with robust trainer bikes. *Buggy access. Mail order.*

Frogs & Fairies

69A Highbury Park, N5 1UA (7424 5159). Highbury & Islington tube/rail. **Open** 10am-5.30pm Mon-Sat; 10am-4pm Sun. **Credit** AmEx, MC, V.

Spoilt for choice
Stoke Newington

Despite significant gentrification over the past decade or so, 'Stokey' still clings to its bohemian identity. Products with green credentials are easy to find round here; on Saturdays, there's a good farmers' market in the grounds of William Patten Primary School.

In an area that's famed for its high concentration of young families, shopping for children couldn't be easier. Most of the action is centred around the pleasant, café-dotted stretch of Church Street, making for a restful afternoon's lunching and browsing.

Toy shop **Route 73 Kids** (*see p284*) is a little less chichi now that Woolies on the High Street has closed, and has a great range of toys and games for under-tens. A few doors away, **Olive Loves Alfie** (*see p269*) is a showcase for the hottest childrenswear designers. **Frère Jacques** (*see p267*) offers distinctive and reasonably priced children's clothes and shoes, and also dispenses haircuts. One of the best children's shops in London is all-rounder **Born** (*see p253*), well-stocked with clothes, prams, accessories, green nappies and more. Church Street is also home to a friendly branch of bike shop **Two Wheels Good** (*see p263*), although savvy parents will make for **D2 Leisure** (*see p263*) on the High Street for cheaper prices.

Down the road on Newington Green, **Three Potato Four** (*see p270*) – selling children's clothes, toys, books and offering haircuts – is a hop, skip and a jump away from kids' café **That Place on the Corner** (*see p237*).

This friendly shop is an excellent place for shoe-shopping, with footwear from Start-rite, Converse, Lelli Kelly, Geox and Crocs. More of interest to children are the toys: goodies by Playmobil, Lego and Galt, plus the ubiquitous micro-scooters. There's also a modest range of clothes for zero to fives, with lines from Petit Bateau and Katvig. An ever-changing selection of cards, gift wrap, party bag-fillers and pocket money toys rounds things off nicely. *Buggy access.*

I Love Gorgeous

52 Ledbury Road, W11 2AJ (7229 5855, www.ilovegorgeous.co.uk). Notting Hill Gate or Westbourne Park tube. **Open** 10am-6pm Mon-Sat; noon-6pm Sun. **Credit** AmEx, MC, V.

Stocking girls' clothes from newborn to 15 years, the rails of this small boutique are full of wonderfully tactile fabrics such as romantic georgette and soft cotton voile. Some of the designs are quite funky, like the hot pink star prints and lurex cardigans; others are much more innocent, with broderie anglaise trims and muted colours. There's a pretty collection of bridesmaid dresses downstairs, with shades to match most nuptial colour schemes. *Buggy access. Mail order.*

Jakes

79 Berwick Street, W1F 8TL (7734 0812, www.jakesofsoho.co.uk). Oxford Circus tube. **Open** 11am-7pm Mon-Sat. **Credit** AmEx, MC, V. **Map** p314 J6.

A percentage of the profits from this shop go towards the future of Jake, a boy with cerebral palsy. Kidswear consists of distinctive 'Lucky 7' slogan T-shirts (£12.50), and sweatshirts. *Buggy access. Mail order.*

Love Me Again

37 Staplehurst Road, SE13 5ND (8244 0172, www.love-me-again.co.uk). **Open** Tue-Sat 10am-5pm. **Credit** AmEx, MC, V.

New and nearly new clothes and toys are the mainstays of this recently opened shop in Hither Green. Expect designer labels such as Kenzo and Burberry, middle range favourites like Gap and Mini Boden and lots of cast off toys. The shop also runs occasional craft workshops for children (see the website for details). *Buggy access. Play area. Mail order.*

Marie Chantal

148 Walton Street, SW3 2JJ (7838 1111, www.mariechantal.com). Knightsbridge or South Kensington tube. **Open** 10am-6pm Mon-Sat. **Credit** AmEx, MC, V.

Consumer

Three Potato Four. *See p270.*

Spoilt for choice
East Dulwich

The buggies began rolling into this suburban patch of south London in the 1990s. Now the sprog scene centres around residential Northcross Road, home of original trendsetter the **Blue Mountain Café** (*see p223*), then spills out on to Lordship Lane. Although local favourite the Never Ending Story Bookshop has sadly now, er, ended, there's still plenty to catch the eye and lighten the wallet.

Swish shoe boutique **Jolie à Pied** (*see p267*), stocks a small range of high-end footwear for toddlers and private-schooled princesses from the likes of Spanish label Maá. The more established **Oranges & Lemons** (*see right*) provides chic maternity and baby wear, while further down Northcross Road, the wonderful **Hope & Greenwood** (20 Northcross Road, SE22 9EU, 8613 1777, www.hopeandgreenwood.co.uk) lures you in with '40s dance tunes on the wireless and shelves stacked with glass jars of flying saucers, gobstoppers and lemon bonbons.

Back on Lordship Lane, the Dulwich branch of **Soup Dragon** (*see p257*) is an Aladdin's cave of groovy clothes, toys and the ubiquitous micro scooters. The south London branch of the **JoJo Maman Bébé** (*see p255*) mini-chain sits at one end of the high street; further down, the sensible **John Barnett** (*see p277*) makes sure little feet have something practical and hard-wearing to put on.

Hope & Greenwood

Immaculate detailing, smart cuts and expensive fabrics, as you'd expect from a range designed by the eponymous Crown Princess of Greece. The collection includes some very high-fashion items such as jumpsuits, though there's plenty to suit more staid tastes; tweed jackets and braces for the boys, for example.
Buggy access. Mail order.
Branches 61A Ledbury Road, W11 2AA (7243 0220); 133A Sloane Street, SW1X 9AX (7730 8662).

Membery's
1 Church Road, SW13 9HE (8876 2910, www.memberys.com). Barnes Bridge rail. **Open** 10am-5pm Mon-Sat. **Credit** AmEx, MC, V.
Membery's stocks a good, solid range of baby gifts and quality clothing for small boys and girls up to six years old. The range includes everything from nightwear to special-occasion outfits; it's also particularly good for children's wedding wear.
Buggy access. Delivery service. Play area.

Oranges & Lemons/ Pretty Pregnant
61 Northcross Road, SE22 9ET (8693 9010, www.prettypregnant.co.uk). East Dulwich rail. **Open** 9.30am-5.30pm Mon-Sat; 11am-5pm Sun. **Credit** MC, V.
This sister establishment to the Pretty Pregnant maternity brand stocks tiny outfits by Petit Bateau and funky Dutch designer Kik Kid, along with animal-motif appliqué T-shirts by Lipfish and some sweet toys. Reggie the Big Eyed Dummy (£16) makes a change from the usual fluffy rabbits.
Buggy access. Mail order.
Branches 102 Northcote Road, SW11 6QW (7924 4850); 13-15 Chiltern Street, W1U 7PG (7486 2531); 186 King's Road, SW3 5XP (7349 7450).

Tots Boutique
39 Turnham Green Terrace, W4 1RG (8995 0520, http://totschiswick.weebly.com). Turnham Green tube. **Open** 10am-6pm Mon-Sat; noon-5pm Sun. **Credit** AmEx, MC, V.
Across the road from Snap Dragon (*see p284*), Tots crams in a broad range of designer gear for babies and children. The frequently changing cache might include the likes of Mini A Ture, Lili Gaufrette, Ralph Lauren and Catimini, with casualwear courtesy of Quiksilver and Roxy. A drawing table and various toys keep the kids sweet as you shop.
Buggy access. Mail order. Play area.

Chain stores

Adams
www.adams.co.uk
A good bet for inexpensive playwear, babywear and school uniforms.

Fat Face
www.fatface.com
Sporty, surf-inspired casualwear including a small range of tops, bottoms, dresses and shirts in muted colours for girls and boys.

Gap Kids
www.gap.com
The pastel-hued babywear makes a safe and practical gift for new parents, while the childrenswear is hardwearing and popular with all age groups.

H&M
www.hm.com
Cheap-as-chips and up-to-the-minute designs for babies, children and grown-ups.

Jigsaw Junior
www.jigsaw-online.com
Thrillingly, the branch at 190-192 Westbourne Grove, W11 2RH (7727 0322) has a silver slide instead of stairs to the basement.

Monsoon
www.monsoon.co.uk
Collections for boys and girls, ranging from simple puff-sleeved T-shirts and turn-up jeans to lavish, sequin-sprinkled party frocks.

Petit Bateau
www.petit-bateau.com
Classic French cotton baby clothes, in floral, plain and trademark milleraies striped designs.

Zara
www.zara.com
The Spanish high street giant offers unusual childrenswear, including some bright and beautiful dresses for girls.

Maternity

Blossom Mother & Child
164 Walton Street, SW3 2JL (7589 7500, www.blossommotherandchild.com). South Kensington tube. **Open** 10am-6pm Mon-Sat; noon-5pm Sun. **Credit** AmEx, MC, V. **Map** p313 E10.
Only the most stylish maternity labels make it on to the hallowed shelves at this über-chic Walton Street boutique. The own-label range offers flattering, perfectly-cut dresses, separates and lingerie, hanging alongside

Consumer

Love me Again: the place for new and nearly new clothes and toys. *See p272.*

pieces by the likes of Missoni, Antik Batik and Clements Ribeiro; the denim bar offers bump-accommodating jeans from the hottest brands (True Religion, Citizens of Humanity, J Brand). Amazing bargains can sometimes be found in the website's sale section.
Buggy access. Mail order.
Branches 69 Marylebone High Street, W1U 5JJ (7486 6089).

Elias & Grace
158 Regent's Park Road, NW1 8XN (7449 0574, www.eliasandgrace.com). Chalk Farm tube. **Open** 10am-6pm Mon-Sat; noon-6pm Sun. **Credit** MC, V.
Perfectly at home amid Primrose Hill's many chichi boutiques, Elias & Grace stocks a stylish combination of high fashion, luxury accessories and gifts. As well as hip labels for mothers-to-be (See by Chloé, Vivienne Westwood, J Brand), there's an international array of brands for babies and under-tens, among them Maan, Bonton, I Love Gorgeous and Quincy. Toys and accessories include bags and dolls from Madame Mo, and quirky Sparrowkids craft sets. A relaxed atmosphere, with plenty of room for pushchairs, a mini play area and friendly assistants make for hassle-free browsing.
Buggy access. Mail order (7483 4334). Play area.

Séraphine
58-62 Heath Street, NW3 1EN (7937 3156, www.seraphine.com). Hampstead tube. **Open** 10.30am-6pm Mon-Wed, Fri; 10.30am-7pm Thur; 10am-6.30pm Sat; noon-5pm Sun. **Credit** MC, V.
This Hampstead boutique looks expensive but stocks surprisingly reasonably priced pregnancy wear from French designer Cécile Reinaud. The emphasis is on co-ordinated smart casual items for yummy mummies, in block colours. A small range of newborn baby clothes and nice Boo Boo smellies for baby and Mama Mio products for mothers mean it's good for presents too. Upstairs is a nursery furniture showroom with decorative white cots, wardrobes and chests of drawers.
Buggy access. Mail order (0844 287 0001).
Branch 28 Kensington Church Street, W8 4EP (7937 3156).

HAIRDRESSING

Several shops listed elsewhere in this chapter incorporate a children's salon, with haircuts available on certain days of the week. See **Harrods** (*see p253*),

Caramel (*see p267*), **Mini Kin** (*see p257*), **Trotters** (*see p271*); **Their Nibs** (*see p270*) and **Igloo** (*see p254*). For the ultimate in children's barnet styling, however, have a **Tantrum** (*see below*).

Tantrum
398 King's Road, SW10 0LJ (7376 3966, www.yourtantrum.com). Sloane Square tube, then 11, 19, 22, 319 bus. **Open** 10am-6pm Tue-Fri; 9am-6pm Sat; 10.30am-4.30pm Sun. **Credit** AmEx, MC, V.
Billing itself as 'a revolutionary new concept in children's hairdressing', Tantrum spoils its young clients rotten with all sorts of bells and whistles. Aimed at an eight- to 14-year-old clientele, the basement area features a juice bar and games room, while the ground floor keeps the under-sevens amused with its buzzing locomotives and starry skies, as well as a general play area. In both areas, each styling chair is equipped with a swanky flatscreen TV and DVDs. The premises can also host children's parties; call for details.
Buggy access. Play area.

SAMPLE SALES

Junior Style
7689 3925, www.juniorstylesales.co.uk
Sharp-eyed shoppers are rewarded by discounts of up to 75% off designer labels at these regular sample sales. Sizes run from newborn to 12, while featured designers might include the likes of Replay, Cavalli, Evisu, Kenzo, Simonetta, Imps & Elfs and Ralph Lauren.

SECOND-HAND

Merry-Go-Round
12 Clarence Road, E5 8HB (8985 6308). Hackney Central rail. **Open** 10am-5pm Mon-Sat; 11am-3pm Sun. **Credit** MC, V.
This environmentally friendly agency trades on behalf of its clients in second-hand clothing, toys and baby equipment. Expect to find lots of high chairs, pushchairs, clothes, books and more, allowing budget- and eco-conscious families to be entirely kitted out with recycled goods. Go prepared for some serious browsing and buying; visitors generally leave with armfuls of purchases. Goods here are of a high quality. All the stock is clean and carefully checked; no missing puzzle pieces or bobbly jumpers here.
Buggy access. Nappy-changing facilities. Play area.

Merry Go Round
21 Half Moon Lane, SE24 9JU (7737 6452).
Herne Hill rail. **Open** 9.30am-5pm Mon-Sat.
Credit MC, V
No relation to its Hackney namesake (*see above*), this place is a fertile hunting-ground for second-hand children's clothes and school uniforms, along with maternity fashion and brand new stock from top-notch names such as Catimini, Molo and Grobags.
Buggy access.

SHOES

Brian's Shoes
2 Halleswelle Parade, Finchley Road, NW11 0DL (8455 7001, www.briansshoes.com).
Finchley Central or Golders Green tube. **Open** 9.15am-5.15pm Mon-Sat; 10.30am-1.30pm Sun.
Credit MC, V.

Founded back in 1970, Brian's has kitted out generations of kids and is known for its expert fittings. D&G and Ricosta are stocked alongside more sober Start-rite and Hush Puppies.
Buggy access.

Cubs
42 Heath Street, NW3 6TE (7431 0018).
Hampstead tube. **Open** 10am-6pm Mon-Sat; noon-6pm Sun. **Credit** AmEx, MC, V.
This compact shoe shop, just opposite the Everyman cinema, has an impressive range of shoes for babies and children. Staff are friendly and patient, calmly measuring feet and fetching numerous pairs out of the storeroom until they are satisfied with the fit. Brands include Start-rite, Ricosta, Babybotte, Geox and Ralph Lauren, and there are plenty of wellies too. Children are enticed into being good with the promise of a free balloon.
Buggy access.

John Barnett
137-139 Lordship Lane, SE22 8HX (8693 5145). East Dulwich rail. **Open** 9.30am-5.30pm Mon-Sat; 11am-5pm Sun. **Credit** AmEx, MC, V.
This long-established Dulwich shoe shop has a great section for children. Brands include Clark's, Ecco, Skechers, Dr Martins and Kickers.
Buggy access. Disabled access.

Little Me
141 Hamilton Road, NW11 9EG (8209 0440). Brent Cross tube. **Open** 10.30am-6.15pm Mon-Thur; 10.30am-3pm Fri; 11am-4pm Sun. **Credit** MC, V.
A wide range of continental children's shoes, fitted with a precision shoe-measuring system.
Buggy access.

Merlin Shoes
44 Westow Street, SE19 3AH (8771 5194).
Crystal Palace rail. **Open** 9.30am-5.30pm Mon-Sat. **Credit** MC, V.
Experienced, patient shoe fitters and a wide range of footwear make this place a firm favourite with local families.
Buggy access. Disabled access.

One Small Step One Giant Leap
3 Blenheim Crescent, W11 2EE (7243 0535, www.onesmallsteponegiantleap.com). Ladbroke Grove or Notting Hill Gate tube. **Open** 10am-6pm Mon-Fri; 9am-6pm Sat; 11am-5pm Sun. **Credit** MC, V.
Live near an outpost of this award-winning children's shoe shop and you'll never have to choose between comfort and style. Summer

---

Spoilt for choice Northcote Road

In stark contrast to the peaceful suburbia that surrounds it, Northcote Road is a buzz of activity. A steady stream of prams and pushchairs trundle along the pavements – so it comes as no surprise to find that the street is bursting with quality children's shops.

Located between Wandsworth and Clapham Commons, the area lays claim to a mix of upmarket clothes shops such as Jigsaw and Whistles, but also to traditional butchers and bakers and small Italian cafés.

Upmarket children's brands such as **Petit Bateau** (*see p275*), **Fat Face Kids** (*see p275*), **Jigsaw Junior** (*see p275*) and shoe-retailing mini-chain **One Small Step One Giant Leap** (*see right*) have all set up shop here, catering to well-heeled Nappy Valley dwellers, alongside a host of imaginative independents.

One of the old-timers is the friendly **QT Toys** (*see p284*); along the road, **Northcote Music** (*see p260*) has long supplied local children with their first recorder. The rails at **Quackers** (*see p269*) offer gorgeous children's labels, while an outpost of **JoJo Maman Bébé** (*see p255*) covers all the basics.

sandals, gumboots, Crocs, football boots, trainers and school sensibles are all present and correct. The Bannock gauge is used for measuring, and staff take time to ensure a proper fit. A thoughtfully assembled range of labels runs the gamut from practical (Start-rite, Ecco, Ricosta) to playful (Lelli Kelly, Pom d'Api).
Buggy access. Mail order.
Branches throughout town.

Papillon

43 Elizabeth Street, SW1W 9PP (7730 6690, www.papillon4children.com). Sloane Square tube/Victoria tube/rail. **Open** 10am-6pm Mon-Fri; 10am-5pm Sat. **Credit** MC, V.
Ballet-style pumps in a rainbow of colours and prints feature largely here, but there are also school shoes and beach sandals for boys and girls, flip flops, moccasins and bridesmaids shoes. Hunter gumboots, socks and tights are also sold, along with tiny, ribbon-tie baby shoes.
Buggy access. Mail order.

Red Shoes

30 Topsfield Parade, N8 8PT (8341 9555). Finsbury Park tube/rail, then 41, W7 bus. **Open** 10am-6pm Mon-Sat; noon-4.30pm Sun. **Credit** MC, V.
Fit and comfort are the key words at this child-friendly shoe shop, where children can match their parents with fashionable big brands such as Crocs, Birkenstock, Ecco and Camper.
Buggy access.

Shoe Station

3 Station Approach, Kew, Surrey TW9 3QB (8940 9905, www.theshoestation.co.uk). Kew Gardens tube. **Open** 9am-6pm Mon-Sat; 11am-5pm Sun. **Credit** MC, V.
Run by two mothers, the Station is a cheery little independent, staffed by trained Start-rite fitters. Children's shoes for every occasion are available, from child's size 2 to adult size 7. Brands include Start-rite (of course), Ricosta, Aster, Naturino, Babybotte, TTY, Giesswein, Mod8, Pom d'Api, Geox, Nike, Puma, Birkenstock, Primigi, Freed and Daisy Roots. Football boots, ballet shoes, slippers and wellies are also stocked.
Buggy access.

Vincent Shoe Store

Westfield Shopping Centre, W12 7SL (7226 3141, www.vincentshoestore.com). Wood Lane tube. **Open** 9.30am-9pm Mon-Fri; 8.30am-9pm Sat; noon-6pm Sun. **Credit** MC, V.
Launched in 1999, this Swedish company prides itself on its affordable, colourful kids' footwear. The range includes appealing gumboots (check

out the flamingo print beauties), leather daisy-dotted baby shoes and patent Mary Janes.
Buggy access. Mail order.

SPORT

Ace Sports & Leisure

341 Kentish Town Road, NW5 2TJ (7485 5367). Kentish Town tube. **Open** 9.30am-6pm Mon-Sat. **Credit** AmEx, MC, V.
Set just opposite Kentish Town tube station, Ace has footwear for all sports, as well as junior rackets, bats and swimming equipment. Brands include Puma, Adidas, Reebok and Nike. There are also small baseball mitts and footballs in all sizes, first cricket bats and balls, ping-pong balls and bats, tracksuits, swim nappies, goggles, earplugs and nose clips – everything, in fact, to get kids active.
Buggy access. Disabled access.

David J Thomas

8 Croxted Road, SE21 8SW (8766 7400). West Dulwich rail. **Open** 9.15am-5.15pm Mon-Sat. **Credit** AmEx, MC, V.
A school uniform and sports kit specialist with a great line in cheap equipment in junior sizes.
Buggy access.

Decathlon

Canada Water Retail Park, Surrey Quays Road, SE16 2XU (7394 2000, www.decathlon.co.uk). Canada Water tube. **Open** 9am-9pm Mon-Fri; 9am-7pm Sat; 11am-5pm Sun. **Credit** MC, V.
The French sporting giant's London outpost occupies two enormous hangars by Surrey Quays, crammed with a huge range of gear. There are hard hats, jodhs, crops and grooming kits for riders, snow-proof gear in all sizes for skiers, bikes, fishing rods, no-nonsense walking boots, trainers of every description, footballs, golf equipment and more. Decathlon has 12 own brands, including the affordable and hard wearing Quechua (for hiking, mountaineering and snowboarding). You'll also find Nike, Reebok and Adidas. The young, often French staff are bright and enthusiastic. Services available include racquet restringing and ski maintenance. Children generally enjoy coming on an expedition here, as there's always plenty of scope to play – trying out gym equipment, bouncing balls and testing bikes.
Buggy access. Disabled access. Mail order. Repair service.

Lillywhites

24-36 Lower Regent Street, SW1Y 4QF (0870 333 9600, www.sportsdirect.com).

Piccadilly Circus tube. **Open** 10am-9pm Mon-Sat; noon-6pm Sun. **Credit** AmEx, MC, V.
A fixture on Piccadilly since 1925, Lillywhites is still good for mainstream sports gear. It concentrates mainly on urban sporting activities, and especially football.
Buggy access. Disabled access. Mail order.

Ocean Leisure
11-14 Northumberland Avenue, WC2N 5AQ (7930 5050, www.oceanleisure.co.uk). Embankment tube. **Open** 10am-7pm Mon-Fri; 10am-5pm Sat. **Credit** MC, V.
Hidden away under the arches by Embankment, this watersports emporium sells all manner of sailing, scuba diving and surfing gear. Some of the stock – including the wetsuits, swimwear, Reef sandals and neoprene Aquashoes – comes in very small sizes. They also stock baby life-jackets, fins, masks and snorkels; and specialist children's scuba equipment can be ordered in.
Buggy access. Disabled access. Mail order.

Slam City Skates
16 Neal's Yard, WC2H 9DP (7240 0928, www.slamcity.com). Covent Garden tube. **Open** 11am-7pm Mon-Sat; noon-5pm Sun. **Credit** AmEx, MC, V.
A well-stocked source of skateboards, sneakers of the moment, rucksacks and accessories, beloved by teen aficionados.
Mail order (7240 2611).

Soccerscene
56-57 Carnaby Street, W1F 9QF (7439 0778, www.soccerscene.co.uk). Oxford Circus tube. **Open** 10am-7pm Mon-Wed, Fri, Sat; 10am-8pm Thur; noon-6pm Sun. **Credit** AmEx, MC, V. **Map** p314 J6.
Scaled-down replica kits, sturdy socks, goalie gloves and more, plus footie and rugby themed gifts and accessories.
Delivery service. Mail order.
Branches 156 Oxford Street, W1D 1ND (7436 6499).

Speedo
41-43 Neal Street, WC2H 9PJ (7497 0950, www.speedo.com). Covent Garden tube. **Open** 10am-7pm Mon-Wed, Fri, Sat; 10am-8pm Thur; noon-6pm Sun. **Credit** AmEx, MC, V. **Map** p315 L6.
Swimming costumes, shorts and nappies, alongside all manner of aquatic accessories: armbands, snorkels, goggles and caps to match your swimsuit.
Buggy access. Disabled access. Mail order.

Consumer

Everything for skating: **Slam City Skates**.

Hamleys

Wigmore Sports

39 Wigmore Street, W1U 1QQ (7486 7761, www.wigmoresports.co.uk). Bond Street tube. **Open** 10am-6pm Mon-Wed, Fri, Sat; 10am-7pm Thur; 11am-5pm Sun. **Credit** AmEx, MC, V. **Map** p314 G6.

Junior stock at London's premier racquet sports specialist (tennis, squash, badminton and more) includes footwear by brands such as K-Swiss, Adidas, Asics and Nike; shorter racquets and softer balls are a speciality. Staff are committed to the tennis cause and are keen to match youngsters up with the right racquet. There's a 'try before you buy' practice wall, which children love when it's not being used by some hard-bitten hitter. Raquet restringing is also offered.

Buggy access. Delivery service. Disabled access. Mail order.

TOYS & GIFTS

Art Stationers/ Green's Village Toy Shop

31 Dulwich Village, SE21 7BN (8693 5938). North Dulwich rail. **Open** 9am-5.30pm Mon-Sat. **Credit** MC, V.

The shop at the front is an Aladdin's cave of arts and crafts-related bits and pieces: pipe cleaners, beads, pompoms, stick on jewels, sequins and beads, along with paints, pastels, stationery, clay and other materials. That's just half the story, though. A big sign bearing the legend TOYS has the children cantering down the passage for the booty: Brio, Sylvanian Families, Playmobil, Crayola, Lego, Warhammer and other big brands. Lesser-spotted companies such as Tantrix and Wow are also represented. The enormous pocket money-priced range goes from a rubber goldfish to a magnetic car racer.

Buggy access.

Disney Store

360-366 Oxford Street, W1N 9HA (7491 9136, www.disneystore.co.uk). Bond Street tube. **Open** 9am-9pm Mon-Sat; noon-6pm Sun. **Credit** AmEx, MC, V.

Children make a beeline for this bright, brash shrine to all things Disney, which sells figurines, stationery, toys, costumes and all manner of merchandise. Enduring favourites are the character dolls, lunch-boxes, costumes and classic DVDs.

Buggy access. Disabled access. Mail order. **Branches** 10 The Piazza, WC2E 8HD (7836 5037); 1090-1091 Westfield Shopping Centre, W12 7GD (8811 1162).

Early Learning Centre

36 King's Road, SW3 4UD (7581 5764, www.elc.co.uk). Sloane Square tube. **Open** 9.30am-6pm Mon-Sat; 11am-6pm Sun. **Credit** AmEx, MC, V.

A presence on British high streets since the 1970s, ELC has stuck to its ethos of encouraging imaginative play for babies and young children. Everything is sturdy, brightly coloured and reasonably priced; on Tuesday mornings (10am-noon), kids can get hands-on with the toys or try some craft activities at the drop-in play sessions.

Buggy access. Delivery service. Mail order (0871 231 3511). **Branches** throughout town.

Fagin's Toys

84 Fortis Green Road, N10 3HN (8444 0282). East Finchley tube, then 102, 234 bus. **Open** 9am-5.30pm Mon-Sat; 10am-3pm Sun. **Credit** MC, V.

Along with toys from the likes of Galt, Orchard, Brio, Lego, Playmobil, Meccano and Sylvanian Families, Fagin's has a central table of penny dreadfuls for party bags. Have fun choosing between little rubber fish and stretching aliens, powerballs, pots of slime, magic screens, colouring sets and silk purses; prices run from 15p for a fortune-telling fish to £1.69 for a pack of magnetic marbles.

Buggy access. Disabled access. Play area.

Hamleys

188-196 Regent Street, W1B 5BT (0870 333 2455, www.hamleys.com). Oxford Circus tube. **Open** 10am-8pm Mon-Fri; 9am-8pm Sat; noon-6pm Sun. **Credit** AmEx, DC, MC, V.

Arranged on seven noisy, bustling floors, with implausibly perky demonstrators showing off selected wares, Hamleys has become a prime tourist draw. Most must-have toys are here – though Hamleys isn't immune to that pre-Christmas panic when the cult toy of the moment becomes scarce. Down in the basement are the gadgets and construction toys, while the ground flooris devoted to soft toys and magic tricks. Floor one is games, science kits and sweets, two is for preschoolers, three is girls' stuff, four hobbies, models and remote control toys, and five is boys' toys and a nice little café. Though racing round the store is thrilling enough for most children, large-scale family events are held on site throughout the year. Check the schedule to find out who's planning to pop in; Scooby-Doo, perhaps, or SpongeBob SquarePants. In-store parties are also offered – although at £7,000 for ten kids, the Hamleys Sleepover is possibly best left to young billionaires.

Buggy access. Café. Delivery service. Disabled
access. Mail order. Nappy-changing facilities.
Play areas.

Happy Returns
36 Rosslyn Hill, NW3 1NH (7435 2431).
Hampstead tube. **Open** 10am-5.30pm
Mon-Fri; 10am-6pm Sat; noon-5.30pm Sun.
Credit MC, V.
This fairly small toy shop doesn't have bags of
choice, but the range is a clever mix of products
with prices to suit everyone. Aimed at the zero
to five age group, the shop is geared largely
towards parties. Stock up on the celebration
essentials then go hunting for presents. Look out
for classics like glow stars or Etch-A-Sketch, or
more modern toys by Jellycat; there's a big
Sylvanian Families collection, plus toys by Galt,
Schleich and Playmobil, doll's house accessories
by Plan and jolly, chunky plastics by Wow Toys.
Buggy access.

Honeyjam
*267 Portobello Road, W11 1LR (7243 0449,
www.honeyjam.co.uk). Ladbroke Grove tube.*
Open 9.30am-5.30pm Mon-Sat; 11am-4pm
Sun. **Credit** MC, V.
Spinning tops, skipping ropes and traditional
wooden toys from companies like Bigjigs and Le
Toy Van delight nostalgia-hungry parents,
while children deliberate over the pocket-money
purchases. You'd need to save for longer to
afford the bigger pieces: the best-selling mini
wooden Aga (£350), for example, which is
exclusive to the shop. In the dressing-up section,
boys can be transformed into knights and
pirates, while little girls are enchanted by the
reversible costumes: Snow White on one side
and the Sleeping Beauty on the other, or
Cinderella in her ballgown and rags. There's a
small collection of baby and infant clothes and
an ever-expanding range of fair trade and eco-
friendly products.
Buggy access. Disabled access.

Just Williams
*18 Half Moon Lane, SE24 9HU (7733 9995).
Herne Hill rail.* **Open** 9.30am-6pm Mon-Sat.
Credit MC, V.
A bright blue-painted child's paradise, Just
Williams has some top names in toys, with
plenty of goodies from Brio, Sylvanians,
Schleich and Playmobil. Traditionalists will
approve of the wooden playthings from te likes
of Bigjigs, Plan Toys, Pintoy and Santas, while
Warhammer enthralls more bloodthirsty boys.
Buggy access.
Branches 106 Grove Vale, SE22 8DR
(8299 3444).

Little Rascals
*140 Merton Road, SW19 1EH (8542 9979).
South Wimbledon tube.* **Open** 9am-5.30pm
Mon-Sat. **Credit** AmEx, MC, V.
Aimed at under-fives, this friendly, family-run
local shop is full of appealing toys and gifts.
Check out the handmade wooden book ends and
money-boxes and colourful greetings cards; for
younger babies, there are snug Grobag sleeping
bags and Taggies comforter blankets.
Buggy access.

Mystical Fairies
*12 Flask Walk, NW3 1HE (7431 1888, www.
mysticalfairies.co.uk). Hampstead tube.* **Open**
10am-6pm Mon-Sat; 11am-6pm Sun. **Credit**
MC, V.
There are several thousand small and pretty
things in this shop, at least half of them
hanging from silver branches overhead. Most of
the merchandise is pink or sparkly and features
princesses, ballerinas, flower fairies, pixies and
elves. The back of the shop is an Aladdin's cave
of costumes (mostly for girls, though there are
some token wizard and pirate outfits). Mystical
Fairies is a shop that's hard to leave empty-
handed; it's full of tea sets, trinkets, books,
sticker sets, stationery, slippers, dressing gowns,
pyjamas and duvet covers, wands, wings, craft
sets and jewellery. Staff also run parties in the
shop's fairy light-decked Enchanted Garden (the
basement). Check the website for details of the
regular fairy schools.
Buggy access. Mail order.
Branch Bluewater Shopping Centre,
Greenhithe, Kent, DA9 9ST (01322 624997).

Patrick's Toys & Models
*107-111 Lillie Road, SW6 7SX (7385 9864,
www.patrickstoys.co.uk). Fulham Broadway
tube.* **Open** 9.30am-5.30pm Mon-Sat.
Credit MC, V.
One of London's biggest toy and model shops,
Patricks is a major service agent for Hornby and
Scalextric, attracting adult enthusiasts as well
as kids. The model department specialises in
rockets, planes, cars, military and sci-fi, while the
general toy department has traditional wooden
toys, board games, soft toys and doll's houses.
*Buggy access. Delivery service (local). Disabled
access. Mail order.*

Postmark
*59 Northcross Road, SE22 9ET (8693 1133).
East Dulwich rail.* **Open** 10am-5.30pm Mon-
Sat; 11am-5pm Sun. **Credit** MC, V.
Unable to live up to its name, the Never Ending
Story Bookshop closed a few years ago. Its
former premises are now occupied by this

Consumer

Consumer

Glove puppets, marionettes and more at **Puppet Planet**. *See p284.*

cheerful card shop, which has a small back room that is full of models, games and toys of an educational bent.
Buggy access.
Branch 123 Balham High Road, SW12 9AR (8675 7272).

Puppet Planet
787 Wandsworth Road, SW8 3JQ (07900 975276, www.puppetplanet.co.uk). Wandsworth Road rail. **Open** by appointment only. **Credit** AmEx, MC, V.
Children absolutely love browsing among the glove puppets and marionettes on the shelves of this puppet emporium, which also has a fabulous array of display puppets from around the world. Within seconds of entering the shop, the youngsters will be creating full-blown productions in the hands-on corner, but be ready for some pressure to purloin a full blown puppet theatre (some of which are designed to hang from doorways) to take home.
Buggy access. Delivery service. Disabled access. Mail order. Play area. Nappy-changing facilities.

QT Toys
90 Northcote Road, SW11 6QN (7223 8637). Clapham Junction rail. **Open** 10am-5pm daily. **Credit** MC, V.
From ever-popular Lego and Sylvanian Families sets to tubs of luridly-hued Play Doh, it's all here. There are also some educational games, craft and modelling kits and stationery for older kids.
Buggy access. Disabled access. Mail order. Nappy-changing facilities.

Route 73 Kids
92 Stoke Newington Church Street, N16 0AP (7923 7873, www.route73kids.co.uk). Bus 73, 393, 476. **Open** 10am-5.30pm daily. **Credit** AmEx, MC, V.
Named after the bendy bus that chugs along Stoke Newington Church Street, this jolly toyshop caters to all budgets. A party-bag-tastic table full of pocket money toys takes centre stage, and there's a great selection of traditional names such as Brio and Galt. It's geared towards parents looking for quality wooden toys rather than tacky plastic goods; Plan Toy's eco-friendly rubberwood designs are particularly popular. Then there are books, puzzles, jigsaws, word games, craft packs, Jellycat animals and Starchild's soft leather baby shoes. The train and racing car tables are there to be played with, along with a bike and scooter to whizz about on.
Buggy access. Disabled access.

Snap Dragon
56 Turnham Green Terrace, W4 1QP (8995 6618). Turnham Green tube. **Open** 9.30am-6pm Mon-Sat; 11am-5pm Sun. **Credit** AmEx, MC, V.
A good general toy shop for big brands, Snap Dragon stocks a bit of everything: Lego, Playmobil, Brio and Sylvanian Families are among the biggest sellers, along with games and jigsaws from Orchard Toys as well as stacks of cuddly toys of all kinds. For rainy days, there's an abundance of classic board games, from Buckaroo to Boggle. There are generally a few sandpits and goalposts on the shop floor, while bulkier trampolines and wooden climbing frames by TP Toys can be ordered in on request.
Buggy access. Delivery service.

Sylvanian Families
68 Mountgrove Road, N5 2LT (7226 1329, www.sylvanianfamilies.com). Finsbury Park tube/rail. **Open** 9.30am-5.30pm Mon-Fri; 9am-6pm Sat; 10am-4pm Sun. **Credit** AmEx, MC, V.
Scores of neatly-attired woodland critters line the shelves at this tucked-away emporium of all things Sylvanian, along with every conceivable accessory. Here you can buy your favourite dressed-up animals from the numerous families, along with their homes, hospitals, schools, cars and furniture.
Buggy access. Mail order.

Toy Station
6 Eton Street, Richmond, Surrey TW9 1EE (8940 4896). Richmond tube/rail. **Open** 10am-6pm Mon-Fri; 9.30am-6pm Sat; noon-5pm Sun. **Credit** (over £8) MC, V.
This bastion of traditional, good-quality playthings has two storeys filled with model animals, knights and soldiers, forts and castles, remote-control vehicles and more traditional wooden toys.
Buggy access. Disabled access.

Toys R Us
760 Old Kent Road, SE15 1NJ (7732 7322, www.toysrus.co.uk). Elephant & Castle tube/rail then 21, 56, 172 bus. **Open** 9am-8pm Mon-Fri; 9am-7pm Sat; 11am-5pm Sun. **Credit** AmEx, MC, V.
The American retail giant generally has industrial quantities of the toy of the moment amid its mighty stockpile, though it can be hard to find an assistant.
Buggy access. Car park. Delivery service. Disabled access. Nappy-changing facilities.
Branches throughout town.

Directory

Directory

GETTING AROUND

PUBLIC TRANSPORT

The prices listed for transport and services were correct at the time of going to press, but do bear in mind that some prices (especially those of tube tickets) are subject to a hike each January.

Public transport information

Full details can be found online at www.thetube.com and www.tfl.gov.uk, or by phoning 7222 1234.

Transport for London (TfL) also runs Travel Information Centres that provide maps and information about the tube, buses, Tramlink, riverboats, Docklands Light Railway (DLR) and national rail services within the London area. You can find them in Heathrow Airport, as well as in Liverpool Street and Victoria stations.

London TravelWatch

6 Middle Street, EC1A 7JA (7505 9000, www.londontravelwatch.org.uk). **Open** Phone enquiries 9am-5pm Mon-Fri.
This is the official, campaigning watchdog monitoring customer satisfaction with transport.

Fares, Oyster cards & Travelcards

Tube and DLR fares are based on a system of six zones stretching 12 miles (20 kilometres) out from the centre of London. A cash fare of £4-£4.50 per journey applies across the tube for zones 1-6 (£3.50 excluding zone 1); customers save up to £2.50 with Oyster pay-as-you-go (*see below*). Beware of £25 on-the-spot fines for anyone caught without a ticket.

Children aged under 11 travel free on buses, DLR and the tube. If you are using only the tube, DLR, buses and trams, Oyster pay-as-you-go will always be cheaper than a Day Travelcard (*see below*). If you are using National Rail services, however, the Day Travelcard may best meet your needs (children travelling with you can buy a Day Travelcard for £1). Under-16s get free travel on buses.

Travelcards, valid for tubes, buses, DLR and rail services, can be the cheapest way

of getting around. Travelcards can be bought at stations, London Travel Information Centres or newsagents.

Day Travelcards

Peak Day Travelcards can be used all day Monday to Friday (except public holidays). They cost from £7.20 (£3.60 for under-16s) for zones 1-2, with prices rising to £14.80 (£7.40 for under-16s) for zones 1-6. Most people use the off-peak Day Travelcard, which allows you to travel from 9.30am Monday to Friday and all day Saturday, Sunday and public holidays. They cost from £5.60 (£2 for under-16s) for zones 1-2, rising to £7.50 (£2.60 for under 16s) for zones 1-6.

Oyster card

The Oyster card is a travel smart-card that can be charged with Pre-Pay and/or 7-day, monthly and longer-period (including annual) travelcards and bus passes. Oyster cards are currently available to adults and under-16 photocard holders when buying a ticket. Tickets can be bought from www.oystercard.com, at tube station ticket offices, London Travel Information Centres, some National Rail station ticket offices and newsagents. A single tube journey in zone 1 using Oyster to pay-as-you-go costs £1.50 at all times (50p for under-16s, children under 11 go free).

Children

Under-16s can travel free on buses and trams; under-11s travel free on the tube (those travelling without an adult, or who look over ten, will need to carry a 5-10 Oyster photocard; call 0845 330 9876 for information). Children aged 14 or 15 need a child – or 11-15 – photocard to travel at child rate on the tube and DLR, and get free travel on buses and trams.

An 11-15 Oyster photocard is required by children aged 11-15 years to get child-rate pay as you go on the Underground or DLR, or to buy 7-day, monthly or longer period travelcards.

London Underground

The tube in rush hour (8-9.30am and 4.30-7pm Monday-Friday) is not pleasant, so it is best to travel outside these hours with children, if possible.

Using the system

Tube tickets can be purchased or Oyster cards (*see above*) topped up from a ticket office or self-service machine. Ticket offices in some stations close early (around 7.30pm); it's wise to carry a charged up-Oyster card to avoid being stranded.

To enter and exit the tube using an Oyster card, touch it to the yellow reader that will open the gates. Make sure you touch the card when you exit the tube, otherwise you may be fined.

There are 12 Underground lines, colour-coded on the tube map; we've provided a full map of the London Underground on the back page of this book.

Timetable

Tube trains run daily from around 5.30am (except Sunday, when they start later). The only exception is Christmas Day, when there is no service. During peak times the service should run every two or three minutes.

Times of last trains vary, but they're usually around 11.30pm-1am daily, and 30 minutes to an hour earlier on Sunday. Debates continue as to whether to run the tube an hour later at weekends. The only all-night public transport is by night bus.

Fares

The single fare for adults within zone 1 is £4 (Oyster fare £1.60); for zones 1-2 it's £4 (Oyster fare £2.20 or £1.60). For zones 1-6 it's £4 (Oyster fare £3.80 or £2.20). The single fare for 11-15s in zone 1-6 is £2 (Oyster fare 65p with a valid 11-15 Oyster photocard), £1.60 for zones 2-6 (Oyster fare 65p). Children under 11 travel free at all times.

Docklands Light Railway (DLR)

The DLR (7363 9700, www.dlr.co.uk) runs driverless trains from Bank or Tower Gateway, close to Tower Hill tube (Circle and District lines), to Stratford, Beckton and the Isle of Dogs, then south of the river to Greenwich, Deptford and Lewisham. Trains run 5.30am to 12.30am Monday to Saturday and 7am to 11.30pm Sunday.

Fares

The single fare for adults within zone 1 is £4 (Oyster fare £1.80). For zones 1-2 it's £4 (Oyster fare £2.30 or £1.80). The zones 1-6 single fare is £4 (Oyster fare £3.80 or £2.20). In zones 2-3 it is £3.50 (£1.30 Oyster). Children under 11 travel free.

Children aged 11-15 pay £2 (Oyster fare 65p) or £1.60 for zones 2-6 (Oyster fare 65p), while zones 2-3 for children is 80p (65p Oyster).

One-day 'Rail & River Rover' tickets combine unlimited DLR travel with hop-on, hop-off boat travel on City Cruises between Greenwich, Tower, Waterloo and Westminster piers. Tickets cost £14.50 for adults, £7.25 for kids and £37 (2 adults and up to 3 children under 16) for a family pass; under-5s go free.

Buses

New buses, with low floors for wheelchair and buggy users, and bendy buses with multiple-door entry and the 'pay before you board' schemes now make up much of the fleet. Buses in central London also require you to have an Oyster card or buy a ticket before boarding from pavement ticket machines. Be sure to have a ticket or swiped Oyster card on you while travelling: inspectors can slap a £25 fine on fare-dodgers. Of the famous open-platform Routemaster fleet, only Heritage routes 9 and 15 remain in central London.

Using an Oyster card (*see p286*) to pay as you go costs £1.20 at all times; the most you will pay a day is £3.90 on buses and trams. Paying by cash at the time of travel costs £2 per trip.

Children under 16 and students up to age 18 and resident in London travel free on buses. New Deal and 16+ Oyster fare is half-price (50p) for those in education outside London.

Night buses

Many night buses run 24 hours a day, seven days a week, and some special night buses with an 'N' prefix to the route number operate from about 11pm to 6am. Most services run every 15 to 30 minutes, but many busier routes have a bus around every ten minutes. Travelcards and Bus Passes can be used on night buses until 4.30am on the day after they expire. Oyster Pre-Pay and bus Saver tickets are also valid on night buses.

Green Line buses

Green Line buses (0844 801 7261, www.greenline. co.uk) serve the suburbs and towns within a 40-mile (64km) radius of London. Their main departure point is Ecclestone Bridge, SW1 (Colonnades Coach Station, behind Victoria).

Coaches

National Express (0871 781 8181, www.nationalexpress.com) runs routes to most parts of the country; coaches depart from **Victoria Coach Station**, a five-minute walk from Victoria rail and tube stations.

Directory

Victoria Coach Station
164 Buckingham Palace Road, SW1W 9TP (0871 781 8181, www.tfl.gov.uk/vcs). Victoria tube/rail. **Map** p316 H1.
National Express, which travels to continental Europe as Eurolines, is based at Victoria Coach Station.

Rail services

Independently run services leave from the main rail stations. Travelcards are valid on services within the right zones. The very useful London Overground network, run by TFL (0845 601 4867, www.tfl.gov.uk/rail) extends across London, skirting the centre, and is currently being expanded.

If you've lost property at an overground station or on a train, call 0845 330 9882; an operator will then connect you to the appropriate station.

Family & Friends Railcard
www.family-railcard.co.uk.
This is worth buying if you make even a couple of long rail journeys per year with the children, as the discounts it gives are substantial. The card costs £26 and lasts one year. Valid across Britain, it gives travellers with children one year of discounts from standard rail fares (a third off adult fares, 60 per cent off child fares, £1 minimum fare). Under-fives travel free. Up to two adults can be named as cardholders – they do not have to be related. The minimum group size is one cardholder and one child aged five to 15; maximum group size with one cardholder is four adults and four children. To pick up a form for the Family & Friends Railcard, visit your local staffed station.

London's mainline stations
Charing Cross *Strand, WC2N 5HS.* **Map** p317 L7.
For trains to and from south-east England (including Dover, Folkestone and Ramsgate).
Euston *Euston Road, NW1 1BN.* **Map** p315 K3.
For trains to and from north and north-west England and Scotland, and a line north to Watford.
King's Cross *Euston Road, N1 9AP.* **Map** p315 L2.
For trains to and from north and north-east England and Scotland, and suburban lines to north London.
Liverpool Street *Liverpool Street, EC2M 7PD.* **Map** p319 R5.
For trains to and from the east coast, Stansted airport and East Anglia, and services to east and north-east London.
London Bridge *London Bridge Street, SE1 2SW.* **Map** p319 Q8.
For trains to Kent, Sussex, Surrey and south London suburbs.
Paddington *Praed Street, W2 1HB.* **Map** p311 D5.
For trains to and from west and south-west England, South Wales and the Midlands.
Victoria *115 Buckingham Palace Road, SW1W 9SJ.* **Map** p316 H10.
For fast trains to and from the channel ports (Folkestone, Dover, Newhaven); for trains to and from Gatwick Airport, and suburban services to south and south-east London.
Waterloo *York Road, SE1 7NZ.* **Map** p319 M9.
For fast trains to and from the south and south-west of England (Portsmouth, Southampton, Dorset, Devon), and suburban services to south London.

Tramlink

Trams run between Beckenham, Croydon, Addington and Wimbledon. Travelcards and bus passes taking in zones 3-6 can be used on trams; cash single fares cost £2 (Oyster fare £1.20 or 50p for 16- to 17-year-old photocard holders).

Water transport

The times of London's assortment of river services vary, but most operate every 20 minutes to hourly between 10.30am and 5pm, with more frequent services in summer. Call the operators for schedules, or see www.tfl.gov.uk. Travelcard holders can expect one-third off scheduled riverboat fares.

Thames Clippers (0870 781 5049, www.thamesclippers.com) runs a commuter boat service. Clippers stop at all London piers, including Embankment, Blackfriars, Bankside, London Bridge and Tower (near Tower Bridge). The names in bold below are the names of piers.

Royal Arsenal Woolwich – **Greenwich** (15mins) – **Masthouse Terrace** (3mins) – **Greenland Dock** (4mins) – **Canary Wharf** (4mins) – **Tower** (8mins) – **London Bridge**

(4mins) – **Bankside** (5mins) – **Blackfriars**
(3mins) – **Embankment** (4mins); Thames
Clippers (see p288).

Westminster – **Embankment** (5 mins) –
Festival (5mins) – **London Bridge** (10mins)
– **St Katharine's** (5mins); Crown River 7936 2033,
www.crownriver.com.

Westminster – **Greenwich** (1hr); Thames River
Services 7930 4097, www.westminsterpier.co.uk.

Westminster – **Kew** (1hr 30mins) – **Richmond**
(30mins) – **Hampton Court** (1hr 30mins);
Westminster Passenger Service Association
7930 2062, www.wpsa.co.uk.

Westminster – **Tower** (40mins); City Cruises
7740 0400, www.citycruises.com.

TAXIS
Black cabs

Licensed London taxis are known as
black cabs – even though they now come
in a wide variety of colours – and are a
quintessential feature of London life.
Drivers of black cabs must pass a test
called the Knowledge to prove they know
every street in central London and the
shortest route to it. If a taxi's yellow
'For Hire' sign is switched on, it can be
hailed. If a taxi stops, the cabbie must
take you to your destination, provided
it's within seven miles. Expect to pay
slightly higher rates after 8pm on
weekdays and all weekend.

You can book black cabs in advance.
Both Radio Taxis (7272 0272, www.radio
taxis.co.uk) and Dial-a-Cab (cash bookings
7253 5000, credit card bookings 7426 3420,
www.dialacab.co.uk) run 24-hour services
for black cabs (there's a booking fee in
addition to the regular fare). Enquiries
or complaints about black cabs should
be made to the Public Carriage Office
(www.tfl.gov.uk).

Minicabs

Be sure to use only licensed firms and
avoid minicab drivers who tout for
business on the street. There are plenty
of trustworthy and licensed local minicab
firms around in all areas, including Lady
Cabs (7272 3300, www.ladyminicabs.co.uk),
which employs only women drivers, and
Addison Lee (0844 800 6677, www.addison
lee.com). Whoever you use, it's always
a good idea to ask the price when you
book and confirm it with the driver
when the car arrives.

DRIVING
Congestion charge

Everyone driving in central London –
an area defined as within King's Cross
(N), Old Street roundabout (NE), Aldgate
(E), Old Kent Road (SE), Elephant & Castle
(S), Vauxhall, Chelsea, South Kensington
(SW), Kensington, Holland Park, North
Kensington, Bayswater, Paddington (W),
Marylebone and Euston (N) – between
7am and 6pm Monday to Friday, has to
pay an £8 fee. Expect a fine of £60 if
you fail to do so (rising to £120 if you
delay payment).

Passes can be bought from newsagents,
garages and NCP car parks; the scheme is
enforced by CCTV cameras. You can pay
by phone or online any time during the day
of entry, even afterwards, but it's an extra
£2 after midnight on the day following the
day of travel. Payments are accepted until
midnight on the next charging day after a
vehicle has entered the zone. A proposal to
scrap the Western extension of the
Congestion Charge zone (covering Chelsea,
Kensington, Knightsbridge, Bayswater and
Notting Hill) is afoot, and may be
introduced by December 2010.

For information, phone 0845 900 1234 or
go to www.cclondon.com. The Congestion
Charge zone is marked on the Central
London by Area map, see p308.

Parking

Central London is scattered with parking
meters, but finding a vacant one can take
ages. When you do, it'll cost you up to £1
for every 15 minutes to park there, and
you'll be limited to two hours on the meter.
Parking on a single or double yellow line,
a red line or in residents' parking areas
during the day is illegal. In the evening
(from 6pm or 7pm in much of central
London) and at various times at weekends,
parking on single yellow lines is legal and
free. If you find a clear spot on a single
yellow line during the evening, look for
a sign giving the regulations. Meters are
also free at certain times during evenings
and weekends.

NCP 24-hour car parks (0845 050 7080,
www.ncp.co.uk) in and around central
London are numerous but pricey. Fees vary,
but expect to pay £10-£55 per day. NCP car
parks can be found at Drury Lane, Parker
Street, Parker Mews, and Upper St Martins
Lane, WC2; and 2 Lexington Street, W1.

Driving out of town

Check your route for possible delays and roadworks. Try the route-planner service available from the RAC (www.rac.co.uk) or the AA (www.theaa.com).

CYCLING

Parents who want to find out more about cycle training can visit www.bikeforall.net for info, or log on to the websites below. Most local authorities include Safe Routes to Schools schemes in their local transport plans. Check the Sustrans website (www.sustrans.org.uk) for details. London Cycle Guide maps are available from some stations and bike shops, or the Travel Information Line (7222 1234).

London Cycle Network
www.londoncyclenetwork.org.uk.
This 560-mile (900km) network of routes for cyclists will be completed in 2010.

London Cycling Campaign
7234 9310, www.lcc.org.uk.
Looks after the city's pedallers.

WALKING

The least stressful way to see London is on foot. A selection of street maps covering central London is on pp308-319 but you'll need a separate map of the city: both the standard Geographers' *A–Z* and Collins's *London Street Atlas* are very easy to use.

The Guy Fox *London Children's Map* is comprehensive and packed with colourful illustrations of city landmarks; buy it at www.guyfox.co.uk at £2.95 or bookshops and tourist attractions.

RESOURCES

Councils

Barnet *8359 2000, www.barnet.gov.uk.*
Brent *8937 1200, www.brent.gov.uk.*
Camden *7974 4444, www.camden.gov.uk.*
Corporation of London *7606 3030, www.cityoflondon.gov.uk.*
Ealing *8825 5000, www.ealing.gov.uk.*
Greenwich *8854 8888, www.greenwich.gov.uk.*
Hackney *8356 3000, www.hackney.gov.uk.*
Hammersmith & Fulham *8748 3020, www.lbhf.gov.uk.*
Haringey *8489 0000, www.haringey.gov.uk.*
Hounslow *8583 2000, www.hounslow.gov.uk.*
Islington *7527 2000, www.islington.gov.uk.*
Kensington & Chelsea *7361 3000, www.rbkc.gov.uk.*
Lambeth *7926 1000, www.lambeth.gov.uk.*
Lewisham *8314 6000, www.lewisham.gov.uk.*
Merton *8274 4901, www.merton.gov.uk.*
Newham *8430 2000, www.newham.gov.uk.*
Richmond upon Thames *0845 744 2442, www.richmond.gov.uk.*
Southwark *7525 5000, www.southwark.gov.uk.*
Tower Hamlets *7364 5020, www.towerhamlets.gov.uk.*
Waltham Forest *8496 3000, www.walthamforest.gov.uk.*
Wandsworth *8871 6000, www.wandsworth.gov.uk.*
Westminster *7641 6000, www.westminster.gov.uk.*

Education

Advisory Centre for Education (ACE) *0808 800 5793, 7704 9822 exclusion advice line, www.ace-ed.org.uk.* **Open** 10am-5pm Mon-Fri.
Phone the centre for advice about your child's schooling; the advice line is for parents whose children have been excluded from school, have been bullied, or have special educational needs. School admission appeals advice is also available.
British Association for Early Childhood Education *136 Cavell Street, E1 2JA (7539 5400, www.early-education.org.uk).* **Open** *Phone enquiries* 9am-5pm Mon-Fri.
A charitable organisation that provides information on infant education from birth to eight years.
Gabbitas Educational Consultants *Carrington House, 126-130 Regent Street, W1B 5EE (7734 0161, www.gabbitas.co.uk).* **Open** 9am-5.30pm Mon-Fri.
The consultants at Gabbitas give advice to parents and students on choosing an independent school.
Home Education Advisory Service *PO Box 98, Welwyn Garden City, Herts AL8 6AN (01707 371854, www.heas.org.uk).* **Open** *Phone enquiries* 9am-5pm Mon-Fri.
Call for information if you want to educate your child at home. An introductory pack costs £2.50, a year's subscription £16.

ISC Information Service London & South-East
7766 7070, www.iscis.uk.net. **Open** *Phone enquiries* 9am-5pm Mon-Fri.
The Independent Schools Council Information Service works to help parents find out about independent schools.
Kidsmart *www.kidsmart.org.uk.*
Kidsmart is an internet safety awareness programme run by Childnet International, funded by the DfES and Cable & Wireless. Its guide is available to all primary schools.
National Association for Gifted Children *Suite 14, Challenge House, Sherwood Drive, Bletchley, Milton Keynes, Bucks MK3 6DP (0845 450 0295, www.nagcbritain.org.uk).* **Open** *Phone enquiries* 9am-4pm Mon-Fri.
Support and advice on education for gifted kids.
Parenting UK *Unit 431, Highgate Studios, 53-79 Highgate Road, NW5 1TL (7284 8370, www.parenting-forum.org.uk).* **Open** *Phone enquiries* 9.30am-5pm Mon-Fri.
Information about parenting classes and support for parents. It was set up for people who work with parents, but parents can call as well.
Pre-School Learning Alliance *Fitzpatrick Building, 188 York Way, N7 9AD (7697 2500, www.pre-school.org.uk).* **Open** *Phone enquiries* 9am-5pm Mon-Fri.
A leading educational charity specialising in the early years. It runs courses and workshops in pre-schools around the country for parents of children under the age of five.

Fun & games

Activity camps
Barracudas Young World Leisure Group *Bridge House, Bridge Street, St Ives, Cambs PE27 5EH (0845 123 5299, www.barracudas.co.uk).*
School holiday camps based in schools in outlying countryside. Children aged five to 16 are welcome.
Cross Keys *48 Fitzalan Road, N3 3PE (8371 9686, www.xkeys.co.uk, www.miniminors.co.uk).*

Day camps in Finchley for kids aged 12 or under and rural week-long camps in Norfolk, for children aged up to 17.
EAC Activity Camps *45 Frederick Street, Edinburgh, EH2 1EP (0131 477 7570, www.eacworld.com).*
Day and residential camps for children aged five to 16 in countryside sites.
PGL *Alton Court, Penyard Lane, Ross-on-Wye, Herefordshire HR9 5GL (0844 371 0101, www.pgl.co.uk).*
Sport and activity camps for children aged seven to 16 in the UK and Europe.
Wickedly Wonderful *Russett Cottage, Itchenor, West Sussex PO20 7DD (0794 123 1168, www.wickedlywonderful.com).*
A holiday company that runs weekly buses from London down to the beach during the summer holidays.

Indoor play
Gymboree Play & Music *www.gymboree-uk.com.*
A parent-and-child play organisation for children aged 16 months to four-and-a-half years.
National Association of Toy & Leisure Libraries *(NATLL) 68 Churchway, NW1 1LT (7428 2286 helpline, www.natll.org.uk).* **Open** *Helpline* 9am-5pm Mon, Tue, Thur.
For information on more than 1,000 toy libraries.
Toys Re-united *www.toys-reunited.co.uk.*
Check the website to see if a missing plaything might have been found.
TumbleTots *0121 585 7003, www.tumbletots.com.*
Open *Phone enquiries* 9am-5.30pm Mon-Fri.
Phone to find out about TumbleTots play centres in your area.

Health
Asthma UK *0800 121 6244, www.asthma.org.uk.*
Open *Helpline* 9am-5pm Mon-Fri.
Advice and help if you or your child has asthma.
Contact-A-Family *7608 8700, 0808 808 3555 helpline, www.cafamily.org.uk.* **Open** *Helpline* 10am-4pm, Mon-Fri.
Support for parents of children with disabilities. This organisation is a valuable resource for those who feel isolated while caring for their disabled children.
Euro Pair Agency *8421 2100, www.euro-pair.co.uk.*
An au pair agency that specialises in French candidates.
Family Natural Health Centre *106 Lordship Lane, SE22 8HF (8693 5515).* **Open** *9.30am-9.30pm Mon-Thur; 9.30am-6pm Fri-Sat; 11am-5pm Sun.*
A wide range of alternative therapies, from acupuncture to osteopathy, are practised here. French classes, sing and sign classes, children's yoga and art therapy are also offered.
Family & Parenting Institute *457 Highgate Studios, 53-79 Highgate Road, NW5 1TL (7424 3460, www.familyandparenting.org).* **Open** *Phone enquiries* 9.30am-5.30pm Mon-Fri; 24hr answerphone other times.
A resource centre that produces factsheets covering all aspects of parenting.
Food for the Brain Foundation *8788 3801, www.foodforthebrain.org.*
The Food for the Brain schools project is designed to help parents throughout the UK make the right

Directory

food choices to help improve their children's brain function, behaviour and intelligence. A downloadable leaflet, the 'Smart Food Smart Kids Shopping Guide', accompanies the scheme.

Greatcare *www.greatcare.co.uk.*
A useful resource for those looking for childcare. Greatcare has 20,000 registered users, including nannies, au pairs, babysitters, mothers' helps and maternity nurses.

NHS Direct Helpline *0845 4647, www.nhsdirect. nhs.uk.* **Open** *Helpline* 24hrs daily.
Confidential information and health advice; an invaluable resource.

WellChild Helpline *0808 801 0330, www.wellchild.org.uk.*
This national charity offers practical and emotional support to sick children and their families.

Help & support

Bestbear *0870 720 1277, www.bestbear.co.uk.* **Open** 9am-6pm Mon-Fri; 24hr answerphone other times.
Information about childcare agencies.

Childcare Link *0800 234 6346, www.childcarelink. gov.uk.* **Open** *Phone enquiries* 9am-5pm Mon-Fri.
Provides a list of childcare organisations in your area.

ChildLine *0800 1111, www.childline.org.uk.*
Confidential 24-hour helpline for young people in the UK. The counsellors are trained to listen and help with all kinds of issues, from bullying and abuse to drugs and STDs. Sometimes they put callers in touch with someone who can help further.

Daycare Trust *21 St George's Road, SE1 6ES (7940 7510, 0845 872 6251 helpline, www.daycaretrust.org.uk).* **Open** 10am-1pm, 2-5pm Mon, Tue, Thur, Fri; 2-5pm Wed.
A national charity that works to promote high-quality, affordable childcare. If you are a parent or carer paying for childcare, the www.paying forchildcare.org.uk site provides easy-to-read introductions to each of the main types of benefits, grants and subsidies that are available to help ease the financial burden of paying for childcare.

4Children *7512 2112, 7512 2100 information line, www.4children.org.uk.* **Open** *Phone enquiries* 9am-5pm Mon-Fri.
4Children is the national children's charity for children and young people aged up to 19. It works with government, local authorities, primary care trusts, children's service providers, and children and parents to ensure joined-up support for all children and young people in their local community.

Kids *6 Aztec Row, Berners Road, N1 0PW (7359 3635, www.kids.org.uk).* **Open** *Phone enquiries* 9.30am-5.30pm Mon-Fri.
An organisation that seeks to enhance the lives of disabled children, through play, leisure, education, family support, information, advice and training, with a view to empowering them in society.

Kidscape *2 Grosvenor Gardens, SW1W 0DH (7730 3300, 08451 205204 helpline, www.kidscape.org.uk).* **Open** *Helpline* 10am-8pm Mon, Tue; 10am-4pm Wed-Fri.
Established by the indomitable child psychologist and mum Dr Michele Elliott, this was the first charity in the UK set up specifically to prevent bullying and child abuse in the family as well as at school. The helpline is for the use of parents, guardians or concerned relatives and friends of bullied children.

London Au Pair & Nanny Agency *www.londonnanny.co.uk.*
Matches families with child carers.

London Mums *www.londonmums.org.uk.*
A group of new mums based in London who support each other by sharing views and tips online and organising activities for mums (and dads) and babies, such as trips to view exhibitions at the National Gallery, movies at the local cinema and nature walks.

Nannytax *PO Box 988, Brighton, East Sussex BN1 3NT (0845 226 2203, www.nannytax.co.uk).* **Open** *Phone enquiries* 9am-5pm Mon-Fri.
For £270 a year, Nannytax registers your nanny with the Inland Revenue, organises National Insurance payments and offers advice.

Night Nannies *7731 6168, www.nightnannies.com.*
Night Nannies provides a list of qualified carers who may be able to offer respite from sleepless nights.

Parent Company *6 Jacob's Well Mews, W1U 3DY (0845 094 4220, www.theparentcompany.co.uk).* **Open** *Bookings* 9am-3pm Mon-Fri.
The company runs first aid training courses for parents and carers of babies and children. The courses are delivered by paediatric nurses, either in the home or workplace.

Parent Courses *Holy Trinity Brompton, Brompton Road, SW7 1JA (7581 8255, www.htb.org.uk).* **Open** *Phone enquiries* 9.30am-5.30pm Mon, Wed-Fri; 10.30am-5.30pm Tue.
Runs Parenting Course for parents with children under the age of 12, and Parenting Teenagers, for parents of children aged 13-18. Each course costs £30 and takes place over five weeks once a year.

Parentline Plus *0808 800 2222 helpline, www. parentlineplus.org.uk.* **Open** *Helpline* 24hrs daily.
Organises nationwide courses on how to cope with being a parent. For more details, call the free helpline.

Parents for Inclusion *0800 652 3145 helpline, www.parentsforinclusion.org.* **Open** 10am-noon, 1-3pm Mon, Wed.
Organises workshops for parents of disabled children as well as providing training for teachers who want to develop inclusion in their schools.

The Parent Practice *8673 3444 bookings, www.theparentpractice.com.*
A support and training group that promises to endow parents with the skills for transforming family life. It also produces CDs (£18.50; £33/pair) that provide harrassed mums and dads with practical strategies to make family life calmer, happier and more rewarding.

Parent Support Group *72 Blackheath Road, SE10 8DA (8469 0205 helpline).* **Open** *Helpline* 10am-8pm Mon-Thur; 24hr answerphone other times.
As well as the helpline, staff run one-to-one support sessions and offer courses on parenting skills to the parents and carers of adolescents who are acting in an antisocial or criminal manner.

Post-Adoption Centre *5 Torriano Mews, Torriano Avenue, NW5 2RZ (7284 0555, 7284 5879 advice line, www.postadoptioncentre.org.uk).* **Open** *Advice Line* 10am-1pm Mon-Wed, Fri; 5.30-7.30pm Thur.
Registered charity providing advice, support and information for anyone affected by adoption, including adoptive/foster parents and their children, adopted adults, birth relatives and the professionals who work with them.

Directory

Simply Childcare *www.simplychildcare.com.*
If you're seeking a nanny, check this website.
Sitters *0800 389 0038, www.sitters.co.uk.* **Open**
Phone enquiries 9am-5pm Mon-Fri.
A babysitting agency with locally based nurses,
teachers and nannies on its books.

FURTHER REFERENCE
Websites

BBC London *www.bbc.co.uk/london.*
London-focused news, weather, travel and sport.
British Pathé *www.britishpathe.com*
Newsreels, from spaghetti-eating contest to pre-war
Soho scenes.
Children First *www.childrenfirst.nhs.uk.*
Run by Great Ormond Street Hospital and
children's charity WellChild, this website has
information on all aspects of healthy living, with
special sections about going into hospital.
Classic Cafés *www.classiccafes.co.uk.*
The city's finest classic caffs.
Department for Education and Skills
www.parentscentre.gov.uk.
Advice on schools and other aspects of education.
Film London *www.filmlondon.org.uk.*
London cinema, information about film in and
around the capital, as well as London's film culture.
Get London Reading
www.getlondonreading.co.uk/books-in-london.
Map of London books by district. Also details
reading events taking place around the city.
Greater London Authority *www.london.gov.uk.*
The official website for the Mayor of London and
the Greater London Authority.
Hidden London *www.hiddenlondon.com.*
The city's undiscovered gems.

Learning Partnership
www.thelearningpartnership.com.
The Learning Partnership's online guide to
parenting, Top Tips for Tiny Tots (www.tt4tt.co.uk),
provides new parents with essential information on
pregnancy, birth and early development in one easy-
to-use downloadable course.
London Footprints *www.london-footprints.co.uk.*
Free walks around London, listed by area
and theme.
London Parks & Gardens Trust
www.parkexplorer.org.uk.
A website designed to help Key Stage 2 children
learn more about the parks, gardens and open
spaces of London.
London Randomness
http://london.randomness.org.uk.
Want to find Finnish food near a music shop? Great
review site-cum-wiki for interesting places.
London Remembers *www.londonremembers.com.*
A guide to the plaques and statues dotted
around London.
London 2012 *www.london2012.com.*
The official website for the 2012 London Olympics.
Deatils on what's happening, how to get involved
and all things Olympics.
London Undergound Blog *http://london-
underground.blogspot.com.*
Daily tube blog.
Meteorological Office *www.metoffice.gov.uk.*
The most accurate source of weather forecasts.
Nickel in the Machine
www.nickelinthemachine.com.
Blog on the history, culture and music of 20th-
century London.
On a Bus *http://onabus.com.*
Enter a bus number and its route is mapped.
Parent Pages *www.parentpages.co.uk.*
A useful listings site for families with children and
professionals working with children.
The River Thames Guide *www.riverthames.co.uk.*
Interesting places to stay, eat, drink and play, all
along the riverbank.
Seety *www.seety.co.uk.*
Navigable photos of pretty much every
London street.
Street Map *www.streetmap.co.uk.*
Grid references and postcodes.
Time Out *www.timeout.com.*
Up-to-the-minute listings, features and reviews, plus
critics' recommendations. The Kids section runs
from info on city farms, workshops, museums and
days out to new films, shows and festivals.
Transport for London *www.tfl.gov.uk.*
The official website for travel information about
tubes, buses, DLR and river services, as well as travel
times and cycle routes. Use the journey planner to
find the quickest routes to your destination, and
check for any disruptions or delays. The planner
can also find you cycling routes.
Visit London *www.visitlondon.com.*
The official tourist board website, full of
information and special offers.
Walkit *www.walkit.com/london.*
Type in your setting off point and destination, and
find out how long it'll take to walk it. It'll even find
you the route with the lowest pollution levels.
Wild Web *http://wildweb.london.gov.uk.*
Wildlife in the city.
Yellow Pages Online *www.yell.com.*
The best online resource for numbers and addresses.

A-Z Index

Directory

Directory

Directory

Directory

Area Index

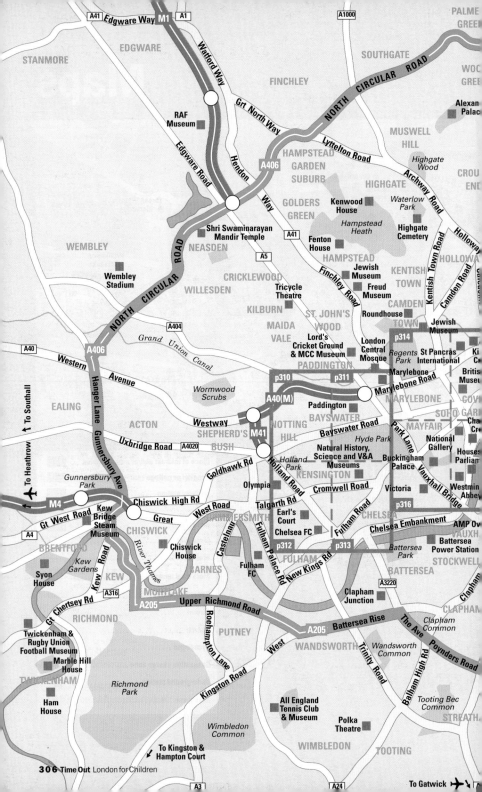

London Overview

© Copyright Time Out Group 2010

Central London
by Area

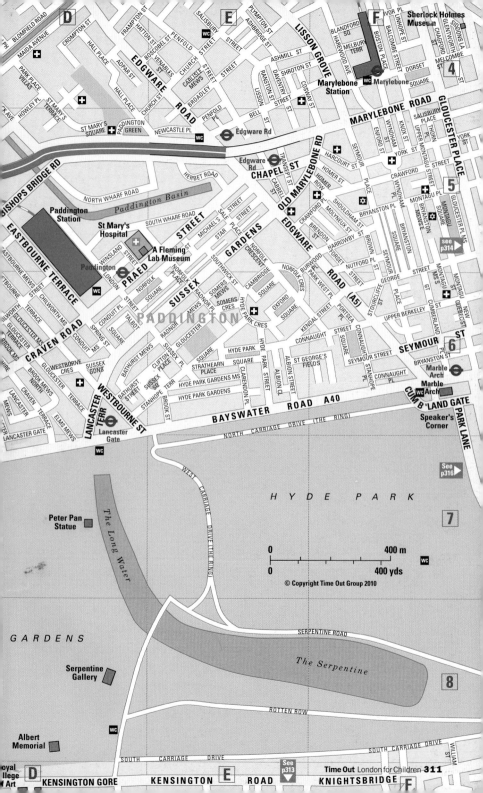

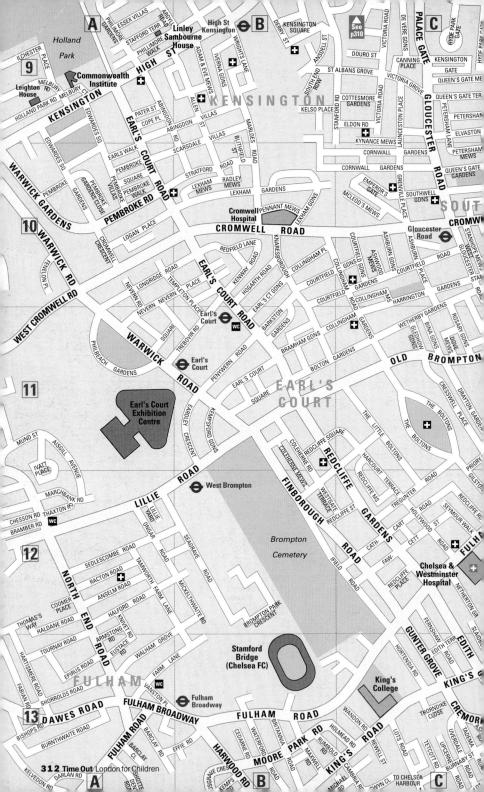

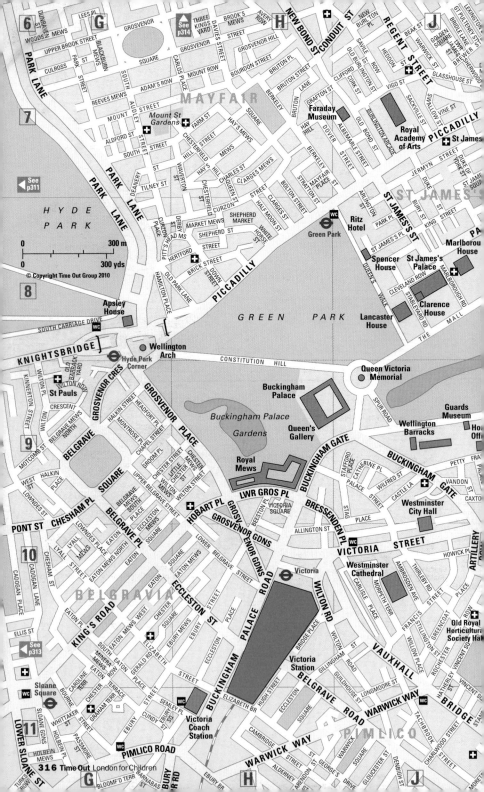

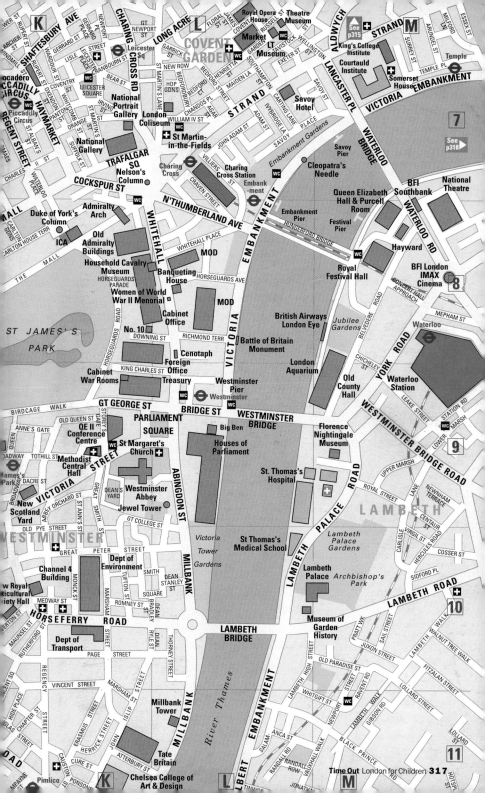

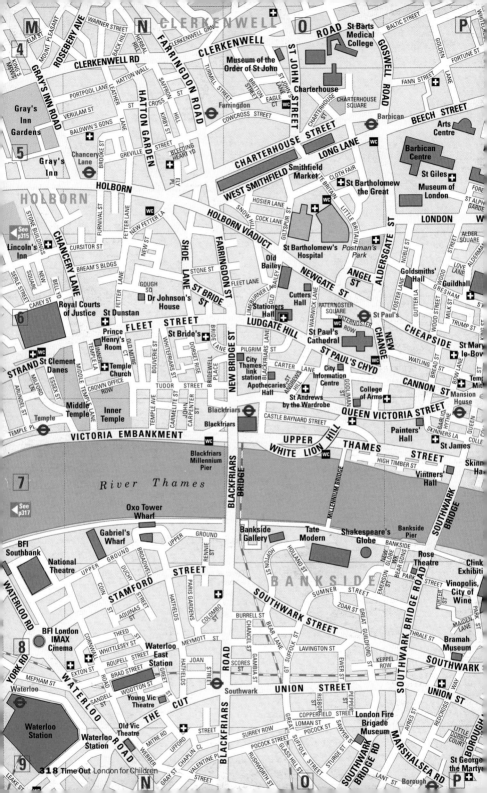